BRITISH TRADE UNIONISM
1750–1850

Note on cover illustration

This pictorial heading from an 1820 resolution shows a journeyman hatter signing in at an inn used as headquarters by the local trade society. He is showing his ticket of membership (blank) issued by his own local society and will receive, if no work is available in that place, a night's lodging and a sum of money sufficient to carry him onto the next town on the official route. The *tramping system* was an important institution in early trade unionism. In some trades, e.g. woolcombing, it went back to the beginning of the eighteenth century. It not only provided the original reason for membership, but was an essential link in spreading information about trade conditions and wage levels.

British Trade Unionism 1750–1850

The Formative Years

Edited by John Rule

Longman
London and New York

Longman Group UK Limited,
Longman House, Burnt Mill, Harlow,
Essex CM20 2JE, England
and Associated Companies throughout the world.

*Published in the United States of America
by Longman Inc., New York*

First published 1988

British Library Cataloguing-in-Publication Data

British trade unionism 1750–1850: the
    formative years.
    1. Trade-unions – Great Britain – History
    I. Rule, John
    331.88'0941   HD6664

    ISBN 0–582–49459–1

Library of Congress Cataloging-in-Publication Data

British trade unionism, 1750–1850.

    Bibliography: p.
    Includes index.
    1. Trade-unions – Great Britain – History – 18th century.
    2. Trade-unions – Great Britain – History – 19th century.
    I. Rice, John, 1944–
    HD6664.B83   1988   331.88'0941   87–22614

    ISBN 0–582–49459–1

331.88

2002949-2

Set in Linotron 202 10/12 pt Bembo

Produced by Longman Singapore Publishers (Ptc) Ltd.
Printed in Singapore

Contents

Preface

These essays originated in the decision of the Society for the Study of Labour History to hold, in 1984, a conference at Congress House to mark the 150th anniversary of Tolpuddle. Planning the conference revealed that despite a considerable amount of research, very little on early trade unionism had been brought together in an accessible form since the Webbs published their celebrated history almost a century ago. The papers have been much revised and rewritten since that conference, and one, that on the Scots miners, has been added from a previous conference of the Society.

Papers given by John Harrison, Robert Leeson and Rodney Dobson at the conference were not in the event available for publication. John Rule's specific contribution has been incorporated into an introductory essay. The very real gap in trade union history which the Conference sought to fill still seems as wide. We offer these essays as a step towards a new history of the formative years of a trade union movement which in Britain perhaps more than anywhere else can only be understood in the light of more than two hundred years of history.

The contributors share an interest in early trade union history and the belief that recent research on it should be more easily available. They do not necessarily agree on matters of interpretation. No attempt has been made to present a 'collective' view in this volume.

List of Abbreviations

Agric. Hist. Rev.	*Agricultural History Review*
Annals of Agric.	*Annals of Agriculture*
BCRO	Berkshire County Records Office
BPP	*British Parliamentary Papers*
Brit. Jn. of Indust. Rel.	*British Journal of Industrial Relations*
Bull. of the Soc. for the Study of Lab. Hist.	*Bulletin of the Society for the Study of Labour History*
Camb. Jn. of Economics	*Cambridge Journal of Economics*
CEHE	*Cambridge Economic History of Europe*
Econ. Hist. Rev.	*Economic History Review*
Econ. Jn.	*Economic Journal*
English Hist. Rev.	*English Historical Review*
ESCRO	East Sussex County Records Office
Flintshire Hist. Soc. Pub.	*Flintshire Historical Society Publication*
GJ	*Gloucester Journal*
GNCTU	Grand National Consolidated Trades Union
GRO	Gloucester Records Office
HCJ	*House of Commons Journal*
HCRO	Hampshire County Records Office
HCSC	House of Commons Select Committee
Historical Jn.	*Historical Journal*
History Workshop Jn.	*History Workshop Journal*
HO	Home Office
Inter. Rev. of Soc. Hist.	*International Review of Social History*
Jn. Econ. Hist.	*Journal of Economic History*
Jn. of Legal Hist.	*Journal of Legal History*

Jn. of Peasant Studies	*Journal of Peasant Studies*
Jn. of Religious Hist.	*Journal of Religious History*
Jn. Soc. Hist.	*Journal of Social History*
Jn. Statistical Soc. of London	*Journal of the Statistical Society of London*
Manchester Stat. Soc. Trans,	*Manchester Statistical Society Transactions*
NAPL	National Association for the Protection of Labour
NAUT	National Association of United Trades
NS	*Northern Star*
PRO	Public Records Office
Proc. Dorset Nat. Hist. and Arch. Soc.	*Proceedings of the Dorset Natural History and Archaeological Society*
Proc. [Second] Inter. Congress of [Historians]	*Proceedings of the [Second] International Congress of [Historians]*
Q.S.	Quarter Sessions
R. Hist. Soc.	*Royal History Society*
S.C.	Select Committee
Trans. Bristol and Gloucs. Arch. Soc.	*Transactions of the Bristol and Gloucester Archaeological Society*
Univ. of Birmingham Hist. Jn.	*University of Birmingham Historical Journal*
WO	War Office
WSCRO	West Sussex County Records Office

CHAPTER ONE

The Formative Years of British Trade Unionism: An Overview

John Rule

INTRODUCTION

After a long interlude since the Webbs wrote their history in 1894, during which no fresh synthesis appeared and their agenda and imposed constraints largely predominated, considerable advances have been made in recent years in our understanding of eighteenth-century trade unionism.[1] Ridding themselves of the pioneering pair's insistence that only *permanent* associations formed to defend or advance the interests of workers could be considered trade unions, historians have discovered collective labour organisations to have been much more widespread, sophisticated and significant than used to be assumed.

To their credit the Webbs, like that insightful historian Lipson, never presented trade unions as being created by the industrial revolution and as accompanying the birth of a 'modern' factory proletariat. They fully realised that it is the separation of labour and capital, irrespective of the form in which the latter exists, which provides the historical context for the emergence of the perception of a distinct labour interest which is the pre-condition for trade unionism. In the early pages of their great work they show the origins of organised labour from at least the beginning of the eighteenth century in workshop trades like tailoring, hat making and printing; among out-working artisans in cloth manufacture; in the 'yard' trades like shipbuilding; in building and, in short, anywhere where a 'craft' could be defined and protected.[2] However, their insistence on permanent organisation invalidated their presentation of the extent of trade unionism before the industrial revolution, for what they dismissed as episodic and spontaneous labour reactions

1

have been re-incorporated into trade union history. Historians now recognise that the basis for collective worker action lay as often in the habitual patterns of association in workplace and community. Translated into collective pressures they provided a continuity against which strikes and related labour actions can be seen as recurrent rather than episodic manifestations of industrial protest.[3]

A count of 383 disputes in Britain between 1717 and 1800 forms the basis of Dr Dobson's recent detailed analysis of eighteenth-century unionism. He has divided them into more than 30 occupational groupings, several of which could well be subdivided, woollen workers such as combers and weavers for example might find themselves at some times making common cause, but when the import of ready-combed wool was the issue, they took each other on in pitched battle.[4] What the total population of reported disputes will reach when more time has been spent on the provincial press can hardly be guessed; the 'dark figure' of those which were never reported is unknowable. Such a revised view of incidence has had an effect on the historiography of early trade unionism. Professor Malcolmson presents labour conflicts as 'fairly common', although not among farm workers – easily the largest single occupational group – and less so than the much studied food riot.[5] Professor Christie finds that trade unions 'played a significant part in the lives of multitudes of craftsmen and artisans during the Hanoverian age'. Seeking to explain why revolution did not come about in England, he finds they were successful enough to 'take the sting out of human discontent' and achieve a tolerable balance of interest. For the London craftsmen at least, whose widespread alienation would have been crucial to any Jacobin movement, there was some degree of confidence in a trade unionism which, although it often failed, was not so ineffective that 'the aspirations of working men' were not often 'at least partially satisfied'. They also provided, he feels, 'an arena for a realistic working-out of . . . the combativeness in human nature'.[6]

Be that as it may, the new work on early unionism has given useful support to Professor Fox's surely proper insistence on the necessity for an historical context if British trade unionism is to be understood: 'The artisan-craft tradition by which the British trade union movement more than any other was deeply marked is a pre-industrial and pre-capitalist tradition.'[7] Some qualification is needed here, or at least amplification. 'Pre-industrial' certainly in the usual applicaton of that label to mean pre-industrial revolution, but pre-capitalist only in a special sense. The rise of a class of capitalist employers predicated the emergence of defensive labour organis-ations. Contrary, however, to the Webbs' insistence on a clear break between the guild organisation of the crafts and the beginnings of trade unionism, it can be noted that it was often the unions which sought to retain the restrictive and regulative customs and practices of the 'trade' over such issues as apprenticeship control, who inher-ited much of ceremony and ritual and who sought from the state that it continue to 'regulate' the market.[8]

A recent, substantially convincing, reassessment of England's occupational structure significantly changes the pattern derived by generations of historians from Gregory King's famous investigation of 1688. England and Wales were much more industrial and commercial than he presented them and than they have generally been described by historians. It would also seem to have been quite possibly the case that what we might, loosely, think of as the 'artisan fraction' of the manufacturing labour force was then not only large, but proportionately increasing. The great expansion of the unskilled non-agricultural workforce, both through demographic increase, through methods of production involving some degree of de-skilling and through changing sexual divisions of labour is a context vital for the understanding of early-nineteenth-century trade unionism. Workers' combinations may well have operated in more propitious circumstances in the eighteenth century, than they did in the first half of the nineteenth.[9] Such a view would have a measure of congruence with Marx's description of a 'period of manufacture' separating the guild form of independent handicraft production from the age of machino-facture and characterised by an increasing division of labour, a related expansion of the workshop as a means of organ-ising production and a continued dependence on the labour of skilled men: 'Inasmuch as handicraft skill formed the basis of manufacture and inasmuch as the integral mechanism which was at work in manufacture had no objective skeleton existing apart from the workers themselves, capital had continually to wrestle with the subordination of the workers.'[10]

Adam Smith, after all, took it for granted that disputes between masters and journeymen were endemic in manufacturing, indeed he would not have had to have looked further than two cities he knew well, Edinburgh and Glasgow, for examples from tailors, shoe-makers, cabinetmakers and masons among others. His fundamental assumption was that it was the normal condition of labour to be waged. Though we need not take his ratio of 20 : 1 as other than impressionistic, he clearly took the existence of a class of permanent journeymen, not destined to become either masters or independent producers, as an evident structural feature of the British manufacturing economy: 'What are the common wages of labour, depends everywhere upon the contract usually made between those two parties, whose interests are by no means the same. The workmen desire to get as much, the masters to give as little as possible. The former are disposed to combine in order to raise, the latter in order to lower the wages of labour.'[11]

While accepting that collective labour action both to defend and improve conditions of hiring and of work was normal, Smith was anxious to present it as necessarily ineffective against the 'laws' of the labour market. Laws against combination were, he argued, ineffective against masters, but a serious sanction on the workers. Further the employer had the resources to hold out while striking labour starved itself into submission. Desperate tactics to pressurise employers only succeeded in bringing the forces of law and order into the conflict, and the penalties prescribed by 'those laws which have been enacted with such severity against the combinations of servants, labourers and journeymen'.[12]

The widespread trade unionism of his time suggests that his insistence on ineffectiveness was overdone. There need be no denial of the very real difficulties which faced early unions to recognise that some degree of qualification is needed. That the law was on the side of the masters does not mean that they always saw it in their interest to use it, nor that it was not in many situations something of a blunt weapon. Reluctance to resort to it might stem from a desire to avoid making martyrs, or from the realisation that the processes of the law took time and prosecutions long after a dispute had ended might do no more than rouse hostilities among the returned labour force. Significantly employers seeking improved legislation wanted not more severe penalties, but speedy summary sentencing.[13]

In the preambles to the various statutes which outlawed trade unionism in specific trades, combinations are already described as 'unlawful'. They were so regarded under the Common Law of conspiracy. In Scotland a judgment in the Court of Session in 1762 specifically declared them unlawful, but in many instances combinations had already been so regarded and treated. Employers did not lack weapons and, as well as the intrinsic difficulties in using them effectively, we have also to understand a more general context which allowed, nevertheless, the persistence and spread of unions of skilled workers. Masters *could* indeed hold out longer in most instances than their workmen, but this does not mean that it was always in their

4

interest to do so. They were always likely to do so when, enforcing wage reductions or infringing established working practices, they provoked defensive strikes, but they were often prepared to do so for only a short time when workmen sought moderate advances in times of good trade. Higher profits were available in expanding markets, and if, as Smith himself argued, in such conditions increasing demand for labour would in any event lead to wage increases, there was no real point in resisting workers' demands when they struck on an upswing. Journeymen understood this. Clothing workers struck in the spring, the seasonal demand peak.[14]

Indeed craft unions showed an appreciation of the need to select the right moment to threaten or implement a withdrawing of labour. Shipwrights in the royal dockyards struck when fleets were being fitted out for war. Fellmongers chose Michaelmas, the time of the pre-winter livestock slaughter when their employers had piles of rapidly deteriorating hides on their hands. Edinburgh's tailors pressed for advances at times of coronation and of general mourning, while Coventry's black-ribbon weavers elected to strike on the death of a popular member of the royal family. Adam Smith also took no account of the importance of previously built-up strike funds, of help from other unions – although this was hardly available before the early nineteenth century – of saving support resources by sending single men on the 'tramp' to find work outside the locality, of subscription funds from local sympathisers, or of the earnings from the setting up of co-operative workshops. When the wool sorters of Exeter went on strike in 1787 against the woolstaplers, they had previously calculated that within a fortnight, given the large wool stocks they had on hand, their employers would capitulate and agree to an increase from 9s. to 10s. 6d. a week. They had built up a strike fund which, despite their belief that it would support those striking at their usual wages, the journeymen spoke of as the 'loaves and fishes'. There seems little doubt that they struck with confidence. They were defeated when the employers, having conceded wage increases in the past, decided to make a stand and secure arrests under the specific statute against combinations of woollen workers.

Two points should be noted: that the employers were using for the first time a statute passed against combining in the woollen manufacture nearly sixty years previously, despite their jour- neymen's successfully combining to secure wage increases on several occasions in the intervening period and that the journeymen's union was taking a risk with the law. Clearly at times either as individuals or, more effectively as an employer combination, masters did make effective use of the law, even in manufactures where they had previously given way to organised journeymen. The Sheffield cutlery trades, London printing and Kentish papermaking provide further examples.[15]

With such a capricious use of the law, unions operated in a context of risk rather than of full constraint. In the very many disputes where the law was not invoked, if the time to strike was well chosen, and they were well organised and adequately funded, they were far from being as hopeless as Smith portrayed them. The account by Francis Place of the strikes of the leather-breeches makers shows how strikes could be sustained beyond the ability or at least the willingness of employers to resist. The union supported itself through a long strike in 1796, setting up its own workshop as well as sending some men away on the tramp and although it did not win that year, the threat of a repeat the following year when funds had been rebuilt was enough to bring concessions from the masters. The hatters managed to pay £1 a week strike pay during one of their early disputes and several trades had by the end of the eighteenth century developed the rolling strike, or 'strike in detail' whereby shops were turned out one at a time so that those in work could support their brothers who had struck. Calico printers, compositors, papermakers and colliers were among them.[16]

Even the 'desperation', which Smith suggested tended to mark the eventual frustration of workers on strike and to complete their defeat by bringing the forces of order against them, can be more functionally viewed as a tactic of intimidation. Hobsbawm and others have commented on the sometimes effectiveness of 'collective bargaining by riot', while Randall has shown how pre-emptive action was used by west-country shearmen against the introduction of shearing frames.[17]

Crucially Adam Smith failed in his main discussion of workers' combinations to draw the distinction between skilled and unskilled workers which he clearly did elsewhere in the *Wealth of Nations*. Discussing apprenticeship, he did say of the wool combers, of whom around six were necessary to keep a very large number of weavers at work: 'By combining not to take apprentices . . . [they] . . . reduce the whole manufacture into a sort of slavery to themselves, and raise the price of labour much above what is due to the nature of their work'.[18] Here he recognised the power (which Marx also saw) resting in skilled handworkers. Since however great their incentive to make maximum use of cheap labour, employers still operated in manufacturing contexts in which they were unable to dispense with essential manual skills, they were 'checked by the customs and active resistance of male workers . . . Thus we find that in England the laws of apprenticeship, remained in force down to the end of the manufacturing period.'[19]

This power depended upon the defence of skill, both aganist deskilling innovation and as a frontier against the unskilled, including large numbers of women workers. Artisans assumed and later, when under pressure, articulated, a 'property of skill', and so long as they were able to restrict entry to their trade by their collective strength (legitimised before 1814 by the apprenticeship requirements of the statute law as well as by the 'custom of the trade') then they were not powerless in the sale of their labour power.[20]

The identification of skill with the apprenticed trades is clearly central, but not complete. As Campbell stresses in the case of the Scots colliers, even where there was no formal system of apprenticeship some work groups regarded themselves as skilled and the value which they put on that skill and their ability to restrict entry and to secure working practices was central to their unionism.[21] We should also remember, as Maxine Berg has pointed out, gender in many instances has as much to do with what was considered skilled as did the requisite degree of manual dexterity and of mental 'cunning'. The journeymen wool sorters of Exeter were by 1787 members of a union with a headquarters in London and tramping links through the country. A running grievance with their employers, the wool staplers, was their refusal to work with those who had not served an apprenticeship to the trade, even if they had so served in another branch of the woollen manufacture such as combing. Yet in Gloucestershire the work which they performed was normally done by women at only 60 per cent of male wages.[22]

Edward Thompson's classic presentation of the 'moral economy' of the eighteenth century was formulated in the context of the grain supply and of food rioting. In so far as it drew attention to customary expectations on the part of the lower orders, the meeting of which should be achieved through regulation of the 'market' and of the activities of those dealers and employers who operated within it, then historians have extended its application to other areas of popular action including industrial disputes.[23] Dr Randall, for example, in studies of the food rioting of 1766 and of the industrial strife of 1765–66 among Gloucestershire's woollen workers, has seen a 'community of shared values and expectations' incorporating beliefs and attitudes inexplicable by purely economic considerations underlying both protest forms. A Norwich wool comber protested to the employers during a dispute in 1752: 'We are social creatures, and cannot live without each other; and why should you destroy Community . . . '.[24]

The language of much eighteenth-century industrial protest signifies the existence of an 'industrial moral economy'. To accept this is not to deny that among well-established groups of urban craftsmen a perception of labour as a commodity which could be bargained with marked a step towards a more 'modern' system of industrial relations. Among the London groups studied in revealing detail by Dr Dobson, such as tailors and compositors, there is clear enough evidence of an arena of interaction within which employers and workers to a degree perceived their roles and the moves which were open to them. Here one can perhaps suggest 'conflict resolution' based upon mutual recognition of bargaining strength.[25]

Nevertheless in general and especially in the rural manufactures where weavers, knitters and the like existed as communities of producers the defence of customary standards and expectations is more evident than calculative bargaining. Even what sometimes appears to be the latter, when workers struck for an advance in wages or reduction in hours, may on further inspection turn out to have been the taking advantage of a strategic moment to *restore* conditions of employment. Employers naturally did not choose to acknowledge such disputes as being remedial action against reductions or impositions made by them at a time when they had been advantaged.[26] Against the regular upward negotiation of their wages through the eighteenth century by some urban artisans must be set the persistence of 'customary' wages in many crafts through decades or even from one generation to another. A west-country weaver stated in 1802 that his rate per yard had never altered: 'nor yet in my father's memory'. Nor were all urban crafts operating within a 'system' which allowed wage adjustment. The London masons complained in 1775 that their 50s. a week had persisted for seventy years.[27]

There is no unequivocal link between the skill level of a craft and its location in either a 'system of industrial relations' or a context of 'moral economy'. Despite their well-organised union, tramping system and apprenticeship control, the wool sorters of Exeter were not considered properly skilled. That they nevertheless acted as a craft group was the running complaint of their employers. Several of their number imprisoned in a dispute in 1787 were unable to sign their names. Yet they had succeeded in getting their wages raised several times in the course of the eighteenth century to levels comparable with those of more skilled groups in the serge manufacture. One of the years in which they secured an advance was 1765, yet in the following year the shipwrights of the port of Exeter, a craft acknowledged as skilled and commanding wages 50 per cent above those of woollen workers, were organising to defend their conditions of employment. In a carefully worded agreement which they drew up binding themselves not to work for employers who were seeking to reduce wages, they used a language redolent with custom and morality. Their employers were attempting to employ them at 'less wages than have been from time immemorially paid to journeymen shipwright' and to be endeavouring to 'deprive' them of 'several of their ancient rights and privileges' and to 'impose' on them longer hours than had been 'usual and customary'. In binding themselves not to accept less than 2s. 6d. a day, 'the usual and accustomed wages', they also insisted upon receiving 'the usual allowance . . . for liquor for every journeyman shipwright'.[28]

The Webbs understood trade unions to exist 'for the purpose of maintaining or improving' conditions of employment. To accept that the former was predominant is not to deny that from time to time some workers achieved success in the latter. Adam Smith noted 'offensive' and 'defensive' combinations.[29] To be effective in either case combined workers needed organisation and strategy. We have already discussed the latter, and we have space to do no other than note that even in the eighteenth century the latter was becoming evident in the emergence of tramping systems, delegate meetings, fund building etc.. Dr Haynes suggests below (Ch. 11) that the Webbs were a little too insistent on the 'primitive democracy' of the early unions and, as Robert Malcolmson has pointed out, it is significant that industrial disputes generally lasted longer than other forms of popular action, the relations of the work place being more continuously present than those of the market place. In a dispute lasting for several weeks there was ample opportunity and incentive for both sides to organise their forces:

One frequently observes at such times clear signs of conscious organisation among the workers: the calling of meetings and the planning of strategy; the drafting of a formal petition . . . for a redress of their grievances; visitations to various workplaces to force a stoppage of labour; the selection of deputies and delegations to represent the collective cause . . . negotiations with the employers or the local magistrates; the preparation of wage-lists and other such formal proposals, with the intention of reaching a long-term agreement in the trade.[30]

While there might still be room for disagreement over what were typical forms, objectives and contexts for eighteenth-century trade unionism, there can be no doubt that by the time of the passing of the Combination Acts in 1799 and 1800, organised labour was an important presence in the manufacturing economy of Britain.

THE COMBINATION ACTS

Clearly employers in a significant range of urban crafts would see in the passage of a general prohibitive combination statute a strengthening of their arm against established trade unionism: the more so because they would be obtaining the expediency of summary proceedings. Lord Holland recognised this in contributing to the parliamentary debate of 1799. The workmen, he argued, laboured under 'disadvantage arising from a certain degree of dread that pervaded all the upper ranks of mankind lest the lower ranks should be seduced' by 'subversive' principles 'particularly afloat at this period'. But, he continued, were not the masters conscious of this 'temporary advantage' and seeking 'to enforce their views and render their workmen more dependent than they had hitherto been, and than in all fairness and equity they ought to be?'[31]

The Combination Acts had two dimensions: the bringing of the state into a more evident repressive role against combinations (though even that was qualified by an ultimate dependence on employer initiation of proceedings) and the withdrawing of the state from an older 'regulative' role in the determination of the price of labour. The second as clearly represents an employer interest as the first does a more general one. It has been pointed out that in choosing a recent specific act against combinations of journeymen papermakers as a model, Pitt and his advisors were electing for a form which specifically broke the pattern of previous combination statutes by being prohibitive without the qualification of prescribing wage-regulation by the justices; even though the wage-fixing clauses of the Statute of Artificers were not to be repealed until 1813.[32]

Furthermore the special significance of the repeal of 1824 and of its modification in 1825 is that while it allowed in Britain, well ahead of any other country, a narrow recognition of trade union activities confined to matters of hours and wages it marked the complete abandonment of wage regulation in favour of a policy of negotiation between employers and their workmen. In out-manoeuvering the first bill for repeal drafted by Gravenor Henson and George White, Place and Hume may well have correctly calculated that it had scant hope of passage, but it remains true that that bill would have under-written some artisan expectations of regulation, circumscribed the free market in labour and imposed a degree of control on the oper-ations of employers. It is noteworthy that, while the Combination laws were in force, a powerful lobby of employers had secured in 1814 a further significant erosion of regulation in the labour market. This was the repeal of the statutory apprenticeship requirement of the Statute of Artificers in the face of organised artisan opposition.[33]

Historians have often repeated the verdict of the clerk to the investigating select committee of 1824 that the Acts had in general been a dead letter against 'those artisans on whom it was intended to have an effect' namely the printers, tailors, shoemakers and ship-builders who had continued their 'regular societies and houses of call, as though no such act were in existence'. The most recent historian of London trade unionism of the period has noted the spread and development in organisation of the city's trades during the period.[34] Outside London, and especially in the outworking trades like weaving and framework knitting and in the new manufacturing districts, it has been argued that the Acts had more effect and indeed by making trade unions illegal forged an association between them and the jacobin republican movement.[35]

The reconsideration of the Combination Acts by Dorothy George was, when first presented, an important qualification of views like that of the Hammonds who wrote of 'the most unqualified surrender of the State to the discretion of a class in the History of England'. Dr George presented the Acts as no new departure and as 'in practice a very negligible instrument of oppression'. Hers is a verdict that seems itself much in need of revision.[36]

That the Acts were not a new departure is an assertion commonly made by historians who draw attention to the pre-existing 'illegality' of trade unions under the common law of conspiracy and to the around-forty statutes prohibiting workers' combinations already in being. In fact of 34 statutes repealed along with the general one of 1800 by the Act of 1824, 20 had been passed since the Hanoverian succession of 1714. Of these, ten had not been passed by Parliament at Westminster at all but at Dublin and were specific to Ireland. One was directed at Scots miners and the nine which applied to England were all specific to particular trades and manufactures, and prior to the passage of the Act against the journeymen papermakers were all qualified by wage-regulating clauses binding on employers. Clearly, even if the Combination Acts did not amount to a wholly new departure, it is seriously misleading to present them as simply more of the same. George points out that harsher penalties were sometimes imposed under older laws than were allowed under the Acts of 1799 or 1800. But they were not for the simple fact of combination. They were imposed for activities linked with industrial disputes which would have attracted penalty as felonies in any legal context: assault, destruction of property etc. In any event the employers could not have it both ways. If the state was offering them speedy summary redress, then it could not attach the penalties imposable by the courts. This leaves the common law of conspiracy, under which prosecutions continued to be brought while the Combination Acts were in force. Common law decisions are not made in vacuum. In the Acts of 1799 and 1800 Parliament had pronounced its opinion about the illegality of trade unions and this was part of the atmosphere producing a situation in which it came to be expected that the courts would find against combined workmen.[37]

Finally it is worth emphasising, as Professor Orth has recently done, that there *was* a class dimension to the passing of the Acts. In 1799 penalties were for the first time prescribed for *workmen*, not as in previous statutes against hatters or papermakers; in other words the statute was couched in terms of a horizontal division of society, not in those of the vertical division of the 'craft'.[38]

English historians have been little concerned to discuss the legal situation of Scottish unionism in this period. It would seem likely that Pitt and Wilberforce envisaged a general prohibition since, after all, the industrial area around Glasgow and the coalfields of Lanarkshire were as 'dangerous' as any in Britain. However the Acts of 1799 and 1800 were not fitted to the Scottish legal system and were 'completely inoperative' there. A Glasgow cotton worker, convicted during a dispute, later told the inquiry of 1825 'of what law I am yet at a loss to know', for there was 'no statute law in Scotland'. Scottish judges could nevertheless take a clear lead from the passing of the laws even if they could not directly apply them. They regularly sought advice from the Home Office and evinced a clear disposition to treat combination as a crime. Significantly, John Burnett's major treatise on Scottish criminal law of 1810 clearly directs to such a verdict. The Scottish situation is made more intriguing by the continued and widespread seeking by artisans and miners of wage regulation by justices. Cases where employers refused to implement such 'fixings' sometimes were brought by organised workers to the Court of Session. Judges were clearly troubled by the difficulty presented by workers combined to secure their legal rights, and a number of cases just before the repeal in 1813 of the wage-fixing clauses of the Statute of Artificers seem to suggest that recent Scottish problems had much to do with the repeal of a legal provision which had long been in desuetude in England.[39]

The repeal of 1824 is correctly seen (see Moher below, Ch. 4) as acknowledging a place for trade unions within a framework of wage negotiation. But we need to stress not only how circumscribed that recognition was in reserving the wider terrain outside wages and hours to employer control, but also the need to recognise that for most employers, unions did not come into their scheme of things. They made hardly any move towards incorporating unions into their management strategies, and furthermore had still available an armoury of legal weapons with which to back their stand.[40]

AFTER THE REPEAL

Historians have not failed to note that the upturn in trade which coincided with the repeal of 1824 produced an outburst of union formation and activity which frightened the legislature into restoring in 1825 the application of common law conspiracy proceedings against workers' combinations, which it had unguardedly allowed to lapse in 1824. Fears that Parliament would go further than this were not realised. In part the downturn of trade at the end of 1825, beginning a depression which lasted to the end of the decade, returned the advantage to the employers. But more important in the longer run was an underlying structural change which had much more impact than the phasing of the trade cycle. This was population growth. The 1821 population of England closely approaching 11.5 million had doubled since 1751. Its rate of growth which had been around 0.5 per cent up to 1770, exceeded 1 per cent by 1800 and was at 1.5 per cent by 1821.[41] The labour market implications are evident. They were certainly taken by Francis Place whose pioneering advocacy of birth control largely stemmed from them.[42]

The responses of workers to technological innovation have been, as Dr Berg has presuasively argued, rather selectively presented by labour historians. That some groups such as shearmen, calico printers and sawyers took action against machinery which made their skills redundant is well known, but on the other hand Birmingham's artisans accepted and learned to work with a constant stream of innovation, in product as well as in machinery. Professor Hobsbawm long ago stressed the distinction between machine breaking where a deskilling machine was the object, and more generally where machinery was destroyed in the process of more generalised labour disputes. Even the classic Luddites, the framework-knitters of the East Midlands, opposed not machinery per se, but the employment on it of cheap labour to make inferior articles.[43]

The other argument, that some technical innovation came about specifically to break the power of organised skilled workmen is less often made. The search for a self-acting mule to dislodge the hold of the cotton-spinners has been most discussed in this context and here the intention seems clear even if the object was not achieved.[44] Equally well-known is the continuing attempt of significant employers in the rapidly developing engineering industry to rid themselves of dependence on skilled men. It had been their petitioning against the millwrights' union which had provided the occasion for the passing of the general Combination Acts; they had been in the vanguard of the campaign to end statutory apprenticeship and they directed much attention to securing a dilution of the labour force with the aid of a stream of newly invented or improved machine tools.[45]

But what more generally challenged the position of the artisan was the huge expansion of the 'sweating system' as the rapidly expanding labour force was tapped to fulfil the growing demand for ready-made clothes, shoes and furniture. For the London trades Mayhew's well-known descriptions of 1849–50 reveal how the expansion of outworking on ever decreasing piece rates had reduced the hold of the unions of skilled tailors, shoemakers, cabinet makers etc. to a bespoke, West End, quality section of the trade, enlisting perhaps as little as 10 per cent of the workers in their respective trades.[46] The same processes were at work in other towns, as McNulty shows below (pp 222) for Bristol, while in the building trades the rise of 'general contracting' was seeking to outmanoeuvre craft autonomy and force down rates. In vainly striking in 1834 for time, not piece, rates and for work on the employers' premises only, the London tailors were looking to uphold the old guarantees of artisanal production and their action had been foreshadowed in Paris in 1830 where merchant capitalists (*confectioneurs*) 'put out' to sweated outworkers to supply the ready-made trade.[47]

The limited nature of the legal recognition of 1824/5; the very considerable powers of using the law left to employers (for example under the Master and Servant legislation or under the recently provided statute against intimidation) and the demographically propelled expansion of the labour force were the main determining factors of trade union development in the next decade.[48] A fourth and related factor was the growth of class consciousness, in its turn dependent on the appearance of a 'language of labour', most evident in Owenism, but far from confined to it.[49]

The circumscribed nature of legal recognition and the accompanying explicit and emphasised outlawing of what had been in the past effective trade union practices encouraged some unions to adopt at least a public face of 'respectability'. But the effect could be quite different. Behagg has pointed to the importance of the related facets of violence and ceremony in trade union history from the 1820s to the 1840s. They were, he argues, consistently misunderstood by contemporaries as they have been by subsequent historians. Violence to 'knobsticks' (strike breakers) and ceremonial forms of initiation with their awesome binding oaths against betrayal; trade funerals with impressive processions revealing the strength and solidarity of the 'brothers of the trade' and workshop courts to try those who broke the 'rules' were all widespread and exhibited marked similarities of form from craft to craft and from place to place: from Leeds woolcombers to west country weavers, from London tailors to the poor labourers of Tolpuddle.[50]

Against the contemporary view that such practices amounted to the terrorising of the generality of workers in a trade into compliance with and membership of trade unions, which were 'the very worst of democracies', Behagg argues that what was involved was a form and practice of participatory democracy which stressed the obligations due to the work group and which underwrote and legitimised the sanctioning of those who in pursuit of individual advantage threatened the well-being of the 'community of the trade'. Elaborate rituals emphasised the sense of that community. Secrecy was essential for its survival and the preserving of its customary practices, norms and values. Essentially they defined the right of the workman to control the nature and pace of work, while allowing to the employer the separate sphere of initiating the process of production and marketing the finished product. To ensure this the world of the workshop had to remain a 'mystery' to outsiders.[51]

Expanding markets gave to early-nineteenth-century employers the incentive to innovate, perhaps through mechanisation, increasing the division of labour or otherwise diluting skills. Faced with such a challenge to traditional artisan status and well-being in a context

15

of a rapidly expanding working-population and of increasing mechanisation, it is not surprising that violence against 'knobsticks' occurred. The misunderstanding of many contemporaries was to represent it as a means by which the trade in general was forced to adhere to the policies of the 'society' rather than as a means by which the generality disciplined deviant individuals, or by which it sought to prevent the importation of cheaper 'unfair' labour from outside. It may have been 'rough justice', but that does not mean that its perpetrators did not consider themselves to be acting in a 'just cause': the defence of the trade and its customary methods of working and expectations of reward.

That the capitalist pressures which brought about these reactions were being felt simultaneously across several crafts was, as Behagg has noted for Birmingham, the condition which superimposed a class dimension on the pursuit of sectional craft interests. The real issue is not whether a class consciousness redefined issues and perspectives to replace a craft consciousness. It is less a matter of submerging the latter in wider ambitions than of the recognition of shared problems and the perception of common solutions. A considerable step towards a class consciousness is taken when artisans can recognise in a general framework of analysis, such as a labour theory of value – however rudimentary – something of their own situation and see in remedies such as co-operative production or franchise extension an appropriate objective. This is a more significant stage than the growth of inter-union co-operation, such as the widespread and well documented financial assistance given to each other in times of dispute. It is approached in organised inter-union pressure, such as in the campaign of 1814 against the repeal of statutory apprenticeship, or in that motivated by fear of repressive legislation from the inquiry of 1838 or against impending changes in Master and Servant legislation in 1844. It is revealed in the support for trade unionists on trial and in the campaign over the Tolpuddle Martyrs.[52]

What is significant about this period of trade union history is the emergence of a 'language of labour' in opposition to the relentless and destructive pressures of 'competitive' capitalism. In this sense Owenism made a major ideological contribution by giving more extensive propagation to ideas already present in the writings of the 'socialist economists'; to practices such as co-operative production and employment exchanges already tried in some local artisan contexts and to already appreciated ways of increasing organised labour's effectiveness through federation into general unions.[53]

It follows that there is a local dimension to the formation of class consciousness. Behagg has pointed to the significance of the 1820s in Birmingham. Fyson suggests that with the potters' union, whose strike and lock out of 1836–37 became a national working-class cause, in the vanguard, 1834–37 were the key years in Staffordshire. Sykes notes that the 1829–34 period was remarkable in the cotton districts of Lancashire for the extent of 'bitter industrial conflict on class lines' over fundamental issues of status, skill and work control over most of the major trades of the area. Textile workers predominated in 1829–31 and artisans in 1833–34. This 'experience of actual class conflict' and practice of trade unionism, linked with 'widespread diffusion of a mode of economic reasoning' deeply opposed to that of dominant ruling-class ideology provided the main economic basis for 'a heightened degree of working-class consciousness'. Haynes indicates such a 'moment' during the strikes of Northamptonshire shoemakers in 1834, while there is some justice in the claim that with the activities of Glasgow spinners and weavers, Edinburgh artisans and papermakers and Lanarkshire colliers to the fore, by 1831 the 'Scottish working class was already the most militant, class conscious and politically aware working-class in Europe'.[54]

Despite this, the Webbs' presentation of the years from 1825 to the formation of the Grand National Consolidated Trades Union in 1834 as a 'revolutionary' period has been much criticised. Oliver has corrected their over-estimation of the size and reach of the GNCTU, while Musson has chided them for their emphasis on 'ephemeral excitements' and neglect of the 'trade aspects' which were 'the most essential, solid and continuous features of trade unionism'. Undoubtedly historians should pay attention to 'patient organisation' and collective bargaining, but it would be misleading to insist on a separation between 'trade aspects' and class or political ones. Even if Owenite ideals and objectives extended beyond the horizons of many trade societies, the tailors, shoemakers, building craftsmen and others who joined the GNCTU most certainly did not dispense with traditional artisan aspirations: rather they sought new ways of realising them.[55]

There was no clear moment of change from 'revolutionary' to 'careful' unionism after the collapse of the GNCTU and the conviction of the men of Tolpuddle in 1834 as the Webbs supposed. As Musson has pointed out, many craft unions had never become involved in the excitement, though why they should be therefore considered more representative of 'real' trade unionism is not clear. Nevertheless a change of mood is unmistakable. The building craftsmen who retreated away from general unionism back to craft autonomy did not do so quietly: they vented strong feelings of condemnation as they left. The language of labour was less publicly articulated as to a more marked degree trade unionism concentrated on the workplace.

There was plenty of industrial conflict, for cautious official presentation contrasted with widespread and frequent local disputes. Even from the print workers, the craftsmen most often used as exemplars by Musson, there were 51 local disputes reported to the National Typographical Association in 1845 and 90 in 1846. The stone-masons had 44 in the north-west alone between 1840 and 1846. It does not seem helpful to dismiss these as 'trivial' or as 'usually small and petty' for many of them, including those in printing over apprenticeship, were, if local, nevertheless over fundamental issues and representative of skilled worker defences against innovation, labour dilution and attacks on traditional forms and levels of pay.[56] The great number of local strikes is symptomatic of employer opposition to unions throughout the period. The problem of suggesting a move in the more 'sophisticated' direction of peaceful negotiation and accepted bargaining procedures before the 1850s lies in the scant evidence of employer reciprocation.

Robert Leeson has applied the phrase 'business as usual' to the post-Tolpuddle years, emphasising developing organisation within the craft unions, and has suggested that the mid-1830s saw the beginning of a new stage, making them 'richly active' years in trade union history. From the late eighteenth century separate trade societies in different towns had begun to 'put themselves in a state of union' with each other. Perhaps 17 trades had achieved this by 1800. By the mid-1830s perhaps 40 had and few, if any, of the town trades had no union of an extra-local character. From that point most embarked on the difficult process of achieving a single union, that is, amalgamation. In 1834 'union' usually implied an organisation with from 20 to 80 member societies and by the 1840s the term 'branch' had come into use. It was adopted, for example, by the cabinetmakers in 1846. Total memberships ranged between 500 and 2000 with average local societies of between 15 and 50, but sharp increases often accompanied particular struggles. The masons claimed 5000 during their struggle against general contracting in 1833–34 and the carpenters 7000, but much of this could be ephemeral and many verbal commitments never finalised into paid-up subscriptions.[57]

Only very gradually did local control give way to centralisation of funds, while rotation of leadership among the branches was only slowly replaced during the 1830s and 1840s by fixed national office-holding. Control and consultation over striking were more a matter of assertion than practice. Few national unions did not attempt the policy of 'No town to stand without agreement' (cabinetmakers), but in practice in this respect national leaderships followed as much as they led, and 'recognised' rather than initiated. Contrast between 'official' disapproval of strikes and their widespread local occurrence is a feature of trade unionism in this period.[58]

As Leeson has suggested, although craft union structure evolved 'undramatically and pragmatically' in the period, the much greater degree of national organisation achieved by the 1850s probably in itself removed the flexibility which had allowed experiments like the GNCTU to happen. Certainly it has become increasingly difficult, as Musson has pointed out, to see what was new about the 'new model unionism' which according to the Webbs was inaugurated by the formation of the Amalgamated Society of Engineers in 1851.[59]

UNIONS AND POLITICS

Involvement with and participation in political movements by early trade unionists has tended to be discussed by historians on a national scale and often simply in terms of discussing the link with Chartism, and in particular the extent to which the 'general strike' of 1842 was politically led or inspired. However that the 'political' dimension needs to be sought in a wider and at the same time more local context has been established by John Foster's powerful study of Oldham. Here, as well as securing mass support by political action to protect illegal trade union practices while the combination laws were in force, the radical 'vanguard' of the working class were able to secure control of key local 'political' institutions, including the police.[60] Much work has been stimulated by Foster's challenging book, and although his claims have been disputed even by historians with a 'left' rather than 'right' inclination (see for example Sykes, below, Ch. 8) the need to study the political involvement of trade unions within a local context has been clearly established.[61] Fyson (in Ch. 9, and see note 62), for example, has instanced in the Potteries involvement in local affairs such as the appointment of parish overseers and poor rate collectors, campaigns against the incorporation of the Pottery towns and the introduction of the New Poor Law in 1836. Dr McNulty (Ch. 10) has described the local politics of trade unionism in Bristol during the same period. In that town at least it was not simply a matter of whether or not the 'organised trades' became involved with Chartism. Their aspirations towards 'respectability' were not the least of the factors which enabled local Liberals to look to them for support even before mid-century; indeed the support of the organised trades seems to have been rather a shifting thing. In that city too, issues were often local, such as the free port agitation in 1846.[62]

So far as national political movements are concerned, as Edward Thompson has pointed out, the failure of general unionism in 1834 probably convinced more of the articulate and thinking vanguard of the skilled working class that more might be expected from securing the vote than from syndicalist alternatives. It is as important to recognise this element of *conviction* as to acknowledge the degree of truth in the suggestion long since advanced by Lord Briggs that a pendulum rhythm produced political actions in bad times and industrial ones in good, that is, that the former was likely to be supported either by those trades, such as handloom weaving, whose circumstances of overstocking militated against effective unionism, or by better situated trades at times when they were disadvantaged by the trade cycle.[63]

Despite a recent insistence on the political nature of Chartism, it is evidently the case that weavers, knitters, and depressed urban groups like tailors and shoemakers sought the vote as a means of securing control over their lives and labour. Chartism may have been a political movement, but its economic vision was artisanal.[64]

Analyses of trade involvement in the widespread strikes in the industrial districts of the north and midlands in 1842, now generally described as a 'general' strike, have tended to diminish a previous scepticism about Chartist involvement, for example, Fyson on the Potteries and Sykes on the cotton districts (Chs 8 and 9). In the case of Lancashire the 'aloofness' claimed by Musson for the craft unions has been questioned, while Foster would seem to have offered a reasonable riposte to Musson's challenge to the significance he placed on Oldham events in 1842 as confirming the existence there of a politically conscious working class.[65] Prothero has further shown that in London the somewhat delayed support for the Charter after 1842 came from groups like tailors, shoemakers, carpenters and masons; the 'older trades' where the structural changes which we have already noted were limiting the effectiveness of industrial action. The future did not lie with such crafts. Mayhew was to show how tightly cornered their unionism had become by 1850, embracing only the workers who still worked in the shrinking West-End bespoke sections of their trade. They were however in the 1830s and 40s much more numerous and in their time accordingly more representative than the 'aloof elites' whose attitudes are sometimes presumed more representative of nineteenth-century unionism.[66]

One of the more notable episodes of the early 1840s was the formation of the Miners' Association of Great Britain and Ireland established in 1842. Early unionism on the Lanarkshire coalfield is described in this volume by Campbell (Ch. 6). In England too the history of colliers' unionism before 1842 is one of struggles on particular coalfields. The eighteenth century saw disputes in Northumberland, Durham and, before it ended, in Kingswood, Lancashire and Yorkshire. Unionism continued through the years of the Combination Acts and the Association of Colliers on the Tyne and Wear which emerged publically in 1824 was very like the Lanarkshire unions described by Campbell, for it was an exclusive union of the skilled hewers and pursued a policy of restricting output. The strikes in the north-east of 1810 and of 1831–32 have been described by the Hammonds, but what distinguished the strike of 1844 was that it was contested in Lancashire, Yorkshire, Staffordshire and Derbyshire as well as in the north-east. The human drama, especially in the north-east, with the bringing in of 'blacklegs' and the eviction of strikers' families is well known. The defeat of the union by 1845 in the north-east marked the beginning of the end, although in Lancashire, where the local market for coal gave the miners a more advantageous bargaining position, the Association held on until 1847. The extent to which, except in the person of its great lawyer, W. P. Roberts, it was linked to Chartism was probably limited, but at its peak with 60,000 members from every major coalfield, it presented one of the most awe-inspiring unions of its time.[67]

After the strike of 1842 and the ending of the first and most dynamic stage of Chartism, the history of trade unionism is usually presented through the growth of organisation and through concentration on several major, but craft-localised disputes such as those in the building trades and the great engineering dispute of 1852. The impression is one of an increasing accommodation to the economic precepts of a successful capitalist economy which became generally characteristic in the mid-Victorian boom. Foster has depicted the labour aristocracy as drawing away in the 1840s in sea change from the confrontation years of the early industrial revolution. This role of a new aristocracy of labour retains a persuasive power, despite challenges.[68] Yet accommodation, even given the growth and spread of arbitration and conciliation procedures and the achievement of a 'respectable' junta in gaining the very significant change in legal recognition in 1871, was at best partial. Craft unions strove to maintain apprenticeship, job demarcation and the closed shop and thus remained fundamentally opposed to basic capitalist assumptions of a free market in labour. They did not completely eschew intimidatory and violent methods. Even if they no longer sought, in Marx and Engels's phrase 'to turn back the wheel of history', but to secure and strengthen a bargaining position in the capitalist economy. Even if employers came to accept and accord them a role in the determination of wages and hours, none of this meant identification with the interest of the employer. As William Allan, the model leader of the model ASE, told the Royal Commission of 1867: 'it is their interest to get the labour at as low a rate as they possibly can, and it is ours to get as high a rate of wages as possible, and you never can reconcile these two things' [69] He spoke words hardly different from those written by Adam Smith nearly two hundred years before (above p. 4).

CONCLUSION

How is the position of British trade unionism in 1850 to be assessed? Its limitations are evident. Essentially it was confined to skilled workers, indeed maintaining a frontier against the unskilled was a central pre-occupation, even a rationale for existence. True the cotton spinners, who were male factory workers, organised under the impressive John Doherty in the early nineteenth century, but they are now considered not to have been a typical factory proletariat, rather as being imbued with the attitudes of the traditional artisan. At times, such as at the peak of Owenism, hints that it might stretch to embrace labourers and even women workers appear, but they were not fulfilled. The unskilled labour force was hardly to develop trade unionism before the last two decades of the century, while attitudes against women hardened rather than softened.[70]

Nevertheless it is a fact of very great significance that British trade unionism has a long history which began before the era of the factory and the formation of the modern proletariat. When unions reached beyond the ranks of the skilled they had much to inherit in attitudes and in tactics. To its craft origins must be attributed British unionism's distaste for industrial unions; its adherence to job demarcation and the 'closed shop' and, not least, its willingness to contest the employers' right to manage in matters of recruitment, working practice and wage forms.[71] For all that its distaste for 'foreign' socialism has seemed a matter for congratulation to some, the British trade union movement has, in important respects, been the least accommodating to the capitalist economy.

NOTES AND REFERENCES

1. **Sidney** and **Beatrice Webb**, *The History of Trade Unionism*, 1894. Recent works are: **C. R. Dobson**, *Masters and Journeymen: A prehistory of industrial relations 1717–1800*, Croom Helm 1980; **J. Rule**, *The Experience of Labour in Eighteenth-century Industry*, Croom Helm 1981 and **R. W. Malcolmson**, 'Workers' combinations in eighteenth-century England', in **M.** and **J. Jacob** (eds) *The Origins of Anglo-American Radicalism*, Allen & Unwin 1984, pp. 149–61.
2. **E. Lipson**, *Economic History of England III, The Age of Mercantilism*, A. & C. Black 1943, pp. 248–9.
3. This point was made by **H. A. Turner** in his pioneering book: *Trade Union Growth, Structure and Policy: A comparative study of the cotton unions*, Allen & Unwin 1962. See also: Rule, *Experience of Labour*, pp. 149–51.
4. Dobson, *Masters and Journeymen*, pp. 22, 24–5; Rule, *Experience of Labour*, p. 183.
5. Malcolmson, 'Workers' Combinations', p. 150. However the various forms of agricultural protest have been under-researched. Tolpuddle should not be considered in isolation from them; see especially the contribution by Roger Wells to this volume.
6. **I. R. Christie**, *Stress and Stability in Late Eighteenth-century Britain: Reflections on the British avoidance of revolution*, Clarendon, Oxford 1984, pp. 124, 141.
7. **Alan Fox**, *History and Heritage: The social origins of the British industrial relations system*, Allen & Unwin 1985, p. xiii.
8. See **E. P. Thompson**, 'English trade unionism and other labour movements before 1790', *Bull. of the Soc. for the Study of Lab. Hist.*, No. 17 (1968), pp. 19–24.
9. **P. H. Lindert**, 'English occupations, 1670–1811', *Jn. Econ. Hist.*, XL, No. 4 (1980), pp. 685–712.
10. **K. Marx**, *Capital*, Everyman, 1930, I, p. 389. For a fuller discussion see: **John Rule**, 'The property of skill in the period of manufacture', in **P. Joyce** (ed.), *Historical Meanings of Work*, Cambridge U.P. 1987.
11. **Adam Smith**, *Wealth of Nations*, ed. E. Cannan, 1904, pp. 74–5.
12. See the discussion in Rule, *Experience of Labour*, Ch. 7.
13. See Ch. 4 by J. Moher in this volume.
14. 'They generally begin in the Spring, when there is the greatest demand for goods and most plenty of work', *Commons Journals*, xx, 31 Mar. 1726, p. 648.

15. For these and other examples see Rule, *Experience of Labour*, pp. 178–9. Early strikes of the Edinburgh tailors were described by **W. Hamish Fraser** in 'Labour Relations and the Courts in Scotland, 1707–1813', a paper presented to the Fourth Anglo-Dutch Social History Conference at Newcastle Polytechnic in April 1983. The strike of wool sorters at Exeter in 1787 is well documented in a bundle of papers in the Devon County Record Office, ref. Law Papers G. 6 1787 (hereafter 'Wool sorters MSS'. For the development of the 'tramping' system see: **E. J. Hobsbawm**, 'The Tramping Artisan' in *Labouring Men*, Weidenfeld & Nicolson 1964, and **R. A. Leeson**, *Travelling Brothers*, Granada 1980. For employers combining against unions see Rule, *Experience of Labour*, pp. 172–4.

16. **Francis Place**, *Autobiography*, ed. M. Thale, Cambridge U.P. 1972, pp. 112–13; *BPP* 1824, v, *Third Report on Artisans and Machinery*, p. 148; Rule, *Experience of Labour*, pp. 182–3.

17. See **E. J. Hobsbawm**, 'The machine-breakers' in *Labouring Men*, and **A. J. Randall**, 'The Shearmen and the Wiltshire outrages of 1802: trade unionism and industrial violence', *Social History*, vii, No. 2, pp. 283–304.

18. Smith, *Wealth of Nations*, i, p. 141.

19. Marx, *Capital*, i, p. 389.

20. For apprenticeship generally see Rule, *Experience of Labour*, Ch. 4 and also 'Property of skill'.

21. See Ch. 6 by Alan Campbell in this volume.

22. **Maxine Berg**, *The Age of Manufactures 1700–1820*, Fontana 1985, pp. 151–3; document in 'Wool sorters MSS'.

23. **E. P. Thompson**, 'The moral economy of the English crowd in the eighteenth century', *Past and Present*, **50** (1971), pp. 76–136. For example see the suggestion by **Keith Snell** that it could extend to popular expectations from the poor law, *Annals of the Labouring Poor: social change and agrarian England 1660–1900*, Cambridge U.P. 1985. pp. 99–100.

24. See Ch. 6 by Adrian Randall in this volume. Quoted in Malcolmson, 'Workers' combinations', p. 149.

25. See Dobson, *Masters and Journeymen*, Ch. 10: 'Epilogue: a conservative interpretation of labour history'.

26. See Berg, *Age of Manufactures*, pp. 159–64. For representations of a defensive strike as aggressive see the petition and counter-petition in **W. E. Minchinton**, 'The petitions of the weavers and clothiers of Gloucestershire in 1756', *Trans. Bristol and Gloucs. Arch. Soc.*, lxxiii (1954), pp. 218–25.

27. *BPP*. 1802/3, vii, *Minutes of Committee . . . on the Woollen Trade*, p. 35; **M. D. George**, *London Life in the Eighteenth Century*, Penguin 1966, p. 166.

28. Devon County Record Office, 'Wool sorters' Mss' and 'Agreement of the Shipwrights', 146 B/ add Z1.

29. Smith, *Wealth of Nations*, i, pp. 74–5.

30. Malcolmson, 'Workers' combinations', p. 154.

31. *Parliamentary Register*, ix (1799), pp. 65–6.

32. For the most recent discussion see: **J. V. Orth**, 'The legal status of

English trade unions, 1799–1871', in **A. Harding** (ed.) *Law-Making and Law-Makers in British History*, Royal Historical Soc. 1980, pp. 195–207. See also Ch. 4 by J. Moher in this volume.

33. See Ch. 11 by Michael Haynes in this volume. For the repeal of statutory apprenticeship see: Rule, *Experience of Labour*, pp. 116–19 and **I. Prothero**, *Artisans and Politics in Early Nineteenth-century London: John Gast and his times*, Dawson 1979, Ch. 3.

34. Prothero, *Artisans and Politics*, pp. 40–3

35. This argument is developed in **E. P. Thompson**, *The Making of the English Working Class*, Penguin 1968, p. 546; **J. Foster**, *Class Struggle and the Industrial Revolution: early industrial capitalism in three English towns*, Unwin 1977, pp. 38, 49–50.

36. A major re-assessment was presented to the Conference on the History of Law, Labour and Crime at the University of Warwick, Sept. 15–18 1983: **J. V. Orth**, 'M. Dorothy George and the Combination Laws reconsidered'. **J. L.** and **B. Hammond**, *The Skilled Labourer* (ed. J. G. Rule) Longman 1979, pp. 80, 89; **M. D. George**, 'The Combination Laws', *Econ. Hist. Rev.*, Ist ser. VI (1935/6), p. 177.

37. Several of these points were made by Professor Orth in his Warwick conference paper. See also Ch. 4 by J. Moher in this volume.

38. Orth, 'Legal status', pp. 205–6.

39. An important discussion was provided by Dr Fraser in his Newcastle conference paper (see note 15). **G. D. H. Cole** and **A. W. Filson**, *British Working-Class Movements. Select documents 1789–1875*, Macmillan 1967, footnote to pp. 98–9. **J. D. Young**, *The Rousing of the Scottish Working Class*, Croom Helm 1979, p. 48; **John Burnett**, *Treatise on the Various Branches of the Criminal Law in Scotland*, 1810. For the significance of the Scottish context in the repeal of statutory wage fixing in 1813 see documents nos. 128–34, 136–9, 141–4. Note the view of J. J. Dillon to the Home Secretary (Doc. 134): 'No lawyer can doubt that a combination of workmen to institute legal proceedings in order to establish through a competent jurisdiction the rate of wages, is a proceeding perfectly justifiable', quoted in **A. Aspinall**, *The Early English Trade Unions*, Batchworth 1949, pp. 137–61.

40. Orth, 'Legal status', p. 206; **W. Hamish Fraser**, *Trade Unions and Society: The Struggle for Acceptance 1830–1880*, Allen and Unwin 1974, pp. 185–6. Lord Melbourne told a manufacturer in 1833 that trade unions were 'inconsistent, impossible and contrary to the law of nature' (**David Cecil**, *Lord M. or the Later Life of Lord Melbourne*, Arrow Books 1972, p. 89).

41. **E. A. Wrigley** and **R. S. Schofield**, *The Population History of England*, Arnold 1981, pp. 528–9.

42. For a discussion of Place and the early birth control movement see: **W. L. Langer**, 'The origins of the birth-control movement in England in the early nineteenth century', in **T. K. Rabb** and **R. I. Rotberg** (eds), *Marriage and Fertility*, Princeton U.P. 1980, pp. 267–75.

43. See Ch. 3 by Maxine Berg in this volume; Hobsbawm, 'Machine breakers' pp. 6–7. For a review of the historiography of Luddism see my introduction to the 1979 edition of the Hammonds' *Skilled Labourer*.

44. For contrasting views on the consequences of introducing the self-acting

mule see: Foster, *Class Struggle*, pp. 231–2 and **W. Lazonick**, 'Industrial relations and technical change: the case of the self-acting mule', *Camb. Jn. of Economics*, **3**, (1979), pp. 231–62.

45. See Foster, *Class Struggle*, pp. 224–9.
46. See **E. P. Thompson** and **E. Yeo** (eds), *The Unknown Mayhew*, Penguin 1973, pp. 218, 223, 276–94, 410, 444, 455–6, 500–11, 536–40, 559–60. For a general discussion of these developments see: **J. G. Rule**, *The Labouring Classes in Early Industrial England, 1750–1850*, Longman 1986, pp. 341–3. For building trade unionism see **R. W. Postgate**, *The Builders' History*, Labour Publishing Co. 1923 and **R. Price**, *Masters, Unions and Men, Work Control in Building and the Rise of Labour 1830–1914*, Cambridge U.P. 1980, pp. 36–8, 41.
47. See **C. H. Johnson**, 'Economic change and artisan discontent: the tailors' history 1800–1848' in **R. Price** (ed.), *Revolution and Reaction: 1848 and the Second French Republic*, Croom Helm 1975, pp. 87–114. For a general European context see **J. G. Rule**, 'Artisan attitudes: a comparative survey of skilled labour and proletarianisation before 1848', *Bull. of the Soc. for the Study of Lab. Hist.*, No. 50 (1958) pp. 22–31. The London tailors' strikes are described in Prothero, *Artisans and Politics*, pp. 300–2 and in **T. M. Parssinen** and **I. J. Prothero**, 'The London tailors' strike of 1834 and the collapse of the Grand National Consolidated Trades Union: a police spy's report', *Inter. Rev. of Soc. Hist.*, xx (1977). For tailors' unionism in Bristol see Ch. 10 by D. McNulty in this volume and for Bath see: **R. S. Neale**, *Bath: A Social History 1680–1850, or A Valley of Pleasure, Yet a Sink of Iniquity*, Routledge 1981, pp. 69–70, 91, 269.
48. For a discussion of the post-1824/5 situation see Ch. 11 by M. Haynes in this volume. The demographic factor is also stressed by Orth, 'Legal status', pp. 202–3, who also discusses the legal situation.
49. See Rule, *Labouring Classes*, Ch. 12.
50. See Ch. 7 by C. Behagg in this volume and also his important article: 'Secrecy, ritual and folk violence: the opacity of the workplace in the first half of the nineteenth century', in **R. D. Storch** (ed.), *Popular Culture and Custom in Nineteenth-Century England*, Croom Helm 1982, pp. 154–79.
51. Behagg, below, Ch. 7.
52. **C. Behagg**, 'Custom, class and change: the trade societies of Birmingham', *Social History*, iv, No. 3 (1979), p. 456. For the significance of these 'moments' in Bristol see Ch. 10 by D. McNulty.
53. On this point see **J. F. C. Harrison**, 'Owenism and the Unions' a summary of a conference paper in *Bull. of the Soc. for the Study of Lab. Hist.*, No. 49 (1984), pp. 21–2; Prothero, *Artisans and Politics*, pp. 239–64 and 332–40; Rule, 'Property of skill', pp. 117–18.
54. See Behagg, 'Custom, class and change', p. 456; Ch. 9 by R. Fyson and Ch. 8 by R. Sykes in this volume; **M. J. Haynes**, 'Class and class conflict in the early nineteenth century: the Northampton shoemakers and the Grand National Consolidated Trades Union', *Literature and History*, No. 5 (1977), pp. 88–91; Young, *Rousing of the Scottish Working Class*, p. 81.
55. **W. H. Oliver**, 'The Consolidated Trades Union of 1834', *Econ. Hist.*

Rev , XVII, No. 1 (1964), pp. 85–8; **A. E. Musson**, *British Trade Unions 1800–1875*, Macmillan 1972, p. 29 ff.

56. Musson, *British Trade Unions*, pp. 29–35; Rule, *Labouring Classes*, pp. 296–8, 325.

57. **R. A. Leeson**, 'Business as usual – craft union developments 1834–1851'. *Bull. of the Soc. for the Study of Lab. Hist.*, No. 49 (1984), pp. 15–17.

58. Leeson, 'Business as usual', p. 17; Rule, *Labouring Classes*, p. 325.

59. Leeson, 'Business as usual', p. 17; Musson, *British Trade Unions*, pp. 51–6.

60. See **F. C. Mather**, 'The General Strike of 1842: a study of leadership organisation and the threat of Revolution during the Plug Plot disturbances', in **R. Quinault** and **J. Stevenson** (eds), *Popular Protest and Public Order*, Allen & Unwin 1974, pp. 115–35. This is the much discussed argument of the first part of Foster's *Class Struggle and the Industrial Revolution*.

61. As well as Robert Sykes's contribution to this volume see his article: 'Early Chartism and trade unionism in south-east Lancashire' in **J. Epstein** and **D. Thompson** (eds), *The Chartist Experience*, Macmillan 1982, pp. 152–93.

62. See Ch. 9 by R. Fyson in this volume and his article: 'The crisis of 1842: Chartism, the colliers' strike and the outbreak in the Potteries', in Epstein and Thompson, *Chartist Experience*, pp. 194–220. Ch. 10 by D. McNulty.

63. Thompson, *The Making*, pp. 908–10; **Asa Briggs**, 'The local background of Chartism', in **Briggs** (ed.), *Chartist Studies*, Macmillan 1962, p. 6.

64. See **G. Stedman Jones**, 'The language of Chartism', in Epstein and Thompson, *Chartist Experience*, pp. 3–58.

65. Sykes, 'Early Chartism and trade unionism', pp. 177–81; **A. E. Musson**, 'Class struggle and the labour aristocracy, 1830–60', *Social History*, **3** (1976) pp. 340–3 and Foster's reply in ibid., 357–60.

66. **I. J. Prothero**, 'London Chartism and the trades', *Econ. Hist. Rev.*, XXIV, No. 2, pp. 202–18.

67. For the Miners' Association and its links with Chartism see: **R. Challinor** and **B. Ripley**, *The Miners' Association: a Trade Union in the Age of the Chartists*, Lawrence & Wishart 1968. See also **A. J. Taylor**, 'The Miners Association of Great Britain and Ireland, 1842–8', *Economica*, XXII (1955). For earlier miners' unions see Hammonds, *Skilled Labourer*, Chs 2 and 3 and Rule, *Labouring Classes*, pp. 313–16.

68. Foster, *Class Struggle*, Ch. 7 and his reply to Musson in *Social History*, **3** (1976), p. 359. For a very useful summary discussion see: **R. Q. Gray**, *The Aristocracy of Labour in Nineteenth-century Britain c. 1850–1914*, Macmillan 1981.

69. Quoted in **H. Browne**, *The Rise of British Trade Unions 1825–1914*, Longman 1979, p. 31.

70. For the suggestion that the cotton spinners were 'factory artisans' see: **P. Joyce**, *Work, Society and Politics: The culture of the factory in later Victorian England*, Methuen 1982, pp. 60–3. For attitudes towards women see: **B. Taylor**, *Eve and the New Jerusalem*, Virago 1983,

pp. 83–117. On Owenism and for the nineteenth century generally consult **E. H. Hunt**, *British Labour History, 1815–1914*, Weidenfeld & Nicolson 1981.

71. See the discussion in Fox, *History and Heritage* pp. 89–91.

CHAPTER TWO

The Industrial Moral Economy of the Gloucestershire Weavers in the Eighteenth Century

Adrian Randall

INTRODUCTION

In recent years social historians have paid increasing attention to popular protest in the eighteenth century. In particular E. P. Thompson's seminal article, 'The moral economy of the English crowd in the eighteenth century'[1] has stimulated a continuing re-appraisal of the character of the food riot, the most typical form of popular disturbance. Research has also extended into the fields of agrarian protests, political disturbances and crime. Yet this awakened interest has to a surprising extent passed the study of eighteenth-century trade unionism by. While social history has spread its nets and analysis wide, eighteenth-century labour history has, with certain notable exceptions, remained closely confined with the box club and the strike.

One reason for this may be traced to the Webbs' pioneering work and their insistence upon the definition of trade unions as 'continuous associations of wage earners' [my italics]. This emphasis on formal and overt organisation, upon regular meetings and orderly negotiations, has (as it did with the Webbs) resulted in a heavy bias towards the study of those Metropolitan artisans whose historically accessible combinations most approximate to this model and in the neglect of the equally typical fragmentary union tradition which was characteristic in a wide variety of trades across the country. Such 'ephemeral combinations against their social superiors', as the Webbs termed them,[2] were deliberately excluded from their remit. This neglect has been criticised by more recent scholars. Thus Turner has shown of the cotton trades that 'continuous association' did not necessarily require formal organisation, rule books or recognised

leadership but rather the 'natural association' of common experience.[3] John Rule echoes this view, arguing 'It is not useful to think
of a polarisation of organised trade union activity at one pole and
sporadic "one-off" actions at the other. Instead there was a spectrum
of responses'.[4] Nonetheless the emphasis upon formally constituted
institutions remains strong. Thus Dobson, while noting the variety
of union structures, emphasises 'the level of organisation achieved
by the early trade unions' and their need for 'a permanent base for
continuous association'.[5] And Musson asserts that 'humdrum
matters relating to wages, hours, apprenticeship etc. and the development of union structures are of more fundamental importance'
than 'violence, machine breaking and mass demonstration'.[6]

A more critical, though related, hindrance to the study of eighteenth-century combinations has been the tendency, again dating
from the Webbs, to view them as dimly flickering antecedents to the
trade unionism of the nineteenth century rather than as products of
their own unique context. Musson, for example, forthrightly echoes
the Webbs, emphasising the progressive nature of orderly unionism
as distinct from earlier 'more primitive aspects'. 'The development
of peaceful constitutional collective bargaining in place of crude violence was part of the progress from primitive barbarism to a more
civilised society'.[7] Hobsbawm's pioneering rescue of the role of violence in eighteenth-century industrial disputes from assertions of
barbarism such as this nonetheless also slides into a developmental
view of early trade unions. 'Collective bargaining by riot' was a
form of combination found among trades where 'organised unions
hardly as yet existed', a transitional stage of growth, or 'proto
unionism' as Hunt has described it.[8] Stevenson takes this line further
and posits a sort of development theory of protest. In this, popular
protest is seen as evolving from spontaneous insurrection, graduating
to orderly and directed price fixing, developing through collective
bargaining by riot and finally culminating in the strike, the
membership card, industrial conciliation and arbitration. Thus he
notes that between 1793 and 1815, 'Not only were food riots
declining in number, but they were being replaced by other forms
of protest more suited to an industrial environment'. In places 'food
riots merged into "collective bargaining by riot" . . . Elsewhere
rioting had already been overtaken by trade union activity and
strikes.' Thus there was, he claims, "a modernisation of protest" as
the patterns of protest appropriate to the "face to face" society of the
small market town gave way to the more permanent and larger-scale
organisations of urban and industrial life'.[9] Again the emphasis is on

seeing trade unionism as an orderly institutional form, a product of coming to terms with capitalism, not as something indigenous to pre-industrial society.

It is the contention of this paper that such approaches may hamper our understanding of both the character and motivation of a large number of eighteenth-century combinations. While an overt formal structure and organisation might be possible and applicable to skilled workshop trades, it was not the only form of combination, nor was it necessarily appropriate to the needs or environments of many industrial groups. Nor was the failure of such trades to establish 'continuous associations' proof of their industrial weakness such that resistance could only occur through rioting. Further, by imposing the straitjacket of a specific, mostly nineteenth-century, image of 'the trade union' or 'the strike' upon eighteenth-century workers, the historian may well restrict his understanding of their motivation, actions and expectations by assuming a certain sort of economic rationality, an awareness of market forces and bargaining strategies, which may in fact have been quite alien to the perceptions and context of pre-industrial manufacture.

It is necessary, I suggest, to see eighteenth-century combinations as products of the workers' communities, not as something independent of them; as organisations which arose from the industrial and social context within which work took place and in which 'work' and 'life' were much less sharply divided than in the age of the factory; and which developed according to the character of need as perceived by those at the time. Such communities, the basis of combination, were also in many cases the source from which other forms of popular protest, and in particular food riots, so often sprang in the eighteenth century. English historians have been reluctant to examine links between the two. Shelton, one of the few to investigate both, nonetheless strictly compartmentalises the 'sophisticated' Metropolitan industrial protestors from the 'unsophisticated' rural food rioters, finding their only common denominator in the depressed economy of 'a decade of social transition'.[10] Bohstedt's approach is much more subtle but he likewise characterises food riots as products of a certain sort of community, seeing their disappearance as indicative in part of a shift from a consumer to a labour consciousness manifested in organised industrial protest.[11] John Rule has perceptively noted the ways in which workers 'preserved in experience and tradition' a pattern of 'recurrent behaviour' in industrial conflicts very like that found in food riots. But he does not develop the idea.[12] The most interesting exploration of such linkages concerns not English workers but the textile workers of Rouen studied by Reddy. By examining the 'language of the crowd' and the symbolism of their actions Reddy notes common themes permeating all sorts of protests and warns against interpreting them solely within a narrow functionalist framework. Behind all protests, he suggests, may be seen a community of shared values and expectations which incorporated beliefs and attitudes inexplicable by purely economic considerations.[13]

Reddy's emphasis on the need to understand the *mentalité* of the crowd within its own context is important, but his interest lies in long-term continuities and changes. The purpose of this paper is rather different: to ascertain how far we may discern common community values and expectations in both the market place and at work within the same time period. The area chosen for study, the Gloucestershire textile-producing region, offers a good example for it experienced a major industrial dispute in 1755–68 and extensive food riots in 1766. I shall suggest that examination of these disturbances indicates that there was indeed such a common perception informing actions in both spheres. In the market place such an ideology has been described as 'the moral economy of the poor'.[14] It will be argued that similar values and imperatives informed conflicts in the workplace, values which may be described as an industrial moral economy, and that these preclude viewing eighteenth-century combinations in isolation from their social context or simply as prototypes for later trade unionism.

THE COMMUNITY CHARACTER OF COMBINATION

The character of eighteenth-century combination depended on the character of the trade. Clearly it was easier to maintain a formal and continuous union presence in workshop trades where skills were at a premium and not easily acquired. Yet we should note that even such combinations were certainly not always overt. The West Country shearmen for example were certainly organised on a parochial basis from at least the 1740s, but their unions' presence was felt only on odd occasions, as in 1769 when a county-wide Wiltshire and Somerset federation was involved in a dispute over incomings. Certainly they left no rule books or written agreements to evidence their 'continuous association'. And in 1802 it was discovered they had joined these parochial branches into a union which embraced all cloth workers in both the West of England and the West Riding and which issued common membership tickets and co-ordinated resistance to machinery. This 'Brief Institution' only came to the notice of the authorities because of the Wiltshire Outrages of 1802. Yet this national union had been set up, as far as can be seen, in 1796.[15] Historians assume (with good reason) that combination was more difficult for outworkers, by virtue of their scattered and dispersed domestic work location and the variety of products and masters. Yet these problems were not insurmountable.[16] And against them must be set the strong community identity of such groups and their need to maintain some control over work and custom.

Take the example of the Gloucestershire weavers: they were certainly widely scattered, working in their own cottages in parishes around the west-facing scarp slopes of the Cotswolds. Yet in times of crisis they were held together by a constant interchange of delegates. And always there was the regular social and industrial interchange of information in the public houses, on bearing home day, at inter-parochial sports or social event, or getting in the harvest. When 'illegal' weavers took up the loom, or when a weaver broke ranks and accepted under-price work or took work from a blacklisted clothier, it was the community which punished him, carrying him around the district seated astride him own stinge, the large pole used for carrying woven cloth, and ducking him in his master's mill pond. It was from this same community basis that the weavers of Bisley in 1802 hired a Cheltenham solicitor and began proceedings against a local clothier for employing illegal weavers in a loomshop, the first engagement in the weavers' unsuccessful campaign to protect the apprenticeship legislation.[17]

The Gloucestershire weavers were also, however, quite able to form effective county-wide organisations. Thus in 1755–6 they united to petition Parliament to enact new legislation authorising the bench to rate wages annually, an action deemed necessary since some clothiers were endeavouring to use poor trade to reduce wage rates, and because previous legislation allowing for the rating of wages had proved ineffective. They established a formally constituted association which embraced all weavers in the county, levied subscriptions (at a time of low work and high prices) and hired a solicitor to help present their case. This association was organised on a parochial basis, each parish sending delegates to a central committee of managers who explained their policy to the members at seven consecutive open meetings at public houses in the major weaving parishes of the county. There was a clear central leadership in which pride of place was taken by a man named John Gay who successfully led the weavers' evidence at Westminster.[18] This same sort of organisation characterised subsequent county-wide unions in 1793, in 1802–6 and in the years from 1825–28 and 1838–39. The number of delegates per parish and the number of principals varied.[19] But the structure, the accountability and the constitutionalist character always remained.

But, while county-wide organisations came and went (and we should remember the legal restrictions on combinations other than for petitioning purposes), the weavers' ability to constitute these combinations so rapidly and effectively is indicative of a lower level semi-permanent organisation. This is much less easy to discern, but the petition to the Quarter Sessions in 1755 requesting the justices to rate wages as they had formerly done which commenced the weavers' parliamentary initiative of that year originated with the weavers of Horsley, who had already held discussions with sympathetic magistrates and had constructed their own table of wage rates.[20] At a local level then some loosely organised presence was probably permanent. Its basis was the local sick club or friendly society, burial club or just a public house at which the weavers regularly met: in other words those local institutions which were a natural product of the daily lives of the local weaving community.

It is clear therefore that the Gloucestershire weavers, like the weavers in the neighbouring counties of Wiltshire and Somerset, had the capacity to organise. But it is also true that their wider organisations were essentially for defensive purposes. Defence – protection of custom, resistance to wage cuts – is indeed characteristic of weavers' unions from the early eighteenth century into the 1830s, as it is of unions of framework knitters and other outworkers. The main role of combination in such trades was to defend customary rates and customary rights. It is worth asking why this should have been so, particularly as Dobson has suggested that the great majority of disputes throughout the eighteenth century involved aggressive strikes for wage increases. The economic circumstances of these industries can offer only a partial explanation. Certainly growing competition for markets was manifested in 'downward pressure on piece rates',[21] and the West of England woollen industry in particular was failing to match the remarkable growth rate of the West Riding. But this decline was relative.[22] Production levels generally at least kept pace with population, though the pattern of booms and slumps was more acute than in most other craft industries. Other trades suffered wage cuts in depressions and like the weavers sought to protect living standards, but they also used booms to claw back lost ground and to improve conditions by striking work. Booms in out-working trades however rarely witnessed such actions. The weavers' failure to use in an aggressive mode a weapon within their compass may therefore be seen as indicative of a belief that it was not an appropriate strategy, indicative indeed of a wider *mentalité* towards industrial relations. How can we discover what were the bases of this *mentalité*? The characteristics of industrial action among the weavers – the community basis, the defence of custom and the repudiation of the erosion of 'rights' – also characterised the eighteenth-century food riot. Comparison of the two indicates an ideology common to both.

THE PROTESTS OF 1756 AND 1766

The Gloucestershire woollen industry, centred around Stroudwater, Wotton and Dursley, was one of the major textile producers of mid-eighteenth-century England. The towns, villages and hamlets which clustered together under the Cotswolds held a population estimated by Rudder in 1779 at around 40,000,[23] and a very large proportion of these were involved in cloth production. Organised on the out-working system, the industry was highly capitalistic and specialised in organisation, and the quality of its products was tribute to the craft skills of its workers who exhibited a strong sense of independence and solidarity. This independence was emphasised in work custom and community values and in a tradition of vigorous resistance to detrimental change both as consumers and as producers.

The Gloucestershire woollen manufacturing districts experienced major food riots in 1766, 1795 and 1800–1, but those of 1766 were much the most extensive.[24] The riots which broke out in September in the Stroudwater area were to last for nearly six weeks. They followed a disastrous but superficially good-looking harvest, rocketing food prices, a rapid movement of grain stocks for export after 26 August and a growing belief that chicanery by middlemen was creating an artificial shortage. The riots in Gloucestershire soon assumed a clear form with large crowds of regulators, summoned by the blowing of horns and led by flags and emblems, marching around the district, setting the price at all the local markets and at markets as far afield as Gloucester, Cirencester and Lechlade. They also systematically scoured farms, shops and factors' warehouses for food stocks, seizing it if they were opposed, but generally paying the owner what they deemed was a 'fair' price. Troops were rushed into the county but were not used to confront the regulators. The riots died down of their own volition by mid-October for, following their actions, food prices fell, tenant farmers under pressure from their landlords were bringing grain to market, and the gentry were organising charities and magazines of wheat for sale to the poor. They were also exercising a firm and very public control over the markets.

The Gloucestershire woollen-manufacturing districts had experienced similar problems of rising food costs a decade earlier. The outcome then had been unrest, disturbance and the influx of troops. But in 1756 the conflict arose not over food prices but over wages as weavers resisted exploitation as producers rather than as consumers.

The early 1750s was a period of generally depressed trade for the industry.[25] As pressures on clothiers mounted, old abuses such as payment by truck, the use of promissory notes and of illegal warping bars by which the weavers were defrauded of a fair remuneration, all increased. The weavers' situation was further worsened by a growing employment of 'illegal' (those not 'brought up in the trade') men and women in looms in master weavers' workshops. All these trends antagonised the weavers. But it was the decision of some clothiers in 1755 to cut piece rates which triggered conflict. Their number was not large, but the weavers recognised that these men put pressure on all other clothiers and that, if they succeeded, other piece rates would begin to spiral down following their lead.[26]

The Gloucestershire weavers' response to this threat was informed by their previous experience of such conflict, in particular in the years 1726–8. Then abuses and wage cuts had led to six weeks of riot. However, the local gentry and bench had shown themselves well disposed to the weavers' case and central government had strengthened legislation against truck and illegal warping bars and, most significantly, had confirmed the power of the bench to arbitrate in disputes and to rate wages annually at the quarter sessions. This the bench had done in 1728. Determined non-cooperation by the clothiers, who were able to adjourn cases for failure to pay the fixed rates to higher courts, and continuing poor trade put an end to such rating after 1732.[27]

But the weavers remained convinced that such a system of determining wages was the most effectual method of protecting their trade. Thus, as noted above, when faced in 1755 by wage cuts, the weavers appealed to sympathetic magistrates who advised them to utilise the existing machinery and request that the Quarter Sessions should again fix a rate, either that of 1728 or a new one, generally some 10 per cent lower.[28] The bench, however, was reluctant to act. Thus, again with the support of some gentlemen, the weavers successfully petitioned Parliament for new legislation. The new Act not only reiterated the right of the bench after due discussion to rate wages but also precluded appeals against conviction for failing to pay these rates going to higher courts.[29] The weavers were jubilant and immediately proposed a new rate for the Michaelmas Sessions' approval.

The clothiers had done little to counter their weavers' petition to Parliament, believing that 'nothing was intended but to amuse the weavers'. They were shaken by the realisation that, amused or not, the weavers intended to take the new Act seriously, and, worse still, so did many members of the bench. They immediately embarked on a major propaganda offensive in an attempt to browbeat the justices and persuade them that regulation was harmful, impracticable and impolitic. In a long memorial, they drafted a strident defence of a *laissez faire* political economy and warned that the result of interference would be social insubordination and the decay of trade.[30]

Faced with two contradictory pressures and divided among themselves, the bench vacillated and agreed to shelve the decision.[31] The weavers were clearly frustrated, but their organisation held firm. They resolved to attempt to force the issue by playing their one remaining card. They struck work. The strike was to last from the second week in October until December in many areas. The clothiers' propaganda stressed violence and coercion, but it is clear that the strike generally was very orderly and highly organised.[32] It was supported by some gentlemen and viewed with sympathy both by the *Gloucester Journal* and by the officer in command of the troops who were dispatched to Gloucestershire in mid-October to maintain order, James Wolfe.[33] The weavers twice endeavoured to find a negotiated settlement with their employers. The majority of clothiers stood firm, but some were prepared to be conciliatory, and, on the basis of an agreement reached on 2 November, a reconvened bench ratified a new rate on 6 November over the opposition of many wealthy clothiers.[34] This denoted the high water mark of the dispute for the weavers. They had worked within due constitutional channels, obtained a new Act and, with a certain use of industrial muscle, had now achieved their aim. They prepared to return to work.

Unfortunately, the clothiers had much less regard for constitutional niceties. Many ignored the rate and tried to pressurise their
weavers into accepting lower wages. Their weavers therefore
continued on strike though their resources were clearly stretched and
some violence ensued when a few decided to work at the proffered
rates.[35] Yet the weavers' leadership held firm and in December they
successfully used the courts to prosecute two very eminent clothiers
for non-compliance with the Sessions' order.[36] This more than
anything else convinced the clothiers that they must ensure the repeal
of the 1756 Act. Publicly most accepted the new rates and the strike
ended, but secretly they orchestrated a petition and lobby of Parliament, and in January 1757 published their own highly biased account
of the dispute. In February their bill for repeal was introduced.
Belated counter petitions from the weavers and also from gentry and
freeholders in the county were ignored and the bill was accepted
by the Commons and Lords by March.[37]

THE INDUSTRIAL MORAL ECONOMY OF THE GLOUCESTERSHIRE WEAVERS

A comparison of these events of 1756 and 1766 reveals many parallels
and indicates a strong underlying unity of participants, actions and
motivation.

It is clear that the participants in both strike and food riots were
the same. In 1756 the strike involved only the weavers, but weavers
constituted by far the largest adult male trade. They also received
considerable support, financial and physical, from all other woollen
workers. In 1766 the food rioters embraced all the woollen trades
though weavers, because of their predominance, played the major
part.[38] It is pertinent to note that while scribbling, weaving and cloth
dressing were distinct trades, inter-marriage and the restricted entry
into the last meant that these woollen workers were far more closely
integrated than strict craft divisions might presume. It was the
woollen-manufacturing community as a whole therefore which was
mobilised in both disturbances, not just individual groups or trades.

This community basis is reflected in the widespread and active
participation of the woollen workers in both strike and food riots.
The strike certainly saw a total cessation of weaving for at least four
weeks. And this meant that there was soon no work for fullers or
dressers either. Yet there is no sign that this led to any internal rift

within the woollen-working community as whole villages ceased work, attended meetings or marched considerable distances around the district collecting funds or seeking charity and food, forcing blacklegs to return their work and confiscating their shuttles.[39] In 1766 the regulators made a particular point of insisting that all cease work and join in the actions of price setting. 'Our trade is and will be at a total stop', wrote William Dallaway. 'The rioters come into our workshops and force all the men willing or unwilling to join them.'[40] In both cases therefore it was believed that all the community should take part in defence of the common good.

This unity of participation cannot be explained simply by reference to a common experience of economic 'distress'. This is not to deny the very real economic pressures behind both crises. But the actions of the Gloucestershire woollen workers were in neither case mechanistic responses to 'the imperatives of the market economy'.[41] The decision of some clothiers to lower piece rates in 1755 affected only some weavers immediately. Indeed other clothiers continued to pay the old rates throughout the dispute. Nor were the abuses about which the weavers complained new. Food prices had risen sharply before the riots broke out in September 1766. But while they had climbed steeply into mid-August, they then remained stable until the disturbances began.[42] In both 1756 and 1766, therefore, though living standards were under considerable threat, disturbances were the consequence of the actions or supposed actions of clothiers, farmers and middlemen which the wider woollen-manufacturing community would not tolerate rather than of economic circumstances which they could not endure. The actions of the crowd in 1756 and 1766 must be seen as conscious and purposeful statements of outraged common values, not as spontaneous reactions to distress.

What were these values and attitudes which informed the woollen workers' actions? E. P. Thompson has persuasively argued of the food rioters:

Grievances operated within a popular consensus as to what were legitimate and what were illegitimate practices in marketing, milling, baking etc. This in turn was grounded upon a consistent traditional view of social norms and obligations, of the proper economic functions of several parties within the community, which, taken together, can be said to constitute the moral economy of the poor. An outrage to these moral assumptions, quite as much as actual deprivation, was the usual occasion for direct action.

The crowd, Thompson argues, derived its sense of legitimacy from the paternalist model of marketing which had a real if eroded existence in statute and common law and customary practice. This model demanded that food should be marketed locally and transparently with primacy being given to the needs of the local poor and restrictions being placed on the activities of dealers and middlemen. Local authorities were thus obligated to monitor and regulate the marketing of foodstuffs for the protection of the consumer. When such obligations were not met, when in times of crisis the model broke down, the crowd intervened to re-establish these norms, 'informed by a belief that they were defending traditional rights and customs'.[43]

The food riots in Gloucestershire in 1766 lend support to Thompson's thesis. The participants displayed a clear belief that shortages and high prices were caused by farmers and dealers stock-piling food and side-stepping local markets to send it for export. They were determined to prevent this and to ensure that food was made available locally at reasonable prices. To this end they marched from market to market setting the price and from farm to farm coercing the owners of large food reserves to sell their stocks or to promise to bring them to market. In carrying out this policy the regulators exhibited an orderliness which impressed even some magistrates. While they seized foodstuffs without compensation where they were resisted or deceived, generally they paid what they deemed the 'just price'.[44] There was very little gratuitous theft of other property. Indeed, one band searched all their members when a farmer's wife accused them of stealing some silver spoons, and, on finding them in one of their number's pockets, they immediately handed him over to the otherwise impotent authorities for punishment.[45] Foodstuffs were not always even seized. When the rioters discovered particular examples of deceit or fraud such as bolting mills containing ground chalk and other materials clearly used to adulterate flour, they would often publicly destroy foodstuffs as an overt punishment.[46] Such actions clearly indicate that it was not just desperate hunger which informed the crowd's actions.

The rioters justified their activities not simply by their need for food. They frequently claimed to have 'all the gentlemen on their side', for they believed they had a constitutional right to protection. The Royal Proclamation issued during the riots denouncing fore-stallers and regraters simply confirmed this belief.[47] It was the failure of the local magistracy to carry out this regulatory function which legitimised the crowd's actions. But while they saw that their form of regulation proved more immediately effectual than the bench's pleas and proclamations, at all times one senses the crowd expected the authorities to take up their own burden of government and to re-establish an order which protected local consumers as the law required.

Some historians have interpreted such legitimising notions more as tactical devices than as the value system which informed those tactics, Thompson's real meaning.[48] It is impossible to prove this either way. But even if the language of the moral economy orig-inated simply as a tactic, its continued 'success' in coercing the bench to uphold a regulatory model of marketing must over time have confirmed it as a basic tenet of economic and political relations. Certainly there is every reason to conclude that the Gloucestershire workers firmly believed that the authorities had no real alternative but to act out a role they had assigned themselves. This notion of a desire for a regulated market has led other historians to question the entire moral economy thesis, pointing out that the crowd 'had long been members of the same marketing system' and that therefore its workings. were both familiar and acceptable to them.[49] This misunderstands the argument. Clearly they did not object to the market as a system of exchange for it was the only such system available. Their opposition was to the growing ideology of 'The Market', increasingly loudly articulated by farmers, dealers and others in 1766, which claimed that only by the unhampered pursuit of individual advantage could the needs of the community be best met. This was an amoral vision of the market as economic arbiter as against the moral imperative of the need for fairness and social and economic responsibility enshrined in the concept of the moral economy. The Gloucestershire crowd showed that they believed the market might operate only within those parameters established by custom and law which should be upheld by the bench. If the bench failed, the crowd should quite correctly take over this role themselves.

How far can these same characteristics be seen in the industrial crisis of 1755–6 when the same workers faced exploitation as producers rather than as consumers? It is clear from the weavers' statements and actions that they saw the cause of their distress not in the autonomous workings of the market economy but in the machinations of unscrupulous men who, like the middlemen in 1766, were taking advantage of the natural disaster of economic recession, as with harvest failure in 1766, to use their power over the market to increase their own profits at the expense of the wider community. The weavers believed that these selfish actions constituted a threat not only to their living standards but to their entire way of life. By cutting piece rates, employing illegal workers in shops and paying truck, these clothiers were seen to be challenging the customary industrial relationships on which the cultural values of the community were established, and placing intolerable pressure upon other employers to follow their lead into an overtly exploitative economy in which the only arbiter was economic power.[50]

The weavers believed that the most effectual way to prevent this was not through violence or industrial action but through the law. Drawing on their experiences from thirty years before, they sought to involve the bench as arbiters. When their initial request was rejected, they petitioned Parliament to strengthen the magistracy's powers to rate wages and to deal summarily with those who evaded their orders. In taking this action the weavers of the county were united. Immediate sanctions against those who were the source of the problem do not appear to have been contemplated. The failure of the Michaelmas Sessions to agree a rate came as a great disappointment to the weavers. While they were only too aware of the considerable pressure exerted on the bench by the clothiers, they nonetheless expected the magistrates to uphold their constitutional duty. Here we see a clear parallel with 1766. While the food rioters were mindful of the existence of the Book of Orders and acts against forestallers and regraters, the weavers in 1756 had a very specific act, little more than four months old, to support them. They were also aware that the acts concerning truck and non-apprenticed workmen were not being enforced with vigour. Thus, just as the failure to regulate the dealings of middlemen in 1766 prompted the crowd to action, so the bench's abdication of responsibility in 1756 left the weavers with no option but to act for themselves.

Just as the food rioters for the most part acquitted themselves in an ordered and disciplined fashion, the characteristic of the weavers' behaviour during the county-wide strike in 1756 was order, discipline and purpose. While the clothiers' propaganda later complained of riots, there were none, not even when many clothiers ignored the rate the bench belatedly settled in November or sought to make their weavers sign agreements to work under-price. The striking weavers certainly made their presence felt at negotiations with the clothiers, on one occasion emphatically rejecting the agreed terms and insisting in no uncertain manner on a complete acceptance of the old rates.[51] But there were no examples of frustrations boiling over into gratuitous violence as had happened in Wiltshire in 1738.[52] The property of particularly hostile clothiers was occasionally attacked and threats made to their persons, but this was very low key. The weavers' leaders maintained a tight control over the dispute. Large numbers attended public meetings, marched in formation around the county seeking financial aid and support and frog-marched blacklegs back to their employers' mills, but in all this the weavers were very restrained. This orderliness was deliberate, an indication that the weavers, like the food rioters, believed that their actions were both legitimate and productive. As with the food rioters, personal violence was usually dealt out only to those within their own ranks who took work under price or who gave evidence for the clothiers.

Certainly there were disparities between the actions of the crowd in 1756 and in 1766. In 1756 the weavers spent many months lobbying and petitioning in an attempt to solve their problems before taking strike action in October. In 1766 there was no such delay as regulators set about the process of setting the price. But the crises were different. The problems besetting the weavers in 1756 had built up gradually, whereas in September 1766 food stocks began dramatically to disappear for export. The practicalities of the situations also differed. It was possible as a consumer simply to seize foodstuffs for future needs and the cost was borne by the owner. The weavers could not seize their own labour, they could only withdraw it and then they bore the cost in lack of income. Again, in industrial conflicts the weavers confronted men who employed them and from whom they might expect to seek work in the future. The farmer and the middleman had no such close or permanent relationship with them. Thus the pattern of protest differed somewhat. (This point should not be over-drawn, however. A comparison of the 1766 food riots with the industrial disturbances in the county in 1726–7 or even those in Wiltshire in 1738 would show even closer parallels of action.) There was certainly no master strategy model of the moral economy which could be dusted down and be immediately applicable to every dispute. But the same underlying values informed both food riots and strike alike.

In 1756 the weavers reacted against the exploitation of the clothiers. In 1766 they reacted against the exploitation of the middlemen. Both groups were deemed guilty of practices which offended those precepts of economic and social relationships which the woollen workers held inviolate. This was in both cases essentially a moral view of what could and what should constitute the parameters of these relationships. This perception clashed with that of the clothiers as with the middlemen for both deliberately ignored or sought to undermine this model, rejecting the whole concept of regulation and holding up in its place the competitive vision of unfettered free enterprise.[53] The woollen workers saw these arguments simply as the special pleading of predatory interests and invoked in their own defence the paternalist model, in 1756 brightly re-minted, of regulation and stability. And when the reluctant paternalists vacillated, they twisted their arms until they took action.

To conclude: the comparison of the Gloucestershire weavers' strike of 1756 and the food riots there in 1766 indicates that the same view informed both protests; the same moral economy determined the character of both market protest and industrial dispute. The same philosophy of the legitimacy of economic and social relations underlay the woollen workers' response to detrimental change. The same moral imperatives were deemed to override market forces. The moral economy was thus not just a view of food marketing. It was a value system of a whole community.

INTERPRETING EIGHTEENTH-CENTURY INDUSTRIAL CONFLICT

The Gloucestershire woollen workers' reactions to exploitation both as producers and consumers in the years from 1755 to 1766 raise issues of wider relevance to the study of eighteenth-century combinations.

Firstly they suggest that it is a manifest error to view trade unionism and the strike simply as representative of a higher stage in a developmental view of the 'modernisation of protest'. On these terms how can we explain why the Gloucestershire weavers, so 'modern' with their county-wide union and strike in 1756, had returned to 'pre-industrial' protest ten years later? The problem stems from the tendency to read history, and particularly labour history, backwards in the search for antecedents and to impose nineteenth-century models of trade union organisation and action upon the combinations of the eighteenth century. Though there were points in common, these combinations operated within a context in which the perceptions of society held by labour were not the same as in the nineteenth century. In that century the strike was to become much more clearly a straight economic contest between capital and labour with the state weighting the scales in capital's favour. In the eighteenth century this conflict was much more blurred for labour was as much concerned to establish rules as it was to engage capital; and to involve the authorities as a sort of Marquis of Queensberry in both drawing up these rules and in acting as a referee to see that they were kept. The clothiers in 1756 rejected such rules and referees out of hand, as did some outspoken farmers and political economists in 1766. In this their attitudes were 'modern' (although in reality the clothiers did tacitly accept many of the rules that the custom of the trade demanded until machinery began to alter the whole character of the industry in the 1790s). But only if we recognise that the woollen workers repudiated such 'modern' views as amoral (as, indeed, they were) and strove to maintain these essentially moral parameters of custom can we really understand their actions and their attitudes.

The strike of 1756, therefore, cannot be seen simply as a piece of industrial *realpolitik* directed at coercing recalcitrant employers into line. All clothiers, both rate-cutting and full-rate-paying alike, found their businesses at a standstill as the entire county's weaving work-force abandoned their looms for upwards of six weeks. Such a total strike was not necessary if the weavers' purpose had been merely to force the under-price clothiers back to customary rates. Selective strikes against such men would have been well within the weavers' capacity and would have proved easier to finance if perhaps some-what harder to police against blacklegs. The purpose of the strike therefore has to been seen as being as much political as economic, aimed as much at the bench as against the clothiers. The weavers' action was a symbolic rejection of a market in which customary and constitutional rules were being flouted while the referee turned a deliberately blind eye. This was why the strikers purposefully assumed a high though orderly profile. Their actions contained a message: play by the rules, enforce the rules or we will not play at all. Clothiers, good honest gentlemen and trucksters alike, were warned that even in a recession, even when food prices were high, they could not ride rough-shod over custom. The magistracy were reminded of their role as rulers and of the precarious hold they main-tained over law and order. It was a message which could not easily be ignored.

The role of the local and central authorities was thus clearly crucial in the strike as in the food riots. They were the direct or indirect recipients of the messages contained in the woollen workers' actions. In both crises they eventually took up their part and set about reimposing order not with a stick but with an olive branch, not as subjugators but as conciliators and arbitrators. Of course in part they did this because of fear of disorder, but the crowd could successfully press them to act because the role of arbitrator was one which they had imposed upon themselves. The model of the moral economy was the obverse of the paternalist model, the execution of which was the justification of their right to rule. And every time the gentry assumed their role they legitimated the moral economy of the crowd. It was to be the overt abandonment of this role which, as much as industrial transformation, was to force labour to accept a new relationship with capital.

In the eighteenth century however labour still believed it had a constitutional right to protection as producers as well as consumers. This view of protection did not imply a complete rejection of market forces for all economic aspects of their lives were subject to them. Thus Reddy notes of the Rouen workers, 'the critical social relationships for their survival were all commercial ones, all focussed on markets of one kind or another'.[54] As producers the woollen workers recognised that markets boomed and slumped, just as as consumers they knew that harvests were sometimes a bumper, sometimes a failure. Neither in 1756 nor 1766 were they seeking to fix wages or prices for ever. They demanded stability, not stasis.[55] What they sought was a market circumscribed by custom and law within which all might compete as equals and where an avaricous few were not permitted to manipulate or monopolise systems of exchange in such ways as threatened to undermine the entire social and economic fabric of the community. The Gloucestershire woollen workers' view was not a class one. They did not oppose capital *per se* nor did they see all the clothiers as enemies. Although nearly all the clothiers, full-rate and cut-rate payers alike, united against the imposition of rating in 1756, the weavers blamed the few rotten apples who broke customary practice for the crisis, not the outworking system. And indeed their aspiration for stability and order was covertly shared by many clothiers as was shown when the great majority continued to pay at the old rates, resulting in a *de facto* success for the weavers' protest if not a *de jure* one. It was also a view shared by the many gentlemen and ratepayers who petitioned Parliament in 1757 'that a power somewhere may be lodged to ascertain and regulate the weavers' wages' should the clothiers' bill 'to divest the justices of the power of regulating the weavers' wages' be passed.[56] Confidence in the beneficent consequences of a completely free market was not widely shared.

Secondly, I have argued that the common basis for both the 1756 strike and the 1766 food riots lay in a strong community consensus. The wide community participation in both protests was impressive and reflected the ways in which the actions of the crowd were a manifestation of a common identity and ideology. The importance of this community basis has long been recognised by historians of social protest. Eighteenth-century labour historians would be well-advised to address themselves to this wider context as well.

This over-spanning ideology informing attitudes as producers and consumers alike was perhaps of more importance in some industries and communities than in others. As noted before, there was a disparity between the essentially defensive character of most outworkers' combinations and the more aggressive attitudes discerned by Dobson of shop-based craft unions.[57] Reddy has reminded us that to strike for wage increases it is necessary that labour should first see itself as a commodity whose value might be increased by withholding it from market.[58] The aggressive strike was thus a market manoeuvre by workers who regrated themselves just as the dealers regrated corn. Such a 'modern' self-perception came more easily in the context of some trades than others. Shop-based workers directly shared a common experience of work and could more easily identify together and against their masters. Here too they might experience more closely the process of selling their labour in a collective context. Here, in part at least, 'the trade' could be identified separately from 'the community'. But we should not over-emphasise this picture of economic rationality in our interpretation even of such craft unions' actions. These artisans were also members of a wider community whose values they shared and in whose actions they participated. The cloth dressers of the West of England are a clear case in point. While their combinations may appear 'modern' in their search for higher wages, they too were more concerned with threats to custom and customary relationships, to non-economic aspects such as apprenticeship and the organisation of work, than a quick glance at a list of 'strikes' might lead us to suppose.

Weavers, however, worked in their homes with their families in communities made up principally of other weavers. Here the identification of a trade consciousness and a community consciousness were synonymous, here the institutions of the social and economic stuctures were the same. Here a man might simultaneously have work from several masters, here there were a multiplicity of cloths of different qualities and work requirements to be woven. Within this society the most cherished of the weaver's 'privileges' was his independence. Weavers saw themselves as independent producers, not as commodities. They did not want to manipulate the market but to ensure that it remained open and stable. Like the moral economy of the consumer, their industrial moral economy of the producer had no place for a model of permanent conflict resolved by economic power, a model in which there were no fixed points, only the ebb and flow of contending interests. Thus the context of their trade and its cultural values echoed and reinforced the values of the community such that their views both as consumers and as producers were the same. As both they resolutely refused to learn what Hobsbawm has termed 'the rules of the game'[59] as dictated by predatory capitalist interests. They had rules of their own. In 1756 they withdrew their labour to ensure that their rules were enforced, not as a tactic in a game which in essence had no rule other than devil-take-hindmost. This more than anything was why aggressive strike action was rare amongst them. Such actions required a complete reappraisal of their entire *mentalité*. Such reappraisal proved painful. Looking back on the history of the Gloucestershire weavers in 1838, Exell recorded how 'peace and content' were destroyed in 1802 when the clothiers promoted

a bill to suspend the weavers' protecting laws and after this the spoilers broke in upon the weavers' rights and privileges – shop looms were introduced . . . and the manufacturers became master weavers themselves. The system of apprenticeship was done away with and things became dreadfully confused – the clothiers looked upon the weavers as an army defeated and taken prisoner and as prisoners they have treated us . . . There is no rule or order among the masters themselves but they appear to be vieing with each other who shall bring wages to the lowest point . . . if the government does not interfere I can see nothing but destruction at our heels.[60]

In the eighteenth century such assaults on custom provoked protest everywhere but some communities were particularly inclined to protest. Weavers in the West Country were. So were the Cornish miners and many others. In such areas a tradition of protest grew up; here that 'rebellious plebeian culture' to which Thompson refers[61] was forged; here the moral economy was reinvoked and reinforced. Protest therefore fostered protest. But protest also fostered concessions. The authorities' and the clothiers' awareness of this readiness to protest influenced their handling of problems and perhaps made them a little more willing to arbitrate or negotiate. Even in defeat protest could be seen to pay dividends. The strike of 1756 failed to secure annual rating for long and in 1757 the machinery for arbitration was repealed. But the clothiers did not follow up their victory and begin a wholesale reduction of wage rates, which in fact stayed fairly stable in the second half of the century. Their victory had been too costly to want such another. It was because protest did offer such dividends therefore that the Gloucestershire weavers, as did many others, continued to invoke the moral economy not only as consumers but also as producers in times of crisis throughout the eighteenth century.

NOTES AND REFERENCES

1. **E. P. Thompson**, 'The moral economy of the English crowd in the eighteenth century', *Past and Present*, **50** (1971), pp. 76–136.
2. **S.** and **B. Webb**, *The History of Trade Unionism*, Longmans Green 1894; 1950 edn, pp. 1, 2.
3. **H. A. Turner**, *Trade Union Growth, Structure and Policy. A comparative study of the cotton unions*, George Allen & Unwin 1962, pp. 45, 50–4.
4. **J. Rule**, *The Experience of Labour in Eighteenth-Century Industry*, Croom Helm 1981, p. 151.
5. **C. R. Dobson**, *Masters and Journeymen: a prehistory of industrial relations 1717–1800*, Croom Helm 1980, pp. 16, 25.
6. **A. E. Musson**, *British Trade Unions, 1800–1875*, Macmillan 1972, pp. 10, 11.
7. Ibid., pp. 14–15.
8. **E. J. Hobsbawm**, 'The machine breakers', in *Labouring Men* (2nd edn), Weidenfeld and Nicolson 1968, pp. 7, 8; **E. Hunt**, *British Labour History 1815–1914*, Weidenfeld and Nicolson 1981, p. 195.
9. **J. Stevenson**, 'Food riots in England 1792–1818', in J. Stevenson and R. Quinault, *Popular Protest and Public Order: Six studies in British history 1790–1920*, George Allen & Unwin 1974, pp. 62–3, 67. See also **Stevenson**, *Popular Disturbances in England 1700–1870*, Longman 1979, pp. 112, 135.
10. **W. J. Shelton**, *English Hunger and Industrial Disorders. A study of social conflict during the first decade of George III's reign*, Macmillan 1973, pp. 158, 200, 201, 205.
11. **J. Bohstedt**, *Riots and Community Politics in England and Wales, 1790–1810*, Harvard 1983, pp. 212–13. It is significant that while Bohstedt identifies Devon as epitomising the 'classic food riot', he ignores the Devon woollen industry's long tradition of industrial protest, noting only that 'strikes gave way to food riots as Devon's woollen industry unraveled' in a 'story of industrialization run backwards', p. 46.
12. Rule, *Experience of Labour*, p. 151.
13. **W. M. Reddy**, 'The textile trade and the language of the crowd at Rouen 1752–1871', *Past and Present*, **74** (1977), pp. 62–89.
14. Thompson, 'The moral economy of the English crowd', p. 79.
15. **A. J. Randall**, 'The shearmen and the Wiltshire Outrages of 1802: trade unionism and industrial violence', *Social History*, **7**, No. 3 (1982), pp. 283–304.
16. Too much can be made of the weavers' isolation. **D. Bythell**, *The Handloom Weavers*, Cambridge U.P. 1969, p. 187, for example, writes that the weavers in north Lancashire were cut off from Manchester 'by

the physical barrier imposed by the Rossendale hills', while the Bolton and Blackburn weavers were 'separated by ten miles of moorland'! Timothy Exell, the Gloucestershire weavers' leader, walked 1000 miles on union business between May and November, 1838.

17. **J. de L. Mann**, *The Cloth Industry in the West of England from 1640 to 1880*, Oxford U.P. 1971, pp. 143–8; see also **A. J. Randall**, 'Labour and the Industrial Revolution in the West of England Woollen Industry', University of Birmingham Ph.D. thesis, 1979, Ch. 6.

18. Gloucestershire Record Office (GRO), Q/SR 1756 D, Petition of the weavers to the Michaelmas Quarter Sessions; *Gloucester Journal (GJ)*, 13 Jan. 1756; *House of Commons Journal (HCJ)*, 27, pp. 468, 503.

19. See Mann, *The Cloth Industry*, pp. 140–5, 234–9; and Randall 'Labour and the Industrial Revolution', Chs 6, 8.

20. *GRO*, 149/B8 Petitions of the poor weavers of Stroud and Horsley, 23 July and 22 August, 1755.

21. Dobson, *Masters and Journeymen*, pp. 28–29, 27.

22. Mann, *The Cloth Industry*, pp. 37–62; **R. G. Wilson**, 'The supremacy of the Yorkshire cloth industry in the eighteenth century', in **N. B. Harte** and **K. G. Ponting**, *Textile History and Economic History: Essays in honour of Miss Julia de Lacy Mann*, Manchester U.P. 1973, pp. 226–35.

23. **S. Rudder**, *A New History of Gloucestershire*, Cirencester 1779.

24. For detailed examination of these riots see **A. J. Randall**, 'The Gloucestershire food riots of 1766', *Midland History*, X, 1985, pp. 72–93.

25. Mann, *The Cloth Industry*, pp. 37–8, 42.

26. *GRO*, D149/B8, Petition of the poor weavers of Stroud and Horsley, 23 July 1755; Q/SR, 1756 D, petition of the weavers to the Michaelmas Q.S.; *HCJ*, **27**, p. 503; *A State of the Case and a Narrative of Facts relating to the late Commotions and Risings of the Weavers in the County of Gloucester*, 1757, p. 23.

27. Mann, *The Cloth Industry*, pp. 67–71.

28. *GRO*, D149/B8 Petition of the poor weavers, 22 August 1755.

29. 29 Geo. II, c. 33.

30. *A State of the Case*, pp. 5–8; *GRO*, Q/SR 1756 D, Memorial of the Clothiers to the Michaelmas Q.S.

31. *GJ*, 12 Oct. 1756.

32. *A State of the Case*, pp. 24–7.

33. *GJ*, 12 Oct. 1756; **R. Wright**, *The Life of Major General James Wolfe*, London 1864, pp. 349–51.

34. *GJ*, 12 Oct. 1756; *A State of the Case*, pp. 24–7, 29–30.

35. *A State of the Case*, p. 30; *GJ*, 23 Nov. 1756.

36. *A State of the Case*, pp. 31–2.

37. *A State of the Case*, pp. iv, 33; *HCJ*, 27, pp. 683, 703, 730–3, 741, 753–4, 757, 785–6.

38. See, for example, *Public Record Office*, PC 1/8/41, William Dallaway to Henry Seymour Conway, 17 September 1766; *GJ*, 15 Sept. 1766; *Gazetteer and New Daily Advertizer*, 22 Oct. 1766.

39. *Salisbury and Winchester Journal*, 25 Oct. 1766; *A State of the Case*, p. ii, 24–7.

40. *PC* 1/8/41, Dallaway to Conway, 20 September 1766.

41. The phrase comes from **D. E. Williams**, 'Morals, markets and the

English crowd in 1766', *Past and Present*, **104** (1984), p. 73. For a critique of Williams' thesis, see **A. Charlesworth** and **A. J. Randall**, 'Morals, markets and the English crowd in 1766', *Past and Present*, **114** (1987), pp. 200–13.

42. Randall, 'The Gloucestershire food riots', pp. 75–6.
43. Thompson, 'The moral economy', pp. 78–9, 83–8.
44. See, for example, *PC* 1/8/41, Dallaway to Conway, 20 September 1766.
45. *British Museum*, Add. MSS. 35607, *Hardwicke MSS.*, John Pitt to Lord Hardwicke, 29 September 1766; see also *PC* 1/8/41, Dallaway to Conway, 20 September 1766.
46. *PRO, TS* 11/1128, Testimony of Edmund Dadge.
47. *TS* 11/1128, case against John Morse; the proclamation, issued on 10 September, was posted and read out at many markets, among others by Dallaway. *PC* 1/8/41, Dallaway to Conway, 20 September 1766.
48. For the most provocative and closely argued example of this line see Bohstedt, *Riots and Community Politics*, especially Chs 2 and 9; see also Stevenson, *Popular Disturbances in England*, pp. 310–12; and **R. Wells**, 'The revolt of the south-west, 1800–1801: a study in English popular protest', *Social History*, **6** (1977), pp. 713–44, who suggests that the moral economy was not always an appropriate strategy for crowd behaviour.
49. Williams, 'Morals, markets and the English crowd in 1766', p. 70. Stevenson, *Popular Disturbances in England*, p. 311, makes much the same point.
50. *GRO*, Q/SR 1756 D, Petition of the weavers.
51. *A State of the Case*, pp. 24–7.
52. **J. de L. Mann**, 'Clothiers and weavers in Wiltshire during the eighteenth century', in **L. S. Pressnell**, *Studies in the Industrial Revolution Presented to T. S. Ashton*, London U.P. 1960, pp. 66–96.
53. In particular, see *GRO*, Q/SR 1756 D, Memorial of the Clothiers to the Michaelmas Q.S.; *GJ*, 8 Dec 1766; *Hardwicke MSS.*, Pitt to Hardwicke, 29 September, 20 December 1766.
54. Reddy, 'The textile trade', pp. 73–4.
55. Cf. Bohstedt, *Riots and Community Politics*, p. 211; Stevenson, *Popular Disturbances in England*, p. 311.
56. *HCJ*, 27, p. 753.
57. Dobson, *Masters and Journeymen*, pp. 27–9.
58. Reddy, 'The textile trade', pp. 77–8.
59. Hobsbawm, 'Custom, wages and work-load in nineteenth-century industry', in *Labouring Men*, p. 345.
60. **T. Exell**, *A Brief History of the Weavers of the County of Gloucestershire*, Stroud 1838, pp. 6–7, 10–11.
61. **E. P. Thompson**, 'Eighteenth-century English society: class struggle without class?', *Social History*, **3**, No. 2 (1978), p. 154.

CHAPTER THREE
Workers and Machinery in Eighteenth-century England

Maxine Berg

Resistance to the introduction of new technology in the extreme form of machine breaking hardly figures in the histories of the Industrial Revolution currently read by students. This is despite the popularity of the history of technology. David Landes in *The Unbound Prometheus* summed up in a misleading sentence: 'the workers, especially those bypassed by machine industry, said little but were undoubtedly of another mind.'[1]

Sustained waves of resistance to machinery swept through the textile manufactures in the later eighteenth and early nineteeth centuries. Where economic historians have not simply ignored this resistance, they have tried to subordinate its significance, and this because they cannot explain it. Mathias, for example, argued that the new technologies of the Industrial Revolution were labour-saving only in terms of labour costs. The great increase of output far outweighed the employment effects of increases in productivity per man to the extent that industrialisation with urbanisation became the 'greatest creator of employment the world has known'.[2]

The economic theory relied upon by most economic historians assumes, if it cannot prove, that new technology creates more not less employment. Hence actions like those of the Luddites are seen as irrational, or mistaken in their lack of foresight. In general, orthodox economists agree on a favourable overall impact of new technology upon employment and income, though their aggregate data leaves no firm conclusions. The more careful counsel the study of individual innovations or industries.[3] But economic historians have followed their lead in their work on individual innovations. Von Tunzelman, for example, sums up the latest ortho-roxy in plumping for long-term considerations of profitability rather than short-term cost-cutting as the inducement for most eighteenth-century innovation. He argues that where labour was adversely affected by technical change, it was in those industries which had been bypassed by new technologies. He gives the example of the Yorkshire cloth dressers but concludes such workers were a small minority.[4]

This complacent attitude towards the beneficence of technical change has unfortunately been absorbed by social historians. Fabian roots have been evident in attempts to separate machine breakers from the rest of the working class. The violence of the Luddites has been seen as the resort of a minority, those unable to develop more sophisticated forms of resistance. Historians have referred to the 'pointless physical violence' of 'helpless victims of distress'. There have also been functionalist explanations such as Hobsbawm's definitive view that it was 'primitive trade unionism' or 'collective bargaining by riot'.[5] Machine breaking has thus been accepted by most social historians as a self-defeating strategy: an embarrassment to the history of the labour movement. Even today trade unionists in a new context of social dislocation caused by restructuring or the new technology preface their remarks by 'We are not Luddites, but . . .'

Recently, however, our view of our industrial past has been changed, making it especially meaningful to raise the subject again. The world economic recession, a new critical approach to the development of the Third World, and wide-ranging debates over the social impact of new technology have all raised questions over those sacred cows of the post-war boom once taken for granted: heavy capital investment, large-scale industry, new technology and rapid economic growth. Doubts about our own time lead to a new questioning of the first experience of industrialisation.

One of these questions is of workers' reception of the first phases of mechanisation and this study will open up a discussion of the machinery issue in its own right – not simply as an appendage to early forms of industrial dispute, nor as an aspect of anti-capitalist struggle. It is clear that workers' reception of new technology spanned the whole spectrum from outright resistance through passive acquiescence even to active participation in innovation. While our main concern will be to describe this range of receptivity, we must also raise questions about what economic, social and cultural factors contributed to the active participation of workers in innovation in some manufacturing communities, while in others they remained entrenched in traditional methods. This reflected the uneven and multi-dimensional character of industrial change. The very diversity of the experience of early industrialisation implied an unevenness in the effects of machinery and between region and gender as well as between different time periods and different industries. Understanding working-class responses to machinery we must set aside a notion of once and for all conflict between traditional technologies and mechanisation. It is not simply that hand and machine technologies coexisted throughout the eighteenth and nineteenth centuries. In itself this is a truism. What matters is rather the range of hand, machine and combined techniques each being developed in their own right; the use to which they were put and the significance attached by workers to their own experience of change.

TECHNICAL CHANGE AND PRODUCTIVITY

New estimates of growth rates and increases in productivity suggest slower growth and limited productivity change before the 1820s.[6] Crafts has revised aggregate estimates of growth to argue that productivity growth in manufacturing was probably very slow until 1830. A small and atypical industry, cotton, probably accounted for half of all productivity change in manufacturing: 'not only was the triumph of ingenuity slow to come to fruition, but it does not seem appropriate to regard innovation as pervasive'. He estimates productivity growth in manufacturing of only 0.2 per cent 1760–80, 0.3 per cent 1800–30 and 0.8 per cent 1830–60.[7]

Though growth was slow, recent revisions have also found the industrial sector to have been very large, much larger than previously thought. The eighteenth century was, according to Crafts, characterised by a large industrial workforce but low levels of productivity. The existence and significance of an eighteenth-century machinery question needs to be explained and assessed in the light of such findings. Widespread and notable occurrences of workers' resistance to machinery appear on this evidence to have happened in a period of very limited innovation. Two possibilities arise. Either workers' fears were groundless, or their resistance did indeed have the effect of checking innovation and of becoming a major cause of slow productivity growth.

The first explanation is unsatisfactory, for there is substantial qualitative evidence and evidence at the microeconomic level of innovation and of restructuring. Whether this had the ultimate effect of substantially raising aggregative growth rates is another matter, for other factors would also have come into play; recent productivity estimates may well, however, underestimate the degree of change. The second explanation is certainly plausible and will be discussed below.

Assessment of the level of technical innovation in the eighteenth century is difficult for there are no satisfactory measures. The economists' catch-all of 'total factor productivity growth' is a very unsatisfactory proxy for technical change. Crafts has argued that the overwhelming concentration of the productivity change which did occur in the cotton industry implies that other manufactures remained traditional with primitive technologies.[8] But technical change in the eighteenth century needs to be understood in a framework broader than that of the artifact. For as long as we look at it purely in terms of artifacts – that is, machinery and fixed capital, – we fail to grasp the essence of technical change – that is, the processes of production. This covers both machinery and tools, skills, dexterity and the knacks and work practices of the trade. These included the improved tools and piecemeal technical changes – dubbed by Nathan Rosenberg the 'continuum' of technical change, or 'anonymous' technical change[9] – and also the social relations which lay behind the skill and intensity with which work was carried out.

A survey of textile technologies points out the impact of early inventions: carding and scribbling machinery and finishing techniques especially in bleaching and calico printing. In these cases and also in those of the major innovations of spinning mule and water frame, there was a very close integration with the development of rural manufacture and artisan industry. We know from Rosenberg, Harris and Mathias of the skill-intensive hand processes and hand tools in the metal-working trades.[10] Birmingham's hardware trades were proverbial for their technical innovation in the development of new tools, materials and skills. The stamp, press, drawbench and lathe were developed to innumerable specifications and uses. New malleable alloys, gilting processes, plating and japanning were just as important. Virtually all of these were handicraft techniques developed before the major era of the cotton factory, or alongside it in so-called traditional sectors. Apart from well-known innovations in textiles and metal processing and working, many industries experienced some form of transformation in materials or of the division of labour if not in the artefacts of technological change.

The leather industry, for example, had no transformation equal to that in paper making with the introduction of new machinery for making pulp, but there were many attempts to speed up the tanning process, although none was successful in terms of quality until the early nineteenth century. A range of traditional industries certainly underwent reorganisation due to changes in materials and processes. New industrial uses for coal affected brewing, brick making, malting, sugar and soap boiling, as well as metallurgy and metal working. Salt refining based on rock salts yielded ten times as much salt as had brine solutions. The division of labour and production time of luxury manufactures like hat-making were transformed by a change in materials such as the replacement of beaver fur by hare.

In traditional textile industries changes in the product, such as the move from heavy serges to mixed stuffs where wool was mixed with silk or cotton, considerably reduced the finishing time. Many of these needed no fulling and were dyed in the wool or printed rather than vat dyed. The success of the calico printing industry later in the eighteenth century did not hinge on new machinery but on new cheaper labour prepared to carry out labour-intensive processes on a new scale and under new organisation and discipline.

The building industry, it is true, did not undergo much change despite the building booms of the 1770s and 1780s. But the reason probably lay in limitations on credit, and the release of these in the early nineteenth century unleashed not new machinery but a major organisational transformation.[11] It is worth reiterating Josiah Tucker's observation of 1757 whose sentiments were widely echoed in eighteenth-century economic commentary:

Few countries are equal, perhaps none excel, the English in the number of contrivances of their machines to abridge labour. Indeed the Dutch are superior to them in the use and application of Wind Mills for sawing Timber, expressing Oil, making Paper and the like. But in regard to Mines and Metals of all sorts, the English are uncommonly dexterous in their contrivance of the mechanic Powers; some being calculated for landing the Ores out of the Pits, such as Cranes and Horse Engines; others for draining off superfluous Water, such as Water Wheels and Steam Engines; others again for easing the Expense of Carriage such as Machines to run on inclined Planes or Road downhill with wooden frames, in order to carry many Tons of Material at a Time. And to these must be added the various sorts of Levers used in different processes; also the Brass Battery works, the Slitting Mills, Plate and Flatting Mills, and those for making Wire of different Fineness. Yet all these, curious as they may seem, are little more than Preparations or Introductions for further Operations. Therefore, when we still consider than at Birmingham, Wolverhampton, Sheffield and other manufacturing Places, almost every Master Manufacturer hath a new invention of his own, and is daily improving on those of others; we may aver with some confidence that those parts of England in which these things are seen exhibit a specimen of practical mechanics scarce to be paralleled in any part of the world.[12]

A sharp contrast in the reception of technical change is manifest in reactions to early textile machinery – notably the spinning jenny, the Dutch engine loom, and the flying shuttle on the one hand, and to innovations in the metal and hardware trades – the press, stamp, lathe and numerous small tools on the other. The former all met with significant, though divided, resistance; the latter were not only sought out by, but developed by, workers themselves. Workers' reception of technical change, even in the earliest days of the Industrial Revolution, was complicated by the many divisions created by the process of industrialisation.

Two major sources of division in response to new technology were to be found in differences between regions and in the characteristics of the labour force. But these provide only the beginnings of understanding responses. For social and cultural factors as well as community traditions played a part in encouraging worker participation in some areas and resistance in others. The two major sources will be considered in detail and some points for discussion on the divisions of culture and community raised.

REGIONS

In a neglected article Sidney Pollard challenged historians to look at the complex regional inter-relationships of Britain's Industrial Revolution.[13] Industrialisation in one region entailed de-industrialisation in others. Factory systems in one area involved extensions of domestic industry in areas round about or further afield. Industrialisation occurred within the framework of a regional symbiosis across Europe – between British yarn and German looms; British iron and German metal goods, British ships and Baltic grain. Equally there was a symbiotic framework within Britain itself.

One result of regionalisation was a growing history of industrial decline across the southern counties of England. Berkshire, Dorset, Hampshire, Wiltshire, Norfolk, Suffolk and Essex dropped an average of eleven places in the county wealth league between 1693 and 1843. Ironworking left Kent, the Sussex Weald then the Forest of Dean in the course of the eighteenth century. The woollen cloth industry disappeared from Kent in the late seventeenth and was finally eclipsed in the late eighteenth century in Surrey, Berkshire and Hampshire. It dwindled in Exeter and by the early nineteenth century was contracting in Somerset, Wiltshire and Gloucestershire.

Carpet weaving, cotton spinning and stocking knitting all failed to sustain a hold in the south. By the nineteenth century boot- and shoe-making had disappeared from Berkshire, the making of wire buttons from Dorset and wool and fur hatting from Gloucestershire.[14]

Von Tunzelman suggests that those adversely affected by technical change were a small minority. But such conclusions have normally been based on the cotton industry, not the woollen – on the experience of the north not of the south. His conclusions have swept from sight all the spinners, weavers and cloth finishers of the most important eighteenth-century industry: the woollen industry, which accounted for over 30 per cent of value added in British industry in 1770 and was not overtaken by cotton until the 1820s. Large declining industrial regions of the south and parts of the Midlands, and even agricultural regions where women's employment in spinning, knitting and lace making had formed a substantial part of the local economy have no part in current optimistic histories of technical change. In the textile industry the spinners in the eighteenth century and the hand loom weavers in the nineteenth were the majority, and spinning and weaving machinery did substitute directly for their labour. Although hand processes continued they did so in competition with machinery and consequently at lower wages and with greater intensity of labour. Adrian Randall has shown that in the west country the spinning jenny displaced nine out of ten warp spinners and thirteen out of fourteen weft spinners. Scribbling engines made fifteen out of sixteen adult male scribblers redundant and the gig mill replaced nine out of ten cloth dressers. The scribblers, before machinery, made up 10 per cent of the adult male workforce; the cloth dressers 15 per cent.[15]

Such a context goes far to explain the acute resistance to machinery in the south. In Essex a major woollen weavers' revolt in 1715 extinguished any idea of a factory system there. In Barking in 1759 weavers fought the introduction of a mill for cleaning and loosening wool. There was some resistance to the flying shuttle, though it was ultimately introduced. Spinning remained backward, and there were no jennies there until 1794, whereas they had been in use in Yorkshire since the 1790s. In the West Country a jenny set up in Shepton Mallet in 1776 was destroyed by a mob. Elsewhere in the south until the 1790s such machines were used only on the fringes of the industrial areas. A mob destroyed an advanced scribbling machine in Bradford on Avon in 1791. Workpeople rioted against the flying shuttle in Trowbridge in 1785–87 and 1810–13, postponing its introduction there and in west Wiltshire until the end of the Napoleonic Wars. Weavers were still rioting against the flying shuttle in Frome in 1822. Woollen cloth finishing machinery, the gig mill and the shearing frame, which also fuelled the classic Luddite attacks in Yorkshire, were fiercely resisted in Wiltshire and Somerset, and clothiers there who wanted their cloth dressed by gig mill had to send it 90 miles away.

Regional decline goes only part of the way in explaining the levels of resistance to machinery in the south. Another part of the explanation lies in the differences in work structures and especially in industrial concentration in different parts of the country. The greater social polarity between employer and employed in the southern woollen industry is proverbial. Tucker summed up the differences from Yorkshire in 1757:

One Person, with a great Stock and large Credit, buys the Wool, pays for the Spinning, Weaving, Milling, Dying, Shearing, Dressing, etc. etc. That is, he is the Master of the Whole Manufacture from first to last, and perhaps employs a thousand persons under him. This is the Clothier, whom all the Rest are to look upon as their Paymaster. But will they not also look upon him as their Tyrant? And as great Numbers of them work together in the same Shop, will they not have it the more in their Power to vitiate and corrupt each other, to cabal and associate against their Masters and to break out into Mobs and Riots upon every little Occasion? . . . Besides, as the Master is placed so high above the Condition of the Journeyman, both their Conditions approach much nearer to that of a Planter and Slave in our American Colonies, than might be expected in such a country as England: and the Vices and Tempers belonging to each Condition are of the same Kind, only in an inferior Degree. The Master . . . however well-disposed in himself, is naturally tempted by his Situation to be proud and over-bearing, to consider his People as the Scum of the Earth, whom he has a right to squeeze whenever he can; because they ought to be kept low, and not to rise up in Competition with their Superiors. The Journeymen on the contrary, are equally tempted by their Situation, to envy the high Station, and superior Fortunes of their Masters, and to envy them the more, in Proportion as they find themselves deprived of the Hopes of advance themselves to the same Degree by any Stretch of Industry, or superior Skill. Hence their Self-Love takes a wrong Turn, destructive to themselves, and others. They think it no crime to get as much Wages, and to do as little for it as they possibly can, to lie and cheat, and to do any other bad Thing; provided it is only against their Master, whom they look upon as their common Enemy, with whom no faith is to be Kept.

In Yorkshire:

Their journeymen . . . if they have any, being so little removed from the Degree and Condition of their masters, and likely to set up for themselves by the Industry and Frugality of a few years . . . thus it is, that the working people are generally Moral, Sober and Industrious; that the goods are well made, and exceedingly cheap.

While in the West Country:

The Motives to Industry, Frugality and Sobriety are all subverted to this one consideration viz. that they shall always be chained to the same Oar (the Clothier), and never be but Journeymen . . . Is it little wonder that the trade in Yorkshire should flourish, or that the trade in Somerset, Wiltshire and Gloucestershire be found declining every Day?[16]

Pat Hudson has described the relatively egalitarian social structure of the Yorkshire woollen industry in the eighteenth century. Low capital thresholds and open access to marketing made entry relatively easy for the small yeoman clothier.[17] Randall's account of the manufacture in the west of England on the other hand shows a degree of extreme concentration, the manufacture being controlled by gentlemen clothiers frequently employing over 1000 workers and with the markets tied up by the Blackwell Hall factors.[18] The small clothiers who had survived into the early eighteenth century were forced out by its end and by the early nineteenth century large factories were supplying proletarian domestic weavers with yarn.

Hudson's work demonstrates that such contrasts can be drawn not just between north and south, but within the north itself. For although the Yorkshire woollen industry was run by independent artisans, the worsted industry on the other side of the Pennines was from the first organised on capitalist lines. Merchant manufacturers and extensive putting out networks ran a tightly controlled market. Extensive putting out systems in both West Country wool and west Yorkshire worsted owed much of their origin to concentrated ownership of land.

Regional contrast in structures of work was also noticeable in the Midlands metal trades. In Birmingham we find the coincidence of economic opportunity and a more egalitarian social structure within a framework of small, medium- and large-scale industry in the eighteenth century at least fostering a positive endorsement and even participation by workers in technological improvement. Such areas were noted for the inventiveness of their workforce. Richard Prosser, author of *Birmingham Inventors and Inventions*, argued that Birmingham had more patents to its credit than any city outside London until the 1850s. Most had been granted for small improvements in the manufacture of trinkets and buttons, in machine tools, in metal compositions and in scientific instruments. Many more improvements were never patented by 'the secretive manufacturers who locked their doors, and found it easier to withhold their innovations by keeping them dark'. These were largely the inventions of small artisans and working men and women and were of the type described by Hawkes Smith as: 'that alone which requires more force than the arms and tools of the workmen could yield, still leaving his skill and experience of head, hand and eye in full exercise.[19] The earliest working equipment of these trades had been anvil, hammer, file and grindstone. But the major eighteenth-century innovations were the stamp, press and drawbench and the lathe. These, along with division of labour, combined to save time and effort. Shelbourne cited mixed metals and stamping machinery used with the division of labour to produce cheap buttons. There were besides 'an infinity of smaller improvements which each workman has and keeps secret from the rest'. In Boulton's Soho works it was not just the skilled artisans who contributed to success, but 'the number of ingenious mechanical contrivances they avail themselves of, by means of Water Mills, which much facilitates their work and saves a great portion of time and labour'. Birmingham machinery was, however, in the main hand-operated, only supplemented in some cases by horse and water power. Steam power, though the engines which produced it were the most famous product of the town, was hardly used before 1800 and by 1815 there were still only forty engines.[20]

Though small-scale and hand-operated, the tools and machinery used in Birmingham were varied and extensive, so that artisans and manufacturers who possessed a remarkable range of them were not insubstantial figures. Buttonmakers typically owned several different size straps, a number of setting out and piercing presses, a variety of different lathes, anvils, bellows, bench vices and other tools.[21]

There seem to have been no instances of resistance to the introduction of this machinery: rather an ethos of active worker participation in invention. The reception of new technology in the town's hinterland does not seem to have been all that different. The nail trade may be an exception with several attempts to introduce cast and machine cut nails going back to the 1780s, but cheap supplies of labour rather than resistance to machinery held the balance and the numbers of hand forges continued to increase despite competition from mechanical techniques. In other trades new techniques assisted the domestic worker. In lockmaking Mason's fly press of 1794 allowed him to cut parts more speedily. By the early nineteenth century chain and bolt makers as well as nailors made use of the Oliver or foot-operated spinning hammer, which allowed a smith to work single-handed.[22]

If Birmingham hardware manufacture displayed something of a

similarity in work structure to the Yorkshire woollen industry, the counterpart to the worsted districts was to be found in the cutlery manufacture of Sheffield and south Yorkshire, where subdivision of skills and trades was far advanced by the eighteenth century. Small masters continued to proliferate, but came increasingly under the thumb of a local group of merchant capitalists who controlled the circulating capital of the trade and the distribution of the finished product.

Regional diversity was more complicated than simple polarities between the south and the midlands, or the south and the north. For there were many anti-machinery espisodes in the north and midlands in the eighteenth century and later during the Luddite period and the machinery disputes of the 1820s and 1830s. Hargreaves' first jenny was destroyed in 1767 and in 1769 more were destroyed at Turton, Bolton and Bury. In 1779 a mob scoured the country for several miles around Blackburn, demolishing jennies, carding engines and every machine turned by water- or horsepower. Hargreaves' move to Nottinghamshire seems unlikely to have been inspired by prospects of a more docile workforce, for Nottingham had a reputation in the second half of the eighteenth century for popular protest, riot and attacks on machinery. And of course it was the West Riding, Nottinghamshire and Lancashire which formed the focus for the disciplined Luddite attacks on machinery, stocking frames and power looms in 1811–12 and 1816. In the event, the textile industries experienced widespread regional differences in their patterns of technological diffusion and labour resistance. Power sources, product choice and employment structure all affected the extent to which a region took up, resisted or ignored any particular technical change. In Yorkshire the jenny and carding engine were introduced by domestic spinners in times of expanding employment, but combing machinery was resisted in the early nineteenth century. In the West Country, after years of resistance, jennies were finally introduced over a wide area, but the scribblers still resisted the use of carding engines. The flying shuttle met a good reception in Yorkshire, but was widely resisted in East Anglia, Lancashire and the West Country.[23] The broader differences in regional economic structures and conditions found their mirror image within the region with the impact of new technology on rising and declining sectors. This goes some way toward explaining the differential.

Apart from regional economic conditions and levels of industrial concentration there was also the different extent of community ties and identities between regions. It was the community identity and endorsement that gave backing to food rioters in the south-west in 1800–1 and to anti-machinery protesters in Wiltshire in 1802. The strength of community relationships and sanctions protected the Luddites. Community solidarity established through forms of land-holding, long industrial traditions and customs and the relative supply and militancy of the local labour force affected forms of industrial organisation and workplace networks: it also affected the reception of new techniques. One explanation for slow productivity growth in the eighteenth century must surely lie in the different local and industrial receptions which need to be located in social and community structure. The personal, kinship and other social connections within a workshop culture or small quasi-peasant community created close working bonds which could dictate local reception. Historians have long pointed to the strength of community structures, and the long historical and deeply held traditions and cultural values of both the Yorkshire and West Country woollen industry. Equally, in the east and west midlands, as Chambers argued over twenty years ago, the values of the domestic worker were also the values of the society in which he lived. Some regions there thus experienced a smooth transition to the factory system, while others supported the resistance of their framework knitters and silk weavers to the advance of machinery.[24]

Randall has described the highly localised nature, but wide ramifications of a 'rebellious traditional culture' deeply rooted in some West Country communities. The riots against the spinning jenny occurred there for the most part in woollen towns and villages, where textile production occupied most members of a family and provided the only source of income. These were textile communities with a strong trade base, able to sustain a long protest and with the connections and experience to organise resistance.[25] But they were also areas where a number of families might clearly benefit from the jenny with its greater output of yarn, at least in its early days.

The real damage was on families in declining agricultural areas, where women's and children's hand spinning helped the rural poor to eke out a living. Yet the jenny encountered little protest in such areas. Passivity and powerlessness went hand in hand, just as they did in some instances of enclosure. Non-textile areas which did protest, however, were those where miners' wives supplemented family earnings by spinning.[26] A Somerset magistrate was called on in 1790 to protect two manufacturers from the depredations of a lawless band of colliers and their wives who had lost work to spinning machinery.[27] Randall argues that this community-based reaction to machinery was also expressed in a common philosophy or political economy based on the defence of the customs of the domestic system.[28]

The explanation for different regional responses tied to strength of community structures provides a vital clue to understanding the reception of the machine. It is an explanation which Randall has closely pursued, but it also raises some fundamental problems about the notion of 'moral economy'. There is the primary and thorny question of the definition of community. There were the divisions between artisans with a long and stable stake in the community or in the trade society and the casual outworkers in temporary residence. There were the divisions created by the differential impact of international price fluctuations on neighbouring communities producing slightly different products. There were the divisions inherent in the division of labour itself, especially between men and women workers. In addition, as Olivia Harris has cogently argued, there was no reason why the existence of kin or community should imply a behaviour code based on mutuality, morality or custom:

> Both the language of kinship and the way co-residence is represented, contain underlying assumptions about the sex division of economic relations based on direct exchange and precise calculation, and the presence of other relations of generosity without calculation. This ideology . . . should not, however, be confused with what relations actually obtain between kin and non kin . . . The degree to which people exhibit such behaviour to each other is a matter for investigation rather than assumption.[29]

Community ties in many areas were most deeply based in agrarian relations. Recently several historians including Keith Snell, Jeannette Neeson, J. M. Martin and Pat Hudson have argued for the close interdependence of common right and the structure and extent of domestic industry. They have also demonstrated how closely connected the decline of rural manufacturing was with enclosure.[30] The destruction of one of the major institutions of community common right seemed to break the resilience of the handicraft sector.

Community was not, however, something simply associated with a pre-industrial past, something bound up with custom and common right and outside of interaction with the market. Nor was it external and unchanging in the way that the concept is often invoked against the market and industrialisation. Community and the custom to which it is related is, rather, a living product. It is not egalitarian nor is it free of relations of power and subordination. Divisions of interest within any one community may well have been marked, yet the 'interests of the community' were defined in terms of the group which at that moment wielded some authority. Community was frequently invoked, for instance, when the livelihood of skilled and craft workers was at stake; rarely when that of squatters, casual labourers and women was threatened. These people were regarded as mobile, anonymous, 'without community'.

The creation of new products, the use of new techniques and access to a whole range of markets could form the basis for different types of community – such as existed in eighteenth-century Birmingham and its hinterland. Here close family connections between town and country, and rural traditions of partible inheritance appear to have allowed the easy transmission of skills and of capital. And a close-knit, but flexible, workshop culture formed the basis of a progressive technological stance.

Industrial concentration and monopolisation of the market cut off the possibility of such flexible community structures in the West Country, and there the textile community became entrenched in its own traditions: traditions which were, however, the artifact of fairly recent processes of monopoly and proletarianisation. On the one hand there was the specialisation of the workforce. On the other, there was the wider impact of settlement legislation. Randall points out that although the workforce of the west of England was extremely specialised it was also stable and craft conscious. Workers drew pride from their shared 'proto-proletarian' experience of waged but autonomous work.[31] It left a workforce which vigorously defended its customs and community from any change. This characteristic of the west of England clothing communities may have been exacerbated by the effects of later-eighteenth-century poor law institutions which considerably reduced mobility, at least in the south. But, as Snell has argued, other institutions came into play – notably the settlement provisions of the old poor law. Outdated legal provisions on settlement, rarely relevant at the time they were introduced in the seventeenth century, came into play in the later eighteenth. They transformed a relatively mobile rural population in the early eighteenth century into the stay-at-home agricultural labourer of the nineteenth. The enforcement of these settlement laws ended the earlier ease in gaining settlements, forcing high proportions of the rural workforce to take their father's settlement. Snell argues that in the case of the artisan and proto-industrial trades, this perpetuated families practising certain trades in the same place over the generations. They developed familiarity with parochial issues stretching back into their family history, creating a community and political consciousness which could never have existed to the same degree when up to 60 per cent of village populations might disappear every twelve years through migration and low life expectancy.[32]

Social and cultural factors such as I have outlined, and others in local workshop and rural handicraft cultures, helped to shape receptivity to technical change and different forms of work organisation, including the factory. They help to provide one explanation for slow productivity growth in a way that appeals to low capital investment do not.

DIVISIONS OF LABOUR

The regional divide in economic opportunity and conditions, in industrial concentrations and in social relations was but one side of the coin. The other was a division in labour markets. The effects of and response to new technology also depended on whose employment was reduced and whose was increased. In other words it affected the division of labour. Linebaugh has pointed to the effects of technological change on the early nineteenth-century. He points to the shipwright whose tools: 'the adze, rasp, clave, auger, chisel, hammer, maul, mooter, saw . . . will suggest a discussion of the degree of specialisation, the changes, the ownership, the employment of these instruments and hence to the social realities of production'.[33] He looks at the effects of such technical innovation on a wider spectrum of the labouring classes than the skilled artisans. In passing he mentions that the world of the London radical artisan was a very male world. Our discussion of technological unemployment and the response of workers to machinery is almost always perceived from the standpoint of the skilled male artisan. But a major factor behind differing responses to machinery was the implications of new technology for the female as well as the male labour market.

In fact, a high proportion of the anti-machinery feeling in the eighteenth century was generated by the taking away of women's labour. In the 1730s engine looms in the silk manufacture dispossessed the buttonworkers of their needlework. In 1737 the women of Macclesfield 'rose in a mob and burnt some looms'. The rioters against the spinning jenny around Blackburn in 1779 included not only the women spinners themselves but also colliers, labourers and weavers. For as Wadsworth and Mann argued, 'the spinners' interests were those of every working-class family'.[34] The introduction of new technology fostered a structural unemployment which was at once based on gender and region. For mechanisation left in its wake the destruction of widespread family based women's trades. As Clapham put it, spinning machinery, knitting and lockmaking implements had left women's hands idle and family earnings curtailed in an age of hunger and high prices.[35] Jones, more recently, has written of mechanisation driving the southern and eastern districts into industrial oblivion: 'On the clays and lowland heath of the south and east with little or no alternative to mother and daughter power . . . cottage industry contracted in the face of competition from machines.'[36]

The response to the spinning jenny is particularly interesting in its effect on female labour markets. Though invented by Hargreaves, it was quickly taken up and improved by hundreds of imitators. As Reddy has suggested, it developed like a folk song passing from one artist to another, so that authorship was an inappropriate concept. The early jenny was cheap, turned by hand and easily tripled the output of the spinner; by 1780 there were 20,000.[37] Initially it seemed a machine well suited to the expansion of cottage manufacture – of a decentralised mode of production. It meant a loss of employment to the women who used the traditional technology of distaff or wheel, but at least the early jenny was a women's technology. It substantially increased the productivity of large numbers of spinners and brought them higher wages. Small country jennies of about twelve spindles were originally operated by children, but an improved version with more spindles, frequently as many as 60 to 80, was operated by women. It was this jenny which spread manufacture in the eighteenth century. Larger jennies of up to 120 spindles and large hand mules were built in the 1790s, but these were thought to need male operatives, and as men's wages cost more than half as much again as those of women, they were not a popular alternative. In Yorkshire the jenny and the carding engine were introduced by the domestic spinners themselves. In one district the eighteen-spindle jenny was hailed as a prodigy: 'Every weaver learned to spin on the jenny, every clothier had one or more in his house, and also kept a number of women spinning yarn for him in their cottages.'[38] The wages of the early jenny spinners averaged 9 to 10s. a week, a big jump from the 2s. 6d. to 3s. earned on the old hand wheel, and they could spin 16, 20 or 30 times as much. The wages of those who could not introduce jennies fell, but before long so too did those of the jenny spinners. By 1780 there were complaints that women who had been earning 8s. to 9s. on 24 spindles could then only get 4s. to 6s. Larger jennies of more than 80 spindles were posing an even greater threat. Those of up to 20 spindles could be used in the home, and in this form were a widespread part of the domestic system, the machine of the poor. The jenny which spread in the last quarter of the century in Lancashire, and later in the woollen industry, was small factory technology, linked to machine carding and installed in so-called jenny factories. It was these larger jennies which evoked resentment against machinery. A petition complained: 'that the jennies are in the Hands of the Poor, and the Patent Machines are generally in the Hands of the Rich; and that the work is better executed by small jennies than by large ones.'[39] The jenny posed the vital issues behind responses to new technology. It clearly improved prospects for some women, but it entailed unemployment or lower wages for many more. Its implications for women's employment were moreover closely bound up with how it was used, that is within the domestic system or the factory system, and with the regional hierarchies on which its introduction was based and which it further reinforced. We thus understand how it was that women both 'hailed the jenny as a prodigy' *and* avowed their 'intention of cutting to pieces the machine lately introduced in the woollen manufacture'.[40]

CONCLUSION

The unevenness inherent in the very structure of industrialisation from its earliest days in the eighteenth century was reflected in the great differences in workers' responses to machinery. A process of industrialisation which took on many forms was a great source of division. This paper has touched on two divisions: between regions and communities and within the labour force. Division in experience and reception at the regional and local level were not just about factors of environment and local economy – it was about the social and economic structure of industry in different places and, equally significantly, about the differences in community structures and traditions. The divisions in the labour force were those between artisans and the rest of the industrial labour force – the growing significance of outwork and its casual labour force and the important place within this 'unregulated' workforce of women's and children's labour. These divisions were not eradicated, but reinforced as the process of technological change became part of the cumulative decline into de-industrialisation or alternatively into the 'benign' spiral of growth.

In *The Machinery Question and the Making of Political Economy 1815–48* I asserted that there was no 'machinery question' in the eighteenth century.[41] I still believe this in the sense that there was nothing like the later widespread public debate. But not only was there a great deal of resistance to machinery, but I now know that there was more discussion of the issue among economic thinkers than I had realised. However, this discussion of the technological unemployment created by cost-cutting innovations took its place alongside an equally or even more important discussion of product innovations, economic expansion and the development of skills.[42]

This discussion of the uneven structures of industries and the two-sided coin of technological innovation was not there in early nineteenth-century working-class discussions of machinery. There is an important case to be made for the differences in the form of debate and the public power of the contenders in the machinery debates of the eighteenth century and those of the nineteenth. Technological unemployment and workers' responses have appeared recently on the agenda of social historians of the nineteenth century, but are almost always perceived from the standpoint of the skilled male artisan. In the eighteenth century much of the new machinery hit female not male labour markets. The great public debates on machinery in the nineteenth century allowed the voices of artisans and sweated handloom weavers, many of them urban male workers, to be heard: 'it was not until the 1820s that workers found access to the media, in particular through the radical press, and were able to articulate wider value systems.'[43] In the eighteenth century protest against the machine – from the countryside and especially from women – was drowned out at the time by the proclamations of the improvers, and has since been largely ignored by historians.

What is striking about both the positive and the negative responses to machinery in the eighteenth century was the explicit discussion of machinery itself, and with this a range of responses and debate which exposed the two-sided coin of innovation. By contrast responses to machinery by the 1830s in a very heterogeneous working class and radical movement had become part of the wider protest against cyclical swings and the factory system, that is, against the machine as an aspect, albeit an important one, of capitalist exploitation. Robert Owen, for example, believed that technical innovation had brought about a new age dominated by great increases in productivity, but an age now out of tune with the old social arrangements and values of an earlier more restricted economy. His socialist alternatives were based on the new social science which he regarded as complementary to the mechanical sciences which had introduced machinery. It would teach men how to redistribute their new found wealth so as to prevent the technological unemployment, underconsumption and poverty which then accompanied the phase of mechanisation.[44]

By the 1830s and 40s the Owenites regarded mechanisation within the framework of their vision of economic abundance; it was also the basis for socialism itself and their vision of social harmony. Once it was known what goods brought the greatest advantage to men, all that was required was the adoption of the best means by which an abundant supply of them might be produced to be accessible to all so that 'no cause may remain for opposition of interests'.[45] The public discussion of machinery among the Owenites and contemporary trade unionists and radicals was thus taken into a discussion of the 'system', and the system as a singular entity. Historians are quick to make the point that it was capitalism to which the workers objected, not machinery per se. Owenites and other radicals in the nineteenth century confirm this. Yet though Owenites and Chartists espoused a form of technocratic socialism while denouncing the machine within the context of capitalist social relations, one wonders to what extent they came to terms with the division of their own membership over technical innovation; divisions embedded in the uneven development and diverse structures of British industry and even more significantly in the social institutions and cultural traditions peculiar to individual localities and workplace settings. Would the divisions reflected in and created by the advance of machinery disappear with the demise of capitalism itself? The Owenites thought so, but I doubt it. The community and labour force divisions outlined in this paper seem to be endemic to industrial change, with roots that go deeper even than capitalism itself.

NOTES AND REFERENCES

1. **D. Landes**, *The Unbound Prometheus: technological change and industrial development in Western Europe from 1750 to the present*, Cambridge U.P. 1969, p. 123.
2. **P. Mathias**, *The First Industrial Nation*, Methuen 1969, p. 144.

3. See **P. Stoneman**, *The Economic Analysis of Technological Change*, Oxford U. P. 1983.
4. **G. N. von Tunzelman**, 'Technical progress' in **R. Floud** and **D. McCloskey**, *An Economic History of Britain Since 1700*, I, Cambridge U. P. 1981, pp. 143–63.
5. **E. J. Hobsbawm**, 'The machine breakers', in *Labouring Men*, Weidenfeld 1964, pp. 5–22.
6. **C. K. Harley**, 'British industrialisation before 1841: Evidence of slower growth during the Industrial Revolution', *Jn. Econ. Hist.*, **42** (1982), pp. 267–89; **P. H. Lindert**, 'English occupations 1670–1800', ibid., XL, No. 4 (1980), pp. 685–712.
7. **N. Crafts**, *British Economic Growth During the Industrial Revolution*, Oxford U.P. 1985, pp. 82, 30–3.
8. Ibid. pp. 84–5.
9. **N. Rosenberg**, *Perspectives on Technology*, Cambridge U.P. 1976, Ch. 1.
10. **J. R. Harris**, 'Skills, coal and British industry in the eighteenth century', *History*, LXI (1976), pp. 167–82; **P. Mathias**, 'Skills and the diffusion of innovations from Britain in the eighteenth century, in *The Transformation of England*, Methuen 1979, pp. 21–44; **N. Rosenberg**, 'Technological change in the machine. tool industry 1840–1910', *Jn. Econ. Hist.* XXIII (1963), pp. 414–43.
11. See **A. Rees**, *The Cyclopedia*, 1819; **A. Ure**, *Dictionary of Arts, Manufactures and Mines*, 1846; *The Useful Arts and Manufactures of Great Britain*, n.d.; **R. Price**, *Masters, Unions and Men, Work Control in Building and the Rise of Labour 1830–1914*, Cambridge U.P. 1980.
12. **Josiah Tucker** cited in **C. Wilson**, *England's Apprenticeship, 1603–1773*, Longman 1965, p. 311; see also **M. Berg**, 'Political economy and manufactures', in **M. Berg**, **P. Hudson** and **M. Sonenscher** (eds), *Manufacture in Town and Country Before the Factory*, Cambridge U.P. 1983, pp. 33–58.
13. **S. Pollard**, 'Industrialisation and the European economy', *Econ. Hist. Rev.*, XXVI (1973), pp. 637–48 and his *Peaceful Conquest*, Oxford U.P. 1981.
14. See **E. L. Jones**, 'The constraints on economic growth in southern England 1650–1850', *Proc. Third Inter. Congress of Historians*, Munich 1965.
15. See **A. J. Randall**, 'Labour and the Industrial Revolution in the West of England Woollen Industry', Ph.D. thesis, Birmingham, 1979.
16. **J. Tucker**, *Instructions for Travellers*, 1757, pp. 23–4.
17. **P. Hudson**, 'Proto-industrialisation: the case of the West Riding', *History Workshop Jn.*, **12** (1981), pp. 34–61.
18. See Randall, 'Labour and the Industrial Revolution'.
19. **Richard Prosser**, *Birmingham Inventors and Inventions*, Birmingham 1881; **W. Hawkes Smith**, *Birmingham and its Vicinity as a Manufacturing and Commercial District*, 1836, p. 18.
20. **Edward Fitzmaurice**, *Life of William Earl of Shelbourne*, Vol. I, *1737–66*, 1875, p. 404; *Victoria County History of Warwickshire*, 1965; **R. A. Pelham**, 'The water power crisis in Birmingham in the eighteenth century', *Univ. of Birmingham Hist. Jn.*, IX (1973/4), pp. 75–90.

21. See **M. Berg**, *The Age of Manufactures 1700–1820*, Fontana 1985, Ch. 12.
22. **M. Rowlands**, 'The metal trades of the West Midlands', Paper to SSRC Conference on Manufacture in Town and Country before the Factory, Oxford 1980. See also her *Masters and Men in the West Midland Metalware trades before the Industrial Revolution*, Manchester U.P. 1975.
23. **C. Aspin** and **S. D. Chapman**, *James Hargreaves and the Spinning Jenny*, Preston 1964, p. 31. See **E. P. Thompson**, *The Making of the English Working Class*, Penguin 1968, pp. 604–82 and **J. de Lacy Mann**, *The Cloth Industry of the West of England*, Clarendon, Oxford 1971, p. 35.
24. **J. D. Chambers**, 'The rural domestic industries during the period of transition to the factory system with special reference to the midland counties of England', *Proc. Second Inter. Congress of Econ. Hist.*, Aix-en-Provence, II, 1963.
25. **A. Randall**, 'Worker resistance to machinery – the case of the English woollen industry', Paper in ESRC Working Group on Proto-Industrial Communities, *Workshop Papers*, 1, University of Warwick, 1987, pp. 86–105.
26. Ibid., p. 94.
27. **J. L.** and **B. Hammond**, *The Skilled Labourer*, ed. J. G. Rule, Longman 1979, p. 149.
28. **A. J. Randall**, 'The philosophy of Luddism: the case of the West of England woollen workers *c.* 1790–1809', *Technology and Culture*, 1986.
29. **Olivia Harris**, 'Households and their boundaries', *History Workshop Jn.*, XIII (1982), pp. 143–52.
30. **K. D. M. Snell**, *Annals of the Labouring Poor: social change and agrarian England 1660–1900*, Cambridge U.P. 1985; **J. M. Neeson**, 'The opponents of enclosure in eighteenth-century Northamptonshire, *Past and Present*, No. 105 (1984), pp. 114–39; **J. M. Martin**, 'Village traders and the emergence of a proletariat in south Warwickshire, 1750–1851, *Agric. Hist. Rev.* XXXII, No. 2 (1984), pp. 179–88; **P. Hudson**, 'Proto-industrialisation: the West Riding'.
31. Randall, 'Workers' resistance'.
32. Snell, *Annals of Labouring Poor*, Ch. 7.
33. **P. Linebaugh**, 'Labour history without the labour process: a note on John Gast and his times', *Social History*, VII, No. 3 (1982), p. 320.
34. **A. P. Wadsworth** and **J. de Lacy Mann**, *The Cotton Trade and Industrial Lancashire 1600–1780*, Manchester U.P. 1931.
35. **J. H. Clapham**, *An Economic History of Modern Britain*, I, Cambridge U.P. 1938, p. 183.
36. Jones, 'Constraints on economic growth'; **E. Richards**, 'Women in the British economy', *History*, LIII (1974), p. 343.
37. **W. Reddy**, *The Rise of Market Culture*, Cambridge U.P. 1984, Ch. 1.
38. **C. H. Lee**, *A Cotton Enterprise 1795–1840; A History of McConnel and Kennedy, fine cotton spinners*, Manchester U.P. 1972, p. 4.
39. **M. M. Edwards** and **R. Lloyd-Jones**, 'N. J. Smelser and the cotton factory family', in **N. B. Harte** and **K. G. Ponting**, (eds), *Essays in Textile History*, Manchester U.P. 1983, pp. 309–14.
40. Lee, *Cotton Enterprise*; and Edwards and Lloyd-Jones, 'Smelser and the factory family'.

41. **M. Berg**, *The Machinery Question and the Making of Political Economy 1815–48*, Cambridge U.P. 1980.
42. Berg, *Age of manufactures*, Ch. 2.
43. Randall, 'Workers' resistance'.
44. **G. Stedman Jones**, 'Utopian Socialism Reconsidered' mimeo, 1983.
45. **C. Claeys**, 'Owenism: a political economy', *Kings College Research Centre Working Paper*, July 1985.

CHAPTER FOUR

From Suppression to Containment: Roots of Trade Union Law to 1825

James Moher

Understanding the situation of workers' combinations in Britain and Ireland requires a grasp of the law relating to such associations. This is complex and confusing because, as often in English law, common and statute law overlap as sources for the various rulings. The application of these rulings from early times, the first statute being in 1305, spanned so many different forms of industrial organisation and relations of production as to compound the legal complexity.[1]

The Common Law, a body of judge-made rules developed over centuries, was fairly clear in its attitude towards workers' combinations:

Combinations in law connoted conspiracy and concerted action by workmen to bring pressure to bear on their employers to secure higher wages or shorter hours was regarded as conspiracy at common law. The very ancient principle on which this construction of the law of conspiracy rested was that such action was a restraint of trade.[2]

This judicial view of combinations as criminal conspiracies punishable as felonies remained a key feature of official policy in Britain and Ireland until the statute of 1824 repealing the Combination Acts. There are two aspects: the doctrine of conspiracy itself and its application to trade combinations. The early statutes captured the sense in which both these aspects had been understood: 'Conspirators be they that do confederate or bind themselves by oath, covenant or other alliance, that every of them shall aid and bear the other falsely and maliciously to indite, or cause to indite, or falsely to move or maintain Pleas.'[3]

This definition, emphasising as it does the secretive nature and malicious intent of the parties conspiring, best illustrates the reasoning behind regarding it as a crime against the state. The well–known journeymen's motto, 'United to protect, not combined to injure', seems a response to such an attitude. This act of 1305 was quoted in many later trials involving charges of conspiracy.[4]

The second aspect, the application of the doctrine of conspiracy to trade combination was also rooted in medieval law:

> For as much as of late days divers sellers of victuals not contented with moderate and reasonable gain, but minding to have and take for their victuals so much as list them, have conspired and covenanted together to sell their victuals at unreasonable prices: and likewise artificers, handycraftsmen and labourers have made confederacies and promises, and have sworn mutual oaths not only that they should not meddle one with another's work, and perform and finish that another hath begun, but also to constitute and appoint how much work they should do in a day, and what hours and times they shall work, contrary to the laws and statutes of this realm, to the great hurt and impoverishment of the King's majesty's subjects.[5]

Raising food prices by sellers in concert was also viewed as a conspiracy against the public interest in times of scarcity, when it not infrequently led to riots. The statute therefore was against restraint of trade by tradesmen, craftsmen or masters as well as journeymen.

The reference to the practices being 'contrary to the laws and statutes' refers to the Statute of Labourers of 1349 which regulated wages and hours of work.[6] Combinations were thus doubly illegal as conspiracies and, in so far as they sought to change wages or hours of work, contrary to statute and punishable by Justices of the Peace. The act of 1548 quoted above established a first offence penalty of £10 or twenty days imprisonment; a second offence £10 or the pillory and for a third £40 or the loss of an ear and infamy. It also decreed that 'Corporations or dealers in victuals so conspiring shall be dissolved.' Most of the elements of government policy towards combinations for trade purposes, therefore, derived from a society accustomed to such laws.

This policy was strengthened in 1563 by the passage of the Statute of Artificers, popularly known as 'the 5th of Elizabeth', which consolidated already established regulatory practices concerning 'the hiring, keeping, departing, working, wages or order of servants, workmen, artificers, apprentices and labourers'.[7] This statute stipulated the main terms of the aptly described Master and Servant relationship. A minimum term of service of one year was prescribed during which the servant could neither be dismissed nor leave, 'unless it be for some reasonable cause' allowed before two Justices of the Peace. Even at the year end a quarter's notice was required

Table 1 Statutes Outlawing Workmen's Combinations (1305–1817)

(1305)	33 Edw. I, st. 2	('Who be Conspirators')
(1425)	3 Hen. VI, c. 1	('Masons shall not confederate')
(1426)	5 Parl. Jac 1, c. 78	(Fees of Craftsmen – Scotland)
	5 Parl. Jac 1, c. 79	(Fees of Workmen – Scotland)
	5 Parl. Jac 1, c. 80	(Writches and Masones – Scotland)
(1427)	7 Parl. Jac 1, c. 102	(Price of Ilk Workmanshippe – Scotland)
(1542)	33 Hen. VIII, c. 9	(Servants' wages–Ireland)
(1548)	2 & 3 Edw. VI, c. 15	(Conspiracies of Victuallers & Craftsmen)
(1551)	5 Parl. Mary, c. 23	(Price of Craftsmenne's Work–Scotland)
(1581)	7 Parl. Jac VI, c. 121	(Ordour 7 Price in all Stuff – Scotland)
(1662)	13 & 14 Car II, c. 15	(Silk Throwing combinations)
(1720)	7 Geo. I, c. 13	(London Journeymen Tailors)
(1725)	12 Geo. I, c. 34	(Woollen manufacturers)
(1729)	3 Geo. II, c. 17	(Unlawful combinations in Ireland)
(1743)	17 Geo. II, c. 8	(Continuing several Irish statutes)
(1749)	22 Geo. II, c. 27	(Dyers, Hotpressers & Others)
(1756)	29 Geo. II, c. 33	(Woollen manufacturers)
(1763)	3 Geo. III, c. 17	(City of Cork combinations – Ireland)
(1763)	3 Geo. III, c. 34	(Linen and Hemp manufacturers – Ireland)
(1766)	8 Geo. III, c. 17	(London Journeymen Tailors)
(1772)	11 & 12 Geo. III, c. 18	(City of Cork, combinations – Ireland)
(1772)	11 & 12 Geo. III, c. 33	(Dublin Tailors & Shipwrights)
(1773)	13 Geo. III, c. 68	(Silk manufacturers)
(1777)	17 Geo. III, c. 55	(Hat manufacturers)
(1780)	19 & 20 Geo. III, c. 19	(General Irish Act to prevent)
(1780)	19 & 20 Geo. III, c. 36	(Silk manufacturers – Ireland)
(1785)	25 Geo. III, c. 48	(Specific Irish manufacturers)
(1792)	32 Geo. II, c. 44	(Extending 1773 Silk Manufacturers Act)
(1796)	36 Geo. III, c. 111	(Paper Manufacturers)
(1799)	39 Geo. III, c. 56	(Colliers in Scotland)
(1799)	39 Geo. III, c. 81	(Unlawful Combinations of Workmen)
(1800)	39 & 40 Geo. III, c. 106	(Repeal and amendment of 1799 Act)
(1803)	43 Geo. III, c. 86	(Unlawful combinations in Ireland)
(1807)	47 Geo. III, c. 43	(Servants' Wages – all Ireland)
(1817)	57 Geo. III, c. 122	(Extended combination laws to Scotland and Ireland)
(1824)	5 Geo. IV, c. 95	(Combination Repeal Act)
(1825)	6 Geo. IV, c. 129	(Combination Repeal Amendment Act)

for termination by either party. A 40s. penalty was imposed on offending masters and imprisonment for servants.

For several centuries these clauses were to have an important bearing on the conduct of industrial disputes, particularly in the cloth-making outwork trades. Gravenor Henson, the noted leader of the framework-knitters' union in the early nineteenth century was to tell the Commons' committee on the Combination laws in 1824:

If any dispute arises respecting the amount and a strike or turnout commences and the men leave their work having words, the master prosecutes them for leaving their work unfinished. Very few prosecutions have been made to effect under the Combination Acts, but hundreds have been made under this law and the labourer can never be free unless this law is modified; the combination is nothing; it is the law which regards the finishing of work, which masters employ to harrass and keep down the wages of their workpeople.[8]

The statute also stipulated the hours of work for all artificers and labourers and empowered the justices, county sheriffs and mayors and other town officials to fix wages annually at the Easter quarter sessions. Penalties were imposed on magistrates who refused this duty. Wage fixing became the practice throughout the country for a century or more afterwards. It continued spasmodically with much regional variation into the eighteenth century, but more importantly remained as a symbol of legitimation, object of restoration to effective implementation and pretext for action for combined workers, notably in the west country woollen districts.[9] The relevant clauses were not in fact repealed until 1813.

Equally important were the clauses governing apprenticeship. These stipulated a minimum of seven years' indentured service before a trade could be lawfully exercised, 'after the custom and order of the City of London'. These clauses were reproduced and strengthened in the rules of most journeymen's societies during the eighteenth century in their increasing conflicts with their masters. They were amended a number of times over the seventeenth century, but remained on the statute book until repealed in 1814 in the teeth of opposition from the organised journeymen.[10]

THE COMBINATION LAWS

It is clear that the main elements of both common and statute laws against workers' combinations were well established before the

beginning of the eighteenth century. There was a conscious government policy which regarded the setting of wage levels and hours of
work as the prerogative of the authorities. There is little evidence
of either active combinations or of vigorous enforcement of these
laws in the sixteenth and seventeenth centuries. The situation
changed in the eighteenth with the emergence of separate and
permanent journeymen's societies for trade union as well as for
benefit purposes in major cities like London, Edinburgh or Dublin.
Now there is increasing evidence of recourse to Parliament by
employers for assistance in the form of more effective laws against
combinations of workers.[11]

The best example is provided by the London tailoring trade. In
1721 the masters of London and Westminster petitioned Parliament
for an Act to suppress combination among their journeymen. They
had failed to overcome this combination by prosecutions under the
common law and by getting sympathetic magistrates to issue
warrants for the arrest of some of the journeymen as loiterers. They
sought to stir Parliament by pointing to the bad example which the
journeymen were setting for all other trades. Parliament went
through a procedure which was to be thereafter followed in other
such cases. A select committee was appointed to hear the masters'
case, but also invited evidence from the journeymen, which was
submitted through counsel. The masters claimed that over 7000
journeymen tailors in London and Westminster had 'lately entered
into a combination to raise their wages, and leave off working an
hour sooner than they used to do'. They then described the system
of 'Houses of Call', public houses where they organised, collected
contributions and communicated to pursue their demands for an
extra 2s. a week (to 12s. 9d.) and to leave work at eight o'clock
instead of nine: 'their usual hour time out of mind'. The masters
sought a specific Act to outlaw any agreements reached formally or
informally with their journeymen for advancing wages or lessening
hours, and that the justices of the peace for London, Westminster
and Middlesex be given power to commit offenders and to 'limit'
the hours and wages of the journeymen. At first the masters
prevailed with the select committee accepting the existence of the
combination as proved and recognising the ineffectiveness of existing
laws and the need for an Act to regulate the trade.[12]

It has been assumed on the basis of Galton's detailed history of
the tailoring unions that the 'Act for regulating the Journeymen
Tailors within the weekly bills of mortality' gave the masters the
one-sided repressive law which they had sought. Closer examination

of the evidence which he has provided suggests that the Act also addressed some of the journeymen's grievances while nevertheless aiming at preventing them from combining to regulate the employment conditions of the trade. In respect of wages they secured the award of 2s. a week plus a breakfast allowance of threehalfpence a day.[13]

Just as importantly the masters were obliged to pay these rates for the full time of hire instead of their previous practice of laying off men half way through the day, which had been a main grievance of the journeyman. An enforcement procedure upon application by either side to the magistrates was provided, indicative of a serious intent that the legal rates should stick. Periodic adjustments at Quarter Sessions were allowed 'according to circumstances of plenty or scarcity'.

Unable to find evidence of further trade union activity by the journeymen tailors, Galton concluded that they were frightened into compliance by the new Act.[14] It could be as easily argued that they had been placated for the time being having obtained most of their demands, with which all masters had to comply within the jurisdiction laid down. Certainly, on the masters' own evidence, they had shown no fear of prosecution before this Act and it is not to be supposed that they simply dissolved their club because of it.

If it is the case that this Act gave the journeymen much of what they wanted, it is more plausible to argue that the outcome was conducive to tranquillity in the trade for some time after, with the journeymen's society now focused on enforcing the legal rates in an undramatic fashion. Overtime rates remained for determination by the two sides, and in times of 'hurry' in the trade (during periods of General Mourning or royal birthdays) double the normal rates were customary and it is unlikely that the Act changed these practices.

The best evidence that the Act of 1720 became the *basis* of legal wage-fixing in the London and Westminster tailoring trades surely lies in the later complaints by the masters that many businesses were moving outside the district covered by the Bills of Mortality, especially to the Marylebone area, to evade it. Accordingly an amending Act was passed in 1766 which extended and unified jurisdiction to five miles around the city under the authority of the Lord Mayor, Recorder and three other Aldermen.[15] In the intervening years the journeymen had made numerous applications and obtained improvements both in hours and in wages.[16]

Detailed examination of this first eighteenth-century Combination

Act shows a more complex pattern of relationships between masters, their journeymen and the state than has been customarily suggested by historians.[17] The next Act, that of 1725 against combinations of west country woollen weavers, was much more repressive.[18] It was aimed primarily at journeyman combinations considered to have been responsible for outrage and widespread acts of violence and intimidation. Yet it also made provision for 'better payment of wages', that is, forbade truck and other forms of payment in kind. Even as late as 1773 a major Combination Act can be found placating the Spitalfields silkweavers with machinery for settling and enforcing wage rates.[19] This Act was to become the envy and desired objective of weavers and other craftsmen in the textile trades generally. The degree to which these scattered handicraftsmen looked to legal regulation of *minimum* rates as an alternative to weak combinations has been obscured by the undue weight attached to the purely repressive features of some Acts.[20] The Spitalfields Act was extended in 1792 to include manufacturers of mixed cloths. The journeymen's attachment to wage-fixing machinery is evident from their indifference to the passage of the general Combination Acts in 1799 and in 1800[21] and their great disappointment and protest over the repeal of the Spitalfields' Act in 1824.

THE PAPERMAKERS' ACT 1796

As an aid to our understanding of the evolution of thinking by masters, journeymen and the government up to the passing of the Combination Acts in 1799 and 1800, we are fortunate in having a detailed study of the background to the Papermakers' Act of 1796, said by Pitt to have been a model for the general Act[22]: 'It is clear that it was the situation created by the steeply rising prices of the later years of the eighteenth century that first brought the papermakers and their doings into the limelight of official disapproval.'[23] The industry was mainly centred in the home counties, especially in Kent. The journeymen had used their strong organisation to compel their masters to concede high and frequent wage increases and generally to dictate the terms of their employment from 1789 onwards. The determination of the journeymen to extract the maximum advantage from their strength seems to have produced a counter-reaction from the masters, who saw the power of the organised journeymen as raising issues of control, and as justifying a stand against the combination. During a dispute which the journeymen started in January 1796 they decided upon a lockout aimed at forestalling the journeymen's tactic of withdrawing labour from targeted papermills. Prosecutions under the common law for conspiracy were also tried. Both approaches were found to be ineffectual in the face of the journeymen's organisational and financial ability to withdraw their labour and to evade the processes of indictment.

In April 1796 the combined master papermakers sought an Act to suppress the journeymen's club and machinery to regulate wages.[24] However due to the opposition of some of the larger papermakers, the wage-fixing clauses were dropped as tending to establish uniform rates contrary to the usual practice and desire of masters to pay differential rates.[25] This omission was significant in that it carried through to the general Act of 1799 giving it an unbalanced suppressive aspect unlike that of most of the previous trade-specific Acts.

The 1796 Act on combinations of journeymen papermakers seems to have had little effect upon their society's very secretive but continuous existence in 1801 and beyond.[26] However its passage and that of a similar bill against the London journeyman millwrights' club in 1799 is indicative of a new mood by the legislators which was unambiguously hostile to the journeymen's interests and operations. The bald Act of 1799 'to prevent unlawful combinations of workmen', introduced as it was by Pitt himself,[27] seems most probably to have sprung from this general mood, inspired by the masters and manufacturers who had by now the ear of government. Wilberforce, close confident of both Pitt and the Yorkshire clothiers, who certainly wanted such legislation, made an intervention during the passage of the millwrights' Bill which probably best expressed their mood when calling for a general measure: 'These combinations he regarded as a general disease in our society; and for which he thought the remedy should be general; so as not only to cure the complaint for the present, but to preclude its return.'[28]

As a government measure these Acts represented a new departure, although how significant remains debatable. Most evidence suggests that it was aimed at an industrial rather than a political problem.[29] The privy council's 'Observations respecting the combinations of workmen', which seems to have influenced the government's decision, listed the bricklayers, carpenters, cloth dressers, weavers, shoemakers, tailors and cabinet-makers as having active combinations: 'All of the above numerated branches have at times turned out and by that means compelled the Masters to consent to the required terms. Some have thus advanced wages twice within four years and whenever advanced no reduction is allowed however unfavourable the times may be for their employers.' It advised that 'combinations among workmen as well manufacturing as others have of late years advanced step by step to a system which calls for the timely aid of the legislature'.[30]

The shape of the Act, placing as it did the onus on the masters and manufacturers to bring prosecutions rather than requiring the law enforcement agencies of the state to do so, is also significant. The government had, in any case, just passed a specific Act against political societies.[31]

Nevertheless the 1799 Act was a straightforwardly repressive one, outlawing all collective agreements concerning wages, hours, quantity of work, apprenticeship or, 'for controlling persons carrying on any manufacture, trade or business in the conduct or management thereof'.[32] Offenders could be committed to hard labour in the House of Correction for up to two months or to the Common Gaol for up to three months on conviction before a single justice on the evidence of one witness or upon confession. Other activities singled out for punishment included combining to prevent other workers hiring themselves or persuading them to quit any employment. Attendance at meetings, payment or collection of subscriptions and maintaining club funds were particularly aimed at and made punishable by fines, seizure and distribution of the funds to encourage informers and defalcators.[33] As with previous private measures, this Act was primarily intended to give masters a speedier and more effective legal remedy than could be provided by the common law. It did not replace it, but the oft heard masters' complaints about the difficulties presented by tardy and cumbersome indictment processes at the next Quarter Sessions encouraged them to think that a summary procedure before a magistrate would be more effective.[34] A right of appeal to all the justices at general sessions was allowed, but not an application to the Court of King's Bench.

On the face of it this was a pretty draconian measure and the surprising thing is that there were not more protests and petitions from the journeymen. Admittedly the parliamentary timetable was short[35], but this was not unusual and did not prevent effective lobbying on other issues. Equally on the government side, there seems to have been a lack of detailed consideration of the measure. One almost gets the impression that they just offered the masters and manufacturers the model of the Papermakers' Act straight off the peg,[36] which in the absence of effective opposition either from the journeymen or in a Parliament in an anti-combination mood passed without scrutiny into law.

Not until the following year was there a significant reaction. This took the form of numerous petitions from journeymen all over Britain, particularly from the Liverpool area. One of the members for that town, General Tarleton, with the support of even the Tory MP Colonel Gascoyne, secured a further committee of inquiry. Its report recommended a number of significant procedural changes such as the right of seeking a judicial review of justices' decisions in King's Bench. Two justices instead of one were now needed to convict and witnesses could give evidence without incriminating themselves. The requirements for the service of summons were strengthened, and a record of convictions and committals kept by magistrates and lodged with the Quarter Sessions.[37] Most of these recommendations were agreed by the government, but Pitt expressly reaffirmed the intended principle of banning collective agreements by trade clubs.

Equally significantly, the opposition was able to exploit the omission of any alternative wage-fixing machinery, and although the government expressly confirmed their opposition to any such clauses being inserted, they eventually agreed to incorporate binding arbitration agreements, albeit in a more limited form than those currently on offer to the cotton weavers in a Bill then before Parliament. The amending Act of 1800 was the one in force until the repeal in 1824.[38]

This outline of the evolution of the laws against combination reveals a definite trend away from mercantilist philosophies which, while definitely wanting to prevent combinations for trade purposes, nevertheless also considered that the state had an obligation to ensure some machinery for regulating wages and industrial relations. The last manifestation of this policy was the Spitalfields weavers Act of 1773 which was rather conceded than willingly granted.[39]

Adam Smith's theories about market forces determining the price of labour like that of any other commodity were now in the ascendant and the Pitt government firmly resisted any moves on the part of the most numerous groups of workers, the agricultural workers and the weavers, to revive the old wage-fixing arrangements to cope with inflationary and depressed trade conditions.[40] This left a lopsided and oppressive armoury of common and statutory law which could be invoked against combinations to promote or defend the interests of workers. By the penal standards of the time, the new statutory offences were to be misdemeanours rather than felonies, as at common law. The intention seems to have been to give masters a speedier but less severe sanction, reserving the common law for more serious incidents. It is unlikely that this 'leniency' was much appreciated by the journeymen. Whether the new procedures were more effective is what we must now consider.

THE OPERATION OF THE COMBINATION LAWS, 1800–24

Assessing the working of the laws is not a straightforward task. Wider controversies among historians in generally interpreting the period have drawn in the Combination Laws to support their different positions without offering any detailed consideration of them in their own right. The traditional view is that they represented a far-reaching change of policy and the 'most unqualified surrender of the State to the discretion of a class in the history of England'.[41] In contrast to this view of the Hammonds, Dorothy George concluded in 1927 that the Combination Acts were 'in practice a very negligible instrument of oppression', and pointed to the very small number of prosecutions and still smaller one of convictions under them.[42] Although many historians since have mulled over the evidence and the conflicting views, little consensus has been reached despite a considerable amount of primary evidence.[43] A definitive study is long overdue of this formative period in the establishment of the political and legal framework of British trade unionism.

An indication of government practice in its treatment of trade unions around the time of the passage of the Act of 1799 is provided by an exchange of correspondence between the Home Office and a Bolton magistrate concerning a combination of weavers in that 'principal part of the manufacturing district'. The local authorities were concerned lest this combination 'ostensibly formed for the regulation of wages' might be a front for radical agitation of the weavers. An informer's account of the proceedings of the Weavers' Association and a copy of their *Address to the Public* were forwarded to the law officers via the Home Secretary, but they concluded that the combination was not illegal within the terms of the 1799 Act. The local magistrate was nevertheless advised to continue his surveillance. In November the weavers were reported to have renewed their opposition to the Act 'to prevent combinations amongst workmen', and although it had nothing to do with their distress, 'yet the ill-intentioned will not fail to take advantage of it as the cause'. This magistrate saw a need for 'rescuing the weavers from the snares which have been laid for them' and 'to prevent any serious or regulated plan of operations from growing out of the temporary difficulties'. In the end the local magistrates were dissuaded from prosecuting the Weavers' Association and instead the weavers were to get a Cotton Arbitration Act. Such incidents possibly educated the government as to the counter-productive aspects of the 1799 Act, disposing them to accept its amendment so soon after its initial passage.[44]

In December 1799, faced with a request from the Lord Mayor of London on behalf of the coal merchants to intervene and enforce the Act against a seamen's combination at Shields, the Home Secretary again declined to act. He relied upon information from the Mayor of Newcastle that it was no more than a traditional wage dispute with the shipowners 'differing as to the quantum of wages'[45]. In January 1800 the master tailors of London tried to enlist help in putting pressure on magistrates to act against their journeymen's houses of call by threatening the publicans' licences. Again the Home Secretary declined to act. However this reluctance on the part of ministers did not mean that local authorities were discouraged from initiating proceedings themselves, as in October 1799 when the Home Secretary encouraged the Lord Mayor of London to prosecute a combination of journeymen bakers under the new Act.[46]

1802 provides an interesting example of the use of the Act of 1800 as an instrument of civil power rather than of masters against a wage combination. This was during the violent campaign against shearing machines and gig mills by the shearmen of the west-country woollen manufacture. The chief Bow Street magistrate, James Read, was sent to Wiltshire to deal with the disturbances and planned to arrest the shearmen's committee. On 1 September he reported that six men had been gaoled under the Combination Act, four for offences and two for refusing to testify: 'I am bringing forward as many cases as I can under the Combination Act, and by forcing some to give evidence against others, I hope to provoke some quarrels amongst them and by that means to be able to bring some of their deeds to light.'

The shearmen's union was suspected to have national headquarters at Leeds, but a much more cautious policy was preferred by the Lord Lieutenant of Yorkshire, Earl Fitzwilliam, and it took some time before he was convinced that nocturnal meetings of the crop-pers, as they were more usually known in the West Riding, were not just for innocuous trade purposes: 'I conceive it to be only the different classes of people for the purpose of raising their wages, and from which nothing is to be apprehended.' He advised the Home Secretary to resist acting on alarmist reports from manufacturers and avoid confusing the inconvenience and mischief caused by ordinary trade disputes with the activities of seditious revolutionaries and conspirators: 'we should not afford them ground of complaint against the Constitution that we should not drive them into the service of the true Jacobin'.[47]

By September 1802, however, he was beginning to have doubts due to information obtained during a dispute between the Leeds manufacturer Benjamin Gott and his shearmen, ostensibly over the issue of apprenticeship:

For a breach of this regulation decreed by their pleasure, Mr Gott is declared by the croppers under the ban of their empire. The striking of workmen is certainly to be considered usually as a business of a private nature . . . but on this occasion I must say it appears to me . . . that the matter, the motives and the nature of the denunciation give it a very different character. It is for infringement of a law made by parties incompetent to make any law; a law . . . subversive of the general rights of all his Majesty's subjects and to be enforced by violence, not only against the party denounced, but against all other people. Single men would not dare to face the menace of so numerous and so powerful a band, without some good assurances of public protection.[48]

This distinction between purely trade disputes, though unlawful, and combinations whose objects or potential were presumed to be sedi-tious, was a crucial one for the authorities.

But what of the employers' use of the Acts? Were the journeymen 'at the mercy of the masters'? In the old trades and manufactures the situation seems to have been the reverse. In the woollen manufacture whose weight was shifting from the west to the north, centuries of detailed legislative regulation and the existence of very strong, stra-tegically placed groups of journeymen like the shearmen, seem to have frustrated ideas for change. Fitzwilliam, who seems to have been both well informed and reasonably unbiassed, concluded:

I know that it has been a measure among some of the Magistrates to stop any merchant from erecting a shearing mill, for fear of the consequences. There must be some strong encouragement held out before anyone will make the attempt. It is indeed unfortunate the masters have yielded so often, that they have lost all superiority. The journeymen are now masters. The masters feel the inconvenience and repine at it, but it appears to me that they have no thoughts of meeting the evil sternly, but are thinking of application to Parliament for further restrictions against the combination of journeymen. Laws to this effect have been amended, and amended over and over again, but still they remain inefficacious. So they will for ever. The system of restriction is vicious. Parliament always feels it so, and whenever it touches upon the subject its better principles are always a check upon its worse propensities. But though masters cannot be vested with an unfitting authority over their servants, they may and ought to be protected in the full exercise of their own just rights against all violence and against the effects of terror.[49]

Without entering into the respective merits in the dispute of the shearmen and their masters, there is little doubt that the situation was far more complex than that presented by the Webbs or the Hammonds as a 'war against trade unions'.

Only very slight use was made of the Act of 1800 in the following two decades, and research has not added very much in the way of fresh evidence in recent years. No doubt an exhaustive trawl of local newspapers and Quarter Sessions records would fetch up some more cases. But it may be more pertinent to ask whether most masters, on whose initiative prosecutions rested, decided not to use the law, and what reason they may have had for this decision.

Take the case of the master millwrights in the London area who had sought an Act for their own trade in 1799. We have evidence of further disputes in 1801, 1805 and 1812, but these were all resolved without reference to the Combination Act despite the masters' earlier lobby for an effective law.[50] By 1813 the masters in that trade seem to have gained the upper hand through *industrial* means. By this time a number of them and other engineering employers such as Galloway, Donkin, Maudslay, Taylor and Martineau had established engineering works, extended the division of labour and flooded the trade with apprentices and semi-skilled engineers.[51] These employers played a leading role in the repeal in 1814 of the apprenticeship clauses of the Statute of Artificers, removing the foundation of the journeymen's cherished restrictions on apprenticeship. The shift in the balance of industrial power is clear from the evidence of both masters and journeymen to the select committee of 1812/13 which investigated apprenticeship prior to the repeal and also from the employers' evidence to the 1824 committee where they unanimously favoured repeal of the Combination Acts, claiming that they had 'broke the neck of all combinations' and had no need of the laws.[52]

Other masters like those in boot- and shoe-making clearly regarded it as a waste of time simply to prosecute some of the ringleaders should they be so unguarded as to expose themselves as targets during disputes. In 1802 the masters drew up another Act 'for the more effectual prevention' etc., in which they aimed at the house of call system by threatening the licences of landlords who allowed meetings of journeymen on their premises. Nothing, however, came of this and in 1804 the masters were still complaining about the 'tyranny' of the cordwainers' union and of the 'thralldom' to which they had been for so long forced to submit:

It may probably be thought that the masters ought to prosecute on these occasions, but a recollection of what was the fate of Mr Newcome who, for undertaking to prosecute, was, being deserted by the masters, entirely drove out of the trade, as no man would afterwards work for him. The masters therefore, fearful of similar treatment, submit to their exactions.[53]

There are frequent references to intimidation from other trades. Trade disputes in Dublin were notoriously violent during this period. The Chief Constable of Police there gave it as his opinion that 'terror among the labouring classes, timidity among the masters' were the major reason that the Combination Laws were rarely invoked there.[54] A similar situation prevailed in the ship building and repair trades of Liverpool, especially among the sawyers and ship-wrights. The town clerk reported that little recourse was had to the Combination Laws 'either from willingness or fear'.[55]

From reading the evidence for these towns from masters, jour-neymen and authorities, one gets the impression of a much deeper struggle over 'control' of the trade with regard to recruitment, payment systems, work practices and a range of other issues. Some masters were trying to change the established system and especially to break down apprenticeship restrictions and increasingly to employ 'non-regular men', but strong societies of journeymen were effec-tively resisting such changes. Violence against those whom the regular journeymen regarded as scabs, blacklegs or 'foreigners' was endemic in desperately bitter disputes over these issues, and if any law was to be used it was more likely to be the criminal law.

Of course for much of the time relationships in most trades were fairly calm. This naturally encouraged most employers to eschew any ready use of the combination laws in the inevitable but spas-modic disputes which did occur, unless they considered that only the *force* of the law would enable them to prevail when other methods had failed.[56]

Masters who invoked the law often found it ineffectual and even counter-productive, inflaming and embittering relationships for years afterwards, especially when gaol sentences were imposed on well-regarded strike leaders, as happened when *The Times* secured conviction under common law conspiracy proceedings of several compositors during a very bitter dispute in 1810. By 1824 a spokesman for the London printers recalled this experience with regret and indicated that as a result of the following period of ill feeling, the employers had unanimously agreed never to use the laws again.[57]

Judicial hostility to the extension of magistrates' powers also seems to have made prosecution under the 1800 Act an uncertain venture, and the higher courts seem to have been strict over the procedural requirements of the Act, so that obtaining a conviction before the justices came to be viewed by some masters as of doubtful value.[58]

EVADING PROSECUTION AND THE CLOUD OF ILLEGALITY

The ability of the journeymen's clubs to evade prosecution and conviction by various means has to be considered a most significant factor in rendering the Act of 1800, like so many before it, ineffective in suppressing trade union activity. The societies in existence before 1799 were already unlawful at common law if their rules could be seen to embrace trade as well as benefit objectives. An Act of 1793 had legalised associations for the latter purpose.[59] Many journeymen's societies had registered under it, ostensibly as friendly societies, but in practice also concerning themselves in the regulation of their trades.[60] Rules governing trade matters and the highly ritualised oath-taking procedures for enrolment and binding of members were probably always kept secret. The effect of the Acts of 1799 and 1800 can only have been to have put a greater premium on secrecy.

This can be seen from the 'Articles of Agreement' drawn up by the Amicable and Brotherly Society of Journeymen Millwrights in 1801 for registration under the Act of 1793 and lodged with the Registrar.[61] All references to trade objectives are crossed out in the original with a handwritten marginal note, 'this has the appearance of an improper combination', presumably on the advice of the Registrar or of an attorney. Rule 6 provides that members of the 'lately dissolved Society of Journeymen Millwrights shall be considered as members of this society without payment of admission money'. In 1805 the journeymen publicly disavowed their membership of any trade club, while at the same time extracting a hefty increase from their masters.[62] In 1801 the journeymen paper-makers' correspondent referred to his meeting at Maidstone with 44 other journeymen who approved and signed 'the sick, and secret articles of our Trade'.[63]

There were many methods of evading prosecution. Certainly very little was committed to writing and demands were conveyed surreptitiously wherever it was thought there might be a danger of prosecution.[64] However it is clear that in most well-organised trades, the masters continued to recognise the authority of the clubs and regularly negotiated with them, usually jointly settling books of prices and other matters, as in the London printing, coopering and brushmaking trades.[65]

Despite such de facto arrangements, the cloud of illegality under which journeymen's combinations had to operate at the turn of the nineteenth century can only be thought of as highly prejudicial to them. And there seems little doubt that it was felt to be so by them. The evidence from both sides to the 1824 committee confirms a widespread sense of grievance. A Dublin master cabinet-maker expressed another aspect from the point of view of a perceptive employer:

In our trade and other trades also there are some of the most respectable part of the Community, who do not wish to take an active part; we generally pay £100 as an apprentice fee and a young man whose friends can afford to pay that must be somewhat respectable; it is not the infliction of the punishment they care about, but these young men do not like to have their names announced in the newspapers as being confined in Newgate; therefore they will not accept any situation as stewards or President; the consequence is, that it falls into the hands of uneducated men who are perhaps of warm tempers, and do not know how to go about the matter; they see no results but in violence. If the Combination Laws are repealed, respectable men would have the upper hand in every trade and all acts of violence would cease.[66]

THE REPEAL OF THE COMBINATION LAWS

Such far-sighted views were gaining ground from 1814 when Francis Place began his campaign for the repeal of the Combination Laws. Despite the vigorous opposition of the organised journeymen, Parliament had swept away in 1813–14 most of the old legislation regulating wages and apprenticeship.[67] By renouncing all responsibility in these matters, whilst retaining laws preventing workers combining to regulate wages and conditions, the state now appeared to be completely on the side of the masters.

The story of the parliamentary campaign to repeal the combination laws which Place master-minded is well known and the credit given to his efforts deserved. However too great a reliance on his own account of the episode has obscured the degree of consensus which by that time existed in Westminster and even among employers for the legalisation of *some* aspects of trade union activity. Huskisson, on behalf of the government, informally facilitated the efforts of those like Joseph Hume to introduce a repealing measure. It is doubtful whether the efforts of Place and Hume would otherwise have been so successful.[68]

A sympathetic Select Committee was set up in February 1824 to look into a range of old laws (such as those preventing the emigration of artisans or the export of some kinds of machinery) and its brief was later extended to include the laws on combinations. Place's boast of having stage-managed most of the evidence from both masters and journeymen seems exaggerated when one considers the full record of the committee's proceedings. Nevertheless it does seem that he succeeded in duping the government as to the precise terms of the Act which followed the committee's recommendation of repeal.[69] For as well as repealing the various statutes against combination, the Act gave immediate immunity from prosecution even at common law for objectives much wider than those considered legitimate by either of the sides in Parliament and certainly by the employers. These included the right to combine 'to regulate the mode of carrying on any manufacture, trade or business or the management thereof'.[70] Although the legitimisation of such broad objectives may seem unremarkable to the modern reader, it was certainly not so in 1824. It was one thing grudgingly to acknowledge the expediency of allowing workers to combine peacefully for wage or other limited purposes, but quite another to legitimise the activities of journeymen's societies aiming at asserting a veto on management powers over such matters as recruitment, discipline, payment systems and work practices generally. But the Act devised by Place went through so quickly that the implications of the clause removing the application of the common law of conspiracy were unnoticed.[71]

The practical implications were soon evident as a rash of turbulent industrial unrest swept the country. There was an immediate clamour from the employers for a re-enactment of the Combination Laws, both statutory and common.[72] Place and Hume much taken aback by the disturbances, remonstrated with the workmen.[73]

A new select committee set up included Hume, assisted still by Place, but was made up largely of members handpicked by the government. Having investigated the combinations most involved in the disturbances, the seamen, papermakers, shipwrights, coach-makers and cotton spinners, they resisted the pressure from employers, like the shipbuilders, to re-impose laws of the old kind. They did, however, recommend the restoration of the common law of conspiracy to trade cases although certain limited objectives were to be immune from prosecution.[74] This distinction between the legitimacy of combination for some objects but not for others was to become the basis of all future policy on the law relating to trade unions in Britain.

It was based on the assessment by the 1825 committee of the nature of the journeymen's clubs of the period:

Their objects appear to be in most instances the regulation of wages, combined with the assumption, in certain particulars of a power of dictation in the conduct of the business of which they are engaged; the effect of which, if submitted to, would be totally to subvert the independence of the masters and deprive them of all means of resistance to the future demands of their workmen of whatever nature those demands might eventually be.

And again: 'It is stated on one side, and distinctly admitted on the other that it is not a question of wages, and is therefore described by masters to be a question of the power of, regulating the mode of conducting the business.'[75] The resulting Act embodied the distinction, legitimising trade union activities only for specific purposes such as the regulation of wages or hours of work. It also stipulated further statutory offences such as intimidation, molestation or obstruction during trade disputes which carried punishments of up to three months' imprisonment. The precise interpretation of what constituted these offences was left to the discretion of the police and judges, a feature which remains to the present day.[76]

CONCLUSIONS

The Combination Laws were a product of a highly regulated medieval society. Originally they were aimed at suppressing associations of both masters and journeymen – traders as well as producers – to prevent them raising the *prices* of their products and services. Apart from being regarded by the courts as a restraint of trade, such combinations were viewed by the legislature as conspiracies and as tending to usurp the wage-setting functions of the State.

The Combination Laws were revived and augmented significantly during the eighteenth century with Acts of Parliament aimed at preventing specific groups of journeymen like the tailors, weavers, paper-makers and millwrights from utilising their organised strength to dominate or regulate their trades in accordance with their practices and customs. However, the wage-fixing aspects of legislation on the model of the Spitalfields Acts were also sought by some like the weavers.

All these laws were largely ineffective in suppressing combinations because unenforceable. With the removal of other medieval industry-regulating legislation in 1813 and 1814 the Combination Laws stood out as anomalous, one-sided and unjustifiable. They were repealed in 1824 following a Parliamentary inquiry which heard a preponderance of opinion – masters, employers and authorities as well as journeymen – in favour of repeal. A more restrictive basis for the lawful operation of combinations was established in 1825. This was the legal framework which the forerunners of today's trade unions had to operate until the newly constituted unions became strong enough to remove many of those restrictions after 1871.

The foregoing interpretation is at odds with the traditional labour historians' view of the Combination Laws, founded on Marx's influential section in *Capital* and eminent works like those of the Webbs and the Hammonds. Yet neither does it accept the view of those like M. D. George that the effect of these acts was 'negligable'. Marx saw the Combination Laws as a continuous barrage of 'legislation against the expropriated wage-labourers', stretching over five centuries of capitalist accumulation. I have attempted to show that a more detailed analysis of those laws reveals a much more complex picture affecting mainly artisans, viz. small masters and journeymen handicraftsmen. Similarities between their associations and those of the emerging trade unions of Marx's time, together with the superficial continuity of the legal form of all combination laws since medieval times, lent plausibility to the traditional view. But we have only to consider such a statement as: 'The barbarous laws against Trades Unions fell in 1825 before the threatening bearing of the proletariat'[77] in order to realise that it is seriously flawed as a historical statement. The trade clubs had only a marginal influence in the repeal of the combination laws as is well known and it would be truer to say that those laws were nearly *re-imposed* in 1825 due to the threatening bearing of the *artisanate*. If this interpretation is sound, it would call in question some received views on the formative period of trade union law and history.

NOTES AND REFERENCES

1. Successive editions of contemporary works such as **Blackstone's** *Commentaries on the Laws of England*, from 1765 are a useful guide. **N. A. Citrine**, *Trade Union Law*, Steven and Sons 1950, has a useful introduction.
2. **M. D. George**, The Combination Laws', *Econ. Hist. Rev.*, VI (1936), p. 172.
3. Ordnance concerning Conspirators 33 Edw. 1, st. 2, 1305 *Statutes at Large*, I, pp. 307–8.
4. Cambridge tailors 1721, 88 *English Reports* 9. *Regina* v. *Eccles* 1783, 168 *Eng. Rep.* 240 *Regina* v. *Hammond* 1799, 170 *Eng. Rep.* 508.
5. Conspiracies of Victuallers and Craftsmen, 2 and 3 Edw. VI, c. 15, 1548.
6. 23 Edw. III, c. 5. These Acts were amended and extended in various directions until the consolidated legislation of 1563.
7. 5 Eliz., c. 4.
8. Place Collection, BM Add. Mss. 27804.
9. See A. Randall's contribution, Ch. 2.
10. For the importance of the statute in the eighteenth century see the recent general studies: **C. R. Dobson**, *Masters and Journeymen: A pre–history of industrial relations, 1717–1800*, Croom Helm 1980 and **J. Rule**, *The Experience of Labour in Eighteenth-century Industry*, Croom Helm 1981. For the contest over statutory apprenticeship see: **I. Prothero**, *Artisans and Politics in Early Nineteenth-century London: John Gast and his times*, Dawson 1979, Ch. 3 and Rule, *Experience of Labour*, pp. 116–19.
11. For seventeenth century see: **G. Unwin**, *Industrial Organisation in the Sixteenth and Seventeenth Centuries*, 1904. For the eighteenth century see: **S. and B. Webb**, *History of Trade Unionism*, Longman 1921.
12. **F. W. Galton**, *Select Documents Illustrating the History of Trade Unionism*, Vol. I, *The Tailoring Trade*, 1923, introduction and pp. 2, 5.
13. Clause 2 of 7 Geo. I, c. 13.
14. Galton, *Select Docs*, p. 9, intro. p. xxv.
15. Ibid. pp. xxi–xxii. The areas excluded were Kensington, St Marylebone, St Pancras, Paddington and Chelsea.
16. *Ibid*, p. 35, 41; C. R. Dobson, *Masters and Journeymen*, Croom Helm 1980, Ch. 5, essentially follows Galton on the oppressive nature of the acts despite many valuable descriptions of a more complex role by the magistrates in trade disputes.
17. Sidney Webb accepted Galton's view in his preface to the 1923 edition.
18. 12 Geo. I, c. 34.
19. 13 Geo. III, c. *68*; Dobson, *Masters and Journeymen*, pp. 85–9; **J. H. Clapham**, 'The Spitalfields Acts, 1773–1834', *Econ. Jn.*, XXVI, (1916).
20. **J. L. and B. Hammond**, *The Skilled Labourer, 1762–1832*, ed. J. G. Rule, Longman 1979, for the various campaigns by textile workers and framework knitters to secure statutory wage regulation similar to that provided by the Spitalfields Act.
21. **M. D. George**, *London Life in the Eighteenth Century*, Penguin 1976, p. 195.
22. *Parliamentary Register*, 17 June 1799.

23. **D. C. Coleman**, *The British Paper Industry 1495–1860*, Oxford U. P. 1958, pp. 258–68.
24. *Commons Journals*, li, pp. 595–61.
25. Ibid, p. 631.
26. **A. Aspinall**, *The Early English Trade Unions*, Batchworth 1949, p. 37.
27. Although he denied having done so less than a year later, *Parliamentary Register*, vol. 12, p. 219.
28. Ibid., 9 April 1799. Wiberforce became chairman of the 1806 Select Committee on the Woollen trade. See also Dobson, *Masters and Journeymen*, Ch. 9.
29. It was certainly the first such general Act applying to England, although Ireland had received one in 1780 (19 and 20 Geo. III, c. 19). But the circumstances of its passing and the preceding events do not give much sense of what the Webbs called a 'momentous new departure'. Pitt's introductory remarks, however, do point towards such an interpretation: 'It was his intention to endeavour to provide a remedy to an evil of very considerable magnitude; he meant that of unlawful combination among workmen in general – a practice which had become too general, and was likely, if not checked, to produce very serious mischief.' *Parliamentary Register*, 17 June 1799, but his statement of a year later (see note 36) and the government's subsequent practice, it will be argued, was much more cautious and discerning between political and industrial combinations. For an interpretation suggesting a primarily political motivation see: **R. A. E. Wells**, *Insurrection: the British experience*, Alan Sutton 1983.
30. P.R.O. PC 1/43/A. 152.
31. 39 Geo. III, c. 79.
32. 39 Geo. III, c. 81, clause 1.
33. The ability to the journeymen to accumulate funds to sustain long strikes was seen as a key factor.
34. The Bills on the papermakers and the millwrights make reference to this need for summary procedure as well as the general Act.
35. The journeymen calico printers were able to petition and be represented by counsel before the passage, see: **J. L.** and **B. Hammond**, *The Town Labourer 1760–1832*, ed. J. C. Lovell, Longman 1978, p. 83.
36. Less than a year later Pitt could not even remember the details of the previous Act. *Parliamentary Register*, vol. 12, p. 220.
37. Hammonds, *Town Labourer*, pp. 86–7. A recent analysis by a legal historian of the Combination Acts was presented to a 1983 Conference at the University of Warwick: **J. V. Orth**, 'M. Dorothy George and the Combination Laws reconsidered'.
38. 39 & 40 Geo. III, c. 106.
39. 13 Geo. III, c. 68 and see: George, *London Life*, p. 186; Clapham, 'The Spitalfields Acts'.
40. In February 1800 Samuel Whitbread had again introduced a Bill to regulate the wages of labourers in husbandry which was lost on its second reading. Pitt expressed his disapproval in principle of 'interference into what ought to be allowed invariably to take its natural course' (*Parliamentary History*, vol. 34, pp. 1428–9).
41. Webbs, *History of Trade Unionism*, p. 64; Hammonds, *Town Labourer*, p. 80.

42. **M. D. George**, 'The Combination Laws reconsidered', *Econ. Jn.*, Supplement, 1927, p. 214.
43. Evidence is easily accessible from the minutes of the Select Committee on Artisans and Machinery, *BPP*, 1824, v; the Home Office documents reprinted in Aspinall, *Early English Unions*, and the Place collection in the British Museum, Add. MSS 27804–.
44. Aspinall, *Early English Unions*, pp. 26, 20–7.
45. Ibid., p. 32.
46. Ibid., pp. 33–5; 28.
47. Ibid., pp. 41, 46.
48. Ibid., p. 62.
49. Ibid., p. 64. Other notable instances of complaints that the journeymen were 'now the masters' can be found from the master tailors and from those in boot and shoe making (ibid., pp. 35, 37). In evidence to the 1824 Committee, John Martineau, an engineering employer, thought the masters in Liverpool were 'under the dominion of the men', (*BPP*, 1824, v, p. 196). Both the lord mayor and the chief constable of Dublin said the masters were in 'constant and very considerable terror of the trades' (*BPP*, 1824, v, pp. 294, 298). The struggles over apprenticeship were very much seen as struggles for power in the trades. The men's recourse to the old laws can be seen as marking their declining ability to control the trades through their system of combination in the face of masters using the vast pool of labour released from the Napoleonic Wars.
50. *Morning Chronicle*, 10 June 1805; Webbs, *History of Trade Unionism*, p. 92.
51. S[elect] C[ommittee] on Artisans and Machinery, *BPP*, 1824, v, pp. 7–42.
52. S.C. on the Apprentice Laws, *BPP*, 1812–13, IV to which more than thirty trades gave evidence. S.C. on Artisans and Machinery, p. 27, evidence of Alexander Galloway.
53. Aspinall, *Early English Unions*, pp. 39–40, 74.
54. S.C. on Artisans and Machinery, pp. 294, 298.
55. Ibid., p. 353.
56. For the situation among London's shipwrights see: Prothero, *Artisans and Politics*. The Scottish situation was also much commented on for the violence of trade disputes, vitriol throwing and other forms of violence were alleged. Aspinall, *Early English Unions*, pp. 232, 392.
57. Quoted in *Mechanics Magazine*, 13 Mar. 1824, no. 29, p. 24.
58. Dr George based most of her case as to the negligible effect of the Combination Laws on this factor, 'Combination Laws reconsidered', p. 177. Orth's recent assessment contests this with some force.
59. 33 Geo. II, c. 54 as amended in 1795.
60. See **R. A. Leeson**, *Travelling Brothers*, Granada 1979, p. 96.
61. PRO. Register of Friendly Societies, F.S.1.
62. Journeymen Millwrights Petition, 1805, in Rennie Collection, National Library of Scotland, MSS 19816 f. 179.
63. Aspinall, *Early English Unions*, pp. 36–7.
64. See S.C. on Artisans and Machinery for examples of trades meeting secretly in fields.

65. Webbs, *History of Trade Unionism*, pp. 74–7.
66. S.C. on Artisans and Machinery, p. 456.
67. 53 Geo. III, c. 40, 1813 repealed the wage-fixing clauses and 54 Geo. III, c. 96, 1814 the apprenticeship sections.
68. **G. Wallas**, *Life of Francis Place*, Allen and Unwin 1925 edn Ch. 8 and **Place's** *Autobiography*, ed. M. Thale, Cambridge U.P. 1972, p. xiii; Aspinall, *Early English Unions*, 'The debate showed it was no party question', intro. p. xxv; Wallas, *Life*, pp. 207–9. Place acknowledged this official assistance and recounts with some satisfaction his connivance in manoeuvres to prevent Peter Moore from spoiling matters with a less practical attempt at repeal.
69. Wallas, *Life*, p. 211, 212–16. Whilst the evidence of the early select committees must be treated with extreme caution, that from both masters and journeymen and the authorities in respect of a variety of trades and locations does seem to corroborate. See for example that of the masters and journeymen shipwrights in S.C. on Artisans and Machinery, pp. 81–138, 188–94.
70. Huskisson later claimed that he had been too busy to keep a close watch on Hume and Place and accused the former of having 'betrayed the Committee and suffered himself to be led by the opinions of others'. The hostility displayed towards Place in the debates on the 1825 Amending Bill is suggestive of feelings that he had put one over on the committee (Wallas, *Life*, pp. 224, 237).
71. Even Hume gave the impression that he had not intended to disturb the reserve powers of the Common Law of conspiracy (*Hansard*, x, p. 146) and the report of the 1824 committee had only recommended alteration in Resolution 8 (*Hansard*, xi, pp. 811–13). See 25 Geo. IV, c. 95 clause 25. Place's objections to continuing the common law sanction were perfectly valid from a journeymen's point of view (Wallas, *Life*, pp. 238–9), but from the historical perspective it was naive to have expected the authorities to relinquish such powers in all circumstances.
72. Webbs, *History of Trade Unionism*, pp. 103–5.
73. Wallas, *Life*, 319–20. Aspinall pointed out the turbulence of some of these strikes: 'There can be no question as to the gravity of the crimes . . . the victims being workers who refused to join the unions, blacklegs whom employers brought in to break a strike. At least two such people were murdered in Dublin; a Stirlingshire miner was almost beaten to death; and between seventy and eighty people in Ireland were wounded, over thirty of them having their skulls fractured. Cases of vitriol throwing had started in Scotland at least as early as 1820, and several people were dreadfully burnt and blinded for life.' (*Early English Unions*, p. xxviii.)
74. Webbs, *History of Trade Unionism*, pp. 107–8; Hammonds, *Town Labourer*, p. 95; Report of S.C. on the Combination Laws. *BPP*, 1825, iv.
75. S.C. on Combination Laws, BPP 1825, pp. 502, 504.
76. Combination Repeal Amendment Act, 1825, 5 Geo. IV, c. 129.
77. Karl Marx, *Capital*, I, Lawrence and Wishart 1965 p. 740.

CHAPTER FIVE

Tolpuddle in the Context of English Agrarian Labour History, 1780–1850

Roger Wells

INTRODUCTION: AN IMPOVERISHED AGRICULTURAL PROLETARIAT

A penetrating enquiry in the late 1780s concluded that farmworkers could 'scarcely with their utmost exertions supply his family with . . . daily bread'. The finding was repeatedly reiterated; in 1794, the chairman of the Oxfordshire Sessions reported that 'the Labourers of this County and part of Bucks are absolutely in a state of starvation from the very low price of labour . . . This morning I have had 30 Labourers to complain . . . The conversation of these People is truly alarming as they plainly state, they cannot be reduced to a more wretched situation.' Observers invariably resorted to graphic descriptions of 'famished Faces', 'Tattered Garments', and 'shivering Nakedness' to convey rural plebeians' 'wretched destitution'. Regional demarcations, emphasised in 1797 by Sir F. M. Eden, added a wealth of empirical detail in confirmation of this depressing picture, notably in the cornlands, south and east of Caird's line linking Scarborough and Weymouth, with which this essay is principally concerned.[1] There is little evidence of significant improvement by 1850. But, despite some historians' suggestions, this cannot be ascribed to apathy and ideological under-development.

The intensification of agrarian capitalism and proletarianisation underlay this rural deprivation. The former penetrated bastions of small-scale farming including Cumbria[2] and the Weald. The tenacity of such 'peasant' farming in many districts may have been underestimated, but even in its strongholds market perceptions were paramount, accounting for increasing specialisation represented by market-gardening in appropriate locations, including Bedfordshire,

Worcestershire and North Kent, and hops and 'chicken cramming' in the Weald.[3] The maximisation of profits accounts for the marked upsurge in cereal farming in response to the pre-1815 secular price spiral, and the post-war struggle to maintain profitability explains the superficially paradoxical upward trend in corn production throughout our period.[4] Enhanced corn production was also central to two more key developments, parliamentary enclosure and what hostile commentators dubbed the 'engrossing of farms', often operative in tandem, and certainly responsible for accelerating the fundamental division between capital and labour.[5] In this context, the relentless growth in population proved the greatest and final force cementing this division and generating the rural proletariat. Its paramountcy is confirmed by a Cambridgeshire study which reveals that even where the unenclosed village survived, static numbers of common rights prevented exploitation of commons and waste by the expanded portion of the population.[6]

If specialisation and greater corn production increased aggregate demand for labour, they also aggravated its seasonal structure; the latter actually reduced demand for female workers.[7] Employment was further jeopardised by creeping de-industrialisation over much of the cornlands. The extinction of Wealden iron and the shrinkage of East Anglian cloth manufacture are well known, but the collapse of branches of the textile industry throughout the cornlands is rarely recognised. The obliteration of the South-eastern domestic textile industry removed a significant vehicle for labourers' transition to the ranks of the numerous small farmers.[8] Rural by-employment in East Anglian textiles was of decreased significance for family incomes by the 1790s; deflated earnings were aggravated by recurrent interruptions to distributions of raw materials by merchants on the verge of bankruptcy.[9] Central southern England was a partial exception, where lace and straw-plaiting came to provide important supplementation of family incomes. Some manufactures, notably the widespread paper industry, created regular local demand for female and child labour, but others, including the growing and widely dispersed brick industry, were largely seasonal.[10]

Manifestations of the oversupply of agrarian labour, serious seasonal under- and unemployment, are evinced from the mid-eighteenth century, especially where the problem was most acute after 1815; complaints were made against Sussex farmers exploiting labour surpluses as early as 1756. Wages failed to rise proportionately, and in places not at all, to grain price rises between 1760 and 1792, when several County Benches formally investigated the problem.[11] Poor relief expenditure rose commensurately with prices; systematic measures to tackle inadequate wages and unemployment, including the immediate antecedents of Speenhamland and the Roundsman scheme, appear in the 1780s, and the latter became quickly entrenched in several counties, including Oxfordshire and Buckinghamshire.[12] Some decline in 'in-service' farm employment, whereby younger workers in their teens and twenties on annual contracts lived in the farmhouse, is encountered: one Sussex parish resorted to clothing youths and paying premiums to employers who would take them for a year as early as 1743. The decline accelerated once farmers appreciated that the abundance of labour enabled them to minimise permanent workers, and hire and fire as dictated by seasonal peaks in requirements and even short-term weather conditions. As a diminishing percentage of an expanding labour force secured permanent employment, summertime and harvest earnings assumed a greater significance.[13] Farmworkers' dependence on the market increased, not just for jobs, but also for housing, clothing, fuel and food. Enclosure consolidated this dependency. Commentators contrasted the roaring cottage fires in areas adjacent to the coal-fields with the cold, damp, 'dreary' housing 'situation of the poor in Buckinghamshire, Bedfordshire, and the neighbouring counties'. Rural housing, never equal to demand, came under increasing pressure from a rising population, and from young unmarried folk forced into lodgings when unable to secure in-service.[14] The greater farmers eschewed poultry and pork production, and abandoned petty retailing functions in favour of exclusive concentration on wholesale trading, forcing workers to depend on the rural shopkeeping sector, which expanded rapidly to fill the void towards the end of the eighteenth century.[15] One ramification of this combination of inadequate housing, expensive fuel, and shopkeeping interests, was the decline of home-baking which so infuriated William Cobbett, and the ubiquitous penetration of the countryside by the baking industry.[16]

If the problems stemming from a labour surplus and falling wages were affecting the cornlands from the 1780s, agrarian history, from a labour perspective, falls into three distinct periods. The first, 1780–1815, is dominated by the French Wars, and is characterised by very high food prices, enhanced profits accruing to the landed interest, massive capital investment in agriculture, and considerable confusion amongst historians. The second, 1815–35, is dominated by prolonged agricultural depression and the centrality of the operation of the old poor law, while the third, 1835–50, witnessed the gradual revival of agrarian capital's profitability during the first years of the workings of the critical Poor Law Amendment Act.

AGRARIAN LABOUR IN WARTIME, 1793–1815

The unprecedented mobilisations during the French Wars, the automatic additional stimulus from war-related requirements to an already booming industrial economy, and the massive investment in agriculture encouraged by soaring grain prices, certainly generated an unparalleled aggregate demand for labour. Marked increases in cereal production were achieved through greater fertilisation to sustain heavier cropping, drainage schemes, conversion to arable, and the rapid enclosure of all types of land, including marginal.[17] Dr Collins is typically categoric about the result; the war 'period is generally recognised as having been one of labour scarcity in agriculture', and Professor Jones asserts that farmworkers' real wages rose.[18] The evidence will sustain neither of these contentions.

Multiple misinterpretations create this illusion. A handful of contemporary claims that agrarian wages in industrial regions were pushed upwards by higher earnings in proximate manufacturing and mining, are assumed to apply to the entire North, and by implication to the Midlands too. However, recurrent industrial slumps tended to flood the agricultural labour market. Detailed incomes data from the mixed agrarian and industrial township of Newbold in Derbyshire reveals that farmworkers living alongside miners and metalworkers earned about the same as their southern counterparts, and similar evidence derives from West Riding estate records. There is northern evidence of periodic shortages of labourers willing to take annual contracts and this reflects a trend for workers to exploit oscillating demands by switching between agriculture and industry.[19] Northern harvests were dependent on migrant labour, but potential difficulties in the 1790s were principally pre-empted by Irish immigrants escaping the serious economic and political problems at home, which inflated the customary summertime migrations of the Irish and Scottish. The only pronounced shortages of labour in the cornlands occurred in recently reclaimed fenland country; 'not yet being peopled', labour was perennially scarce, especially at harvest when 'Irish and Scotch labourers are very serviceable'.[20] Elsewhere, labour shortages were localised and ephemeral, with the partial exception of the harvest.[21] The principal cause was other proximate labour-intensive projects, reflected by Arthur Young's rage that a Bill suspending canal-construction during harvests was lost in 1793. Harvesters from Norfolk and the West Country were among those finding advantages in seasonal migrations to Yorkshire.[22] In aggregate, mobilisation effectively terminated *abundance* of harvest labour; uncertainty over the supply of labour pushed harvest rates up especially between 1807 and 1813.[23]

Increased harvest earnings dovetailed with other factors caused by greater cereal production and heavy capital investment in agriculture, notably a pronounced switch to piece rates. Advantages for farmers included the attraction of requisite workers for short-term labour-intensive operations, without jeopardising the reductions achieved in the permanent workforce; they encouraged maximum *per capita* productivity, permitted employers to 'vary the price' relative for example to the quality and condition of the harvest, and they facilitated the effective payment of differential rates commensurate with individual hands' abilities. The switch was expedited by wartime inflation, and piece rates rose disproportionately to day rates.[24] But it was only the 'strong working men, who always chose to work by the measure', 'prime workmen, in the meridian of health and strength', who benefited through seizing the 'opportunity . . . of earning greatly more than day by day labour', commonly double. Piece rates 'operated greatly to the injury of . . . Men in the decline of life', middle-aged and elderly men's incomes were often reduced by piece rates, and attempts to rationalise this by claims that their family commitments were reduced with age conveniently overlooked the severe pressures of inflation.[25] For the fitter and younger, increased harvest earnings and inflated piece rates when employed during the remainder of the year, operated to preserve low living standards. Moreover, the piece-rate worker became eligible for poor relief during spells of unemployment. Unmarried roundsman John Judge receiving 5s. per week, obtained work 'by the Great' at 14s. 6d. weekly, and re-engaged as a roundsman on completion of this work.[26] Even more critically, these developments freed young men from the lengthy degradation of in-service.

Idealistic nonsense was expressed by contemporaries – usually retrospectively – about the beauties of in-service. Romantics, including Cobbett, blamed the social aspirations of *nouveau riche* farmers for the system's decline. Some historians have uncritically endorsed this interpretation, including Dr Snell who adds that its demise stopped workers obtaining settlements to Cobbett's claim that it was also cheaper to pay pitiful wages than meet the social and economic costs of providing good food and accommodation for labourers in the farmhouse.[27] But in-service was not an invariable guarantee of a pleasant existence; farmers, and their wives, were often dictatorial, and in-servants regularly had poorer food, and uncomfortable sleeping accommodation, in addition to long hours and strict discipline, especially against socialising.[28] The life may have been tolerated by adolescents and even youths, but people in their twenties resented these restrictions, and in wartime, non-comparable earnings: 'young men . . . would not do anything but task work', recalled farmer Field of Rumboldwick,

> if they were [living] in the [farm] house [they] had only 4L or 5L [a year]; a good man could only get his 8l or 10l a year, and board and lodging for his salary . . . if a man could earn 2s 6d or 3s a day . . . he would not abide in the farmhouse for 2s 6d or 3s a week, and his board; it was they who broke through that and not the farmers.[29]

The change is occasionally revealed, for example by the prosecution of three Sussex servants in 1809 for quitting their hiring early to secure inflated harvest wages, the same year that a report of the Chichester hiring fair noted the presence of 'lads and lasses', but not more mature workers. And the greatest of all freedoms achieved, was the freedom to marry at a relatively early age, and to set up house where the man at least could be master. The transformation put extra pressure on rural housing stocks, the 'miserable state' of which was already 'the greatest disgrace to this country' in 1803, to create a relentlessly intensifying 'want of cottages' thereafter. Partial solutions derived from widespread subdivision of existing cottages, speculative building notably by village tradesmen, with additional constructions 'on parish land by permission', and erections of 'mere mud cottages' by workers themselves through considerable 'encroachment on waste ground'.[30] Reduced average age of marriage fuelled even faster demographic growth.

Real wages declined despite any tendency money wages had to increase. Arthur Young and Malthus both recognised that enlistment 'rendered it extremely difficult to keep down the price of labour', and in 1803 Young registered a 40 per cent rise in 'husbandry labour' since 1793. In 1812 he categorically asserted that food prices had risen 'in every case more than labour' since 1770, and reiterated this in 1815. Both men emphasised the soaring costs of poor relief, and ascribed them to farmers preferring low wages and high poor rates.[31] The critical factors were the pronounced rise in food prices in 1792–93, and the three famines of 1795–96, 1799–1801, and

1810–12. Although prices fell in between these distinct but devastating crises, the overall trend was markedly inflationary. Agrarian wages were generally, if exceedingly reluctantly and inadequately, raised in 1793[32] and again in 1795, in tardy reponse to massively increased subsistence costs. Farmworkers' real wages were not preserved by these increases, and slipped further after 1795. Farmers, fearful of the difficulties in reducing wages once famine conditions passed, eschewed direct responsibility for the maintenance of earnings, and transferred responsibility to the poor law bolstered by widespread charitable initiatives. The notorious Speenhamland decision by the Berkshire Bench in May 1795 was part of this process. The Berkshire policy was not typical because it derived principally from the energetic chairmanship of the Whig MP, Charles Dundas, a supporter of Samuel Whitbread's attempts to legislate for minimum wages for farm-workers. The Speenhamland decision was an attempt to put the responsibility for the welfare of employed workers squarely on their employers. It failed signally because farmers, faced under the Bench's sliding scale with formidable additional labour costs if they paid the prescribed incomes for family men, exploited the fruitful ambiguities in the official directive, and shifted the burden on to the poor law. Dundas did not intend to compose a charter for allowances-in-aid-of-wages; the Bench's direction was speedily converted into one.[33] The perversion accorded with the crisis management ideas of many Tories; a Suffolk magistrate reported in December 1795 that 'the rise of wages to labourers hath been trifling, as I approve much more of showing indulgence in the purchase of the necessaries of life, than in raising wages in these times' of famine prices. The Rev. Rowley concurred: 'It is judged more prudent to indulge the poor with bread corn at a reduced price' with subsidy costs falling on the parish, 'than to raise the price of wages'.[34] The Hampshire Bench, also chaired by a Whig, conceded defeat in its campaign to get farmers to pay wages equal to subsistence prices in July 1795, with the announcement that living costs must be calculated and labourers'

income rendered adequate to their necessary expenditure – first by the wages from their employers; or where that is impossible through infirmity or the number in the family . . . the difference between the highest income from the best employment, and the lowest outgoing under the best management should be made up in relief granted by the parish officers.[35]

Moreover, during the 1799–1801 crisis, government policies enhanced the role of public authorities; Pitt aimed to spin out limited cereal stocks by the introduction of substitute foodstuffs, especially potatoes, fish and soups, a campaign best advanced through charities and especially poor law authorities, who received executive directions to this effect and eventually statutory support. This ended residual arguments that wages ought to rise to safeguard farmworkers' living standards. Whitbread's attempt to relaunch his campaign in 1800 was quickly eclipsed, and his supporters, even where strongly entrenched, relinquished their position.[36] The crisis sealed the development of ultimate parochial responsibility for the support of agricultural labourers. If famine retreated, prices failed to fall to previous levels; pre-crisis wages determined that subsequent dependency on the parish varied in rough proportion to the size and earning capacity of families. Significantly, allowances in-aid-of wages with respect to children, emphasised by Mark Blaug for the post-1815 period, already obtained, and were confirmed by a repetition of the measures of 1799–1801 in 1810–12. The increased significance of the poor law was recognised by the rider, added in 1800 to the Norfolk Agricultural Society's advertisement of annual competitive premiums for farmworkers with families 'who have not at any time, received Relief', 'that termed Bread-money in times of Scarcity excepted'. 'Times of Scarcity' was dropped, with the Sussex equivalent typically announcing similar prizes for family men in receipt of 'the least proportionate relief' in 1805. The winner that year was a Ringmer man with nine children, who had received subsidised flour from the parish since April 1795, rent of three pounds per year since 1799, an annual quarter of beans since 1800, and over two pounds in doctor's bills.[37]

Escalating poor-law expenditure is a more telling testimony of the realities of the wartime labour market than the odd complaints of agrarian capitalists in the partisan press, so exclusively cited by historians convinced of shortages.[38] Cobbett's polemical strictures on collapsing 'cottage comforts' have considerable substance. Other evidential snippets, like the pronounced move by Sussex farmers in 1807 against the employment outside haymaking and harvest of workers without character references, and the growing need for parishes to pay premiums to those contracting to employ youths, do not suggest shortages.[39] Nor does the diffusion of threshing machines. Few were erected in the major cornlands during the war, and their significance in Scotland and northern England reflects farmers' determination in regions relatively remote from the centres of consumption, and without pools of under-employed labour, to be able to respond quickly to volatile markets which required rapid threshing. Southern and eastern farmers could exploit the seasonally unemployed, rather than resort to expensive technology.[40] Wartime employment was relatively buoyant, compared with pre-1793 experiences, and in stark contrast to post-1815 developments. Essex reports typically juxtaposed 'almost constant employment' deriving from 'the expensive way in which the cultivation is carried on', with strictures against deflated real wages, farmers' hire and fire mentalities, and enhanced dependence on social security. Better cornland demand for labour compromised 'the key supply of migrant labour to London', reflected by advertisements for labourers for massive urban projects, including metropolitan and Bristol dock constructions carried by the rural press.[41] But the fullest employment accrued to the better and younger men; later, an experienced farm-surveyor recalled that there was no 'good labourer unemployed' during the war.[42]

Rural artisans fared better. If their numbers were relatively undepleted owing to the aversion of skilled men to enlistment, demand for their services peaked. They benefited disproportionately from heavy capital investment in agriculture, not only in enclosure but in farming implements, haulage equipment, extended farm buildings, (notably granaries), and from inflated agrarian profitability, underpinning rebuilt and refurbished farmhouses, finer clothes and carriages, and all those appendages expressive of the farmers' new consumerism which so outraged traditionalists.[43] Such sources of increased demand were inflated further through the inevitable chain reaction through this economic sector caused by the multifarious demands of war, from martello towers, docks and barracks, shoes for soldiers and harnesses for armies, and Volunteer uniforms. The 'immense government works going on all over' Kent helped put a premium on all skilled labour, exemplified by the huge wages paid to attract carpenters to Chatham. Advertisements for building craftsmen to work in London were carried by the Sussex press while barrack-erection at Horsham and Lewes was delayed by shortage of skilled men, and by contractors' difficulties in obtaining sufficient bricks in competition with builders in the private sector.[44] Buoyant demand ensured that prices and wages rose. Masters in the rural South-east, including weavers, wheelwrights, carpenters and shoemakers, publicly announced price increases, which were partly legitimised by the stated need to preserve journeymen's standards of living from inflationary pressures. Industrial action in the market towns, notably in the building, tailoring and shoemaking trades, is frequently evinced, and Hertfordshire bargees struck too. Collective action by employees in the countryside included Sussex building crafts, blacksmiths and wheelwrights, Cambridgeshire 'carpenters, bricklayers, blacksmiths etc.' and Kentish and Hampshire corn-millers. Paper-makers in south-eastern and central southern England mounted recurrent wage campaigns.[45] Even workers in declining rural industries, including Surrey hosiers and East Anglian cloth-makers, adopted imitative initiatives.[46] As early as 1794 agricultural surveyors reported increased wages 'paid to the bricklayer, his labourer and mechanic in general', in stark contrast to farmworkers 'who have not the means of enforcing an increase . . . which the mechanic has'. In West Norfolk prices paid for blacksmiths', wheel-wrights', and harness-makers' products rose more than living costs, because 'all day work and jobbing work by the above . . . branches of trade, are advanced in a much higher proportion'.[47] Healthy rural craftsmen were rarely recipients of parochial aid apart from limited assistance during the famines.[48]

FARMWORKERS IN THE AGRICULTURAL DEPRESSION, 1815–35

Labour conditions during the 1815–35 period, dominated by the agricultural depression, are less contentious. The geographical extent and intensity, and the duration of the depression, have been exaggerated in classic accounts like Ernle's, to the exclusion of regional disparities. Cereal production on the light lands increased, while cereal acreages on heavy lands shrank, especially where only wartime prices sustained the economics of intense grain production. The price nadir of 1822 is no more representative than the 1816–17 peak.[49] Geographical contrasts are starkly revealed by the relative equilibrium maintained on Coke's Norfolk estates,[50] and the prolonged Wealden crisis. While Coke had a waiting list of aspirant tenants, Wealden landlords were plagued by vacant tenancies; here recurrent investment, vital for corn production, terminated, with most land 'less drained than it used to . . . because they have no money to expend, and there are no ditches opened . . . or drains'. The cancer continued; by the early 1820s it was difficult 'to get tenants at all; the farms are not in a condition, and nobody will take them'. The sheep rot at the end of the decade even compromised more profitable downland farming, and created longer-term problems in the Weald where it was said in 1833 that farmers 'do not keep sufficient quantity of sheep to give a remuneration in the loss of their corn'. In aggregate, rent rebates, even complete waivers, landlord assistance with some investment, and tithe reductions, were mild palliatives.[51]

Regional disparities must not obscure major common factors; demobilisation, aggravated by relentless demographic growth, swamped cornland labour markets, and facilitated the cost-cutting exercise vital to all farmers irrespective of district. Wages and piece-rates were forced down; seasonal unemployment soared and perennial unemployment boomed. Threshing machines were more broadly diffused, further reducing demand for winter-time labour, though conversely some resurgence of in-service on heavy land farms enabled farmers to pay in kind with produce at diminished market values, and also reduced cash-flow problems.[52] Labour shortages were virtually unknown; repetitive reports relate harvest-time surpluses, exemplified by major altercations between indigenous and migrant labour, especially Irish, even in fenland districts.[53] The enhanced significance of the poor law's functions, developed during the war, intensified to an unparalleled degree. Unemployment's centrality was reflected by the scale of publicly directed, systemised, make-work schemes; labour rates, roundsmen's registrations, parish farm tenancies, the highways, and generous provision of premiums for the hirers of labourers' youthful offspring, all those 'abuses' denounced by the Poor Law Commission, abounded. Allowances in-aid-of wages assumed a key significance for many family men. This represented a massive extension of farmers' pre-war and wartime labour policies, creating poverty through real wage cutting and minimising the permanent work-force, and forcing the poor law to contain the resultant problems. The poor-rate burden became intolerable, nowhere more so than in the least profitable districts. In the 1820s, many vestries with their oligarchic structure and powers reinforced by the Select Vestries Act, including those in 'open' parishes on which the Poor Law Commissioners focused their critique, took stringent action to contain and reduce poor relief expenditure. Poor-law administration was thereby turned into a battleground for class warfare; greater recourse to the settlement laws added another inflammable ingredient.[54]

Two final points require emphasis. First the depression struck smaller farmers harder in general, and in the most unfavourable districts in particular, especially where increased hop-production failed to provide the anticipated compensations. Secondly, the complete reversal of those factors generating wartime prosperity for the rural craft sector, extended the depression's devastations to it.

Farmers relentlessly 'reduced their price to the blacksmith and wheel-wright, and so on'. In Hampshire during the 1820s waggon prices fell from 40 to 30 pounds, carts from 16 to 12, while harness and plough costs plummeted by 25 per cent.[55] In places price wars flared, while some of the most enterprising craftsmen tried to rationalise their situation by experimental production of cheaper threshing machines, only to expose themselves to the difficulties and even futility of competition with the fast-developing, more technologi-cally orientated, specialist agricultural engineering industry.[56] 'Mechanics and persons employed in trade' in the countryside were forced to solicit poor relief, and the indignity of losing their status was inflamed when they were put to work on the roads alongside unemployed labourers. Unemployment among skilled journeymen achieved such a peak in the Weald that a roundsman system for 'all Tradespeople applying for work' to Burwash vestry, was introduced.[57]

THE EXPERIENCE OF THE NEW POOR LAW, 1835–50

The gradual return of agrarian prosperity between 1835 and 1850 did not extend to the farmworkers. The Poor Law Amendment Act's attempt to sanitise the rural poor by the statutory induction of free-market economics through the termination of outdoor relief to able-bodied males, failed to produce the Act's architect's ideologically determined expectation of raising agrarian wages. The Act failed to restructure fundamentally the agricultural labour market; the imple-mentation of provisions for internal migration and emigration was too slight to reduce the labour supply radically. The survival of the Settlement Laws, and the specification that component parishes contributed to poor law union finances on a *per capita* basis, retained the parochial structure for meeting the cost of poverty relief; this in turn conditioned the ways in which the Act was circumvented. Initially many farmers adhered to their entrenched employment policy of keeping permanent labour forces to a minimum, while augmenting them to accommodate seasonal factors and the dictates of the weather.[58] Fears over the cost of incarcerating family men in the workhouse sustained the practice of discriminatory employment in their favour. Wages were regularly adjusted commensurately with individual's precise family commitments, and further slight alterations were conditioned by cereal price movements. Many East Anglian parishes resorted to 'ticket' schemes, derived from labour rate and roundsmen systems, to distribute unemployed family men round farms in the village. In terms of employment and wages, single men were discriminated against; it was regularly decreed that their summer and harvest wages, with casual earnings at odd times during the remainder of the year, would sustain them.[59] Married men were the main beneficiaries of illegal manipulations of the new law. Outdoor relief could be disguised as sickness benefit to children. In the South, aid was effected by supporting two or three children from large families in the workhouse, and by putting temporarily unemployed fathers in, while relieving the family at home. Mass unemployment, generated by adverse weather was contained by the introduction of wholesale out-door relief by Boards of Guardians in the face of Somerset House injunctions.[60] Resort to parochial charitable subscriptions was another favoured mode.[61] But the most sustained circumvention of the Act derived from the retention of parochial autonomy over the highways; the unemployed were put to work on the roads. 'In fact', said a Kent farmer, 'the highways have become the workhouse'.[62]

The workhouse was not, however, marginalised; it and the Act were used *in terrorem*. Union Boards responded positively to official advice to enhance the workhouse's punitive character,[63] and Guardians conspired with parish officers and employers to discipline the working class; 'labourers of bad character' were 'kept in a workhouse by farmers solely because' they 'will not employ men' with poor reputations or 'who will not do justice to their employers'. Subsequent rehabilitation turned on good behaviour; as one Sessions chairman opined, 'violations of the workhouse rules, were just the most likely means to prevent' the insubordinate 'getting work'. Employment, on the farms or on the roads instead of the workhouse, depended on subservience. As a Bedfordshire farmworker put it, 'the men now had to be more subservient than they used to be, because there were so many out of employment, and the masters knew it'. An employer gave a typical explanation: 'we select the best characters, and do all we can to find them work, and they are grateful for it . . . labourers are thankful to us for giving them employment; before that Act they would use abusive language, and state that they must be kept, whether they work or not, and would not do work in a proper manner'. The depth of popular aversion to even temporary workhouse residence encouraged farmers to maintain their employment policies; only 7 of 400 Hampshire men thrown out of work by heavy snows in the harsh winter of 1836–37, accepted the offer of the house, a reaction paralleled elsewhere.[64] Labourers tried to join the nucleus of permanently employed, and even housing was distributed discriminately, nowhere more fiercely than in 'close' parishes.

In the country villages the cottages are kept for the choicest men; those who are remarkable for strength, skill or character. The reduced cottage-room in the close parishes, with a selection of the tenants, acts as a premium for good character, as the superior men have always the preference of a cottage when one falls vacant. The inferior labourers, whether as regards strength, skill or character, are compelled to reside at a distance . . . and to walk to and from their work daily

when they secured employment. Establishing and maintaining the requisite reputation required herculean self-discipline, especially when farmers cruelly exploited their mastery. It was not uncommon for a labourer to be sacked 'only for saying that he was threshing for 2d a load less than some' workers on adjacent farms. Farmer and overseer Sampson of Blakington employed two family men at 8s. a week in 1844, and then reduced their wages by switching to derisory piece-rates; admitting that average wages were about 12s., Sampson asserted that 'I don't feel obliged to give every man the same', adding venomously, 'I am not bound to employ.' 'Labour is a marketable article', insisted another farmer; asked 'If the labourer had demanded higher wages' since the new law, he replied, 'He would not have had it . . . we could get them at our own price'.[65]

The new law made payments for rent, fuel and pig provender illegal and these losses were but partially compensated for by wider, if localised, allotment provision, which was also distributed discriminately, to divide the agrarian working class further. Divisions which were emergent before 1835 were solidified thereafter and repeatedly evinced often in the form of village 'roughs' and 'respectables'. Asked if the rural proletariat was 'dissatisfied' once the new law became operative, one authority replied, 'Those that are out of employment are.'[66] The sole mitigating economic force in the corn-lands before 1850 stemmed from railway construction. It proved a godsend for the most vulnerable farmworkers, the young and the less subordinate, who flocked to become navvies. Wage rates usually rose in the immediate vicinity of the works, as in Essex where weekly wages rose from 8s. and 10s. to 12s.; but the specialist press remained confident that labour shortages would not materialise.[67] The northern situation was very different, and the major disparities between wages there and in the cornlands become fully apparent in the 1830s.[68] Railway construction proved a boon for craftsmen too, as did the return of agricultural prosperity, though neither must be exaggerated. When artisans lost many days' work owing to bad weather, their fragile finances were revealed by the absence of fuel stocks, and it was said in Bedfordshire in 1838 that 'tradesmen, carpenters, collar-makers and blacksmiths work at harvest; they can earn more money in harvest than they can at their own trade'.[69] Only the most localised labour shortages occurred between 1835 and 1850, as when freak weather conditions saw haymaking and reaping overlap; when different conditions extended the period between these operations in 1843, farmers laid off extra hands, in confidence they could be re-engaged once required. Indeed such was the supply of labour, which 'came from all quarters', that the average harvest period contracted. The incidence of conflict between indigenous labour and migrant Irish harvesters was roughly conditioned by the alternating supply of the latter.[70]

PROLETARIAN RESPONSES, 1780–1830

Historical perceptions of a lack of resistance to, and absence of, protest over farmworkers' grievances appear to originate in the relative acquiescence in enclosure and the broader erosion of customary rights, and in notions of rural isolation. Certainly, enclosure did not galvanise prolonged overt resistance outside a few untypical locations, and if opposition over the customs issue was more prolonged, especially in forest regions, the effects of both were essentially too diffused to generate sustained protest movements.[71] However, common conceptions that rural isolation preserved the agrarian proletariat from newer trade union and democratic political ideologies in the post-1780 period are a serious distortion. There was too much socio-economic intercourse between town and country to prevent the latter's penetration by unionist mentality and populist political perceptions.[72] Vast numbers of countrymen served in the armed forces during the war; the degree of political radicalism, recurrent attempts to improve conditions, and insubordination in the army and navy, is only beginning to come to light.[73] Ideological penetrations of the countryside were reinforced by the multifarious wartime experiences of many thousands on their demobilisation and return after 1815.[74] Occasionally the evidence is superb. For example, Robert Price, a 'stout heavy looking man . . . dressed in the garb of a labourer', had spent fourteen of his forty-eight years in the navy; in January 1831 he received prison sentences totalling five years for leading three distinct Swing mobilisations in Kent, during which his republican politics and his class-consciousness were repeatedly articulated. And Price was neither idiosyncratic nor unique.[75]

Categorisation of farmworker responses reveals a parallel chronology to that relating to conditions. The latter were only remotely favourable for action to improve wages and other prospects during the war. From labour's perspective, the decline in in-service and the marked turnover of yearly servants with fewer staying for more than a year, represent distinct pressure for better terms.[76] Northern indoor servants were probably more successful,[77] but contemporary cornland complaints at rising labour costs may partly reflect the better contracts exacted by those still willing to undertake yearly hirings; such people were also protected from inflated wartime food prices. The expanding majority who were not made a number of sterling collective efforts to increase wages under the stimulus of post-1792 inflation, which were not confined to summertime peaks in labour demand. Sussex labourers went on the offensive in November 1792 and in November 1794; Bedfordshire and Hertfordshire witnessed wages campaigns in March 1793, the year that Isaac Seer achieved his reputation as the 'first known farmworkers' leader' for spreading an Essex strike.[78] Famine conditions in 1795 generated unrest and serious disturbances throughout the country; despite their complexities, clear indications of a rural collective response are represented by strikes at Edenbridge in Kent, and the Spilsby region of Lincolnshire, attempts to organise them in Berkshire and Hertfordshire, and a more ambitious programme in Norfolk to unite labourers into a county-wide organisation under the slogan 'the Labourer is worthy of his hire'.[79] The second famine of 1799–1801 produced a crop of apparently localised wage campaigns, notably in Surrey, Sussex, Hertfordshire, Berkshire and Essex. The fiercest transpired in the latter two counties with attempts to spread strikes outwards from epicentres in two villages, Thatcham and Steeple.[80] These spectacular moves, which do not appear to have recurred in 1810–12, should not obscure the probability that less dramatic thrusts, not threatening the peace, succeeded in gently prising out higher wages. One squire's estate manager received a deputation of labourers in December 1799 complaining 'that their Wages were not sufficient to support their families, as every Necessary of Life was so extravagantly dear'; the claim was met after initial resistance.[81] Many observers reported a new belligerency among farmworkers, an 'unseemliness of manners' in one observer's parlance. An East Anglian clergyman typically claimed in 1805 that before the war 'Our servants or labourers were . . . more content with their wages, less ready to murmur in accidental advances in the price of provisions and more willing to work extraordinary hours as the exigencies of their masters might require, than they are at present'.[82]

There are suggestions that farmworkers were encouraged, and perhaps aided, by militant craftsmen, transport, textile, and paperworkers; in two such locations, Hertfordshire and Norfolk, such encouragement was possibly politically inspired, either to galvanise support for Whitbread's minimum wage proposals, or behind democratic politicisation, and probably both.[83] However the 1790s was hardly the decade for labourers to suddenly perceive that living standards turned exclusively on wages.[84] Recurrent serious food shortages, with prices commonly rocketing by 200 per cent in a matter of months, stimulated orthodox plebeian reactions in the form of the food riot. If the geography of the food riot exhibits a profound urban bias, with intensities concentrated in industrial districts, hardly a market town escaped totally; important communication centres for the wholesale grain trade were repeatedly affected, and if the record is hopelessly defective especially for lesser towns,[85] riots are known to have occurred at Chichester, for example, on 13 April and 10 October 1795, 4 and 7 May 1796. Many agricultural labourers were as exposed to food market forces as urban workers, and both were involved in disturbances. Using the Chichester example again, handbills inviting a maximum turnout for a demonstration circulated in neighbouring villages, and people who responded positively were responsible for informing the crowd of a local farmer who had grain stockpiles in flagrant contravention of the 'moral economy', and then directing protesters to his premises.[86] Cambridge rioters succeeded in winning Corporate bread subsidies, but peace did not return, as the concession was not extended to villagers who had contributed to the popular force, and they rioted again. Minor explosions occurred in smaller exchanges, including Petworth, and even in the villages; itinerant bakers were subjected to *taxation populaire* in Essex, Cambridgeshire and Dorset, and the stoppage of a range of foodstuffs in transit on the roads in the countryside included flour in Hampshire, butter in West Sussex, potatoes in Somerset, and meat in Suffolk.[87] The stoppage of grain shipments in the cornlands achieved such a pitch in the midsummer hypercrisis of 1795, that the regions were effectively blockaded from the rest of the country, whereupon urban Volunteer regiments threatened to march on the villages to release stocks for starving proletarians in populous centres, including Birmingham and Leicester.[88] Nor were village shopkeepers immune from *taxation populaire* as ugly incidents at Brank Broughton, Lincolnshire, and Easebourne, Sussex, reveal.[89]

Some of this recourse to traditional action was juxtaposed with protest over inadequate poor relief. Labourers from several rural parishes who converged on Lewes in 1801 included a Buxted contingent which 'set out with a Determination of Lowering the price of Provisions' in customary style, while others from Chid-dingly, East Hoathly and Framfield intended to lobby Petty Sessions for increased poor relief. The latter party 'had determined unless they lived better "to throw off labour"' too. Other protesters confined themselves solely to relief levels; a 'riotous' assemblage confronted Cocking overseers in December 1794 to demand 'an Increase in their weekly pay over and beyond what the' vestry had stipulated. Seeking magisterial intervention frequently succeeded, as in March 1795 when twenty-five Hurstpierpoint labourers and their wives, with 104 children between them, were ordered weekly wage supplements totalling £4 13s., and £5. 1s. 6d. paid immediately 'for loss of Time' in presenting their case to the Bench.[90]

However, if wartime economic conditions made it the most favourable period for collective action, politically it was the least conducive. Indeed, the need to secure pre-publication clearance for the Rev. Davies's pioneer investigation into farmworkers' conditions with prime minister Pitt in 1795, symbolises the tone of the 1790s, as do the fears of a major East Riding landowner that the work would reinforce the impact of 'Thos Paines Books . . . and make the common Labourers dissatisfied and unhappy': 'to detail' rural wage rates was 'to serve every bad purpose'. The Duke of Portland, Home Secretary during the major periods of food rioting 'displayed . . . a quite new firmness' in orchestrating their suppression, policies uniquely facilitated by the propertied's fears of revolutionary portents in every form of mass mobilisation, and the creation of the Volunteers as a politically motivated counter-revolutionary force whose opportunities to display their mettle were restricted to riot-containment.[91] If these forces were stretched, even with the regulars in support, in places like Sheffield, their counterparts in smaller centres including New Alresford, Banbury and Holt, were not.[92] Volunteers easily suppressed the Berkshire farmworkers' strikes, and the essential weakness of their Essex counterparts was tellingly revealed when the Steeple 'Insurrection' was stopped by the anti-quated *possé comitatus*.[93] The notorious Combination Laws were a further sign of the state's commitment to suppression. For farm-workers increasingly dependent on the poor law, responsibility for subsistence incomes devolved on public agencies. The magistracy accepted this, and seized the chance to hold the balance between agrarian capital and labour; unable and often unwilling to compel employers to pay living wages, they forced vestries to provide subsistence incomes. Criticism of judicial generosity over-ruling cost-conscious parish officers dates from this period.[94] The marked development of arson as a vehicle for rural protest also dates from the 90s; covert terrorist tactics, were a response to the repressive successes of the establishment. Wartime correlations of high prices, inadequate wages, and insufficient relief, were real because agrarian capitalists were identified as the authors of all three. The principal victims of incendiarism were village oligarchs whose parsimonious poor-law administration was commonly the final factor behind arson attacks.[95]

The wartime emergence of the vestry as a theatre for conflict was consolidated by the massive extension of poor-law operations to contain the post-war effects of under- and unemployment. The latter, and the secular decline of prices, principally replaced the issue of food costs, though their significance was reimposed by the 1816–17 peak, and the upward swing at the end of the 1820s. Rural proletarian reactions are coloured by the East Anglian risings of 1816, and the Swing explosion of 1830. In the former, the swamping of the labour market by demobbed servicemen, and the *coup de grâce* delivered to the rural textile industry by the rapid intensification of all the existing factors promoting its decline, explains the focus of immediate post-war protest. Food prices, low wages, inadequate poor relief, and unemployment – which threw the threshing machine issue into sharp relief – comprised the central grievances. The leading role of textile workers suggests that 'the protests of the agricultural labourers acting *alone* in 1816 . . . [were] rather tentative'.[96] The threshing machine retained its significance for the latter, reinforcing the centrality of the employment issue; all factors contributed to galvanise the East Anglian riots of 1822, and the omnipresent Swing movement of 1830.

However, these momentous events must not obscure the day-to-day importance of the employment issue, on which levels of wages *and* public assistance turned, as poor-law administrators confronted the contradictory problems of containing poverty *and* relief costs.

The inevitable conflict was at its fiercest in the most impoverished districts like the Weald, but its intensity there was only an exaggeration of parallels elsewhere, at their most muted in tightly run estate villages. Wealden vestry meetings were beset by recurrent demonstrations, which regularly degenerated into stone-throwing attacks, and also exhibited examples of organisation as at Hellingly where 'in consequence of a preconcerted conspiracy' a possé of claimants, 'some of them armed with cudgels . . . violently and tumultuously rushed into the parish vestry . . . with intention of intimidating the vestry into greater allowances for relief'. Parish officers were repeatedly beaten up; claimants became hopelessly insubordinate, and conflict literally spread up the administrative hierarchy. Petty Sessions were 'tumultuously and alarmingly beset' by protesters 'bursting into the Sessions Room'. On his appearance before the Uckfield Bench, John Hobbs of Buxted struck the accompanying overseer of the poor 'with a . . . Walking Staff with considerable Violence . . . in the presence of Five Justices attending'. Recurrent collapses of public order were aggravated by seemingly endemic crime waves; one authority typically asserted that 'the labouring Class . . . appear to be ready for extreme acts of depredation'.[97]

A premium was placed on increased policing. Special constables, drawn principally from the farmers, with handfuls of permanently employed hands, anxious to safeguard their jobs in an apparently chronic economic crisis, were enrolled, and many vestries further compromised their liquidity with the appointment of paid constables. The besieged Battle Bench ordered the arrest of protesters, but 'a great Number of their Associates being in the Town it was deemed expedient to commit and send' prisoners off to the county jail 'without delay and it was necessary to hire Post Chaises etc and Assistants'. Assaults on the police multiplied by way of response, with scores of vestries depleting their funds by financing the prosecution of offenders, which further reduced vestrymen's socio-political position. A Wadhurst example typifies a common process: 'Labourer & Pauper' (to cite the exact description of witness, victualler Isaac Burt), Samuel Harvey exclaimed, that farmer and overseer '"Baldwin is the Man that sent me to Gaol and I'll do him"'. Baldwin genuinely feared for the 'Safety of himself his Family & Property'. The lead was often taken by youths and young unmarried men, who bore the brunt of unemployment, and were the largest category put to parish work; hooliganism engulfed even 'close' villages in Cambridgeshire: 'the Wimpole boys are growing progressively more wicked & lawless. They go about

. . . in Shoals of 20 or 30 & amuse themselves in Breaking Gates, Fences & Bridges & other Wanton Mischief'.[98]

Parts of East Anglia, notably those which were not seats of the 1816 revolt, rioted against threshing machines in 1822: 'There was no marked distinction between "closed" and "open" villages in the distribution', but incendiarism was the alternative 'in villages where there were no reports of machine-breaking'. If arson peaked in East Anglia and other regions during the depression's nadir in 1822, the numbers of cases reveal that it became a continuous mode of protest. Only its intensity varied.[99]

Cornland urban centres witnessed industrial disputes over wages and the employment of unapprenticed workmen between 1815 and 1830, and some upsurge in trade union activity is detectable here after the 1824 repeal of the Combination Acts.[100] The scale of unemployment, and continued magisterial hostility to any form of rural combination, exemplified by the Bench who stopped relief to youths who struck against work negotiated by their vestry, ensured that farmworkers were prevented from adopting a unionist response. Indeed, the centrality of the poor law was reflected by the fact that more strikes involved labourers working for parishes, than harvesters mobilising to exploit peak demands for labour. Isolated attempts at the latter were also the objects of judicial intervention. These incidents certainly suggest that unionist mentalities were not dead in the countryside, as does the increasingly militant opposition to Irish harvesters between 1828 and 1834.[101]

Unionist mentalities were central to Swing. The demand for work, at improved wages, was repeatedly made, but the insistence on increased parochial allowance did not represent ideological confusion or mitigate the former demands, because it was manifestly obvious that seeking wage rates adequate to the support of men with large families was unrealistic.[102] With Swing we enter changing historical territory because the revolt comprised an integral part of the total crisis which terminated in the demise of the British ancien regime. The recurrent campaigns of agriculturalists for concessions from successive Tory governments between 1815 and 1830 certainly generated exaggerated evidence of the geographical and chronological extents of the depression;[103] they failed and the resultant frustrations were felt by all farmers, whatever their precise economic situation. Failure turned significant sectors of the agricultural interest against the Tories, and Swing rapidly transformed it into hostility against the existing political structure, with positive support for the

Whig's reform proposals accruing from thousands of farmers and their landlords.[104]

Moreover, the radical popular campaign for reform on democratic principles, traditionally associated with metropolitan, urban and industrial centres, was also penetrating the countryside; Swing can camouflage this development. Of the 216 men from three Hampshire villages who had petitioned the king to act against poverty, low wages, high taxes, state pensions, the standing army, tithes, an arbitrary magistracy and the game laws, and advocating radical political reform, 19 were convicted of subsequent Swing offences. This was not an isolated political initiative in places soon to be Swing epicentres. Examples include the creation of a populist society and reading room dominated by the unstamped at High Wycombe, and the agitations for press freedom and the rights of all to full citizenship at Battle, which included praise of proletarians who had engineered the continental revolutions of July 1830.[105] Articulations of radical political sentiments comprised an important element in Swing. They were seriously underestimated by recent experts, and much remains to be discovered, but Mr Charlesworth ascribes much of the diffusion of Swing to the creation of rural political nuclei.[106] Taxation levels, rent and tithe exactions, the fact that the entire rural community was in crisis, strengthened pro-reform political tenets, and galvanised the unity manifested between labourers, craftsmen, the petty rural bourgoisie, and the smaller farmers. The threshing machine issue was a further source of unity. It reduced demand for labour, its cost disadvantaged lesser farmers, and its technology was beyond the capacities of most rural craftsmen. This put these categories of rural society on a rough par with paper-makers and sawyers whose own position was jeopardised by their employers' current heavy investment in new technology, the apparently global potential of which extended fears to almost every skilled trade. Swing's attack on technology extended beyond threshing machines to the premises of the new agricultural engineers, and to saw and paper mills. In many localities the mobilisations of agricultural labourers and rural craftsmen were joined by a miscellany of urban craftsmen, sawyers and paper workers; 'down with all the foundries', said blacksmith and Swing rioter John Aldridge.[107] The political dimension to all this is also revealed by the marked acceleration in rural working-class consciousness achieved by Swing; the 'peculiarity of the present feeling' in the countryside in late 1830 was characterised by plebeian belief 'that the cause of the distress is the unequal division of property'. The rich, on sight, were 'frequently hooted as usurpers of the produce of others labour' and the authors 'of all the suffering the labourer endures'. The Rev. Dr Hele of Brede was forced to admit to the crowd invading his tithe audit day proceedings that he was 'in the possession of a large share of the labour of the industrious classes'.[108]

Swing's revolutionary over- and undertones fundamentally shook the greater agrarian capitalists, and their entrepreneurial counterparts in the agricultural engineering, paper-making, and timber-processing industries. Their increasing identification with the Whig's reform programme was reinforced by the notoriously harsh response of the new Whig government against Swing. The likes of Grey, Brougham and especially Melbourne, calculated on making political capital, cementing support where they had it, and stimulating it where they lacked it most, in rural England. Hence the fiercest repression of all labour, agricultural and craft, for participation in Swing.[109] And hence the severe denunciation of that handful of petty farmers tried for breaking capital's solidarity by supporting Swing.[110] The Whigs, by excluding most of the industrial, and the entire rural proletariat from the post-reform electorate, contrived to strengthen the political significance of the industrial middle class, while maintaining the aristocratic and therefore the agricultural interest's domination of the political system, thus preserving the hegemony of agrarian capital. Ironically, it was a Tory compromise, the Chandos clause, which clinched the latter.

The politicisation of rural labour flourished in the pregnant atmosphere created by the nature and duration of the Reform Bill crisis, and was further enriched by the political lessons emanating from the treatment of Swing, as specifically recognised by authorities in Norfolk and Hampshire.[111] Robert Mason, one of the most politicised Swing leaders, speculated in jail while awaiting transportation in February 1831, that 'there must be a reformed Parliament or a Revolution before next summer is over, and if the former' he advised petitions for the release and return of exiles like himself; if the latter transpired he had no doubt that his Sutton Scotney friends would contribute, but in the event Cobbett chose his village to celebrate the Reform Act publicly.[112] Urban-based Political Unions extended their activities into their rural hinterlands. The Winchester Union's 'delegations . . . obtained a great many members and roused the farm labourers'. Its Chilbolton members typically united political and economic objectives, exposing plebeian living standards through contributions to the *Poor Man's Guardian*. The farmers retaliated with a lock-out, and the Bench compliantly stopped poor relief; the *Guardian* channelled cash collected for their assistance.[113] Maintaining concessions won during Swing necessitated collective action to resist vestries reducing relief, farmers cutting wages, and re-engaging itinerant labour. Kent and Sussex labourers liaised across considerable distances, and shadowy organisations were behind renewed machine-breaking in the former, and successful intimidations of migrant labour in the latter in 1831. 1833 saw sporadic summertime strikes, notably in Norfolk. Supportive arson campaigns affected much of the cornlands.[114] These movements had their successes. 'Intimidation' was said to have stopped wages falling to their pre-1830 levels, and a south-eastern authority said in 1833 that threshing machines were 'generally exploded now; it is considered that where they are kept they may expect a visit'.[115]

The early 1830s saw a massive upward surge in trade unionism climaxed by the foundation of the Grand National Consolidated Trade Union. Many cornland towns had repetitive industrial disputes between 1830 and 1834. Brighton for example, experienced strikes by most building trades, tailors, shoemakers, saddlers and harness-makers. The funeral of a leader presented a vehicle for displays of inter-union solidarity and strength, with a procession of representatives from the trade and political unions. Counter-offensives, principally lock-outs, began to extend to the countryside, as at Uckfield where all master-tradesmen agreed not to employ trade unionists. The GNCTU began to establish branches in some of these towns, and farmworkers were involved as the momentum accelerated, revealed for example by agricultural labourers flocking to Brighton in the spring of 1834 to join the GNCTU and to take its propaganda back to the villages. Challenged by the defence if he knew 'the meaning of the word strike', John Lock who turned King's Evidence against the Tolpuddle men, replied 'it is to stop work'.[116]

This great thrust by the labour movement comprised Tolpuddle's immediate context. The Wareham and Dorchester divisions of Dorset had experienced disturbances during the Reform Bill crisis.[117] One of the Loveless family had been arrested as a Swing rioter, though he escaped,[118] and Dorset also had had its Special Commission. George Loveless first emerged as a spokesman during wage negotiations in 1831–32 'when there was a general movement of the working classes for an increase in wages'.[119] The prosecution of Carlile and Cobbett for publications concerning Swing consolidated urban radicals' interest in agrarian labour; speakers from the countryside were given platforms in London and elsewhere, and the GNCTU on its foundation decided to try 'to get up a Union among the agricultural labourers'.[120] In 1833 Loveless was in touch with men soon to be involved in the GNCTU's formation, through brother John, a Bridport flaxdresser, a unionised trade, and brother Robert, domiciled in London, but about whom nothing is known.[121] Initially, in January 1834, the Dorset Bench reported that 'Societies are forming . . . in parts of' the Dorchester and Wareham divisions, with *known* activities centred on Tolpuddle in the former and Bere Regis in the latter; initiates planned to strike over wages and were 'bound by Oaths administered clandestinely'. James Frampton, the JP who spearheaded the Bench's anti-union onslaught, had cut his teeth against Swing three years earlier. In the 1833–34 winter, Frampton feared a recurrence of Swing, and infiltrated 'trusty persons' into the new organisation. The Home Office's first and low key response supported the deployment of spies, but added that Frampton's proposed recourse to the obsolete 1797 Act against unlawful oaths was 'quite unnecessary'. The 'frequently' used 1817 legislation against corresponding societies was more appropriate.[122] After three more weeks of union organising Frampton placarded the district with judicial warnings on 22 February; it made no difference to the delegates reputedly active in the 'Villages . . . who appear to have districts allotted to them' who 'taught' the labourers 'to consider' magisterial postures 'as a mere invention . . . and not worthy of attention'. Frampton struck with the arrest of the Tolpuddle leadership against whom he had intelligence of illegal oath-administration. Two prisoners cracked immediately and gave sworn evidence which confirmed Frampton's preference for the heavier penalties under the 1797 Act. A sceptical Home Office demanded copies of written evidence, plus additional intelligence, but refused to embroil itself directly with proclamations against the union or rewards for information, as Frampton desired, as this would publicise Dorset events, which to Whitehall eyes were isolated and had 'not yet spread to any other County'.[123]

Frampton was enraged at his apparent inability to intimidate the unionists; on the 25th, the day after the arrests, a meeting convened on 'Bere Heath by the Sound of a Horn', and secrecy retreated with members going 'together in bodies loudly without constraint'. Meanwhile farmworkers had 'become very markedly restless & unsettled', excited at the prospect of striking. At the beginning of March the Home Office, having studied Frampton's sworn evidence, suddenly appreciated that Dorset events were *not* isolated; Dorset information 'afford sufficient proofs that these proceedings . . . are part of a general system, which is now attempted to be established in many parts of the Kingdom, and that they proceed from some general directing authority'.[124]

Secret oaths were one hallmark of several unions powering the GNCTU, which also had an initiation ceremony. That 'directing' body *was* the GNCTU; its rules, thrashed out at the end of February, and published on 1 March, proposed a massive alignment of labour. The Tolpuddle events apparently confirmed secret intelligence simultaneously reaching the government that the GNCTU intended to extend its organisation to the countryside. Melbourne also knew that the Poor Law Amendment Act, then passing through Parliament, was under fierce attack in the radical press. The implementation of the lynch pin of Whig socio-economic policy was seriously, if potentially, jeopardised by the GNCTU's rural initiative. Frampton had fortuitously provided government with the means of a pre-emptive strike against the incorporation of the Act's principal target, the rural proletariat, into a solid phalanx of labour orchestrated by the GNCTU.[125]

Melbourne now accepted prosecutions under the 1797 statute; the trial would produce 'the most authoritative exposition of the law', and stop the GNCTU's penetration of the countryside. But Melbourne refused the official sanction of Frampton's proposed lock-out of obdurate Dorset unionists, and once the storm broke over the sentences the Home Secretary pragmatically stressed that unions were not illegal *per se*, and that industrialists rarely sacked workers for membership alone. Frampton had to rest content with hints of Melbourne's private anti-union sympathies. But if he ever intended to reprieve the Martyrs, Frampton's subsequent intelligence that none of the convicted had either 'acknowledged their error or shown the least sign' of denouncing the union, that local rumour had it that government would commute the sentence to 'only a slight punishment', and *crucially* that 'the Unions were so powerful that the Government would not venture to put the Sentence in force', sealed the Martyrs' fate.[126]

It did not seal the fate of agrarian trade unionism; farmworkers exhibited a marked truculence in many districts over the summer of 1834 as the 'principles of Trades' Unions' were adopted in the countryside, and autumnal wage-cutting produced several strikes.[127] Rural combination was re-invigorated by the implementation of the Poor Law Amendment Act from 1835–36 which unleashed waves of protest throughout the cornlands; riots against workhouses, union officials and Boards of Guardians, arson, animal-maiming, and other forms of 'malicious damage' were all fierce, but a conflagration of Swing's proportions was prevented by piecemeal implementation in the chronological and geographical senses, and by staggered intro-duction of the most radical, rigorous, and penal changes. Admin-istrative untidiness, with major disparities in the experience of neighbouring unions, and even adjacent parishes, at any moment in time, were reinforced by the Poor Law Commission's step-by-step approach. All of this militated against another rural explosion, and mass mobilisations were relatively easily contained by the forces of law and order.[128]

The Act's central principle of forcing labour to depend on employment rather than public aid theoretically created a fertile environment for rural unionism. The challenge was taken up in some regions. In the South-east the United Brothers was formed in conscious anticipation of the Act's implementation. A recruitment drive through public and private meetings and propaganda was launched; aid came from craft unions and political organisations from as far afield as Manchester. The Brothers aimed to consolidate its membership before the summer of 1835, complete negotiations for improved wages and conditions over the summer, expediting them by a threatened withdrawal of key harvest labour. Despite deliberate rumours to the contrary,[129] the Union obeyed the law by the simple expedient of eschewing oaths. The region's farmers imposed a lock-out in the spring and early summer. The essential weaknesses of farmworkers' combinations were quickly exposed. Activists were easily victimised and recruitment collapsed owing to the new premium upon jobs in the threatening atmosphere created by the new Act. Workers who rejected the union enhanced their job pros-pects, while those locked out, or on strike, were easy targets for selective incarceration in the workhouse as union funds were unequal to their support. The union's programme of expansion from its south-eastern bases proved impossible. It contracted and in its death throes weakly resorted to campaigning for old poor law payments for children and house-rent.[130] The Poor Law Commission cleverly exploited the issue in its first annual report, claiming erroneously that 'delegates from some trades' unions in the manufacturing districts' were the United Brothers' architects, and that the local helmsmen were drawn exclusively from the 'ringleaders' of Swing. The further claim, that the anti-new poor law stance of the union saw its rejection by farmworkers 'freed from the parish' by the Act, was ridiculous. The new law's role in defeating the union was of importance in quickly swinging the greater agrarian capitalists solidly behind the Poor Law Amendment Act.[131]

The Act's implementation generated strikes in Hampshire and Wiltshire in the autumn of 1835, but they were easily crushed at this inauspicious season. Parallel action in parts of Norfolk was swamped by violent protest against the Act.[132] Renewed, and more determined efforts with the formation of the Essex 'County Union', which claimed 1100 members in twenty-three parishes in 1836, again exposed weaknesses despite a leadership dominated by craftsmen, shopkeepers, and beer-retailers. The latter's role facilitated the representation of the agitation as a vehicle for depravity and inflated profits in the despised and feared beer-shop trade. Violence over recruitment, and strike-breakers brought from Suffolk for the harvest, enabled prosecutions, with Lord Chief Justice Abinger obligingly lecturing on the 'subversion of all property' by 'foolish' workers whose 'property alone consisted in the labours of their own hands, conspiring to prevent the right use of such property by others'; this was the greatest 'tyranny'. The fears of Essex farmers were revealed when the county Agricultural Society tried to augment the supply of harvest labour with premiums for female reapers under the spurious pretext of 'increasing considerably the earnings of the poor'.[133] Occasionally, and locally, notably in the vicinity of railway construction, the failure of negotiations over harvest contracts permitted collective action. Labourers in parts of Essex adopted militant postures again in 1837, reputedly 'taunting their masters with limited numbers who would stay at home' rather than become navvies. There were strikes by Kentish hop-pickers in 1836 and 1839, but attempts to break formal contracts to exploit local labour shortages frequently exposed workers to prosecution.[134] The United Brothers' last recorded localised strike, at Wilmington in July 1835, collapsed when non-local labour was brought in. This pattern was systematised. The Rev. Huxtable, who farmed at Sutton Waldron, near Shaftesbury, explained that 'At first I did not employ . . . out-parishioners, but I found them necessary for at certain crises, harvest etc, my own parishioners would threaten to strike, and make their own terms, but now this extra-parochial force keeps the other labourers in order'.[135]

Huxtable typified those agriculturalists who extended their corn acreages under the stimulus of post-1837 price rises, reinforced in less favourable arable districts by the Tithe Commutation Act.[136] The labour supply easily accommodated this, and effectively prevented agrarian labour from successful confrontations with agrarian capital. The almost universal struggle to avoid the work-house by the unemployed, especially the perennial victims of discriminatory provision of jobs, poor-law administration, and work on the parish roads, saw a widespread adoption of multifarious expedients. The recurrent cornland crime waves were directly attributable to that struggle, a fact conceded by all sectors of the press, and others including assistant poor-law commissioners and Quarter Sessions chairmen.[137] Thousands tried petty entrepreneurial activities ranging from hawking a multiplicity of goods, to the production of brooms and other implements from whatever materials came to hand – legally or otherwise.[138] Vagrancy increased, not only in the countryside, but also in the towns, seasonally flooded by labourers in search of work. Many settled there; higher rents and longer walks to work, might be compensated by alternative employment, and the greater availability of jobs for wives and children. Urban migrations were accelerated by landowners tackling poverty on their estates by demolishing cottages, which was also responsible for the intensification of the nefarious gang-system, especially in East Anglia, which eventually came to haunt the Victorian conscience.[139]

The Poor Law Amendment Act inspired freeing of the agrarian labour market failed to harmonize supply and demand. Capital retained its supremacy, reflected for example in the stark contrasts drawn by those who took the plunge and emigrated; in Australia, if 'masters say anything' workers 'don't like, they say "pay me my money, you may get somebody else"'. Incendiarism, and to a lesser extent animal-maiming, quickly emerged as rural labour's most effective form of protest. Both achieved a 'fearful . . . preponderance' in Essex in the late 1830s, before the notorious East Anglian arson campaigns of the early 1840s; if the latter's intensity was rarely experienced in other cornland regions, it was equally endemic.[140] Assessing the success of covert protest is problematic, but the evidence suggests ameliorations in the forms of less rigorous poor-law administration, and a reluctance to beat wages down to levels theoretically dictated by free-market forces. This must be contrasted with the ruthless suppression of rural Chartism through blacking men participating in the thrusts of 1838–40, which finally drove plebeian radicalism underground. In Dorset, where Chartism generated an intense, but brief overt response, radicalism was subsequently muted, though a reporter in 1849 was 'astonished to the extent to which . . . socialist doctrines prevailed among the rural poor'.[141]

The final reflection of labour's unequal struggle literally stared observers in the face, 'famine in the countenance' of farmworkers and their families, 'reduced to starvation on the first disaster'. Indebtedness, periodic resort to begging, and savage dietary expediency characterised the experience of life. The Coppard family was reduced to a potato diet and 'even of potatoes they have frequently had but two meals a day . . . often without salt, he not liking to be continually begging it'. 'The children live very much upon potatoes', confirmed a Surrey farmer, and Thomas Gory's 'children would be naked but for gifts'. Nor were journeymen craftsmen immune, notably those with large families who were also hit by the termination of child allowances. Carpenter Towner bought bones which he crushed and 'stewed' for 'Broth', and suet for 'Cakes for the Children which was cheaper than Bread and Cheese and Meat'.[142] Among agricultural labourers, the main exceptions to this picture of 'rags and potatoes', were the permanently employed elite, and those domiciled in districts where alternative employment had a positive effect.[143]

Improved conditions on a broader scale are detectable in the 1850s once rural depopulation began to drain the massive pools of labour. Greater militancy accompanied the 1860s. Earlier experiences produced contradictions. Rural trade unionism had exposed debilitating weaknesses, but it fuelled the growth of unionist mentalities, established the farmworkers as legitimate objects of aid from industrial unions, and advanced politicisation. Somnolent radicalism reinforced unionist mentalities, and with the experiences of dire poverty, created an ideological base ready for activisation once economic change engineered a more favourable environment. Experience also taught that capital was the enemy, and that improved living standards would have to be fought over every inch of the way. In 1868, Canon Girdlestone, that indefatigable campaigner for farmworkers, told the British Association meeting at Norwich, that 'Nothing short of combination would effect any improvement in the deplorable condition of the peasantry.'[144] The achievements of the 1870s owed much to the experiences of agrarian labour during the formative years, not least the acceptance of aid from industrial unions.

NOTES AND REFERENCES

1. **D. Davis**, *The Case of the Labourers in Husbandry* 1795, esp. pp. 8–13, 19, 28–36. Rev. Howlett to Moore, 1 December 1792, B(ritish) L(ibrary). Add(itional) MSS. 16920, ff. 17–20, Sir C. Willoughby,

Oxfordshire, to H. Dundas, 19 November 1794, Scottish Record Office, Melville Mss. GD.51/1/372. **F. M. Eden**, *The State of the Poor*, 3 vols 1797, *passim*.

2. **G. Lawson**, Westmorland, 21 January 1803, in *Annals of Agric.*, **40** (1803), pp. 53–63. Cf. **J. V. Beckett**, 'The decline of the small landowner in eighteenth and nineteenth-century England: some regional considerations', *Agric. Hist. Rev.*, **30** (1982).

3. **M. Reed**, 'The peasantry in nineteenth-century England; a neglected class', *History Workshop Jn.*, **18** (1984). **F. Beavington**, 'The development of market gardening in Bedfordshire 1799–1939' *Agric. Hist. Rev.*, **23** (1975); **B. Short**, '"The art and craft of chicken cramming"; poultry in the Weald of Sussex 1850–1950' ibid., **30** (1982); **J. M. Martin**, 'The social and economic origins of the Vale of Evesham market gardening industry', ibid., **33** (1985).

4. **N. R. Wilkes**, 'Adjustments to arable farming after the Napoleonic Wars', *Agric. Hist. Rev.*, **28** (1980). **M. J. R. Healey** and **E. L. Jones**, 'Wheat yields in England, 1815–1859', *Jn. of the Royal Statistical Society*, series A, CXXV, (1962).

5. **M. E. Turner**, *English Parliamentary Enclosure*, (1983) is the most recent authoritative statement on the subject. A different approach, by **J. M. Martin**, 'Village traders and the emergence of a proletariat in south Warwickshire, 1750–1851', *Agric. Hist. Rev.*, **32** (1984) reveals a *process* which must have been *form ative elsewhere*, if less intensely than in the Fielden district, which is not representative of the cornlands.

6. **D. R. Mills**, 'The quality of life in Melbourne Cambridgeshire in the period 1800–1850', *Inter. Rev. of Soc. Hist.*, **23** (1978), p. 398. Cf. **J. A. Yelling**, *Common Field and Enclosure in England 1450–1850* (1977), pp. 226–8, and **W. A. Armstrong**, 'The influence of demographic factors on the position of the agricultural labourer in England and Wales *c.* 1750–1914', *Agric. Hist. Rev.*, **29** (1981), esp. pp. 79–80.

7. **K. D. M. Snell**, 'Agricultural seasonal unemployment, the standard of living, and women's work in the South and East: 1690–1860', *Econ. Hist. Rev.*, 2 ser. xxxiv (1981). **Snell**, *Annals of The Labouring Poor: Social change and agrarian England 1660–1900*, Cambridge 1985, Ch. 2.

8. **E. Turner**, 'Ancient parochial account book of Cowden', *Sussex Archaeological Collections*, xx, (1868), pp. 96–7. **P. Amsinck**, *Tunbridge Wells and Its Neighbourhood*, 1810, p. 42. B(ritish) P(arliamentary) P(apers), 'Poor Law Report', (1834), Appendix A, pp. 19–20.

9. *Annals of Agric.*, **20** (1793), pp. 410–12; **21** (1793), pp. 379–81. **N. Evans**, *The East Anglian Linen Industry. Rural industry and local economy 1500–1850*, Aldershot 1985, Chs 5 and 6.

10. **P. Horn**, 'Child workers in the pillow lace and straw plait trades of Victorian Buckinghamshire and Bedfordshire', *Historical Jn.*, **17** (1974). **G. F. R. Spenceley**, 'The origins of the English pillow lace industry', *Agric. Hist. Rev.*, **21** (1973). **D. C. Coleman**, *The British Paper Industry 1495–1860*, Oxford U.P. 1958, pp. 147, 151, 195, 224–6. **R. Samuel**, 'Mineral workers', in **Samuel** (ed.), *Miners, Quarrymen and Saltworkers*, 1977, pp. 4–5, 25–6, 31–2.

11. **D. Vaisey** (ed.), *The Diary of Thomas Turner 1754–1765*, Oxford U.P. 1984, pp. 67–8, 238–9. **G. A. Body**, 'The Administration of the Poor

Laws in Dorset 1760–1834 with Special Reference to Agrarian Distress', Ph.D. thesis, University of Southampton 1966, pp. 90, 205. **M. Neuman**, 'A suggestion regarding the origin of the Speenhamland plan', *English Hist. Rev.*, **84**, 1969, pp. 317–22. **E. M. Hampson**, *The Treatment of Poverty in Cambridgeshire, 1597–1834*, Cambridge 1934, pp. 189–90.

12. **G. W. Oxley**, *Poor Relief in England and Wales, 1601–1834*, 1974, pp. 110–11. Willoughby to Dundas, *loc. cit.*

13. Balcombe vestry minutes, W(est) S(ussex) C(ounty) R(ecord) O(ffice), Par. 21/12/3, f. 36. **D. H. Morgan**, *Harvesters and Harvesting 1840–1900*, 1982, pp. 88–9. Snell, *Annals of the Labouring Poor*; Ch. 2.

14. **A. C. Wood** (ed.), 'G. M. Woodward: Nottinghamshire (1797–8)', *Transactions of the Thoroton Society*, LXI, (1957), p. 48. *BPP*, H(ouse) of C(ommons) S(elect) C(ommittee), 'Emigration from the United Kingdom', 1826, vol. IV, Q(uestion)s, 1401, 1960. *Brighton Gazette*, 5 Dec. 1833.

15. **R. Claridge**, *A General View of the Agriculture of . . . Dorset*, 1793, pp. 24–5. **D. Walker**, *A General View of the Agriculture of the County of Hertford*, 1795, pp. 24–5. *Reading Mercury*, 21 Dec. 1795.

16. **R. A. E. Wells**, 'The Grain Crises in England, 1794–96, 1799–1801', D.Phil. thesis, University of York, 1978, pp. 52–3.

17. **M. E. Turner**, *English Parliamentary Enclosure*, Ch. 5. A. H. John, 'Farming in Wartime 1793–1815', in **E. L. Jones** and **G. E. Mingay** (eds), *Land Labour and Population in the Industrial Revolution*, Edward Arnold 1967, pp. 30–2, 37–47.

18. Collins lists a number of claims by contemporaries and historians. **E. J. T. Collins**, 'Harvest Technology and the Labour Supply in Britain 1790–1870', Ph.D. thesis, University of Nottingham, 1970, esp. pp. 150–3, and notes 1 and 8 pp. 162–3. **E. L. Jones**, 'The agricultural labour market in England 1793–1872', *Econ. Hist. Rev.*, 2nd ser., XVII, 1964, pp. 323–5.

19. Newbold corn committee administration book, 1795, 1800, Nottinghamshire CRO, DD. CW. 8fl. Battie-Wrightson, Cusworth wage book, 1780–1813, A/200; Harewood deposit, box 223, Leeds City Archives. *Annals of Agric.*, **15** (1791), pp. 490–2, **20** (1793), pp. 184–5; **24** (1795), p. 241. **T. Brown**, *A General View of the Agriculture of the County of Nottingham*, (1794 edn), p. 47; (1798 edn), p. 133. **A. W. Dyson** (ed.), *William Metcalfe – His Book*, Leeds 1931, p. 40.

20. *Annals of Agric.*, **19** (1793), pp. 188–9; **24** (1795), pp. 121, 133. **I. Leatham**, *A General View of the Agriculture of the East Riding of Yorkshire*, 1794, p. 31. Boston petition, 10 August 1795, P(ublic) R(ecord) O(ffice), W(ar) O(ffice) 1/1086, ff. 549–52. *Boston Gazette*, 11 September 1811. **R. Wells**, *Insurrection: the British Experience, 1795–1803*, Gloucester 1983, esp. p. 166.

21. Complaints about labour shortages require careful evaluation. John Boys, who claimed that labour 'always was scarce' in Kent, juxtaposed 'labourers in husbandry and journeymen mechanics'. The different wartime situation respecting rural craftsmen is examined below. *Annals of Agric.*, **20** (1793), p. 183. *Sussex Weekly Advertiser*, 7 July 1794 and 17 September 1810.

22. *Annals of Agric.*, **20**, (1793), pp. 385–9. Battie-Wrightson wage book, *loc. cit.*

23. Reflected for example in the rising harvest earnings of families who competed for Sussex prizes for those who earned the most: £8 1s., 1807; £9 10s., 1808; £13 12s., 1809; £10 3s., 1810; £13 7s., 1811; £18 11s., 1812; £16 1s., 1813; £10 9s., 1814; £6 7s., 1815: *Sussex Weekly Advertiser*, 9 Nov. 1807, 21 Nov. 1808, 30 Oct. 1809, 5 Nov. 1810, 28 Oct. 1811, 16 Nov. 1812, 7 Nov. 1813, 30 Oct. 1814, 30 Oct. 1815.

24. *Annals of Agric.*, **24** (1795), p. 63; **25** (1796), p. 631; **26** (1796), p. 136; BPP, HCSC 'Settlement and Removal' (1847), vol. xi, Q. 7351.

25. *Annals of Agric.*, **24** (1795), pp. 159–61, 284; **25** (1796), pp. 630–1. Rev. Forth to Lord Carlisle, 17 November 1800, York City Archives, Mumby deposit, Acc. 54/112. **M. Reed**, 'Indoor farm service in nineteenth-century Sussex; some critiques of a critique', *Sussex Archaeological Collections* 1986. My thanks to Mr Reed of the University of Sussex for permitting me to consult this paper before publication.

26. Witnesses against Judge for forging an employment certificate, E(ast) SCRO, QR/E770.

27. 'The farmer sat at the head of his thick oak-table, his men arranged on each side of him, and were served with huge slices of fat pork and solid pudding. By seven o'clock every soul was in bed, locked up under the eye of the master . . . and out in the morning by three to feed the horses and go to plough . . . There is no education like that of keeping young country "chaps" . . . constantly under the eye of a master, who is deeply interested in their welfare, their character, and their pursuits'. *Brighton Gazette*, 5 Nov. 1833. *BPP*, HCSC 'Poor Law Amendment Act' (1837), vol. xvii, Qs. 3003–6. Snell, *Annals . . .*, Ch. 2. esp. pp. 84–93.

28. Reed, 'Indoor farm service'.

29. A Sussex squire penned a more balanced appraisal: 'the feeling of both master and servant during . . . the war led to the same result; the high wages and great demand for labour (as they appeared comparatively and retrospectively) . . . made the good workmen desirous of independent labor and the farmer was . . . improving his circumstances he found his farming servants residence in the house interfere materially with the comforts of his family'. Others stressed the additional strains of wartime taxation, including taxes on malt and 'indoor servants' which allegedly created ambiguities despite the exclusion of agricultural labourers. *BPP.*, HCSC 'Poor Law Amendment Act', (1837), vol. xvii, Qs. 3008, 14905; *BPP*, HCSC 'Emigration', (1826–7), vol. v. Q.1208. Draft reply to Poor Law Commissioners by G. Courthope, 1832, ESCRO SAS. Co/C/230.

30. Cottages containing one family in the 1780s commonly housed five by the 1820s. Mary Mason, who lived with her mother in a Kent cottage split into four tenements, 'slept in the same Room . . . on chairs close to the Window which has no Shutters to it'. *BPP* HCSC 'Emigration', (1826–7), vol.v, Qs. 608–9. Prosecution brief, November 1830, PRO T(reasury) S(olicitor). 11/943/3413. *Sussex Weekly Advertiser*, 18 Aug. and 16 Oct. 1809. *Annals of Agric.*, **40** (1803), p. 284. *BPP*, HCSC 'Emigration from the United Kingdom' (1826), vol. iv, evidence of

C. J. Curteis. *BPP* HCSC 'Emigration' (1826–7), vol. v, Qs. 1572–3. *BPP* HCSC 'Agriculture' (1833), vol. v, Qs. 9896–7, 9908. *BPP*, 'Report of the Special Assistant Poor Law Commissioners on Employment of Women and Children in Agriculture' (1843), pp. 148–9.

31. *Annals of Agric.*, **43** (1805), p. 38. **A. Young**, *An Enquiry into the Progressive Value of Money in England*, 1812, pp. 90–1. **Young**, *An Enquiry into the Rise of Prices in Europe*, 1815, pp. 175, 210. **T. R. Malthus**, *A Letter to Samuel Whitbread MP*, 1807, reprinted in D. V. Glass (ed.), *Introduction to Malthus*, Watts 1953, p. 201.

32. Falling living standards evoked repeated concern. In April 1793 the Rev. Valney of Berkshire acknowledged 'the loud complaints which have been frequent among the inferior ranks of people', and drew a common but key contrast; agricultural 'labourers have generally been patient, and endured the hardships with the dearness of provisions, with less dissatisfaction than the manufacturers'. *Annals of Agric.*, **20** (1793), pp. 179–82. Cf. *Reading Mercury*, 24 Dec. 1792 and *Sussex Weekly Advertiser*, 19 May 1794.

33. The Bench's sliding scale represented the 'calculations and allowances for the relief of all poor *and* industrious Men and their Families'; the justices' prescribed income levels applied to both families supported wholly by the parish *and* those supported by employed men. The clumsily demarcated directive would, as correctly stated by the county press, permit 'labourers in husbandry to *increase their pay* so as to enable them to *provide sufficiently for themselves and families*, in proportion to the present unavoidable high price of bread and other provisions' (my italics). B(erkshire) CRO Q/SO8, pp. 4–5. *Reading Mercury*, 11 May 1795. No historian, including the Berkshire poor-law specialist **M. Neuman**, 'Speenhamland in Berkshire', in **E. W. Martin**, (ed.), *Comparative Development in Social Welfare*, (1972), appears to have recognised the Bench's real policy. For a more detailed reinterpretation see R. Wells, *Wretched Faces. Famine in Wartime England, 1793–1801*, Gloucester, Alan Sutten, 1988, pp. 291–4.

34. *Annals of Agric.*, **24** (1795), pp. 53–7, 154–7, 169; **25** (1796) p. 178. For an analysis based principally on parochial poor-law records for the East Riding, Lincolnshire, Norfolk, Suffolk, Essex, Berkshire, Oxfordshire and Sussex, with further material from counties outside the cornlands, see Wells, thesis, Ch. 21 parts i and ii.

35. This superseded a May directive to regulate wages by wheat prices, and was reiterated, after further investigation, in December 1795. *Reading Mercury*, 11 May, 27 July, 2 and 16 Nov. and 21 Dec. 1795.

36. Thus on 14 January 1800 the Berkshire Bench 'recommended to Overseers and to all Persons giving Assistance to the Poor during the present Scarcity, to give such Assistance in other Articles of Food as Potatoes Pease Soup Meat Herrings, Rice etc rather than Bread, or an Increase of Pay'. BCRO Q/SO8, pp. 411–13. **M. Neuman**, *The Speenhamland County: poverty and the poor law in Berkshire, 1782–1834*, 1982, totally misses the implication for the survival of Speenhamland scales in the county of their birth. On poor relief during the 1799–1801 crisis, see Wells, *Wretched Faces*, pp. 298–302.

37. The Norfolk format was repeated annually, and adopted elsewhere, for

example by the Bramber Agricultural Society on its formation in 1809. *Norfolk Chronicle*, 17 Sept. and 27 Dec. 1800. *Sussex Weekly Advertiser*, 16 Dec. 1805, 2 Mar. 1807, and 6 Nov. 1809.

38. Collins, 'Harvest Technology' thesis., note 8, p. 163, lists these, and John, 'Farming in Wartime', p. 33 relies almost exclusively on the *Farmer's Magazine*.

39. G. Spater, *William Cobbett: the Poor Man's Friend*, 2 vols Cambridge 1982, II, p. 409, citing *Political Register*, issues 38 and 44 for 1815. *Sussex Weekly Advertiser*, 6 and 13 Apr. 1807, and 19 Apr. 1813.

40. **J. Tuke**, *A General View of the Agriculture of the North Riding of Yorkshire*, 1794, p. 73, but cf. Leatham, *Agriculture of the East Riding.*, pp. 30–1, *BPP*, HCSC 'Poor Law Amendment Act', (1837), vol. XVII, Qs. 8239–41. **S. MacDonald**, 'The progress of the early threshing machine', *Agric. Hist. Rev.*, **23** (1975), esp. pp. 71, 76; **N. E. Fox**, 'The spread of the threshing machine in Central Southern England'; **MacDonald**, 'Further progress with the early threshing machine; a rejoinder', ibid., **26** (1978). MacDonald and Fox flatly contradict John's belief, ('Farming in Wartime', p. 35) in widespread cornland adoption before 1815.

41. And occasionally for smaller labour intensive projects in the countryside, like those for underwood cutters in 1807, and for ten to twenty labourers for a new Kent turnpike in 1810. **A. F. J. Brown**, *Essex at Work*, Chelmsford 1969, p. 130. *Annals of Agric.*, **24** (1795), p. 167. **L. D. Schwarz**, 'Conditions of Life and Labour in London *c.* 1770–1820, with Special Reference to East London', unpublished D.Phil. thesis, University of Oxford, 1976, esp. pp. 91–2, 99–104. *Sussex Weekly Advertiser*, 9 July and 22 Oct. 1804, 30 Nov. 1807 and 16 Apr. 1810.

42. He also implied that the ablest men could pick and choose masters. *BPP*, HCSC 'Agriculture', (1833), vol. V, Qs. 7436, 7444, 7449.

43. The increasing significance of farmers as consumers of manufactured goods before 1780 has been emphasised by **D. E. C. Eversley**, 'The home market and economic growth in England 1750–80', in Jones and Mingay, *op cit*. Their importance can only have increased, and another symptom was the burgeoning service sector in many cornland market towns, identified by **A. Everitt**, 'Country, county and town; patterns of regional evolution in England', *Transactions of the Royal Historical Society*, 5th ser. **29** (1979).

44. *Sussex Weekly Advertiser*, 2 Apr. 1792, 14 Apr. 1794, 19 and 26 Sept. 1796 and 24 Aug. 1801. *BPP*, HC 'Emigration from the United Kingdom' (1826), vol. IV, p. 137.

45. *Annals of Agric.*, **16** (1791), pp. 316–17. *Reading Mercury*, 19 Nov. 1792. *Sussex Weekly Advertiser*, 3 Sept. 1792, 9 and 16 Dec., 1793, 8 Feb., 7 Mar. and 25 Apr. 1796, 13 Feb. 1804, 10 June 1805, 11 July and 1 Aug. 1808, 3 June, 15 and 22 July 1811. Brown, *A General View.*, pp. 116, 130. **H. Perkin**, *The Origins of Modern English Society 1780–1880*, 1969, p. 189. **Williams, James, and Malcolm**, *A General View of the Agriculture of the County of Buckingham*, 1794, pp. 176–7. **D. C. Coleman**, 'Combinations of capital and labour in the English paper industry 1789–1825', *Economica*, **21** (1964), pp. 46–52. **A.**

Aspinall (ed.), *The Early English Trade Unions*, 1949, pp. 36–7, 181–2. **J. Rule**, *The Experience of Labour in Eighteenth-Century Industry*, 1981, pp. 182–3. **E. Melling** (ed.), *Kentish Sources: Crime and Punishment*, Maidstone 1969, p. 152, **W. le Hardy** (ed), *Calendar to the Hertfordshire Sessions Books* (1752–99), Hertford 1935, pp. 477, 514–18. H(ampshire) CRO Quarter Sessions Roll, Michaelmas 1800.

46. That is outside its Norwich epicentre, where labour and capital were in perennial struggles across this period. **A. F. J. Brown** (ed.), *Essex People 1750–1900*, Chelmsford 1972, p. 110.

47. *Annals of Agric.*, **42** (1804), p. 174. **W. Malcolm** and **W. James**, *A General View of the Agriculture of . . . Surrey*, 1794, p. 54.

48. Imprecise documentation obscures the extent of this relief. However, Worlingworth (Suffolk) vestry specified that 'the Tradesmen' were to be assisted, and half the claimants at Plympton, Devon, were craftsmen; many small-masters were unable to pay rate demands during the crises. Ipswich and East Suffolk R.O., FC. 94/1/2. Plymouth City Archives, PSM/4. Wells, thesis, pp. 125–6.

49. Ernle's 'most purple passages' cited by **E. L. Jones**, *The Development of English Agriculture 1815–73*, 1968, pp. 10–17. Cf. the important revision in **A. R. Wilkes**, 'Adjustments to arable farming after the Napoleonic Wars', *Agric. Hist. Rev.*, **28** (1980), pp. 93–100.

50. The real crisis here was essentially limited to 1820–23. **R. A. C. Parker**, *Coke of Norfolk: a Financial and Agricultural Study 1707–1842*, Oxford 1975, Ch. 10, esp. pp. 147–52, and cf. pp. 188–98.

51. Ibid. Wilkes, Adjustments to arable farming', esp. pp. 93–5, 97–100, curiously ignores the Weald, perhaps the only region to sustain Ernle's simplistic, over-pessimistic picture. *Sussex Weekly Advertiser*, 20 Oct. 1815, 7 Oct. and 23 Dec. 1816, 30 Apr. and 4 June 1821, 21 Jan., 4 Feb. and 13 May 1822, and 16 June 1823. Estate-manager Bishop, Northiam, to Mrs Frewen Turner, 21 January 1830, ESCRO. Frewen MSS., 7859. *BPP*, HCSC 'Emigration' (1826–7), vol. v, p. 114. *BPP*, HCSC. 'Agriculture' (1833), vol. v, Qs. 7234–74, 12682–4, 12686, 12700–12, 12805, 12847.

52. The fastest annual population increases ever recorded in English history belong to 1811–31. **N. Tranter**, *Population Since the Industrial Revolution*, 1973, pp. 41–2. MacDonald, 'Rejoinder . . .', p. 29. Fox, *op. cit.*, pp. 26–8. Draft reply to the Poor Law Commission by G. Courthope, JP of Ticehurst, Nov. 1832, ESCRO. SAS Co/C/230. **B. Short**, 'The decline of living-in servants in the transition to capitalist farming; a critique of the Sussex evidence', *Sussex Archaeological Collections*, **122** (1984), p. 163.

53. Letters to Melbourne from W. Maxfield, Middlesex, 25 June 1831, Rev. Dr Moore, Spalding, 6 and 9 August, and G. Brownlow, Lincolnshire, 9 August 1832, PRO, H(ome) O(ffice), 52/14, ff. 297–302; 52/18, ff. 402–9. *Sussex Advertiser*, 24 July 1826, 19 July 1826, 19 July 1827, 8 Sept. 1828, 9, 16 and 23 Aug. 1830, and 6 July 1835. *Maidstone Gazette*, 1 Mar. 1831. *Brighton Gazette*, 23 Aug. 1832. *Poor Law Report*, (1834), Appendix B. p. 266.

54. The Poor Law Commission's notorious perversion of its own evidence, compounded by its ideological position, emphasised the cost-

containing successes only of famous poor-law reformers like Nottinghamshire's Rev. Becher, principally to demonstrate, by example, that poor-law management on utilitarian principles was possible without the widely feared social explosion. The 1834 Report deliberately exaggerated the impression of isolated, practising reformers like Becher, and this aspect of the report is reflected in the historiography, partly through older histories' uncritical use of the Report, and further, no doubt unintentionally, by subsequent studies of Becher. For an alternative view of cost containment under the old poor law see **R. A. E. Wells**, 'The development of the English rural proletariat and social protest 1700–1850', and **Wells**, 'Social conflict and protest in the English countryside in the early nineteenth century; a rejoinder', *Jn. of Peasant Studies*, **6** (1979), and **8** (1981), but cf. **D. A. Baugh**, 'The cost of poor relief in South-east England 1795–1834', *Econ. Hist. Rev.*, 2 ser. xxviii, (1975), pp. 62–8. For the settlement ingredient see Courthope's return, *loc. cit.*

55. *BPP*, HCSC. 'Agriculture', (1833), vol. v, Qs. 9919–21, 10094. *BPP* HCSC. 'Agricultural Distress', (1836), vol. viii, Qs. 903–6, 914, 3084.

56. **R. Wells**, 'Rural rebels in Southern England in the 1830s', in **C. Emsley** and **J. Walvin** (eds), *Artisans, Peasants and Proletarians, 1760–1860*, 1985, pp. 129–30. Fox, *loc. cit.*

57. Some tradesmen retaliated with overt support for anti-corn law campaigns. *Sussex Advertiser*, 26 Mar. 1826. Burwash vestry minute, 5 March 1831, ESCRO. Par. 284/12/1. Cf. account of a clamp-down on semi- and skilled poor relief claimants in the Chichester area in 1832, *BPP*, HCSC. 'Poor Law Amendment Act', (1837), vol. xvii, Qs. 14963–15057.

58. Hawley to Lefevre, 18 January 1838; Tufnell to the Poor Law Commission, 1 May 1839, PRO, M(inistry of) H(ealth), 32/39, 70. *Brighton Patriot*, 27 Feb. 1838.

59. **A. Digby**, 'The labour market and the continuity of social policy after 1834: the case of the Eastern counties', *Econ. Hist. Rev.*, 2 ser. xxviii, (1975), esp. pp. 73–80. *BPP*, 'First Annual Report of the Poor Law Commission' (August 1835), vol. xxv (1835), pp. 5–6. *BPP*, HCSC, 'Settlement and Poor Removal' (1847), vol. xi, Q. 3468. Hawley quarterly report 1 January, and to Lefevre, 18 January, 1838; Tufnell to the Poor Law Commission, 1 May 1839, PRO, MH. 32/38–9, 70. Newhaven Union to Hawley, 2 November 1835, ESCRO, G7/8/1. *Brighton Patriot*, 27 Dec. 1836. *BPP*, HCSC, 'Poor Law Amendment Act', (1837), vol. v, p. 25.

60. Uckfield Board of Guardians, minutes 14 and 28 April, 7 July and 1 December 1838, and 25 April 1840, ESCRO, Gll/la/1–2. Hawley to Nicholls, 10 September 1835, quarterly reports, 1 January and 31 March, and to Lefevre, 18 January 1838, PRO, MH. 32/38–9. *Kent Herald*, 13 Dec. 1838.

61. *Sussex Advertiser*, 28 Jan. 1839. Salehurst voluntary rate, 1 November 1837, ESCRO, Par. 497/30/5/1.

62. Hawley to the Poor Law Commission, 18 November 1836 and 5 May 1838, and to Lefevre, 18 January 1838, PRO, MH. 32/38–9. **J. V. Mosely**, 'Poor Law Administration in England and Wales 1834–50

with Special Reference to Able-bodied Pauperism' (Ph.D. thesis, University of London, 1975), *passim*. **R. Wells**, 'Resistance to the New Poor Law in Southern England', in **M. Chase** (ed.), *The Victorian Poor Law*, Leeds U.P. 1985.

63. Hawley typically persuaded one Hampshire Union that their proposed sack-manufacture was not 'sufficiently undesirable' for inmates; oakum-picking was. Hawley to the Poor Law Commission, 17 May 1837, PRO, MH. 32/39.

64. *BPP*, HCSC, 'Settlement and Poor Removal' (1847), vol. xi, Q. 3161. *Brighton Gazette*, 23 Feb. 1843. *BPP*., HL(ords)SC, 'State of Agriculture' (1837), vol. v. Qs. 1478, 1480. Cf. *BPP*, HCSC, 'Poor Law Amendment Act' (1837), vol. xvii, Q. 8903. Hawley to the Poor Law Commission, 18 Jan. 1837 PRO, MH. 32/39.

65. *Brighton Gazette*, 8 June 1843 and 6 June 1844. *BPP*, 'Reports of the Poor Law Board on the Laws of Settlement and Removal of the Poor' (1850), vol. xxvii, p. 95. *BPP*, HCSC, 'Poor Law Amendment Act' (1837), vol. xvii, Qs. 614–9, 8903.

66. Wells, 'Rural rebels . . .', pp. 149–50. **A. Howkins**, *Poor Labouring Men: rural radicalism in Norfolk 1870–1923*, Routledge and Kegan Paul 1985, pp. 30–4. For pre-1834 divisions, see Wells, '. . . rejoinder', pp. 525–6.

67. *Farmer's Magazine*, vi, **5** (May 1837), p. 389. Hawley to the Poor Law Commission, 31 October 1837, PRO, MH. 32/38. *Sussex Advertiser* 29 Apr., 17 June, 8 July and 26 Aug. 1839, and 30 Mar. 1840. *Brighton Gazette*, 17 Mar. 1842, 21 Mar. 1844, 10 Apr. and 8 May 1845.

68. *Farmer's Magazine*, vi, **5** (May 1837), p. 390; vii, **3** (Sept. 1837), p. 225; **4** (Oct. 1837), p. 407. **R. P. Hastings**, 'Essays in North Riding History 1780–1850', *North Yorkshire CRO Publications*, **28**, (1981), pp. 62–8.

69. *Sussex Advertiser*, 6 Apr., 25 May and 28 Dec. 1840. *Brighton Patriot*, 9 Oct. 1838. *Brighton Gazette*, 13 Mar. 1845. Tufnell to the Poor Law Commission, 21 January 1837, PRO, MH. 32/69. *BPP*, HCSC, 'Poor Law Amendment Act', Q. 14169.

70. Localised shortages occasionally derived from abnormally low numbers of migrant Irish harvesters. *Farmer's Magazine*, vii, **3**, (Sept. 1837), p. 224, *Brighton Patriot*, 5 July 1836. *Sussex Advertiser*, 12 Aug. 1839 and 25 May 1840. *Brighton Gazette*, 6 July and 19 Oct. 1843. *Kent Herald*, 5 Sept. 1839. *BPP*, HCSC, 'Agricultural Distress' (1836), vol. v, Q. 4555. *BPP*, HCSC, 'Poor Law Amendment Act' (1837), vol. xvii, Qs. 13027–35. **R. Schofield** and **C. Barham**, 'Extracts from the parish registers from Barming Kent (1788–1812)', *Local Population Studies*, **33** (1984), p. 147

71. **R. Bushaway**, *By Rite*, Junction Books 1982.

72. This topic is briefly explored in Wells, 'Rural rebels . . .', pp. 126–8. It demands systematic exploration.

73. Again, systematic investigation is required. Wells, *Insurrection . . .*, esp. Ch. 5. **R. Wells**, 'The militia mutinies of 1795', in **J. G. Rule** (ed.), *Outside the Law*, University of Exeter 1982, and **Wells**, '"King-killing": assassination attempts on George III; politics or madness?' (forthcoming).

74. Cf. Snell, *Annals of the Labouring Poor*, p. 342, though this is one of his few unsubstantiated claims.
75. *Maidstone Gazette*, 4 Jan. 1831. **E. Melling** (ed.), *Kentish Sources: the poor*, (Kent County Council 1964), pp. 186–9. **E. J. Hobsbawm** and **G. Rudé**, *Captain Swing*, Penguin (1973 edn), esp. p. 76.
76. Reed, 'Indoor farm service'. **A. Kausmaul**, *Servants in Husbandry in Early Modern England*, Cambridge U.P. 1981, pp. 113, 131. A. F. J. Brown, *Essex at Work 1700–1815*, Chelmsford 1969, p 131.
77. In February 1793, before the annual March hiring day, several hundred 'Hinds or Bond Men' held various meetings in Northumberland, and drafted written details of a complex wage claim, worth an estimated, 25 per cent; one copy was endorsed, 'You must send this Paper About to your Brother Hinds and let it go from place to place A true copy.' Col. J. Reed, Alnwick, to Dundas, with enclosures, 8 February 1793, PRO, HO. 42/24.
78. *Sussex Weekly Advertiser*, 26 Nov. and 3 Dec. 1792, and 24 Nov. 1794. West Sussex Quarter Sessions Minute, Epiphany 1795, ESCRO, QO/EW31, and roll, WSCRO, QR/608, f. 58. Sir P. Mantoux, to Dundas, 21, 26 and 27 March 1793, PRO, HO. 42/25. Brown, *Essex at Work*, pp. 131–2.
79. PRO, Assi (zes), 35/235. *Reading Mercury*, 30 Mar. 1795. Sir A. Hume, and W. Baker, to Portland, both 6 July 1795, PRO, HO. 42/35; Nottingham University Library, Portland deposit, PwF. 233. *Norfolk Chronicle*, 14 Nov. 1795. E. Walls, Spilsby, to Sir J. Banks, 30 May 1795, cited **J. W. F. Hill**, *Georgian Lincoln*, Cambridge U.P. 1961, pp. 167–8.
80. W. Wilsher, Hitchen, to the Marquis of Salisbury, 13 February, Lord Leslie, Dorking, to Portland, 7 March 1800, PRO, HO. 42/49. *Sussex Weekly Advertiser*, 21 Apr. 1800 and 16 Mar. 1801. *The Times*, 14 and 26 June, 9 and 13 Aug. 1860. *Chelmsford Chronicle*, 13 June 1800. *Morning Chronicle*, 26 June 1800. PRO, Assi. 31/8. Essex Quarter Sessions papers, E(ssex) CRO, Q/SMF/29; Q/SBb/381/20. Newbury Bench to Windham, 10 June 1800, PRO, WO. 40/17. *Reading Mercury*, 16 June 1800.
81. Steward Smith to R. Pole Carew, 6 December 1799, and subsequent letters, Cornwall CRO. Carew MSS, CC/K/30. Norfolk examples which involved the Bench include the July 1805 refusal of labourers to work for '*customary wages*', and the imprisonment of two men in farmer Lindley's 'permanent employment' for conspiring with colleagues to shorten hours in February 1811. **C. Mackie**, *Norfolk Annals*, 2 vols (1901), I, pp. 42, 89.
82. Cited by **A. D. Gilbert**, 'Methodism, dissent and political stability in early industrial England', *Jn. of Religious Hist.*, x (1979), p. 386; whether the ascription to Methodism was correct is immaterial, for it is irrelevant whether the insubordination was cause or effect. Williams, James and Malcolm, *op. cit.*, p. 176. Cf. *Annals of Agric.*, **27**, (1796), pp. 215–21.
83. See esp. Hume to Portland, 11 July 1795, PRO, HO. 42/35, where he anticipated strikes in the Hoddesdon district by 'Farmers servants and other workmen', including paper-makers, who had withdrawn

friendly society deposits to sustain themselves while on a strike which they intended to extend 'to all persons of their own description'. Whitbread's personal connection with the corresponding societies at Hertford and Royston is revealed by J. Uskerne to Reeves, 8 January 1793, BL, Add. MSS 16928, ff. 16–17. On Norfolk reform meetings see R. Fellowes to Portland, 19 October, Sir J. Rous to Pitt, 7 July 1795, PRO, HO. 42/36; Chatham Papers, 30/8/178, ff. 108–9, and trial of J. Breezer for publishing offences, 18 October 1795, N(orfolk and) N(orwich) RO, Quarter Sessions Roll, Epiphany 1796. In the Commons Whitbread claimed that 'artisans and other working people . . . compel their employers to make . . . advances; such proceedings were totally out of the power of the husbandmen'. *Debrett's Parliamentary Debates*, 2nd ser., **43**, pp. 247–8

84. Ironically, events during the East Anglian risings of 1816 are said to reveal 'much about popular perceptions of the changing situation', a clear sign of the 'convergence of rising union mentality with declining *taxation populaire*'. **E. F. Genovese**, 'The many faces of moral economy; a contribution to a debate', *Past and Present*, **58**, (1973), p. 165.

85. **R. Wells**, 'Counting riots in eighteenth-century England', *Bull. of Soc. for Study of Lab. Hist.*, **37** (1978).

86. *Sussex Weekly Advertiser*, 20 Apr. and 5 Oct. 1795, 9 and 16 May 1796. ESCRO, QO/EW/32. Cf. New Alresford riot, September 1800, before which 'some Farmers were very positively charg'd by the Labourers . . . with possessing much unthresh'd' old wheat. Three of the four men arrested were farmworkers from 'neighbouring parishes'. Rev. North, harvest return, 6 November 1800, PRO, HO, 42/54. *The Times*, 30 Sept. 1800. HCRO, QR, Michaelmas 1800.

87. *Bath Chronicle*, 22 July 1795. *Sussex Weekly Advertiser*, 25 Apr. 1796. ECRO Michaelmas 1795 Quarter Sessions Roll, 362/84; Q/SBb/361. *Sherborne Mercury*, 20 July 1795. Somerset Assize indictments, PRO Assi. 25/1/3; 25/1/12. Somerset CRO, Easter 1800 Quarter Sessions Roll, CQ/3/1/368. Committals, 5 April 1800, HCRO, Easter 1800 Quarter Sessions Roll. Horsham jail calendar, July 1795, WSCRO, QR/610, f. 21. *Lincoln Rutland and Stamford Mercury*. 22 May 1795.

88. Wells, *Wretched Faces*, pp. 108–11.

89. Many incidents must have been too minor to warrant legal proceedings, let alone communication with Whitehall. Lincolnshire CRO, Kesteven Division, Quarter Sessions minutes, 1798–1802, pp. 454–6. Indictments of two paper-makers and a labourer, September 1800, WSCRO, QR/W631.

90. H. Shadwell, Lewes, to the Duke of Richmond, 15 February 1801, PRO, HO, 42/61. WSCRO, QR/608, f. 62; 609, ff. 51–2; Par. 400, 12/1/2; 37/33–62.

91. W. Morton Pitt to W. Pitt, 5 May 1795, PRO. Chatham Papers, 30/8/167, ff. 205–6. Sir C. Sykes to W. Wilberforce, 27 January 1796, Humberside CRO, DD. SY. 101/54. **E. P. Thompson**, 'The "moral economy" of the English crowd in the eighteenth century', *Past and Present*, **51** (1971), p. 129. **J. R. Western**, 'The Volunteer Movement

as an anti-revolutionary force 1793–1801', *English Hist. Rev.*, LXXI (1956).

92. *The Times*, 30 Sept. 1800. W. Walford, Banbury, to Portland, 15 September 1800, PRO, HO, 42/51. **B. Cozens-Hardy** (ed.), 'Mary Hardy's diary', *Norfolk Record Soc.*, **37** (1968), pp. 90–1. The sole major exception were fenland drainage workers 'called Bankers . . . employed in cleaning out Drains and in embanking; these are the most to be dreaded . . . being for the most part Strangers from different Counties are not so easily quieted as those that live on the spot'. Boston petition, and B. Clayton to Sir P. Burrell, 10 and 11 August 1795, PRO, WO, 1/1086, ff. 549–52. HO, 42/35. **W. Gooch**, *A General View of the Agriculture of the County of Cambridge*, 1813, p. 289.

93. *Reading Mercury*, 16 June 1800. *Morning Chronicle*, 26 June 1800. Formal Quarter Sessions' thanks to Rev. Bate Dudley, ECRO, Q/SBb/381/20.

94. **J. R. Poynter**, *Society and Pauperism: English ideas on poor relief 1795–1834*, Routledge and Kegan Paul 1969, Ch. 5. For an example of a very long struggle between Broadwater and the local Bench, see the details emerging when the dispute turned into a public slanging match involving Sir C. Goring, a JP for nearly fifty years. *Sussex Weekly Advertiser*, 18 and 25 Jan., 1 and 8 Feb. 1819.

95. Wells, 'English rural proletariat . . .', pp. 128–31.

96. **A. Charlesworth**, 'A comparative study of the spread of agricultural disturbances in 1816, 1822 and 1830', *Liverpool Papers in Human Geography*, **9** (1982), p. 11. **A. J. Peacock**, *Bread or Blood: the agrarian riots in East Anglia in 1816*, Gollancz 1965, *passim*.

97. This and the following paragraphs are based principally on the Sussex, Kent and Hampshire press, the records of Sussex vestries, Quarter Sessions, and the Home Circuit Assizes. For specific incidents in the text see, *Sussex Weekly Advertiser*, 24 Dec. 1821 and 3 June 1822. Overseer French, Buxted, deposition, 28 August 1818; Burt and Baldwin statements, September 1821; Constable of Battle, bill, October 1821, endorsed by the Bench: Burwash vestry minutes, 3 July 1819, ESCRO, QR/E.757, 769; Par. 284/12/1. For East Anglian evidence see **A. J. Peacock**, 'Village radicalism in East Anglia 1800–50', in **J. P. D. Dunbadin** (ed.), *Rural Discontent in Nineteenth-Century Britain*, Faber 1975, and **P. Muskett**, 'The East Anglian agrarian riots of 1822', *Agric. Hist. Rev.*, **32** (1984), pp. 1–4.

98. R. Withers to Hardwicke, 19 February 1828, BL. Add. MSS 35691, ff. 208–9.

99. Muskett, 'East Anglian agrarian riots', pp. 6–7, 11–12. Charlesworth, 'A comparative study', p. 12. Wells, '. . . rejoinder', pp. 526–8. **A. F. J. Brown**, *Chartism in Essex and Suffolk*, Essex and Suffolk County Councils 1982, pp. 23–4.

100. *Sussex Weekly Advertiser*, 10 July 1815, 24 Apr. 1823, 2 Feb. and 17 May 1824, 14 Mar. 6, 13 and 20 June 1825, and 15 Jan. 1827. *BPP*, HCSC, 'Combination Laws' (1825), vol. IV. pp. 29–30, 45–9, 87–92, 135–9, 146–54, 172, 177–81. Brown, *Chartism*, pp. 31–4.

101. Harvest wages in Kent were widely reduced with little recorded resistance in 1822. *Sussex Weekly Advertiser*, 27 Nov. 1815, 27 Aug. 1821

and 8 July 1822. *Sussex Advertiser*, 21 July 1828, 23 Aug. and 29 Nov. 1830. *Morning Chronicle*, 3 Dec. 1830. *Maidstone Gazette*, 1 Mar. 1831. *Brighton Gazette*, 19 May 1831. G. Spater, *William Cobbett: the Poor Man's Friend*, vol. II, p. 489. Hobsbawm and Rudé, *op. cit.*, pp. 61, 72.

102. For example, the Newick meeting between labourers and farmers, chaired by a squire, was 'strongly impressed with the necessity of keeping the question of fair wages as distinct as possible from that in which the administration of the poor rate is involved; the embroiling of the two questions having had the pernicious effect . . . of lowering . . . wages . . . Thus remuneration of labour, in reference to real value, has been lost sight of, and the necessities of the industrious man have been ministered unto from the . . . fund set apart for other purposes'. Recognising the need to 'value labour in reference to the produce of that labour, and not in reference to the circumstances which different labourers may incidentally be placed', men over twenty were to receive 2s. per day; youths and boys were to get less. Nevertheless the resolutions acknowledged the retention of the poor law's importance for 'rendering assistance to aged persons, women and children', a thinly disguised admission that allowances in-aid-of wages for children would continue. Demands circulated in the Mayfield district demarcated differential wage increases for married men and bachelors 'so that all may live by there labour', but also included house-rent reductions, work for children aged over twelve, *and* family supplements for younger children. *Sussex Advertiser*, 29 Nov. 1830. Sir C. Webster to Peel, with enclosure, 12 November 1830, PRO, HO, 52/10, ff. 397–9.

103. Notably Wilkes, 'Adjustments to arable farming'

104. For example, the massive majority supporting reform in counties like Herefordshire which were not centres of the agricultural depression. Sir G. Cornewall to Lord Holland, 14 October 1831, BL Add. MSS 51837, ff. 140–1. Cf. **J. Cannon**, ' New lamps for old: the end of Hanoverian England', in **J. Cannon** (ed.), *The Whig Ascendancy*, Arnold 1981, pp. 102, 113–144. In many villages farmers responded to Swing by petitioning for parliamentary reform. *Maidstone Gazette*, 16 Nov. 1830. *Morning Chronicle*, 23 and 27 Nov. and 9 Dec. 1830. *Political Register*, 27 Nov. and 4 Dec. 1830.

105. **A. M. Colson**, 'The Revolt of the Hampshire Agricultural Labourers and Its Causes' (MA thesis, University of London, 1937), pp. 146–7. Duke of Buckingham and Chandos to Peel, 9 November 1830, PRO, HO, 52–11, ff. 376-7. *Sussex Advertiser*, 13 and 20 Sept. and 11 Oct. 1830.

106. **A. Charlesworth**, 'Social protest in a rural society: the spatial diffusion of the Captain Swing disturbances of 1830–1831', *Historical Geography Research Series*, **1** (Norwich, 1979), esp. pp. 45–6. Charlesworth, *Liverpool Papers* . . ., pp. 26–7. **A. Charlesworth**, 'Radicalism, political crisis and the agricultural labourers' protests of 1830', in **A. Charlesworth** (ed.), *Rural Social Protest and Conflict since 1550*, Humberside College of Further Education 1982, pp. 48–9.

107. *The Times*, 22 Dec. 1830 and 3 Jan. 1831. *Herts. Mercury*, 20 Nov. 1830. *Southampton Mercury*, 27 Nov. 1830. *Sussex Advertiser*, 29 Nov.

1830. E. Bicton, Trowbridge to Col. Mair, 27 November and Gosport postmaster to Sir F. Freeling, 2, 3, 4 and 7 December 1830, PRO, HO, 47/25(5), f. 38; 52/10, ff. 323–8, 338.

108. *Morning Chronicle*, 6 Dec. 1830. *Kent Herald*, 18 Nov. 1830.

109. Colson, 'The Revolt', p. 178. **A. Aspinall** (ed.), *Three Early Nineteenth Century Diaries*, Williams and Norgate 1952, pp. 19–20, Ellenborough's, 18 November 1830.

110. Judge Taunton told farmers implicated in encouraging Swing that 'As holders of property themselves, they ought to have respected the property of others, for it tumultuous assemblies of persons in the defendants' rank of life, were thus permitted to enforce a reduction of tithes, the farmers themselves would the next day be forced to yield to the demands of their labourers, and thus an indiscriminate confusion would ensue', *Maidstone Gazette*, 28 Dec. 1830.

111. Rev. Dallas, Wonston, and J. Enser, Acle, to Melbourne, 8 January and 26 November 1831, PRO, HO, 52/13, ff. 113–15; 52/14, ff. 8–9.

112. Mason to J. Ray, 7 February 1831, Colson, 'The Revolt', pp. 288–92. Spater, *op. cit.*, ii, p. 503.

113. *Poor Man's Guardian*, 29 Sept., 3 Nov. 1 and 8 Dec. 1832, 23 Feb. and 27 Apr. 1833. For similar rural penetrations elsewhere see Wells, 'Rural rebels . . .', pp. 138–42.

114. Burwash vestry minutes, 22 January, 9 July, 16 November and 29 December 1831, ESCRO Par. 284/12/1. *Kent Herald*, 18 Nov. 1830. *Maidstone Gazette*, 31 May, 9, 16 and 30 Aug., 6 Sept. and 25 Oct. 1831. Sir G. Webster, Battle, and Major Lamb, Rye, to Melbourne, 28 March and 7 November 1831, PRO, HO, 52/15, ff. 15, 97. J. B. Freeland, Chichester, to the Duke of Richmond, 14 July 1831, WSCRO, G(oodwood) MSS 635.

115. *BPP*, HCSC, 'Agriculture', (1833), vol. v, Qs. 7287–7301, 7385–6. *BPP*, HCSC 'Agricultural Distress' (1836), vol. viii, part ii, Qs. 13169, 13172.

116. *Brighton Gazette*, 3, 17 and 24 Apr., 1, 8, 15 and 22 May, 12 and 19 June 1834. *Hampshire Telegraph*, 25 May 1835. **W. Maitland Waller**, 'An impartial appreciation of the Tolpuddle Martyrs', *Proc. Dorset Nat. Hist. and Arch. Soc.*, **55**, (1933), p. 62. *Kent Herald*, 15 Aug. 1833.

117. J. Brown, Wareham, to Melbourne, 8 January 1833, PRO, HO, 52/22, ff. 50–1.

118. Daily police report, 4 November 1830, PRO, HO, 62/6 no. 882.

119. **G. Loveless**, *The Victims of Whiggery*, 3rd edn, 1837, p. 5.

120. 'SS' report on Rotunda meeting, *c.* 19 April 1831; informer G. M. Ball report, n.d., but late February 1834, PRO, HO, 64/11, f. 229; 64/15, f. 106.

121. Loveless, *The Victims of Whiggery*. **J. Marlow**, *The Tolpuddle Martyrs*, Panther 1974 edn, pp. 41–2.

122. Frampton to Melbourne, Melbourne's endorsement, and reply from under-secretary Phillipps, 30 and 31 January 1834, PRO, HO, 52/54, ff. 45–6; **W. Citrine** (ed.). *The Martyrs of Tolpuddle*, TUC 1934, p. 172. **M. Frampton**, *Journal*, 1885, pp. 378–81. Melbourne had earlier told Wellington to use this Act to defeat political unionists in Hampshire. **P. Hollis**, *The Pauper Press*, Oxford U.P. 1970, pp. 35–6.

123. Depositions of E. Legge and J. Lock, 24 and 26 February; W. Wollaston, Dorchester, to Melbourne, enclosing 'Substance' of Legge's information, 26 February: Frampton to Melbourne, 1 and 5 March 1834; Phillipps of Frampton 3 (draft) and 6 March 1834, PRO, HO, 52/24, ff. 24–7, 36–43, 53–6; Citrine, *The Martyrs*, p. 175.

124. Frampton to Melbourne, 1 and 5 March; Phillipps to Frampton, 6 March 1834 (cf. draft), PRO, HO, 52/24, ff. 29–30, 38–9; Citrine, *The Martyrs*, pp. 176–7.

125. **G. D. H. Cole**, *Attempts at General Union*, Macmillan 1953, pp. 122–6 and Appendix 7. **W. H. Oliver**, 'The consolidated trades' union of 1834', *Econ. Hist. Rev*, 2nd ser. XXVII (1964), pp. 79–80. Ball reports, 11 February, n.d. but late February, and *c*. 5 March 1834, PRO, HO, 64/15, ff. 105–8.

126. Frampton to Melbourne, 22 and 29 March; letters to Frampton from, Phillips, 6 March (and draft), Howick, and Melbourne, both 26 March 1834, PRO, HO, 52/24, ff. 29–30, 51–2; Citrine, *The Martyrs*, pp. 176–82.

127. Including Devon, Hertfordshire, Bedfordshire and Sussex. *Farmer's Magazine*, I, **5** (Sept. 1834), pp. 64, 352; 6 (Oct. 1834), p. 446. *Brighton Gazette*, 6 Feb. and 15 Nov. 1834. *Poor Man's Guardian*, 15 Nov. 1834. Indictments of W. Boiling, and N. Denyer; Freeling, 5 and 6 November, and F. Lewis, to Richmond, 6 November 1834, WSCRO, QR/W 775; G. MSS 1477.

128. For southern resistance see Wells, 'Resistance . . .', for East Anglian, **A. Digby**, *Pauper Palaces*, Routledge and Kegan Paul 1978, pp. 218–24, Brown, *Chartism in Essex* . . ., pp. 27–9, and **J. E. Archer**, '"A fiendish outrage?": a study of animal maiming in East Anglia: 1830–1870', *Agric. Hist. Rev.*, **33** (1985), pp. 148–9, and for central southern England, **A. Brundage**, *The Making of the New Poor Law, 1834–9*, Hutchinson 1978, Ch. 5.

129. Assistant-poor-law commissioner Hawley was quickly off the mark in his first letter on the subject to the Poor Law Commission, 19 March 1835, PRO, MH, 32/38, that orators were masked and oaths were taken, a view soon echoed by the press, and farmers, who were transparently lobbying for further martyrs under the 1797 Act. *Kentish Chronicle*, 5 May 1835.

130. Wells, 'Rural rebels . . .', pp. 144–7; Wells, 'Resistance . . .'. **J. Lowerson**, 'The aftermath of Swing; anti-Poor Law Movements and rural trades unions in the south-east of England', in Charlesworth (ed.), *Rural Social Change* . . .

131. *BPP*, 'First Annual Report of the Poor Law Commission', 1835, p. 36.

132. Letters to Russell from chairman, Hampshire Sessions, 10 October, and J. Barr, Warminster, 20 and 22 November 1835, PRO, HO, 52/26, ff. 80–1; 64/5, ff. 66, 235. Digby, *Pauper Palaces.*, pp. 212–13, 221–2.

133. *Chelmsford Chronicle*, 15 and 22 July, and 5 Aug. 1836. *Essex Herald*, 19 July 1836. *Essex Standard*, 15 July 1836. *Farmer's Magazine*, V, **3** (Sept. 1836), p. 194. Brown, *Chartism in Essex and Suffolk* p. 27.

134. *Sussex Advertiser*, 26 Sept. 1836. *The Champion*, 20 Oct. 1840. *Farmer's Magazine*, VI **5** (May 1837), p. 389. **D. H. Morgan**, *Harvesters and Harvesting 1840–1900*, Croom Helm 1982, esp. pp. 125–9.

135. I. Thomas, Lewes, to Lord Chichester, 2 July 1835, WSCRO, G.MSS, 1575. *BPP*, HCSC, 'Settlement and Poor Removal' (1847), vol. XI, Qs. 5664–5.

136. Ibid., Q. 7103.

137. *BPP*, 'Second Annual Report of the Poor Law Commission' (1836) vol. XXIX, p. 215. *Brighton Gazette*, 8 Dec. 1842. *Brighton Patriot*, 23 Feb. 1836 and 8 May 1838.

138. Ticehurst Union to the Poor Law Commission, 30 June 1836, PRO, MH, 12/13138. *Sussex Advertiser*, 11 Mar. and 6 May 1839.

139. *BPP*, HCSC, 'Settlement and Poor Removal' (1847), vol. XI, Qs. 3072–3, 3412–9, 3629–30, 7266–70.

140. *Farmers' Magazine*, VI, 5 (May 1837), p. 389. *Sussex Advertiser*, 29 June 1840. Archer, '"A fiendish outrage?".', pp. 148–52. **Archer**, 'The Wells – Charlesworth debate: a personal comment on arson in Norfolk and Suffolk', *Jn. of Peasant Studies*, Vol. 9, **4**, (1982). **D. J. V. Jones**, 'Thomas Campbell Foster and the rural labourer; incendiarism in East Anglia in the 1840s', *Social History*, **1** (1976). Wells, 'Southern resistance . . .'

141. Brown, *Chartism in Essex . . .*, *passim*. Wells, 'Rural rebels . . .', pp. 150–4. *Morning Chronicle*, 7 Nov. 1849.

142. *BPP*, HCSC, 'Agricultural Distress' (1836), vol. VIII Qs. 3076, 3098. *BPP*, HCSC, 'Poor Law Amendment Act' (1837), vol. XVII, Qs. 1580, 1589; 5062, 6077, 5645, 5982, 12402–14. *Brighton Patriot*, 13 Mar. and 3 Apr. 1838. Confession of James Towner, 28 October 1839, ESCRO, QR/E865. Petworth Union to Hawley, 21 July 1836, PRO, MH, 32/38. **J. Evans**, *Time and Chance*, Longmans, Green and Co. 1943, p. 74.

143. Ibid. J. Horn, 'Child workers in the pillow lace and straw-plait trades of Victorian Buckinghamshire and Bedfordshire', *Historical Journal*, XVII (1974).

144. **M. Gibson**, 'The Treatment of the Poor in Surrey under . . . the New Poor Law between 1834 and 1871', (Ph.D. thesis, University of Surrey, 1978), p. 45. **F. G. Heath**, *The English Peasantry*, 1874, p. 187.

CHAPTER SIX

The Scots Colliers' Strikes of 1824–1826: the Years of Freedom and Independence

Alan Campbell

Between 1824 and 1826, the Scottish coalmining industry experienced widespread labour unrest as the miners took advantage of the
repeal of the laws against Combination and an upswing in the trade
cycle to organise trade unions rapidly. By 1825 they had federated
their local organisations in the Associated Colliers of Scotland, the
first national union of Scottish miners. This union excercised a
powerful control over the coal industry, using strikes or the threat
of strikes, apprenticeship controls and restriction of output to force
wage increases of up to 80 per cent. But its power was short-lived.
The larger coal and ironmasters launched a counter-offensive during
the winter of 1825–26, using unskilled blacklegs to break the
domination of the Colliers' Association in a series of disputes
throughout the Scots coalfields.[1]

This episode of industrial conflict is worthy of detailed consideration for a number of reasons. First, the policies pursued by the
Colliers' Association, such as defence of apprenticeship, allow an
insight into the occupational consciousness of the miners at this time.
Moreover, this period signified the zenith of the organised power
of the Scots miners during the nineteenth century. At the level of
British politics, the ability of the Scots miners to regulate the coal
trade was one of the major examples cited by the Government and
its supporters during the passage of the Combination Law Repeal
Amendment Act in 1825, which restricted the broad trade union
freedoms granted by the initial Repeal Act in the previous year.
According to Robert Peel, the Scots Colliers' union rules constituted
'an abominable assumption of power' by the miners.[2]

This analysis of the Scots miners' strikes therefore provides a
useful case study of union organisation and tactics during the general

143

upsurge of industrial conflict in the years after 1824. More specifically, it is useful as a study of a miners' union; for despite the miners being the most extensively researched group within British labour historiography, the early history of their unions remains at worst ignored or at best treated in impressionistic fragments. This is perhaps due to the institutional focus of much of the writing, which, dependent as it is an official union records, has neglected those areas and periods for which such records do not exist. Yet this neglect may well have obscured themes in the miners' consciousness and in their union strategies which persisted into later periods.

This chapter is in three main sections. The first describes the work situation and the associated work culture of the Scots colliers in the early years of the nineteenth century; the second analyses the ways in which this work culture informed the policies of the miners' early attempts at union organisation and section three considers in detail the conflicts of 1824–26. In conclusion, we briefly indicate the significance of these strikes for future union policy and suggest the need for historians to look for similar movements and traditions in other coalfields.

THE WORK CULTURE OF THE 'INDEPENDENT COLLIER'[3]

One of the keys to understanding the mentality of the Scots collier in the early decades of the century is to realise that his work was not only arduous and performed under restrictive circumstances, but also *skilled*. Thus, Archibald Alison, in his writings on industrial Scotland in the 1830s, located colliers and miners in the category of 'skilled labour' alongside cotton-spinners, iron-founders, engineers, tailors and bakers. The collier's skills included judging which tools to use in particular conditions, how far the coal face might be safely undercut, when the workplace would need timbering. He had also to be able to predict when the coal seam might become gaseous or wet, or how the lumps of coal would break, for he was paid more for 'great coal' than for small. 'The art of the collier', claimed Robert Bald in 1808, 'is to hew down immense blocks of coal'.[4]

In addition to hewing coal, colliers were required to perform a variety of other tasks underground, for the Scots coal industry at this time was characterised by a relatively undeveloped division of labour. At the large Calder colliery near Glasgow in 1834, colliers represented 68 per cent of the total labour force of 213 above and below ground; at the neighbouring Rosehall colliery in 1840, the colliers amounted to 74.5 per cent of the workforce of 157.[5] At smaller collieries, which were common, the proportion of colliers was likely to be higher. As well as colliers performing routine tasks such as drawing tubs of coal, the most skilled and experienced would contract to undertake work of an exceptional character such as constructing new levels.

A second influence on the work culture of the miners was their freedom from managerial control. The hewers were paid on a piecework basis for the amount of coal they produced, the rate being negotiated according to conditions in particular seams. Piecework provided a financial incentive to maximise effort and thus obviated the need for close supervision. Furthermore, the physical conditions of underground labour rendered such supervision impractical. By far the most common system of mineworking in Scotland was pillar and stall, or 'stoop and room' as it was known locally. Miners, working as individuals or in pairs, were scattered in 'rooms' about 12 ft wide which were separated by 'stoops' or pillars or coal which remained unworked. The collier's freedom from control was commented upon by a number of observers in the 1840s: 'The collier is his own master and may work out as much as he likes, and is paid by the piece', stated one witness before the Children's Employment Commission in 1842, while a sub-commissioner noted that 'the only way in which his work is at all regulated by the coal owner' was that the pit engine started at 6 a.m.[6] Around this independence was erected a culture of custom and superstition which depended on the colliers being able to stop work when they pleased, for example in the event of an accident, however trivial, or to celebrate (with copious amounts of whisky) such events as births, marriages or the opening of a new seam.

Because of the skill and experience necessary to perform as a coal-hewer, and lack of supervision, it was rarely a job which untrained men could successfully undertake. A historian writing in the 1860s described the informal system of training which had existed in Scots mines from 'time immemorial':

The old Scottish colliers . . . looked upon their profession as a sort of hereditary right, which had descended from generation to generation, and for which they had to undergo a regular apprenticeship. At the age of 8 or 9 a boy was sent to work in the pit as a trapper . . . In a couple of years he became a putter and assisted in pushing the loads of coal . . . In a couple of years more he was termed a half man when he assisted the working colliers and after another two or three years he was entitled to rank as a man . . . at the coal wall. Thus step by step he was trained to the work.[7]

The young collier's attainment of the status of a 'full man' was celebrated by a ceremony known as 'brothering'. As part of the 'mysteries' of the colliers' trade, this ritual was shrouded in secrecy, but in 1818 several colliers stated that when they had been 'made a brother' about the age of 18 years, they had sworn an oath read from the Bible.[8] In 1825 a Stirlingshire collier declared that as 'an established and full man, or collier by profession, he had of course known the Colliers Word, sign and grips'[9]. As Eric Hobsbawm has pointed out, such 'rites of passage', often borrowing from Masonic ceremonial, were 'almost universal' among tradesmen in Britain during the first half of the nineteenth century.[10]

The reference to 'hereditary right' suggests a further factor informing the occupational consciousness of the Scots colliers: their recent memory of colliery serfdom. This serfdom was a result of legal enactments in the seventeenth century which allowed miners to be bound for life to the coal works of their masters, and which meant they could be leased or bought and sold with the colliery. This system of serfdom was initially intended to ensure a constant supply of labour to what was an unpopular occupation, but during the latter part of the eighteenth century, when the demand for coal rapidly increased, particularly in the industrialising west of Scotland, it proved to be an inadequate solution to the problem of labour recruitment. The stigma of serfdom prevented entry to the trade from outside the existing mining population and masters increasingly attempted to poach labour from each other by offering colliers financial inducements to desert.[11] 'The slavery of the slave', noted one writer, 'had become his strength in the battle for wages. It gave him the advantage of a monopolist. It frightened competition away.'[12] Serfdom was finally ended by Act of Parliament in 1799 but its abolition did little to diminish the Scots coalmasters' problems of labour recruitment. As a consequence, colliers were generally among the best paid tradesmen in the Scottish working class during the early years of the nineteenth century.

In summary, the colliers should not be regarded as unskilled wage labourers, but rather as skilled semi-independent contractors, paid by piece or bargain-derived contract rates which provided a relatively high standard of living. This situation was protected by a general antipathy to colliery work which the tradition of serfdom had fostered, and, so long as this antipathy persisted, the colliers' 'monopoly' of the trade was assured. Like the urban artisan he regarded his skill as his property which he sought to pass on to his sons. Their informal system of training was perhaps the inevitable result of the colliers existing as an hereditary caste under serfdom. But what began as a reflection of their servile status became transformed, after emancipation, into a concern to perpetuate the privileges of their skilled monopoly. As we shall see in the following sections, this concern was a major influence on the aspirations of the miners' unions.

EARLY ATTEMPTS AT UNION ORGANISATION

In many ways, the colliers' independence encouraged collective activity, as a writer in the *Glasgow Herald* in 1825 clearly perceived:

Of all trades the colliers possess the greatest facilities for associating together; and are placed in circumstances the most apt to promote strength and intimacy of coalition. Isolated, in a manner during their labour, from all society with men of other occupations, and dwelling in bodies by themselves around the pits, the colliers, as it were, form one family. They are removed, during the greatest part of their time, from the superintendence of their masters, and may concert their measures together without fear of interference or disturbance. If too, they will exclude the introduction of unassociated workmen among them, how much more easily and effectually can this be done where a coal pit is the scene of labour, than where there is a mill or any place above ground.[13]

One of the bases of this independence, the piecework system, could sometimes foster individualism, but it took little reflection for miners to appreciate that individual manipulation of piecework rates could easily be transformed into a collective control of output. The rationale for this policy, aimed at maintaining high prices in the coal markets through an artificially enforced scarcity, was the convention that colliers' wages generally followed the selling price of coal.

The fundamental rule was to set a maximum level of individual output. In 1842 a government observer noted that rules 'for stinting or limiting each other's earnings' were widespread amongst Lanarkshire miners: 'The general rule is that a man shall not earn above from 3s 6d to 4s a day . . . this is fixed by the men as a man's darg or day's work. No collier is allowed to deliver more than this, though the employer were willing to pay him for it.'[14] The colliers also adopted informal working rules to encourage adherence to the darg. 'The rule is', stated an Ayrshire owner in 1825, 'to relieve the collier of his coals in rotation; a collier who gets his coals taken from him first today is second the following, and so it goes on till the last'.[15] In this way output and earnings were equalised, but, when setting the darg, some allowance was made for men with families to put out more than the standard amount. If sons were working alongside fathers as quarter or half men, the teams were allowed to put out a correspondingly larger darg.

Collective limitation of output was already a weapon in the armoury of the colliers as early as the 1790s, when there were frequent complaints of collieries only working for three days per week as the miners sought to restrict production. In the highly localised markets of the eighteenth century, such a policy might be successfully implemented by the men in a single pit, but by the beginning of the nineteenth century improved transport was beginning to erode local compartmentalised markets. This provided a stimulus to greater coordination between colliers in different districts, since restriction of output was a feasible policy only if the majority of miners in the production area of a particular coal market adhered to it.

An inflow of new labour could also influence the policy's success. During the 1790s and early nineteenth century this problem scarcely arose because of the general scarcity of colliery labour throughout Scotland. In the years after 1815, however, a motley collection of destitute weavers, the urban unemployed and the first trickle of Irish immigrants were creating the beginnings of a pool of surplus labour which could not indulge the luxury of a dislike for underground labour. For the first time there was a threat of competition to the 'hereditary caste'. Such untrained men could not adequately replace skilled colliers, but in the short term masters might employ them during a strike. In the long term such labourers could not perform the variety of tasks needed to keep a pit operating or themselves free from injury. Here lay the vulnerability of the skilled status of the Scots collier after 1815, the Achilles' heel which threatened his standard of living and way of life. The colliers became acutely aware of this threat and sought by their union organisation to construct defences against it.

Formal union organisation was rare in the Scottish coalfields before the repeal of the Combination Acts. Ephemeral organisations tended to be limited to either individual or to small groups of collieries. But it should be remembered that formal organisation is not a necessary preconditionion for a 'continuous association of wage earners'. As H. A. Turner has suggested, 'people of the same occupation, who are regularly brought together in the same workplace or town, may acknowledge regular leaders, develop customs of work regulation and systematic "trade practices", and can produce a disciplined observance of the latter without embedding these procedures in any formal records'.[16] The adoption of similar policies at different times and places by Scots miners' combinations suggested that they were indeed drawing upon 'systematic trade practices' normally submerged in a shared work culture but which developed into an organisational form at times of crisis.

The first recorded instance of a widespread and formally constituted association occurred in 1817 when colliers around Glasgow formed the Glasgow and Clydesdale Association of Operative Colliers which claimed to represent 2000 miners at some 38 collieries. After a three week strike at a number of them, the colliers secured wage increases. A similar association developed in Ayrshire, where there were also partially successful strikes. In October 1817 these two associations merged, but scarcely had this merger taken place when leading officers of the association were arrested and the union appears to have soon been dissolved. The significance of these bodies derives from their having given in their rules a programmatic coherence to the colliers' attempt to regulate both the markets for coal and for labour.

The 'articles' or rules of the Glasgow Association began by calculating the number of carts of coal required for the Glasgow and export markets, and by emphasising the necessity 'to guard against any infringement that would otherwise tend to destroy the prices obtained'. The first rule sought to formalise the traditional training stages of colliers' sons by setting precise age limits to be applied in each colliery, while the second demanded an entry fee of £7 from any person wishing to learn the trade 'who never was in the line thereof before', and required them 'to serve two years to [their] said master'. All eight of the rules related in some way to entry to the trade and they concluded by stating that 'were the above articles strictly observed, the operative colliers never would experience those fluctuations as they have done within these few years past, from low wages'.[17] The demise of the association rendered this a vain hope in 1817, but it was to be dramatically realised seven years later.

THE COLLIERS' ASSOCIATIONS, 1824–26

In the intervening period there is little evidence of organised trade union activity among the colliers, but in 1824 the situation was transformed. Within the space of a few months, the foundations were laid for a national network of organisation throughout Scotland's coalfields. One of the first to be organised was Lanarkshire and the area around Glasgow, and in October 1824 the *Glasgow Herald* speculated that a 40 per cent increase in the price of coal had been due to 'the combination of operative colliers'.[18] In December, the paper published the rules of the Lanark, Dunbarton and Renfrew Association of Colliers and it was later reported that 80 collieries in the West of Scotland has been combined since the repeal of the Combination Acts in the year.[19]

The rules reveal a more elaborate organisational structure than the previous Glasgow and Clydesdale Association. The interests of each 'private association' or colliery branch were in the hands of twelve elected 'managers' and a 'preses' or chairman. The 'general interest' of the Association was under the supervision of a general committee of delegates, consisting of the preses, treasurer and clerk of each private association, and 'as many of the managers as may be found necessary'. The initiation of strikes to resist the 'tyrannical measures' of a master could only be taken by a local association in consultation with this general committee, and provision was also made for strike payments: 'men thrown idle for refusing to work at a lower rate than the wages fixed by the general committee' were to be allowed 10s. per week or alternative work would be found for them.

The policies of the Association were also summarised within these rules. One aim has already been suggested in the statement that the committee was to fix wage rates. The Association also sought to exclude 'irregular men, such as have not served their time as an apprentice'.[20] The sons of associated men were admitted to the Association on the payment of a few shillings as they passed through the respective training stages. Boys not the sons of operative colliers were required to pay sums amounting to £8 for the same 'rights', while adult men wishing to become colliers were required to pay £5, and 'serve an apprenticeship of three years'. Such rules, claimed the Association were intended to remedy the situation in which 'a number of men without proper principles . . . often practice such actions as leaves a stigma upon the whole Body, or Trade at large'.

The Association was fortunate in attempting to implement its policies when the economic boom of 1824–25 created a buoyant market for coal. 'In consequence of this increased demand for coal', stated a correspondent in the *Glasgow Herald*,: 'and the want of a stock to keep the colliers in check, the coalmasters had no alternative but to give the colliers their demands, and the latter have ultimately succeeded in getting three, and in some instances, four and five times more advance than ever they got before'.[21] This statement was corroborated by the the Sheriff of Renfrewshire, who claimed that between October 1824 and January 1825 the colliers received increases of 'about 80% on the wages, and they reduced their hours of work very considerably at the same time'.[22]

The example of the Lanarkshire men was quickly taken up in the neighbouring county of Ayr. Delegates from 27 collieries met in October 1824 to discuss 'several abuses which have gradually crept into the trade' and adopt a set of rules broadly similar to those discussed above. One was singular to Ayrshire and demonstrates the colliers' desire to control the coal trade. 'Is it not evident', asked Article XI:

that there are masters in the coal trade who are constantly running a race in the deduction of wages and are never satisfied unless they are paying below their neighbours . . . This is a case that requires immediate attention and it becomes the duty of this association to point out such masters, and after being duly warned, if they continue in such a career, so hurtful to the trade in general, then it will be our duty to put them out of the trade.[23]

In the following weeks the Ayrshire colliers set about constructing their union and, according to their general secretary, membership amounted to about 1200 by April 1825. In November 1824 the Ayrshire masters had volunteered an advance of 1s. per wagon. The following month, the colliers at Ayr Colliery sought a reduction in the standard output and the right to appoint checkweighers at the pithead. In addition, claimed George Taylor, the colliery's owner, the men's 'great object was the exclusion of other workpeople', presumably those who had not served an apprenticeship.[24] By choosing Ayr as the site of their first battle, the colliers may have been attempting to penalise Taylor, for it is likely that he was one of the masters they considered to 'endanger the trade'. In 1817 he had successfully broken a strike by employing labourers; in November 1824 he had chaired a meeting of coalmasters which had considered ways of combating the colliers' union, and which had resolved 'to oppose all interference on the part of the workmen in the management or conduct of the work'.[25]

The attempt by the colliers to appoint checkweighmen was seen by Taylor to constitute such interference. He refused the colliers' demands and they went on strike. However Taylor once again succeeded in recruiting blacklegs, 'principally Irishmen', and by February the strike was broken. In other collieries, the Ayrshire Association maintained a considerable degree of control; for example, Alexander Guthrie, manager of the Duke of Portland's collieries, admitted that he could only recruit men to his pits with the colliers' 'permission'.[26]

Other counties were also affected by union activity over the winter of 1824–25. In November the manager of the Duke of Hamilton's pits at Redding and Brighton in Stirlingshire observed that his colliers 'were frequently occupied in holding meetings and carrying on a correspondence . . . with people or delegates from the West'.[27] In early December the colliers in these pits embarked on what was to be a long and bitter strike for an increase in wages.

The collieries at Redding and Brighton had only been opened after the completion of the Union Canal in 1822. This canal, which joined the Forth and Clyde Canal, provided a direct waterway link with Glasgow and Edinburgh. One of the primary aims of its construction was to increase the supply of coal to Edinburgh, and, before the strike, most of the weekly output of 8000 tons from the Redding Collieries were sent there. As a result of the strike, the price of coal in both Glasgow and Edinburgh increased, and the dispute highlighted the integration of Scotland's coal markets by improved transport systems. Equally clearly, greater cooperation between the colliers of the different districts was required if the various associations were to succeed in their policies.

In February 1825 the Lanarkshire colliers took the first steps towards a national federation by despatching delegates to every colliery in Scotland. According to an anonymous pamphlet of the time:

The colliers in the West of Scotland have laid, and are at present maturing and extending an artful plan to overturn the usual relation between employer and employed: to place the control of all the collieries in Scotland in the hands of the workmen: to enable the workmen to monopolise the working of coal to the present possessors of that occupation and to limit or extend the quantities brought to market, so as they may have the power of regulating the rate of wages according to their own pleasure.[28]

On 3 May the Sheriff of Stirlingshire, Mr Macdonald, wrote to the Home Office informing Peel that a national association of colliers had in fact been organised. After 'the most absurd and excessive' wage increases had been given to the colliers of both east and west, the miners, claimed Macdonald:

resolved to make their measures general, and accordingly systematised a plan and accordingly organised a confederacy of colliers which they reduced into a sort of small republic, consisting of the Head Freeman, or Dictator, secondly his Grand Central Committee, thirdly that committee again subdivided into provincial committees, and from these committees emanated delegates, preses, treasurers to the association's fund and clerks of districts, etc, etc.[29]

Macdonald's letter might at first sight appear to be the fanciful report of a magistrate haunted by the spectre of trade unionism. He was, however, the magistrate with responsibility for maintaining law and order at Redding, and the events which occurred during the four month strike there go some way to confirming his report. The strike at Redding was to prove an important testing ground for the new national union and an examination of events there provides an insight into the Association's operations.

The Redding colliers, along with those in the neighbouring pits of Parkhall and Rumford, struck on 1 December 1824 for a wage increase of 75 per cent. After eight or nine weeks the manager at Parkhall submitted to the men's demands, and the colliers at Carron, a few miles to the north, also gained an increase. The owner of the Redding and Brighton pits was the Duke of Hamilton, who remained adamant in his refusal to meet the colliers' claim. In an attempt to break the strike, he mustered a force of some 60 or 70 miners and labourers from his Lanarkshire estates and marched them to Redding, some twenty miles away, on 14 March. A mile distant from their destination, three of the blacklegs paused at the roadside to rest and were violently assaulted by a crowd of colliers from Rumford. The following day, all the colliers of the district assembled on Redding Moor, six or seven hundred strong and armed with cudgels. As a result, the Hamilton men refused to commence work, but this was only temporary. Macdonald visited the works daily, promising them the full protection of the law, and the manager employed guards. A number of the colliers involved in the assaults were arrested and the blacklegs began work. By early April, the manager claimed that upwards of 200 colliers had returned to work and the strike was over.

The Redding strike provides an example of the way in which the Colliers' Association spread its influence during the winter of 1824–25, for the majority of the strikers joined during the dispute.

San Sneddon, who was later convicted of assaulting the blacklegs, declared that it was during the strike that he and other men 'joined for the first time the Brethren of the Colliers Association . . . all the colliers of Parkhall and Rumford were sworn in Brethren of the associated colliers and the oath administered to the greater number of them'.[30] Two weeks later, those who had been sworn in were formally enrolled as members of the Associated Colliers of Scotland. This account indicates how the Association incorporated the Scots colliers' traditional 'brothering' rituals into the practice of the union. By reiterating the oath taken at the end of apprenticeship, the union could symbolically emphasise the importance of protecting the colliers' skilled status. Such oathtaking was confirmed by a number of witnesses interrogated by the Sheriff. James Wilson admitted that when he joined the Association he had received 'the grips' and the 'colliers' word' and thus became 'a free man and one of the brethren'. Andrew Benny, a Rumford collier, explained 'that each each member of the association takes the name and designation of a freeman'.[31]

Such terminology evokes clear parallels with Freemasonry, but may also have represented a rhetorical celebration of the colliers' post-emancipation freedom. A number of the Sheriff's informers referred to the Association's aim as the establishment of their 'Freedom and Independence', and 1825 was described as 'this second year of the Constitution of Freedom and Independence'.[32]

These rituals were not simply an eccentricity of the local association at Redding. The Sheriff was informed that when the Grand Central Committee discovered that the Association's secrets had been revealed, a meeting of delegates from every part of Scotland was convened at Redding and the 'Collier's Covenant', which began: 'If a man vow a vow unto the Lord . . . he shall not break his word', was readministered to the strikers.[33]

This was not the Central Committee's only intervention during the dispute. From the beginning it had assumed more than a parochial significance. The Duke of Hamilton's resistance threatened the Association's apparent invincibility. Moreover, had the strike succeeded, Redding wage rates would have been the highest in Scotland and would have provided the basis for similar demands elsewhere. Because of these considerations, the Association extended considerable aid to the struggle at Redding. From a number of informers, Macdonald estimated that £1500 in cash had been sent from all over Scotland's coalfields.[34] The Association's funds were not inexhaustible, however, and as the strike dragged on, other work was provided for the strikers. In March delegates met at Redding to distribute the strikers amongst collieries elsewhere 'under the superintendence of the association'. The power of the Association to do so is demonstrated by the statement of the manager of the nearby Parkhall and Rumford colliery:

The association had apportioned as many of the strike workmen colliers of Redding upon (him) as they had thought he had lost of colliers from his works in consequence of the number of (his) colliers who had fled or who have been apprehended owing to the riot and assault . . . in consequence of the above arrangements and the extensive distribution of the Redding colliers amongst all the other collieries throughout the country, they have all been provided for.[35]

Despite the assistance given, the solidarity of the strikers began to weaken as the strike entered its fifth month and as the blacklegs continued to produce coal. Scottish delegates attending a meeting at Redding in early April were arrested, and, although no charges were ultimately brought, this legal intimidation effectively isolated the strikers and they returned to work. On 23 April Macdonald was able to report that several cargoes of coal were being sent to Edinburgh and that the price of coal there had fallen by 20 per cent.[36].

Although the failure of the strike was a considerable setback for the Colliers' Association, it maintained its power in other districts of Scotland over the summer of 1825. In June the colliers at Hamilton Farm colliery near Glasgow struck in support of a long list of demands including a reduction in output. Their employer, Colin Dunlop, retaliated by evicting them from their company houses. The Association escalated the dispute by bringing out all the colliers at Dunlop's other pits and succeeded in stopping production at Dunlop's Clyde Iron Works. The 300 strikers were maintained by the Association at the rate of 10s. per week and by August Dunlop had been forced to accede to the men's demands.[37]

It was the intention of the combination after this victory, claimed the *Glasgow Herald*, 'to strike against the rest of the coalmasters one by one, till they get all completely under their control as to measurement (i.e. of output) and price. The Grand Stand is to be made this winter'.[38] The ever-attentive Macdonald, who continued to monitor the union's activities, had received reports of a similar plan for a 'general strike' by colliers if their demands for a wage of 11s. per day, and employment to be restricted to association members, were not met.[39]

In the meantime the Association progressively extended its control by a strict policy of output restriction, Glasgow colliers producing only 32 hutches per week compared with 50 normally. In October, Macdonald visited between 40 and 50 pits at 17 collieries in the western counties and found that at none was there more than 12 hours' stock of coal in excess of the daily demand. 'So very tenacious is the committee in the west to enforce the most rigid adherence to this regulation', he reported, 'that they have within the last three weeks appointed a Committee of Inspection who go round to see that every coal pit . . . does not exceed the prescribed quantity of coals to be put out.'[40] He proceeded through the Lothians to Fife and found a similar scarcity of coal in the east.

The escalating demands of the colliers, and the fear of a general strike in the coalfields in mid-winter, galvanised a number of masters to launch a counter-attack. When colliers at William Dixon's pits at Faskine, near Airdrie, struck for an advance in October, he evicted them from their houses and employed new hands under the protection of a strong body of guards. When the Association sent delegates to Dixon's Govan collieries to attempt to spread the strike, he had them arrested and imprisoned.[41] By November it was reported that at Faskine there were now large stocks of coal and ironstone 'so that quarter is quite beyond the reach of the combination'[42]. Dixon's success encouraged a number of other masters to follow suit. In October Lord Belhaven dismissed the entire workforce of his collieries and recruited new men; similar action was taken by the owners of the Muirkirk Iron Works in Ayrshire, and the large Hurlet Coal and Lime Works in Renfrewshire, where it was reported that for the previous 12 months the Association had exercised an almost total control: 'No new hand could be taken in without the concurrence of the combined. Six times this year did they demand an advance of prices and each rise was accompanied by a corresponding diminution in the hours of labour.'[43]

The decisive battle was not fought until April 1826 at the Clyde Iron Works. Until that month, the colliers there, according to the *Glasgow Herald*, had 'wrought when they pleased, demanded what wages they pleased, and had the complete ascendancy of the works'. When they struck to resist a wage reduction on the orders of the Central Committee, Dunlop evicted them from their houses and set about hiring 'labourers, weavers and able-bodied workmen of all descriptions to replace them'.[44] The general economic depression of 1826 created a pool of unemployed in the Glasgow district, and the coalmasters quickly took advantage of it: in one day, nearly a hundred men, mainly unemployed weavers, applied for work at the Clyde pits. The union colliers did not give up without a fight, and for weeks the colliery resembled a fortified camp, protected by guards with pistols. But the strike ended in total defeat, and when other masters gave notice of reductions the Association was unable to resist them.

The great number of men now learning the trade [gloated the *Glasgow Chronicle*] will also render nugatory every effort of the combined colliers to maintain a monopoly. There are 3000 associated colliers in this county. The new hands amount to 1000 . . . [the] additional quantity of coal thrown upon the general market by the introduction of new hands gives a fatal blow to the combination.[45]

This analysis proved correct. Colliers along the Monkland Canal struck to resist reductions in May but with no apparent success, and in the following months there was an absence of any reports of Association activity. Although trade union activity persisted in subsequent years at pit and local level, there is little doubt that the employers' offensive over the winter of 1825–26 succeeded in breaking up the national organisation of the 'Associated Colliers of Scotland'.

Within this counter-offensive, several distinct forces can be discerned. One group notable for its resistance to the colliers was the aristocratic coal owners such as the Duke of Hamilton, Lord Belhaven and the Earl of Elgin (who waged a two-month dispute at his Fife collieries at the same time as the Redding strike). Since mining was only one component of their financial interests, they were in a stronger position to resist strikes than smaller coal masters.

A second major group was the increasingly influential iron companies, such as Dixon, Dunlop and Muirkirk, who were themselves the consumers of coal produced in their pits. While other coal-masters passed on increased labour costs to the public consumers, a sharp decline in the price of iron made confrontation in the iron-masters' pits inevitable. In order to control labour costs, they were forced to challenge the source of the union's power, its control of entry to the mines, by recruiting blackleg labour. Thus, in May 1826, Colin Dunlop resolved 'to make his pits a nursery for colliers, and to rear such a body of new workmen as will be a complete coun-terpoise to the combination at all times'.[46]

In addition to physically protecting such men, the main difficulty with this strategy was the skilled nature of the colliers' work, and this was underlined by the fact that at many of the collieries where it was adopted there were specific circumstances which facilitated the introduction of untrained blacklegs. One feature common to many of them was a more developed division of labour which could provide a nucleus of semi-skilled potential strikebreakers. Thus George Taylor's Ayr Colliery was one of the largest in the county and worked under a more systematic hierarchy of skilled and semi-skilled workers. 'Mr Taylor', stated one of his neighbours, 'has a facility for making colliers which we have not; his colliers simply work the coal and he has men employed to drag the coal from the colliers to the pit bottom.'[47] Such men might be only too willing to earn a collier's wage in the event of a strike.

A number of pits operated by William Dixon were worked by the long wall system, which was associated with a greater division of labour than the more common 'stoop and room'. 'By this mode', commented one observer, 'there is a saving of two-thirds of pick work, and of course the art is much sooner acquired. This is a fortunate circumstance for the new colliers as they will learn much sooner.' Even so, when the new hands commenced work, 'they were accompanied by several regularly bred colliers who put things in order for them, and are to instruct them in their business'.[48]

The years 1824–26 marked a climax in the Scots colliers' attempts to regulate the trade, when their artisanal hopes developed an aggression which almost amounted to a form of syndicalism, aiming to overturn 'the usual relations between employer and employed'. The messianic undertone of phrases such as the 'second year of the Constitution of Freedom and Independence' suggests that the sons of the collier-serfs believed that at last they could receive the rewards of the 'profession' they regarded as their hereditary birthright; however, their temporary mastery of the coal trade was soon broken. Nevertheless, the Scots colliers' aspiration to control both coal output and entry to their trade remained a central feature of the culture of the 'independent collier' and of the policies of successive miners' unions which that culture informed for the greater part of the nineteenth century. Apprenticeship regulations remained in Scots miners' rule books (albeit often unfulfilled) until the 1880s and resolutions for high entry fees to exclude the unskilled from the mines were still being passed at Scottish Miners' Federation conferences as late as 1911.[49] Restriction of output was also a major tactic employed throughout the century, and as late as 1914 the Scots miners attempted to maintain coal prices and wages by the adoption of a four-day week.[50] For decades after the 1820s conflict between the colliers' unions and the coal owners, especially the increasingly powerful iron companies, focussed on these issues of job control.

The resilience of the culture of independence was due to a variety of factors, such as the uneven development, chronologically and geographically, of the Scottish coalfields by large-scale colliery companies, but we should not ignore the extent to which later generations of trade union activists consciously modelled their tactics upon the temporary but nonetheless remarkable successes of the Associated Colliers of Scotland. The Free Colliers, whose lodges spread throughout the coalfields in the 1860s, were a deliberate attempt to revive the early colliery brotherhoods, complete with their traditional masonic rituals, and to recapture that 'freedom and independence' which by then had been vanquished in many areas by the new serfdom of the iron companies' brutal industrial discipline.[51]

Persistence of the policies pioneered in the 1820s also suggests the need for historians to look more closely for similar movements and traditions in other coalfields. As yet, there is still a dearth of systematic studies of early colliers' union organisation in England and Wales. It is perhaps symptomatic of this situation that one of few, good existing analyses, David Jones's account of 'The Scotch Cattle' in Wales in the 1830s, is part of a study of the social history of popular disturbance rather than of mining trade unionism.[52] But even a cursory survey suggests similar concerns with issues such as restriction of output and apprenticeship controls in other parts of Britain. The South Wales Friendly Society of Coalmining included the following ritual declaration in its catechism for new entrants in 1831: 'I will never instruct any person into the art of coal-mining, tunnelling or boring . . . except to an obliged brother or an apprentice – So help me God.'[53] Such aspirations persisted into the latter half of the nineteenth century. The rules of the Ogmore District in Glamorganshire of the Amalgamated Association of Miners in 1874 included 'apprentiship' provisions prohibiting any miner 'to take a person to learn' unless he paid £10 to the lodge funds. These rules sought to restrict entry to the trade to the sons of miners, and laid down training stages for boys, as did the rules of the Abersychan District in Monmouthshire in 1873.[54] Restriction of output was also widely adopted as a strategy in the 1860s and 1870s by both the Amalgamated Association of Miners and the Miners' National Association, whose President, Alexander MacDonald, was also Secretary to the Scottish Miners' Association.[55] Superficial and fragmentary through such strands are, they suggest the need for Welsh and English historians to dig more deeply into the bases and motivations of miners' union organisation and the underlying causes of industrial conflict in the coalfields.

NOTES AND REFERENCES

1. A full account of trade unionism among the Scottish colliers is provided by the author's, *The Lanarkshire Miners: a social history of their trade unions 1775–1874*, John Donald Edinburgh, 1979.
2. *Parliamentary Debates*, NS, xii, 4 May 1825.
3. The idea of the 'independent collier' is further developed in **A. Campbell** and **F. Reid**, 'The independent collier in Scotland', in R. Harrison (ed.), *Independent Collier*, Harvester, 1978, pp. 54–74. See also Campbell, *Lanarkshire Miners*, Ch. 2.
4. **R. Bald**, *A General View of the Coal Trade of Scotland* Edinburgh 1808, p. 44.
5. *BPP*, 1836, xxxiv, R. C. on State of the Irish Poor in Britain, minutes of evidence, p. 588; *New Statistical Account of Scotland*, Edinburgh 1845, vi, p. 646.
6. *BPP*, 1842, xv, Childrens' Employment Commission, First Report, p. 133.
7. **A. Miller**, *Coatbridge: its rise and progress*, Glasgow 1864, p. 187.
8. Scottish Record Office (SRO), AD14/18/112.
9. SRO, RH 2/4, no. 156.
10. **E. J. Hobsbawm**, *Primitive Rebels*, Manchester U.P. 1971, pp. 150–74.
11. For an account of serfdom see: Campbell, *Lanarkshire Miners*, Ch. 1.
12. Anon. 'Slavery in modern Scotland', *Edinburgh Review*, **189** (Jan. 1899), p. 144.
13. *Glasgow Herald*, 7 Mar. 1825.
14. *BPP*, 1842, xvi, Children's Employment, p. 325.
15. *BPP*, 1825, iv, S.C. on the Combination Laws, p. 634.
16. **H. A. Turner**, *Trade Union Structure and Growth*, Allen & Unwin 1962, p. 51.
17. SRO, JC26/396. 'Articles . . .'.
18. *Glasgow Herald*, 25 Oct. 1824.
19. Ibid. 17 Dec. 1824; *Scotsman*, 12 Nov. 1825.
20. Place MSS. BM Add. MSS. 27, 805, 'Practical uses and remarks on the articles of the operative colliers'.
21. *Glasgow Herald*, 24 Dec. 1824.
22. *BPP*, 1825 on Combination Laws, p. 891.
23. *An address to the colliers of Ayrshire*, Kilmarnock, 1824.
24. *BPP*, 1825, on Combination Laws, pp. 634–5.
25. Ibid.
26. Ibid. p. 642.
27. SRO, RH 2/4, 156.
28. Anon. *Observations on the Laws relating to the Colliers*, Glasgow 1825, p. 4.
29. SRO, RH 2/4, 144.
30. Ibid.
31. Ibid., 145.
32. PRO (H)ome (O)ffice 40/18.
33. SRO, RH 2/4, 147.
34. PRO, HO 40/18.
35. SRO, RH 2/4, 145.

36. Ibid. 146.
37. *Glasgow Herald*, 15 Aug. 1825.
38. Ibid.
39. SRO, RH 2/4, 147.
40. Ibid.
41. *Glasgow Herald*, 31 Oct. 1825.
42. *Scotsman*, 12 Nov. 1825.
43. Ibid. 2 Nov. 1825.
44. *Glasgow Herald*, 14 Apr. 1826.
45. Quoted in *Glasgow Herald*, 12 May 1826.
46. Ibid.
47. *BPP* (1825), on Combination Laws, p. 642.
48. *Glasgow Herald*, 21 Oct. 1826.
49. Ibid. 18 Aug. 1911.
50. Ibid. 16 July 1914.
51. See Campbell, *Lanarkshire Miners*, Ch. 11.
52. **D. J. V. Jones**, *Before Rebecca*, Allen Lane 1973.
53. **J. R. Raynes**, *Coal and its Conflicts*, Ernest Benn 1928,. p. 24.
54. PRO, FS 7.4/172 and 135.
55. **C. Fisher** and **J. Smethurst**, 'War on the Law of Supply and Demand: the Amalgamated Association of Miners and the Forest of Dean Colliers, 1869–1875', in Harrison (ed.), *Independent Collier*, pp. 114–55.

CHAPTER SEVEN
The Democracy of Work, 1820–1850

Clive Behagg

The first half of the nineteenth century witnessed a contest for the control of work between capital and labour and also an extensive and active public debate on the nature of the political order. Historians have become so used to assuming that these were separate issues that it sometimes comes as a surprise to find that, generally speaking, contemporaries did not share this view. To many of them there was a clear and reciprocal relationship between the organisation of work and the organisation of society as a whole. Conventional trade union history has tended to fragment and distort this apparent unity since its concentration on the formal organisations of the trades has consistently undervalued the importance of the more informal kinds of organisation. This, and an emphasis on the dramatic moment of conflict, often means that the day to day structuring of work, where conflict was endemic, has been ignored. As a result the workplace organisation has been frequently seen as the preserve of a small elite of skilled workers whose limited and sectional aims expressed their distance from the universal objectives of a movement like Chartism.[1] This chapter, however, aims to explore the class specific notions of social order which were embedded in labour's attempt to control all aspects of the labour process and the relationship between these configurations and a wider perception of the political ordering of society. I have drawn extensively on examples from the trades of the Birmingham area but since the intention is to introduce a theme of relevance to all areas a range of material has been used where appropriate.

THE ORGANISATION OF WORK

As other studies in this volume demonstrate, the years between 1820 and 1850 saw an escalation in conflict, over a variety of workplace practices, between masters and their workforces in a great range of industries.[2] The issues raised by these multifarious confrontations are not reducible to so many sectional disputes over the distribution of rewards within production (as wages *versus* profits, for example). Rather, the ground which was being contested concerned the issue of autonomy over work itself. The workforce, in their various ways, claimed the right to control the nature and pace of work as it was performed within the workplace. The argument was that the employer had his rightful part to play, but it lay physically outside the workplace. His role was to initiate the process of production and to market the finished product. What came between, the nature and pace of production, was the province of labour to be organised on the basis of a series of agreements within the workgroup involved. These were largely tacit, only rarely being given the status of the written word. Thus, when William Broadhead was asked, later in the century, if 'rattening' was allowed by any rule of the Saw Grinders Society, he responded that it had 'simply been an understanding'.[3] There was much of the same sense of informal agreement in the evidence given to a Royal Commission in 1868, by T. J. Wilkinson, Secretary of the Flint-glass Makers Society. Asked if it was the union rules that regulated the capacity of production he answered, 'I may simply say that the old custom of the trade, independently of the union, before the union came into existence, in a great measure brings about the two moves or journey system, and it regulated a certain amount of produce per turn, that is according to a given time.'[4]

Recently historians have become more aware of non-continuous kinds of organisation at points of conflict. John Rule has drawn attention to what he calls the 'habits of association' within the workforce, which resulted in a 'spectrum of responses with *recurrent* forms linking the ephemeral with the continuous'. Richard Price, in his study of the building trades, argues that even by the middle decades of the nineteenth century it was rather more important for workers to be 'in union' than that they be 'in the union'. David Wilson coined the term '*ad hoc* unionism' to describe the extensive activities of Portsmouth dock workers who lacked formal unions until the late nineteenth century.[5] It is quite clear that this kind of activity formed a large part of the structure of early-nineteenth-century industrial relations. Thomas Winters, corresponding secretary of the National Association of the United Trades, made precisely this point to a Select Committee, in referring to an outbreak of strikes in 1853: 'there were strikes in every town, whether the workmen were in society or out of society. I think there were more strikes among those out of society than among those in society'.[6]

Yet it is not enough to argue that, in order to complete our understanding of trade-based organisations, we need a history of 'informal' or '*ad hoc*' unionism to lay alongside the more accessible history of formal trades' unions which already exist. The missing dimension is far broader than such an analysis would suggest, since both 'formal' and 'informal' modes of organisation were merely the most obvious expression of that whole network of 'understandings' through which labour attempted to organise production. Perhaps the example of Birmingham's heavy steel tool trade, producing a range of workmen's tools, will illustrate this point. In 1810 employers were lobbied by workers in the trade for 'an advance on the price of our work'. There is no evidence to suggest that a trade society existed but a memorial to the employers, which appeared in the local press, was signed by ten workmen 'on behalf of our brother journeymen'.[7] Possibly the lack of formal organisation could be explained by the existence of the Combination Laws yet the memorial itself contravened this legislation since it constituted an action 'in restraint of trade'. In 1825 employers in the trade introduced a system of deducting discount from the prices paid to workers. This was widely resented and gave rise to a protracted strike in 1833.[8] Immediately following this successful action a union was formed. This in itself is a notable sequence of events; the strike creating the union rather than *vice versa*. After two years, however, the union was discontinued. Despite this the prices, reluctantly acceded to by employers in 1833, were still being paid by the middle of the century. In addition labour also clearly had some control over the pace of work since it was customary at this time for the men to play cricket on a Monday afternoon if the weather was fine.[9] Needless to say the weather was not usually a variable factor of production where the labour process was controlled by capital. Yet if labour's ability to control work is to be judged on its ability to create formal organisations then clearly this trade has an unimpressive record since it possessed a trade union for only two years of the first half of the century. In this case, however, we can see a process operating whereby ground gained by an '*ad hoc*' strike was then held through the informal structures of 'understandings' which made up the face-to-face relationship of the work-force at the point of production. It is, however, not unlikely that the historian of conventional trade unionism would select the two-year period of formal organisation as the most significant development in the trades' labour organisation in this period. To the workers involved it must have seemed otherwise.

The British workforce, of course, was used to establishing its own rhythm between work and non-work. 'Saint Monday' was only the most regular of a series of informal holidays.[10] The working week was also broken by a range of collective celebrations; 'foot-ales', apprenticeship rituals, 'marriage ales' or other forms specific to particular trades or localities. As a result the manufacturer invariably found himself in an increasingly competitive economic universe but unable to guarantee output from one week to the next. In Birmingham John Goodman, a gun manufacturer, sub-contracted his work through a plethora of small workshops where traditional work patterns were strong. His workforce produced, in their best week, 1755 guns, but in their worst only 93.[11] Goodman's problem was not only the variation in productive level but also that he did not play a determining role within that fluctuation. Charles Walters, who ran a workshop producing iron screws, revealed similar difficulties with his workforce in a series of letters written to a creditor in the first six months of 1832. His workers clung tenaciously to their 'task oriented' work rhythms which reflected both a weekly and a seasonal irregularity. 'Sunday appears to indispose the people and Monday, being a sort of Saint Holiday – among the working classes of this town Thursday generally arrives before all are capable of moving on – one day is a day of exertions, Friday and the quantity set is exceeded – some steady ones approximate daily – I endeavour to move *en masse*.'[12] In February 1832 he wrote, of a workforce he once referred to as 'riff-raff', that 'Shrove Tuesday broke in upon the "even tenor of their sway" and the march of the 7th Hussars complicated our embarrassment. Four of our hands (females) are induced to enter His Majesty's Service.'[13] Then, in April: 'In consequence of Good Friday being a holiday 533 gross were made . . . 647 should have been . . . This week we commenced working today, Wednesday, Monday and Tuesday being termed "heaving days".'[14] Such was the cost in terms of weekly production that he noted by 1 May that, 'The holidays, I am sorry to observe, have brought us back into the worst times – and a loss of £4 14s 2d.'[15]

The early industrial workforce was accustomed to formulate its own, often unpredictable, work pattern and complemented this by asserting its right to organise work when it did take place. This was done by retaining a traditional system of sub-contracting. As the work of Lazonick on cotton spinning demonstrates, this was as prevalent in the large factories as it was in the small workshops of the period.[16] The terminology used to describe the sub-contracting unit varied; in Birmingham alone they were called 'gangs', 'sets', 'chairs', 'shops' or 'crews' according to the trade, but the mode of operation was universal. The 'gang' produced an article and then 'sold' it to the employer through the intermediary of the skilled worker at its head. Although the gang was a hierarchy its endeavours were collective. One observer in the 1830s found this ethos of mutuality to be strongly expressed among the less skilled in cotton spinning: 'a piecer may be a little indisposed and yet not like to stay away and so lose a half or a quarter of a day; then the others will help him in his work and enable him to get full wages'.[17]

In the metal button trade of Birmingham, work was organised around four processes: cutting and soldering, both carried out by women paid a weekly rate, stamping carried out by men on a higher weekly rate and burnishing, the most skilful operation, carried out by men working by the piece.[18] Button shanking was a separate trade with its own hierarchy. Within the button-making gangs only the burnishers were formally organised and they carried responsibility for the organisation of the work groups. As an observer noted of the horn button trade, 'The manufacturer . . . has merely a nominal control over a large proportion of the persons who work in his establishment. He neither engages them, pays them nor dismisses them. They are the servants of his servants'.[19] Len Smith's work on Kidderminster shows that the carpet trade relied on sub-contract units consisting of weaver, half weaver, drawer (or drawers) and bobbin winder. A Factory Commissioner in 1833 found that workmen often held the keys to their employers' loom shops.[20]

As far as labour was concerned the utility of such a traditional form of sub-contract lay in the fact that the employer was kept away from the product during the process of production. Increased competition, particularly in the 1830s and 1840s, meant, however, that employers were more likely to intervene in the workplace and attempt to introduce, what were referred to at the time as, 'readier methods of working'. These kinds of innovations, including mechanisation, the dilution of skill and the increased division of labour, all pre-supposed that the employer possessed enough authority to introduce them in the first place. In re-organising production such that it served the needs of capital rather than labour the employer found himself confronted by the collective culture of the workplace. It was often the onset of depression which, in this respect, gave him the upper hand, a point made by a Birmingham lamp manufacturer T..C. Salt in 1833:

There are many inferior parts of the work that used to pass through men's hands; we take as much as we can off the men and have it done in parts by the boys or the women and then give it to the men to finish; which when trade was good the men would not submit to . . . formerly when trade was good we did not resort to that screwing system; if we had done so we should not have had a single workman to work for us next day.[21]

A Sheffield workman recalled the case of an employer, 'obliged to leave that town because he substituted a bellows for the ordinary blow-pipe used for soldering. He could do the work much quicker by means of the bellows.'[22] When it was possible the process of innovation was the object of collective resistance involving the wider working community. The same workman recalled that 'In Sheffield I have known the children hoot a workman in the streets who did not belong to the union of his trade.'[23] This seems to suggest a closeness between the formal and informal mechanisms of control within the working class.

Since this was the case it was always likely that the system of subcontracting work would come under pressure in this period. Where possible employers either abolished it or distorted it in ways that fragmented the collective unity of the workforce. This was certainly the case with Joseph Gillott's new large scale steel-pen manufactory. The *Morning Chronicle* investigator was struck when he visited the establishment in 1850 with the absence of sub-contracting, noting that 'There is no sub-employing. Every person is directly hired and paid by the manufacturer', and that consequently 'all the workpeople are directly responsible to the employer'. As a result there was much about the conduct of the workforce that the investigator admired, particularly in the discipline of the unskilled female labour:

Unlike too many of the women employed in the manufactories of Birmingham, they are extremely neat in person and attire . . . There is no talking in the room. The only sounds to be heard are the working hand press and the clinking of the small pieces of metal as they fall from the block into the receptacle prepared for them.[24]

This all contrasted markedly with other establishments where the small gang system held sway and the employer's presence was less in evidence. In Gillott's works the role of the 'ganger' was replaced by a supervisor, in this case an engineer: 'Each division of the workshop is superintended by a tool-maker, whose business it is to keep the punches and presses in good working condition, to superintend the work generally and to keep order among the workpeople.'[25]

In fact the abolition of sub-contract and the gangs, and their replacement with direct employment and a system of paid supervisors, was an unusual achievement. Working people clung tenaciously to the traditional system, despite all the pressure, but in the process the system underwent profound changes. The attempts that have recently been made to focus on continuities in work structures throughout the nineteenth century have led some historians to underestimate the significance of these changes.[26] The working-class perception of the 'gang' or 'set' was of a small group of perhaps half a dozen people at the most. The 'chair' of the glass trade (workman, servitor, footmaker and taker-in) seems fairly typical in this respect.[27] The smallness of the group tied the skilled to the unskilled in a direct way. This might facilitate a promotional scale within the group or enable a family to work together. As far as the employer was concerned, however, the larger the gang the better. Skilled work remained an essential element of production throughout the period, of course, but a larger gang increased the supervisory role of skilled labour and its social distance from the unskilled.

The brass lamp trade, in Birmingham in the middle of the century, illustrates the complex of variables involved in the organisation of work. One worker in the trade spoke of the traditional workgroup: 'The wages of the piece-workman differ according to his ability, and to the number of men or boys working under him. A workman has ordinarily from three to six persons working under him called his "crew". By the aid of his crew he may earn from 35s to £2 a week.'[28] The same workman also observed that in his trade, 'There are some manufactories in the town where the crew or gang system is not admitted.'[29] Some manufacturers, however, found the system of sub-contract a useful artifice of management, but their projection was of a larger gang and greater rewards for the ganger. One employer in the trade explained how this operated in his firm:

The 'gang' system . . . is the only one which can be satisfactorily adopted in a large establishment, because of the infinite variety of work required to make a lamp. There may, for instance, be a score of men occupied upon different parts of one lamp burner, and these being placed under one person the work is greatly facilitated . . . The heads of the gangs make from £2 to £3 per week. One man in our employ has invested his savings so well that he is the owner of eleven small houses.[30]

Thus in one trade in one town there were three different forms of work organisation in existence; the traditional and worker-favoured small gang, the employer-favoured large gang, and the direct supervision of work where gangs were abolished. A worker in the brass-thimble trade made a similar point:

> The proportion of men varies *according to the manner in which the manufactory is conducted.* In some cases the men are said to number one-third of the whole, and in others it is stated that men are only employed as tool-makers, and to superintend in the workshops in the same manner as in the principle steel pen and Florentine button manufactories.[31]

The organisation of work, as this statement suggests, varied from factory to factory and workshop to workshop, reflecting the extent to which small groups of workers were able to enforce a collective view of how production should operate. The Chartist John Mason called upon 'the working men of all trades to combine to secure proper and just protection for labour generally and to protect those employers who, in the legitimate pursuit of trade, acted honourably, equally to the interests of other employers and to his workmen'.[32] The *Pioneer* advocated that those employers who operated in the approved fashion be initiated into the unions being set up in the early 1830s, as an expression of their role in the organic community of work.[33] During a prolonged strike in 1828 the carpet weavers of Kidderminster advertised in the local press for employers who were willing to accept a labour-oriented concept of production and to invest their capital in the trade.[34] To the workers who experienced the process of innovation there was nothing fixed or inevitable about the changes taking place. Whatever might be said about the logic of the market or the laws of political economy, work was re-organised because manufacturers took particular decisions on how they wished to operate and utilised the moment to re-structure the labour process to their own advantage.

THE WORKPLACE AND NOTIONS OF SOCIAL ORDER

As I have argued elsewhere, the emergence of particular rituals within the burgeoning workplace organisations of the 1830s reflected labour's claim to control production.[35] Initiation ceremonies and trade funerals expressed the separate and distinct nature of the working community and in so doing reinforced the territorial imperatives of the workplace as that community perceived them. Within the territorial control of the workplace labour organised itself in ways that reflected a very particular perception of social order and political form. Put simply this organisation (both formal structures and informal 'understandings') stressed the obligations which membership of the group imposed upon the individual rather than asserting the freedom of the individual to act, without restraint, according to conscience or pocket. Within these constraints, and in large part because of them, discussion, access and participation were vital components in these organisational forms. A customary work pattern could only operate successfully if everybody participated and if it could be clearly demonstrated that the pattern reflected the wish of the work group as a whole. This can be seen most obviously in the relatively few written rules of formal trades' unions which were drawn up in the period. These carefully protected the process of debate. The stone masons fined men 1d. if, when they spoke at meetings, they did not address the President as 'Worthy President' and fellow masons as 'brother'.[36] In the Lancaster Associated Coal Miners only the President was allowed to keep his hat on during meetings, while the carpenters stipulated that 'no member be allowed to speak twice on one subject except the proposer and seconder of the motion who will be allowed to reply'.[37] These kinds of provisions, and the rotation of executive posts throughout the membership, are familiar enough to trade union historians.[38] Some have been moved to describe this kind of approach as a 'primitive democracy' a rather condescending term which implies a linear development from these forms to the more 'sophisticated' represen-tational structures of later unions.[39] In fact these early-nineteenth-century formal practices were part of a broader notion of partici-patory democracy that was reproduced wherever labour organised to control its own environment. In 1832 one Lancashire manufac-turer complained to Nassau Senior that: 'One of the last strikes was among the piecers, boys from nine to twelve years old. They elected their delegates and President, held their meetings under a gas lamp, stopped the work of their parents by refusing their services and succeeded in their object.'[40] Similarly, in 1844 the *Birmingham Journal* reported on a strike by a small group of workers in the shoe trade:

It appeared that four or five weeks ago forty or fifty shoemakers took an empty house in Pinfold Street where they commenced meeting every other day to regulate what they termed their trade affairs. They elected a President and moved resolutions to the effect that there should be a turn out and strike for higher wages.[41]

In both of these cases groups of workers, organising to take advan-tage of a specific moment, sought to legitimise their demands by a transitory formalism which embraced a clear democratic form.

The same principle operated through the workplace courts of justice whereby workers with a grievance against fellow workers had the right to be heard by the work-group as a whole. Lovett's experience in London is probably the best known example of this, but James Hopkinson, working in the Nottingham cabinet trade in the 1830s, confirms the detail presented by Lovett. Such activities, since they involved the cessation of work and heavy drinking, at once assumed labour's control of work and protected the collectivity by which it was legitimised. Hopkinson suggests that his employer did not object to such trials interrupting the flow of work since 'in our shop the men worked piece-work and not by the day so that the master did not mind so much about it'. He adds as an afterthought however, 'they were such an independent lot of men that they would not have cared much if he had'.[42] This workplace system of justice implies that the lore of the shop might support what the law of the land condemned. It was for this reason that the Barnsley linen-weavers spoke of 'loom law' which they considered more binding in certain respects than statute law.[43] Yet as Pollard's work on Sheffield and Price's work on the brickmakers suggest, violence to the deviant was generally the last resort within a system which stressed public accountability and debate.[44]

Wherever workers organised to control the labour process they referred to an ethic of social responsibility that was clearly antithetical to liberal notions of personal freedom. Violence to the 'knobstick' and the 'secret' ceremonial form marked the paranoid outer-boundary of middle-class sympathy with the working community. Nowhere is this better expressed than in Elizabeth Gaskell's *Mary Barton*. Here John Barton, formerly a paragon of all the working-class virtues admired by Gaskell, is led to an act of cold-blooded murder following an oath-taking ritual. The message is clear; where the freewill of the rational individual is subsumed within the collective identity of the trade association, morality is likely to be threatened. In fact, wherever labour organised its own environment middle-class observers invariably recognised this threat to morality and the economic order in some form. One Birmingham manufacturer interviewed in 1851 saw this entirely in terms of work control: 'there are many trades in which the workmen are very intemperate. These are principally the trades in which the work is given out, and no regular factory discipline is observed.'[45] As the employers of striking locksmiths· put it in 1835, 'they want to get as much money in three days as will support their families and supply them to get drunk and attend men fights, dog fights, etc., the other three days of the week'.[46]

There was, of course, more to this kind of criticism than a simple re-affirmation of the doctrine of original sin. Capital's claim that it should rightly control the labour process was partly the argument of the market: that economic survival in a competitive world was contingent upon innovation carried through by those who appreciated the complexities of credit and marketing in the real world. 'I never see my tall chimney with its full and curling volume', argued one manufacturer in 1831, 'without thinking of the industry it betokens – of the wages it raises for my forty pairs of hands and of the comforts it diffuses amongst the families of my workpeople'.[47] Such logic was transmitted through dominant property relations: that the employer owned the means of production and therefore should determine their use. Yet the equation between public and private interests, which validated the employer's autonomy over work, depended on a notion of representation that was qualitatively different to that reproduced through the workplace organisations of the day. In place of the participatory forms of the working class, employers offered a bourgeois democracy with representation qualified by property. The employers' control of work would, in this sense, reflect the dimensions of the political world as defined by the Reform Act and the Municipal Corporations Act. The structures which working people established between themselves, both the formal trade societies and the informal 'understandings' of the workplace, threatened this whole rationale because they acted through an alternative projection of the social and political order.

Much of this can be seen in the critique of workplace organisations offered by outsiders to the working community in this period. Sir Archibald Alison, Sheriff of Glasgow, commenting on the spinners' associations of the 1830s, declared them to be 'an example of democratic ambition on a large scale'. In a powerful association of ideas he declared that among the Glasgow spinners, 'a committee for assassination was appointed by universal suffrage'.[48] Factory Commissioner E. C. Tufnell was equally succinct in his review of workplace organisations: 'Were we asked to give a definition of a trades union', he wrote, 'we should say that it was a society whose constitution is the worst of democracies – where power is based on outrage, – whose practice is tyranny – and whose end is self destruction.'[49] In much the same vein the *Birmingham Advertiser* commented on the shoemakers' practice of stationing a man outside shops working below the price to note the names of men reporting to work: 'Here is an enemy secretly and silently at work undermining the dearest right of the whole community and bending our best interests to suit the convenience of a set of democratical tyrants.'[50]

These were the key anti-union images of the period: their existence represented 'democratic ambition', their organisations were 'the worst of democracies' and their organisers, 'democratical tyrants'. What comes across strongly here is not simply that the demands of workplace organisations were considered to be unreasonable because they flew in the face of market logic, but rather that the demands had no legitimacy because they stemmed from organisations based upon illegitimate notions of representation. Sir David Sandford, who had been an active supporter of the Reform Bill, put forward a widely held view of the unions in 1834: 'This I cannot avoid designating as the tyranny of the multitude: and that man is ill versed who does not hold the tyranny of the many to be equally hateful with the tyranny of the few'.[51] Writers addressing the issue of trades unions in *Blackwood's Magazine* referred, in 1834, to 'a tyranny of numbers'[52] and, in 1838 to the 'unrestrained and irresistible tyranny of the majority'.[53] During a trial of striking glassworkers in 1848 Birmingham magistrate and manufacturer Charles Geach argued the reverse case, based on the same concept of illegitimacy. 'It was not even, in many cases, the tyranny of the many over the few', he explained to a courtroom packed with union members, 'it was, from their peculiar organisation, the tyranny of the few over the many.'[54]

To the middle-class observer these workplace organisations were living proofs of the impracticality of a more extensive representation than that achieved in 1832. The apparent ambiguity over whether they embraced the 'tyranny of the few' or the 'tyranny of the many' was actually a dispute of degree, rather than kind, which, in itself, echoed Burke's classic attack on representation by right: 'In this political traffick the leaders will be obliged to bow to the ignorance of their followers and the followers become subservient to the worst designs of their leaders.'[55]

CONCLUSION

Labour's attempt to control production in this period clearly cannot be reduced to a crude head count of formal organisations. The time has probably come to stop thinking of workplace organisation as the occasional characteristic of certain aristocratic groups of craft workers. It is more constructive to think in terms of a continuous process involving a network of tacit agreements on workplace procedures, based on common assumptions and deeply embedded at all levels of the working community. These procedures operated, with varying degrees of effectiveness, to enhance labour's control of work and occasionally they were formalised. Unfortunately historians have often taken these comparatively rare occasions of formalism in this period and called them, effectively, the 'history of early nineteenth century trade unions'. They then ask subsidiary questions, for example, 'how does the "history of trade unionism" relate to the "history of Chartism"?'. The search for formal links between the two has never been particularly rewarding and this fact has informed a series of interpretations which cast doubt on the class consciousness of Chartist and trade unionist alike.[56] Yet when the working people of Birmingham contributed extensively to the Chartist National Rent in 1839 they did not, in the main, do so through identifiable trade societies. Rather they contributed politically as they acted industrially, through the informal organisation of the work group. Thus the list includes (to name but a few typical entries): 'Workmen of Mr. Griffiths, £2'; 'Messrs Perton and Sabins workmen, Caroline St, 15s'; 'Ladies clog makers, Park St, 10s'; 'A penny subscription, Mr. Ratcliffes workmen, 5s 10d'; 'Mr. Edwards and shopmates, 10s'; 'Journeymen and assistants of Messrs Gilberts platers, £1 13s 11d'; 'George Pitt, plasterer and shopmates, 17s'; 'Workmen of Mr. Thomas Smith, Holloway Head, 10s 2d'.[57]

This may not be the spectacular demonstration of solidarity between formal and continuous organisations which has often been held to be the measure of class awareness. Yet there is still an important relationship here between the way the working community organised itself at the point of production and the way it thought politically. Exploration of, not only the moment of confrontation, but also the less dramatic yet no less significant day-to-day construction of work, will give us the broader view that was apparent at the time. Strikes may have been specifically about hours, wages, apprenticeship, or a host of other concerns, but what is more important, and most frequently lost from sight, is the perception of the social order which enabled labour to confront capital and the State on any of these issues. Contemporary critics were aware that the construction of personal liberties, which workplace organisations represented, was at odds with the dominant liberal orthodoxy. There is a clear resonance between the workplace as a democratic forum, the 'worst of democracies' as critics would insist, and a political vision with an emphasis on participation and accountability brought about by universal suffrage and annual Parliaments.

NOTES AND REFERENCES

1. This approach has a long pedigree. See particularly **A. E. Musson**, *British Trade Unions 1800–1875*, Macmillan 1972, 'Class struggle and the labour aristocracy 1830–60', *Social History*, 3 (Oct. 1976); **M. I. Thomis**, *The Luddites*, Schockes, New York 1972; *The Town Labourer*, Batsford 1974. The issue is discussed in **F. K. Donnelly**, 'Ideology and early English working class history: Edward Thompson and his critics', *Social History*, II (May 1967). Most recent re-working of the theme is **C. Calhoun**, *The Question of Class Struggle*, Blackwell 1982. Recent work on the labour process has stressed the distance of the artisan from the rest of the working community. See, for example, **W. Lazonick**, 'Industrial relations and technical change: the case of the self-acting mule', *Camb. Jn. of Economics*, vol. 3, no. 3 (1979); the same, to some extent, is true even of the most sympathetic treatment of the artisan in **I. Prothero**, *Artisans and Politics in Early Nineteenth Century London*, Dawson 1979.
2. See also **C. Behagg**, 'Custom, class and change; the trade societies of Birmingham', *Social History*, 4, 3 (October 1979).
3. **S. Pollard**, *The Sheffield Outrages*, Eyre and Spottiswoode 1971, XXII.
4. *BPP, Royal Commission on the Organisation and Rules of Trades Unions*, 1867–68 (3952) XXXII, Q18,706.
5. **J. Rule**, *The Experience of Labour in the Eighteenth Century Workplace*, Croom Helm 1981, p. 151; **R. Price**, *Masters, Unions and Men*, Cambridge U.P., 1980, 54–79; **D. Wilson**, 'Government Dock-yard Workers in Portsmouth (Ph.D. thesis, University of Warwick 1975), 314–317.
6. *BPP, Report from Select Committee on Masters and Operatives (Equitable Councils of Conciliation)*, 1856 (343) XIII, 498.
7. *Aris's Birmingham Gazette*, 14 May 1810.
8. *Birmingham Journal*, 23 Nov. 1833.
9. *Morning Chronicle*, 20 Jan. 1851.
10. See **D. A. Reid**, 'The decline of Saint Monday', *Past and Present*, **71** (May 1976).
11. *BPP*, Report of Select Committee on the Manufacture of Small Arms, 1854 (12), XVIII, Q3473.
12. Walters to Musgrave, GRO, 7 February 1832. The problems of the small producer and the imperatives to innovate are discussed more fully in **C. Behagg**, 'Masters and manufacturers: social values and the smaller unit of production in Birmingham 1800–50' in **G. Crossick** and **H. G. Haupt** (eds), *Shopkeepers and Master Artisans in Nineteenth Century Europe*, Methuen 1984.

13. Walters to Musgrave, 13 March 1832.
14. Ibid., 25 April 1832.
15. Ibid., 1 May 1832.
16. Lazonick, 'Industrial relations'; Lazonick, 'Production relations, labor productivity and choice of technique; British and U.S. cotton spinning', *Jn. Econ. History*, XLI, **3** (Sept. 1981).
17. *BPP, First Report of the Central Board of His Majesty's Commissioners for Inquiring into the Employment of Children in Factories*, 1833 (450) XX, Evidence of John Redman, D1, 46.
18. *Morning Chronicle*, 21 Oct. 1850.
19. Ibid.
20. **L. Smith**, *The Carpet Weavers of Kidderminster 1800–1850*, (Ph.D. thesis, University of Birmingham 1982), 225–7.
21. *BPP, Report from the Select Committee on Manufactures, Commerce and Shipping in the United Kingdom*, 1833 (690) VI, QQ4564, 4565.
22. *Morning Chronicle*, 20 Jan. 1831.
23. Ibid.
24. *Morning Chronicle*, 16 Dec. 1850.
25. Ibid.
26. Price has recently argued that the continuity of sub-contract has been over-estimated, **R. Price**, 'Theories of labor process formation', *Jn. Soc. Hist.* (Fall 1984), p. 101. He particularly cites the work of Littler in this respect, e.g. **C. Littler**, 'Deskilling and changing structures of control', in **S. Wood** (ed.), *The Degradation of Work?*, Hutchinson 1982.
27. See **T. Matsumura**, 'The Flint-Glass Makers in the Classic Age of the Labour Aristocracy, 1850–1880, with Special Reference to Stourbridge' (Ph.D. thesis, University of Warwick, 1976).
28. *Morning Chronicle*, 6 Jan. 1851.
29. Ibid.
30. Ibid.
31. *Morning Chronicle*, 13 Jan. 1851 (my italics).
32. *Northern Star*, 1 Mar. 1845.
33. *Pioneer*, 21 Sept. 1833.
34. Smith, *Carpet Weavers*.
35. **C. Behagg**, 'Secrecy, ritual and folk violence: the opacity of the workplace in the first half of the nineteenth century', in **R. Storch** (ed.), *Popular Culture and Custom in Nineteenth Century England*, Croom Helm 1982.
36. 'Byelaws to be strictly observed by the Operative Stone Masons', MSS, Modern Records Centre, University of Warwick.
37. 'Report on Combinations by Nassau Senior Esq. and Thomas Tomlinson Esq.', HO 44/56; *Bye Laws for the Government of the Operative Carpenters and Joiners Society of Birmingham*, Birmingham 1833.
38. For example, **H. A. Turner**, *Trade Union Growth, Structure and Policy: a comparative study of the cotton unions*, Allen and Unwin, 1962, pp. 87–9.
39. Matsumura, 'The Flint-Glass Makers'.; PHJH. Gosden, *Friendly Societies in England 1815–1875*, Manchester U.P. 1961, p. 7.
40. 'Report on Combinations', *op.cit.*
41. *Birmingham Journal*, 23 Nov. 1844.

42. **J. Hopkinson**, *A Victorian Cabinet Maker*, Routledge and Kegan Paul 1980.

43. **F. J. Kaijage**, 'Labouring Barnsley 1816–56' (Ph.D. thesis, University of Warwick 1975).

44. **S. Pollard**, 'The ethics of the Sheffield outrages', *Trans. Hunter Arch. Soc.*, VII, **3** (1954); **R. Price**, 'The other face of respectability: violence in the Manchester brick making trade 1859–70', *Past and Present*, **38** (Dec. 1967).

45. *Morning Chronicle*, 6 Jan. 1851.

46. *Aris's Birmingham Gazette*, 27 Apr. 1835.

47. Ibid., 11 July 1831.

48. **Sir A. Alison**, *Some Account of My Life and Writings*, Edinburgh 1883, p. 350.

49. **E. C. Tufnell**, *Character, Objects and Effects of Trades Unions: with some remarks on the law concerning them*, London 1834, p. 125.

50. *Birmingham Advertiser*, 20 Feb. 1834.

51. *Blackwood's Magazine*, Mar. 1834.

52. Ibid.

53. *Blackwood's Magazine*, Mar. 1838.

54. *Birmingham Journal*, 24 June 1848.

55. **E. Burke**, *Reflections on the Revolution in France*, Penguin, Harmondsworth 1983, pp. 128–9.

56. For the most productive attempt to link the two organisations see **R. Sykes**, 'Early Chartism and trade unionism in south-east Lancashire', in **J. Epstein** and **D. Thompson**, *The Chartist Experience*, Macmillan 1982.

57. *Birmingham Journal*, 2, 16, and 23 Feb.; 2 and 25 Mar. 1839.

CHAPTER EIGHT

Trade Unionism and Class Consciousness: the 'Revolutionary' Period of General Unionism, 1829–1834

Robert Sykes

INTRODUCTION

A relatively short period at the onset of the 1830s has frequently been seen as a crucial one in the development of class consciousness. The centrally important factor was obviously the Reform Crisis of 1830–32. However, in rural England this was also the time of the Swing Riots. In the manufacturing districts there was not only a surge of industrial conflict, but also new national unions of individual trades and general unions combining diverse occupations. In their pioneering history of trade unionism, the Webbs designated the time from 1829 to 1842 as the 'revolutionary period', and overwhelmingly concentrated upon the particularly eventful years from 1829 to 1834.[1] The main contours of developments from 1829, and the beginnings of the Lancashire based general union, the National Association for the Protection of Labour (NAPL), continuing with the emergence of the national Operative Builders' Union and general unions in Yorkshire, and culminating in the Grand National Consolidated Trades' Union (GNCTU) of 1834 were subsequently mapped out by G. D. H. Cole.[2] Several early labour historians placed great emphasis upon the involvement of Robert Owen as indicating the importance of socialist and syndicalist influence in a particularly heroic phase of trade union history.[3]

Of course this same period is the terminal point of Edward Thompson's seminal work, the *Making of the English Working Class*. For Thompson, the working-class consciousness which blossoms at this point was, in large part, the culmination of a long process of political struggle given new and precise definition by the franchise set by the 1832 Reform Act. Yet in demonstrating a 'consciousness of the identity of interests between working men of the most diverse occupations', and indeed in illustrating the existence of class-conscious alternatives to the prevailing social system, the general unionism of the early 1830s is ascribed an absolutely vital role.[4] Owenite involvement in this general unionism has also continued to be the critical element underpinning the grander claims about the influence of Owenite Socialism on the working-class movement in especially 1833–34.[5] This apparent phenomenon of a burst of working-class political action during the Reform Crisis of 1830–32 being succeeded, after disillusionment with the Reform Act set in, by a swing towards industrial and even syndicalist action, has generated a debate about pendulum swings in working-class political and economic action.[6] A legacy of the pioneering interpretations has been a continued tendency to view the ostensible interest in Owenism and syndicalist tactics as representing an albeit temporary shift in popular attitudes away from constitutional radicalism towards a more specifically working-class ideological standpoint. In his innovative and controversial study, John Foster has also envisaged a dramatic transition from 'trade union to class consciousness' in his case-study town of Oldham, at the onset of the 1830s, and presented an 1834 general strike in the town as the critical evidence to support this claim.[7]

On the other hand, some important revisionary work has certainly undermined some of the earlier grandiose claims about the scale of the GNCTU.[8] Likewise the very detailed biography of the Lancashire labour leader, John Doherty, whilst showing the relative importance of the NAPL compared with the better known but certainly more ephemeral GNCTU, has also tended to play down the scale, novelty and significance of general unionism. Professor Musson has indeed generally emphasised the importance of the continuities in trade-union history at this time, and insisted on the essential separation of the strands of working-class political and economic action.[9] The events of these few years certainly raise vital questions of theory and evidence about the nature of the interplay between consciousness, experience, ideology and tactics. This study is rooted in the evidence of one region, for only such a local perspective reveals the interactions between diverse movements, trades and ideological perspectives, which are of crucial importance in an understanding of the development of class consciousness at this time. However, it is concerned with a region, the cotton district of the North–west, which is probably more important than any other both in the developments considered and the studies which are reassessed. It is certainly hoped that the ensuing discussion of firstly the NAPL and its impact on developments in 1829–32, secondly the influence of Owenism and the various events of 1833–34, and finally the importance of the overall experience of conflict in the 1829–34 period does raise issues of more than local significance.

THE NATIONAL ASSOCIATION FOR THE PROTECTION OF LABOUR, 1829–32

The NAPL originated in Manchester in later 1829.[10] It spread first to the neighbouring cotton towns in early 1830, and subsequently extended elsewhere in the manufacturing areas, especially in the East Midlands. The basic aim was to raise a fund which could be drawn upon by its constituent unions to resist wage reductions. The strength of the association, as measured by weekly subscriptions, peaked in the late autumn of 1830, when membership claims of 60,000 then 80,000 were quite compatible with the extant accounts. Early in 1831 confidence was badly damaged when some funds were embezzled and subsequently local branches retained their own funds, an arrangement which hindered effective co-ordination. In fact the funds were never used for the purpose originally intended, because at no one time was the £3000 deemed necessary before operations could begin, available for use. The subscriptions began to lapse because of union defeats in strikes, in which the NAPL was damagingly only involved informally, attempting to raise money by ad hoc appeals alongside the regular subscriptions. As disillusion set in, the very fall-off in contributions ensured that a large enough fund to begin formal operations was never built up. In the autumn of 1831, when the association's newspaper, the *Voice of the People*, ceased publication, and the key organiser, John Doherty, resigned, most of the remaining energy went out of the association, An attempt by the Manchester committee to revive it in the spring of 1832 came to nothing and it subsequently disintegrated totally.

Nevertheless the NAPL had lasted much longer than the more famous GNCTU, had a larger paying membership, developed a firmer organisational structure and in many respects achieved a broader coverage in terms of different trades and geographical extent. What then were the forces and rationale behind arguably the most impressive exercise in inter-trade co-operation in the first half of the nineteenth century? Firstly it is very clear that the NAPL, and indeed the other general unions, can only be satisfactorily explained if placed in the context of the longer tradition of formal and informal inter-trade co-operation, in particular crises and key strikes.[11] Secondly the NAPL was firmly rooted in the everyday economic experience of the textile workers and was not the result of extraneous ideological influence. It arose directly out of the failure of the 1829 Manchester spinners' strike. The fate which befell even the well-organised spinners was held to prove the inability of any one trade to prevent wage reductions. Hence there was a need for a more general union to prevent reductions spreading from firm to firm, town to town and trade to trade, ultimately reducing all to the deplorable condition of the hand-loom weavers.[12]

The NAPL plan gained such a ready acceptance precisely because the analytical premises upon which it was based were so familiar to local textile workers. There was a widespread belief that excessive domestic competition was producing systematic exploitation. 'It is a uniform system; not something uncertain, accidental, temporary and unavoidable; it is what it is most appropriately termed – a "system" and a *grinding* system.'[13] This whole analysis underpinned the hand-loom weavers' proposals for Boards of Trade to equalise and fix piece rates, the constant stress in spinners' strikes for an equalisation of wage rates between different machines, firms and towns, the stress on the need to limit and equalise working hours in the factory movement and the general attachment to 'standard' lists of piece rates. The NAPL was intended to concentrate resources on preventing the initial reduction and to be large enough to sustain opposition to combinations of employers. In textiles, conflict very frequently crystallised over piece-rate reductions, even when on closer examination other issues concerning de-skilling, control over the labour process and intensification of labour emerge as powerful, underlying animating forces. The NAPL was essentially the product of the experience of workers in an industrial sector where intensive domestic competition, fear of foreign competition in vital export markets, declining profit margins and constant technological innovation had produced a downward spiral of piece rates.[14]

In origin, and in basic aim and ideology throughout, the NAPL was definitely not an Owenite union, and nor did Doherty 'really become a convinced Owenite'.[15] Even the understanding of competition as a systematic phenomenon, often regarded as an innovative contribution of Owenism, more obviously drew upon everyday experience in the workplace. The manner in which the hostility to capitalist competition did not absorb the Owenite communitarian ideals of a co-operative re-organisation of society ensured that it did not take on a quasi-socialist form. The popular analysis was in a sense more limited, concentrating upon the more bread and butter issues of defending workers against excessive competition. But it was also more class conscious than mainstream Owenism, which laid persistent emphasis on a rationalist strategy of attempting to enlighten and unite all classes. The whole point of the NAPL was to make workers strong enough to *beat* the masters. As befitted an organisation constantly beset by lock-outs, bitter strikes and middle-class opposition, the association was demonstrably infused with a spirit of fierce working–class independence.

The particular aims and strategy of the NAPL conditioned the pattern of membership in ways which the main historians of the association do not mention. In consequence they perhaps overstate the significance of sectional feeling, which they present as the reason for trades not joining, as a limitation on class solidarity. Kirby and Musson's painstaking calculations from the extant accounts (£3067 recorded, out of which the trade is specified for £1667) reveal that the cotton spinners and calico printers were the largest contributors. They subscribed £252 each, which together amounted to 30 per cent of the total subscriptions for which the trade was specified. But Kirby and Musson also very plausibly infer that, in fact, the Rochdale flannel weavers actually subscribed even more.[16] Kirby and Musson certainly note the general predominance of the textile trades and the combination of both factory and out-workers. But they cloud the issue by using the category of 'hand-workers', in which they include the calico printers who worked at the heart of large factories, and by laying too much stress on the involvement of declining out-workers. The spinners and calico printers were the two most numerous and economically important *adult male* factory trades, and in addition no significant *adult* factory trade was missing from the accounts.

Kirby and Musson's explanation of the absence of other skilled trades in terms of aloof sectionalism is certainly convincing for a small, truly aristocratic grouping of trades, headed by the letter press printers (who did not participate in any part of the scheme.)[17] However there is evidence of real interest from Kirby and Musson's other example of aloof workers, the engineers. Delegates from the ironfounders, millwrights, machine makers, whitesmiths and brass moulders attended the inaugural meeting about the general union. The total subscription of textile machine makers was quite appreciable (£67), and other metal-working trades are known to have joined.[18] Given the still fairly limited numbers of engineers, the nascent state of their unions and the fact that ultimately there was little for them in an association intended only to fight reductions, the scale of their involvement was quite significant. Moreover intrinsic, aloof sectionalism hardly explains the relatively weak contribution of the lower paid builders, tailors and shoemakers (who all subscribed much less than the engineers), and who in fact dominated the general union movements of 1833–34. Kirby and Musson's interpretation places too much explanatory stress on implied, deep-seated divisions in class situation and attitudes within the mainstream of the working class. In fact the NAPL, designed only to prevent wage reductions, had a limited attraction for many trades for very practical reasons. In many of the largest artisan trades, which remained overwhelmingly unmechanised and orientated towards the domestic market, wage reductions were frequently not the critical issues. Instead conflict often focused more upon economic re-organisation (as in worker opposition to the rise of general contracting in building and increased out-work in tailoring), division of labour, defence of customary practices, control over the labour process, and apprenticeships. In addition the timing of the NAPL, which emerged in a trade slump, further limited its attraction for artisan trades. They tended to restrict their more ambitious exercises in trade unionism to boom periods. It was significant that in the clothing sector, it was not the rather weaker shoemakers and tailors, but the more advantaged hatters, who participated most strongly in the NAPL (subscribing £61, the highest total of any single, non-textile trade). For the hatters, in 1830, experienced precisely the process of reductions spreading from area to area, which the NAPL was designed to prevent.[19] It was the relevance of the NAPL to the precise economic needs of individual trades, which most satisfactorily explains its pattern of membership and not the existence of widespread feelings of excessive sectionalism. As was to be the case in the pattern of trades involving themselves in Chartist activities, there were only a small number of truly 'aristocratic', aloof trades.[20]

In two important cases, the Lancashire miners and the involvement of Yorkshire, Kirby and Musson have also been rather too ready to underplay their contribution on the basis of subscription statistics alone, when other evidence does indicate a positive commitment.[21] For example, a delegate conference of miners from throughout the North-west explicitly declared in favour of alignment with the NAPL.[22] In any case the low level of known subscriptions by the miners can be explained in terms other than hesitancy about general union. For the Lancashire union was possibly only formed in early 1830, resources were instantly needed for a strike for advances (for which the NAPL rules forbade help), and in early 1831 for a life and death struggle to preserve the union, after which it was smashed.[23] In general, from the early spring of 1831, when local districts began to retain their own funds, the published central accounts became decidedly unreliable as a guide to membership trends. There are certainly solid indications that in the final stages Yorkshire played a much more important role than is indicated by its meagre contributions to the central accounts.[24] Indeed this whole issue can be taken further to raise broader questions about the meaning and significance of 'membership' in early labour movements. For Oliver has also used the fragmentary extant accounts to belittle the GNCTU to perhaps too great an extent.[25]

At this time unions were frequently episodic formalisations of pre-existing informal practices. In key confrontations the numbers taking action were frequently vastly larger than those known to be long-term subscribers to formal trade societies. Solidarity with regard to general unionism needs to be placed more in this context. Evidence other than proven subscriptions should not be assumed to pale into complete insignificance in the cold analytical glare of the historian as compared with more tangible financial accounts. Most early labour organisations existed in a perpetual financial crisis. An approach which insists upon reducing the significance of such movements to the level of their formal organisation risks missing so much of what actually made them so important at the time. On the other hand, figures of subscriptions do demonstrate the failure of the NAPL, the GNCTU and indeed the later Chartist organisation, the National Charter Association, to operate according to their original, ambitious intentions. They do illustrate the huge problems encountered when poorly and irregularly paid workers attempted to sustain formal organisations ambitiously seeking a national coverage. For they were necessarily distanced from the community and workplace, where informal networks of solidarity so powerfully reinforced collective working-class action.

Nevertheless the NAPL had a major impact on provincial trade unionism, stimulating surges of unionisation in the East Midlands and Potteries especially, and being more important in inspiring inter-trade co-operation in Yorkshire than has previously been acknowledged.[26] In Glasgow, also, an inter-trade organisation emerged and it was said that in all matters the example of Manchester should be followed.[27] In the cotton district the NAPL did, for a time, encom-

pass all the major, organised textile trades. It took pride in stimulating organisation in previously unorganised trades.[28] It also
generated very significant support amongst those non–textile trades,
where its particular structure and strategy had economic relevance.
Its journals popularised the trade union reasoning, which underpinned working class rejection of middle-class forms of political
economy in the 1830s and 1840s.[29] There was very real alarm
amongst local employers, the middle-class press, and the local and
national authorities.[30] The association was indeed constantly
presented by its leaders in class terms, and as having the ultimate
aim of uniting the entire working class. This was true at the start,
and even more so later on when there was talk of uniting all
working-class societies into 'one grand and stupendous aggregate'
and of uniting 'all Trade, Benefit, and Co-operative Societies, and
Political Unions, in one great cause, and as one Society'.[31] The
NAPL simply as a general union was not unprecedented, but in size,
geographical extent, duration, sophistication, ambitions and class
outlook, it did represent much that was new. It was not merely a
stage in an unchanging tradition of inter-trade co-operation. It both
signified and in turn helped to generate a heightened degree of
working-class consciousness.

However, the political implications of this development were
limited and structured by external factors. Neither the NAPL, nor
the economic reasoning on which it was based, became the basis for
a more distinctly proletarian programme of political action. The
cotton district was probably the most important centre of working-
class opposition to the Reform Bill.[32] However, those radicals
actively campaigning against the Bill were mostly hand-loom
weavers, with minimal connections with the NAPL. Their rhetoric
and strategy revealed no new, more economic or more sophisticated
analysis of society. Instead their motivation arose from a rigorous
attachment to a tradition of ultra-radical independence stretching
back to 1819 and beyond, and from loyalty to Henry Hunt, who
became the national figurehead of radical opposition to the Bill. The
NAPL's journal supported the Reform Bill as a first step, and the
association's central committee specifically endorsed this position.[33]
The attempts by the Huntites in Lancashire to generate a national
campaign for universal suffrage, in explicit hostility to the Bill,
floundered badly. The very structure of the political debate in the
Reform Crisis left no real room for a plausible, but distinctly
working-class political stategy. The choice in terms of practical
politics was ultimately between the Bill and the boroughmongers.

The events of the Reform Crisis period in fact illustrated the importance of the national political framework in conditioning the forms
of working-class political action, irrespective of developments in the
economic sphere.

OWENISM, GENERAL UNIONISM 1832–4 AND THE OLDHAM GENERAL STRIKE OF 1834

The five years from 1829 to 1834 are also the time when it has been
claimed that the working-class movement was 'dominated by
Owenite theories', with a climax being reached in 1834, when
'Owen was for a few months at the head of a great national federation of trade unions and was the acknowledged leader of the
working classes'. Professor Harrison made a great advance by
expertly setting Owenism in the context of a whole complex of
trans-Atlantic social and intellectual forces. However whilst showing
how narrow and misleading was the perspective which viewed
Owenism only as a stage in the development of the working-class
movement, he still tended to take earlier claims about the actual
extent of Owenite influence on the working class too much at face
value. This has continued to be the case in more recent work on
Owenism in which the main focus has been on Owenite theories.[34]
In 1829–34 Owenite endeavour also found expression in the establishment of many co-operative shops and a few labour exchanges.
But it is the connection with trade unionism which provides the real
basis for claims that Owenism indelibly coloured popular attitudes,
and that it is possible to speak of an Owenite mass movement. In
Lancashire the influence of Owenism on trade unions was, in fact,
very patchy and limited. The NAPL was never an Owenite union.
On the other hand two important textile unions, the dyers and calico
printers, did forge links with local Owenites when they established
their own major co-operative production schemes in 1830–33.
However in both cases the schemes were galvanised by strikes, and
related to the need to employ union members as an adjunct to
industrial action.[35] It is not the case that co-operative production was
necessarily a sign of Owenite influence, for it was a persistent artisan
strategy in strike situations. In the cotton district in the 1830s and
early 1840s, there were examples of co-operative production
involving shoemakers, tailors, hatters and sawyers, when there was
no hint at all of Owenite influence or involvement.[36] The Operative

Builders Union, a national federation of all the main building trades established in 1831–32, has frequently been blanketly labelled Owenite. Yet the crucial Lancashire builders' strike of 1833 (the failure of which effectively sealed the fate of the union) is entirely explicable in terms of changes within the industry. In none of the local discussions of the strike and the propaganda produced by either the masters or men was there any mention or real sign of Owenite influence.[37] Owenite sources also indicate an initial, near total ignorance of Owenism amongst the local builders, but then do show that Owenite influence helped to secure agreement on changes in the union's structure and aims in the last stages of the strike. Owen himself attended the delegate meeting, the so-called Builders Parliament, in Manchester in September. He then complained about the ignorance of the vast majority about his views.[38] The Manchester strike collapsed in the very week of the meeting.[39] Subsequently Lancashire was criticised for refusing to fit in with the Owenite plans for the union.[40]

Apart from these cases there is no evidence of Owenite involvement with individual local unions. Of course it was the famous GNCTU of 1834 which has been seen as the high point of Owenite influence with a mass trade union movement. Yet it has now been clearly established that the pioneering accounts exaggerated the scale of the union, and the extent to which the Owenite beliefs of several key leaders pervaded the broader movement. The known paying membership was a little over 16,000, and the union was primarily based upon the London tailors and shoemakers (both of whom were preparing for strikes). A broader structure grew out of the trade union committees established to support the 1833–34 Derby strike, and then the Tolpuddle Martyrs.[41] The GNCTU was therefore a much more familiar trade union phenomenon, recognisably part of the established tradition of inter-trade co-operation in crisis situations, than the emphasis upon Owenite influence and utopian aims in the early accounts would lead one to believe. Nevertheless the atmosphere created by the very existence of the GNCTU had a marked effect in encouraging unionisation and alarming middle-class opinion in many areas. However, it did make few inroads into Lancashire. One vital reason for this was the same as elsewhere in the country. The GNCTU simply did not last long enough to put down firm roots. It was only formally established in February 1834 and was seen by sympathetic observers as little more than 'a name' by July.[42] In Lancashire there were also the additional factors of the spectre of the NAPL, the weakness of the cotton unions after the serious strike defeats in 1829–31, and the involvement of many local activists in the National Regeneration Society.

This body was established in Manchester in November 1833, with the aim of enforcing a universal eight-hour day by direct action. It is another society still frequently labelled Owenite.[43] Certainly Owen was involved at the very beginning, but it was the radical MP for Oldham, John Fielden, who proposed the basic plan. Fielden was no Owenite, and indeed considered Owen had 'some very peculiar opinions'. Furthermore, as Fielden made very clear, the plan was very much a means to continue the short-time agitation.

I thought it desirable to suggest a mode of procedure on the part of the workpeople in factories, which, if successful, would supply the defect in the factory bill passed last session, and do away with the necessity of further legislation on the subject.

The plan is, that about the 1. of March next, the day the said bill (now act) limits the time of work for children under eleven years of age to eight hours a day, those above that age both grown persons and adults, should insist on eight hours a day being the maximum of time for them to labour'.[44]

The Regeneration Society offered a tactical way forward at a time when renewed petitioning of Parliament was obviously pointless, with an as yet untried Factory Act (which the operatives viewed as a defeat) having been passed so recently. It was effectively a choice between attempted direct action and doing nothing. Owen was of course a very long-standing advocate of shorter working hours, so his endorsement of the scheme was perfectly understandable. But after an initial burst of effort publicising the society, Owen moved on to other schemes. Some Owenites were in the Regeneration Society, but the bulk of the activists were familiar figures from the local radical and short-time movements.

In a remarkable burst of activity between the summers of 1833 and 1834, Robert Owen then did flit from organisation to organisation in Lancashire as he did nationally. He hardly stayed long enough in any locality or scheme to be an effective leader. In a close parallel with the Tory-radical Richard Oastler, he was widely respected as a man genuinely seeking to improve the situation of the working class, but he cannot be said to have affected deep or widespread changes in popular beliefs. The spring of 1834 has been seen as the high point in the influence, not only of Owen, but also the Owenite journals, the *Crisis* and *Pioneer*, with their neo-syndicalist ideology and strategy. It was significant that at precisely this time the speeches at the Manchester trades union meeting protesting about the Dorchester prosecutions were most obviously in line with the more familiar radicalism of the *Poor Man's Guardian*. The *Crisis* and *Pioneer* were unmentioned at the meeting, as they were in a thorough survey of the circulation of the most popular unstamped papers in Manchester at this time.[45] It was the *Poor Man's Guardian*, which was singled out for thanks in a resolution passed by that meeting praising the unstamped, and which emerged as having easily the highest circulation in the unstamped survey. All this local evidence is significant, for Manchester has been presented as the 'strongest Owenite centre' in the provinces, a place where 'the trade unions under the leadership of John Doherty went Owenite'.[46] The actual situation of Owenite influence being genuinely important with a few specific leaders and organisations, but certainly limited and ambiguous in its general impact does moreover fit with recent re-assessments of London and Yorkshire.[47] The evidence from critical localities suggests that Owenism cannot be seen either as a coherent mass movement or a predominating intellectual force at this time. The ideological swing away from radicalism towards Owenism and syndicalism was more illusory than real.

Irrespective of the question of Owenite influence, 1834 was genuinely a climactic year in the trade union world in many areas. This was much less the case in Lancashire. Even the Manchester trade union meeting about the Dorchester prosecutions was seen by the local radical newspaper as a disappointment. The rest of the local press and the authorities saw it as a failure not a threat.[48] Nevertheless twenty-two trades were represented, with the tailors' contingent being the largest. For the Manchester tailors, as for the London tailors, 1834 was a crisis year with a long and bitter general strike.[49] It is a serious error to ignore the importance of the artisan trades in the manufacturing districts, and the Manchester tailors were a numerous and important group. But it cannot be said that their strike came anywhere near reproducing the convulsive effect on the local economy of the textile and mining strikes of 1829–31. The tailors certainly expressed firm interest in joining the GNCTU, as did trade delegates from Oldham.[50] In Oldham there was the added motivation of a genuine if local crisis, the remarkable general strike which erupted in the town in April 1834.

This 1834 strike is the key episode which John Foster uses to sustain his Leninist interpretation that, 'in just three or four years' after 1830, a revolutionary 'vanguard leadership' guided the Oldham working class from 'trade union to class consciousness'. In Foster's formulation the Regeneration Society was a 'lever for fundamental political mobilisation', with the local, Oldham branch directing the strike.[51] Professor Musson has persuasively argued that Foster has exaggerated the power of the Regeneration Society and its revolutionary intent. However he has not been able to challenge Foster effectively on the events in Oldham, because he has not consulted the crucial Oldham source, the Butterworth diaries.[52] In fact the very detailed account in these diaries clearly shows that the strike began as an essentially spontaneous response to what was seen as a Dorchester style arrest of two spinners' union officials by the Oldham police. The strike became a general one the next day when crowds rescued the prisoners, with cries of 'no more Dorchester', and attacked a mill where there had been a long-running strike. The massive public meetings which assembled on the first two days of the strike decided upon no positive policy beyond remaining on strike and condemning the police. It was only on the third day, when Manchester speakers arrived, that resolutions were passed in favour of striking for an eight-hour day if other areas would support them.[53] The extent to which the local radical leadership provided the strikers with a clear strategy is in very considerable doubt. James Mills, one of the key radical leaders and delegate to the prior Manchester Regeneration Society meeting, wanted the workers to return to work. The Oldham Regeneration Society did not assume leadership of the strike. Instead a trade union committee emerged, and they decided that unless other areas joined them, they would return to work on 22 April, a week after the strike began. Butterworth also recorded 'they have no present objection to the hours of labour, but they are concerned the masters are for putting down their Unions'.[54]

It is very difficult to see how this strike does establish the element Foster sees as 'the key one in establishing class consciousness, that of intellectual conviction', or show that the development of the mass movement was 'closely linked to the careful, conscious process by which the radicals guided mass understanding from one level to another'.[55] There was in fact a high degree of spontaneity in defensive, largely improvised community-based action, which can only be understood if placed in the context of Tolpuddle and the wider events of 1834, which Foster largely ignores. On the other hand to insist upon a rigid compartmentalisation of trade and political action, and reduce the strike to being 'fundamentally trade unionist',[56] is to miss all that made it so extraordinary. It was a general strike involving 'all descriptions of workpeople' and all the factories.[57] The strike in fact illustrated the intensity of working-class communal solidarity in the face of aggressive action by the authorities.

Nevertheless the fact that no other town went on strike emphasised the essentially local and fortuitous reasons for the Oldham strike. The Regeneration Society decided *not* to take advantage of the Oldham events in a general attempt to put the eight-hour plan into immediate effect. It did increasingly attempt to involve itself with local trade unions. But even the interested trades wanted a delay, and the target date was endlessly postponed.[58] An Oldham central committee was definitely corresponding with the GNCTU in July, and delegates from seven cotton towns attended a GNCTU delegate meeting in London in August.[59]

But the various strands were coming together too late. By this time the GNCTU and the Regeneration Society were spent forces. In fact in general the sense of crisis in the cotton district in 1834 was muted compared with 1829–31. Then the locally rooted NAPL and numerous large strikes had seriously alarmed the authorities. In 1834 the authorities were confident.[60] Thus in Lancashire it is even very dubious whether a pattern of political action followed by a swing to trade unionism was the predominant pattern. It is certainly very doubtful whether the forms of action taken just after the Reform Crisis were conditioned by a change in popular consciousness brought about either by Owenism, or, as in Foster's arguments, a progression to a fully revolutionary class consciousness. Everywhere in the country it was obvious that, on tactical grounds, further suffrage agitation was pointless until the Reform Act had been given a trial. Likewise the direct action tactics of the National Regeneration Society were a response to the similar situation existing in the immediate aftermath of the 1833 Factory Act. In many areas a trade union upsurge in 1832–34 was a product of artisans attempting to take advantage of the upturn in trade. Tactical considerations were a major force shaping forms of working-class action, which were not a simple reflection of the nature of mass consciousness.

EXPERIENCE AND IDEOLOGY: FROM INDUSTRIAL CONFLICT TO CLASS CONFLICT

The outburst of general unionism was a marked feature of trade union developments in the 1829 to 1834 period, but so also was a very marked surge of industrial conflict and unionisation, often of a very unexclusive character, in diverse trades. In the cotton district in 1829 to 1831, there was not only the creation of a national spinners' union, but also massive, often violent spinners' strikes in Manchester, Stockport, Bolton, Ashton and Oldham. In 1829, there were serious hand-loom weaver strikes and riots in Manchester and Rochdale. A widespread silk weavers' union emerged, then failed after an 1829 strike. Thousands of flannel weavers were involved in near continual conflict in Rochdale in 1829–31. There was an unprecedented surge of unionisation amongst bleachers which culminated in widespread strikes in 1831–32, a county-wide strike by calico printers in 1831, and very widespread strikes by dyers in 1833–34. An explosion of unionisation amongst the miners in 1830 subsequently led to bitterly fought strikes in the winter of 1830–31. In 1833, there was the Lancashire builders' strike, and, in 1834, very long tailors' strikes in Manchester and Bolton. A new national union of hatters was created at a Manchester conference in 1833, and a trial of strength was precipitated with the giant firm of the trade in the Stockport area in 1834.[61]

The pattern was one in which the textile and mining disputes were concentrated in 1829–31, and the artisan disputes in the trade upturn of 1833–34. This of course paralleled the involvement of these groups in the respective surges of general unionism. More generally it is clear that there was a very widespread experience of bitter conflict on class lines *within* most of the major industries of the area, in a remarkably short period of time. There were several instances of combinations of the main employers facing unions incorporating a clear majority of the workers. The issues characteristically concerned not only pay, but also status and skill. In such cases the very unions of the workmen became the issue in a struggle focusing on control over the work process. The strikes revealed great differences in the economic reasoning of masters and men, even in unmechanised artisan trades. Serious violence was commonplace. Large numbers of workers experienced not only industrial conflict, but also the use of troops, what was seen as the unfair, class-biased operation of the law, the clear hostility of the authorities and the constant criticism of the middle-class press. It was a radicalising experience, which was perhaps particularly intense in the cotton district, but also visible in many other areas of the country. In Yorkshire and London also, alongside the general unionism, there was a very marked upsurge in conflict and unionisation across the whole spectrum of trades in 1832–34.[62] In 1830–32 there were also serious miners' strikes and disturbances in Wales, the Midlands and the North-east. Potters' unionism revived strongly in 1831–32, promoted local enthusiasm for general unionism in 1834 and was only finally smashed by the strike of 1836–37.[63] In Birmingham, '1833–35 saw a great burst of trade society activity with strikes and prosecutions in a wide variety of trades'. In Northamptonshire, the scale of unionisation amongst the shoemakers was unprecedented, and there were also arrests for oath taking.[64] In 1834 legal action by the authorities against trade unionists was by no means restricted to the Tolpuddle case, but also occurred, as we have seen in Oldham and Northampton, and indeed in Nantwich and Exeter.[65] A real sense of crisis in the relationship between trade unionism, the employers and the State, in the spring of 1834, emerges from the reports in the *True Sun* and *Weekly True Sun*, which provided a national coverage of trade union developments. This was also a time when bitter attacks on trade unionism were especially prominent in the national press, and indeed generally the early 1830s saw a marked increase in the publication of anti-trade union pamphlets and propaganda.[66]

Of course it is possible to find examples of middle-class hostility to trade unionism and bitter strikes at almost any point in the nineteenth century. But there does seem to have been a particularly intensive and embittered spell of conflict at the onset of the 1830s. This whole experience, at precisely the time when the Reform Crisis had such a politicising effect on all sections of urban society, deeply influenced class attitudes and relationships. The importance of this experience of economic conflict must serve to qualify some of the propositions advanced by Gareth Stedman Jones in his recent, penetrating analysis of radical ideology. He has convincingly argued that radicalism consistently emphasised that political rather than economic causes lay at the root of exploitation, and that the radical tradition never fully transcended the ideological limits imposed by its eighteenth-century origins. In consequence he is at pains to show that, in the vital period of the later 1820s and early 1830s, neither trade unionism nor Owenism nor indeed Ricardian Socialism produced a breakthrough to a more distinctly proletarian ideology. However, in his discussion of trade unionism, the claim that neither 'a trade union practice' nor 'a trade union theory' in fact 'contradicted or went beyond radical assumptions' goes too far. For surely the *practice* of trade unionism did frequently go beyond the political analysis described by Stedman Jones.[67]

Many trade union leaders were radicals, and therefore they often tended to accord political causes, such as the pressure of taxes, the pride of place in their general analysis of society's ills. Yet the reality of what trade unions were doing in practice was conditioned by conflict rooted in the productive process, in which workers as workers faced employers as employers. It was about economic roles rather than political relationships. Trade union ideology did not produce a genuinely socialist analysis, but rival political economies were espoused by masters and men. The central contentious issues were ones of control rather than ownership of the means of production.[68] This must cast doubt on the view that in the early 1830s, 'the battle for the minds of English trade unionists, between a capitalist and a *socialist* political economy, had been (at least temporarily) won', or that the issue can be even posed in those terms.[69] Nevertheless the conflicts were sufficient to generate very visible class antagonism. Furthermore if the point is certainly conceded that language structures the understanding of experience, that the 'language of class was not simply a verbalisation of perception', still the language can also be given distinctive meanings by the social context. In this case that was the widespread experience of actual conflict. Stedman Jones writes that 'in strikes themselves and the battle for public opinion that surrounded them, the enemy was not the employers as a class, but rather the grinding and tyrannical employers in contrast to their honourable associates'.[70] Is this not what trade unions were bound to say, that it was not the honourable but the dishonourable employers they opposed? Such statements are surely recognisably from the same stable as those by employers arguing that their action was directed not against the respectable workmen but the tyrannical union (often organised by 'paid' or outside 'agitators') which had misled them. Both sets of statements were a complex mixture of propaganda and genuine belief. Yet in both cases the logic of class division in the workplace communicated the real meaning. Who were the honourable employers? They were the ones doing what the workers wanted. The whole point of trade union battles over rules in the workplace, standardised wage rates and hours was that all employers should conform. Ultimately whether they were called honourable or dishonourable at a particular point in time was, in a very real sense, beside the point.

It is vital not to lose sight of the importance of experience and exaggerate the role of ideology. From a Marxist perspective the labour movement of this time was perhaps ideologically underdeveloped, but in terms of actual class conflict it was by no means backward. A tone of class antagonism arising from economic conflict did infuse political relationships. An understanding of this point helps to explain the actual pattern of politics in the 1830s and 1840s. For in fact, irrespective of the ideological failings of radical thinking as analysed by modern historians, this was a time when the labour movement maintained a fierce, class-conscious independence. The real significance of the events of 1829–34 in terms of mass attitudes may well be more in the realm of experience rather than in ideological advance.

CONCLUSION

Overall the many defeats of 1829–34 did set definite limits on popular perceptions of the potential of trade unionism as a mechanism for social advancement in the face of a hostile State. This was a factor of real importance in the resurgence of political action in the form of Chartism in 1838–42 when, also, long continued trade depression hopelessly undermined the bargaining position of most trade unions. On the other hand the general union defeats certainly did not signify the demise of more orthodox trade union action. Nor did they end the phenomenon of inter-trade co-operation in crisis situations although they did result in a reluctance to create formal general unions on pragmatic grounds. The general weakness of workers when reliant upon formal organisation far removed from workplace and community had been clearly revealed. Nevertheless the whole outburst of general unionism and the linked phenomenon of the creation of new national unions and the tendency towards unexclusive, 'all grades' unions in 1829–34 were indicative of a greater degree of class solidarity. Nor were they just a reflection of deeper social trends, but they also actively helped to generate a more intensive working-class consciousness in the 1830s and 1840s.

There is, however, little evidence to sustain more ambitious claims for a dramatic, qualitative shift in mass consciousness either towards a neo-syndicalist Owenite alternative to radicalism, or towards a full, revolutionary class consciousness in the sense adopted by Foster. There was a broadening of analysis and concerns in the labour movement in the 1830s. However the crucial development was the political definition imposed by the 1832 Reform Act. Chartist ideology continued to be grounded upon an essentially political analysis of society. Nevertheless the labour movements of the 1830s and 1840s were infused with a tone of class hostility, which was in large part rooted in economic conflict. Actual experience helps to explain the actual pattern of political developments (in which attempted class alliances constantly floundered) in a manner which an overdue stress upon ideology perhaps obscures. Although certainly the gap between ideology and social reality led to serious tactical confusion in Chartist times.[71] Finally, and especially in the early 1830s when historians have read much into apparent swings between political and economic action, we need to be more aware of the extent to which mobilisation and strategy are dependent upon power relationships, expectations of success and the constraints imposed by the overall political and economic framework, rather than being a straightforward reflection of the nature and theoretical rigour of popular consciousness.

NOTES AND REFERENCES

1. **S.** and **B. Webb**, *The History of Trade Unionism*, Longmans, Green and Co. 2nd. edn. 1920, Ch. 3.
2. **G. D. H. Cole**, *Attempts at General Union, 1818–1834*, Macmillan 1953.
3. See e.g. **M. Beer**, *A History of British Socialism*, Allen and Union, 1 vol. ed, 1940, pp. 326–35 on the 'syndicalist phase'.
4. **E. P. Thompson**, *The Making of the English Working Class*, Penguin 1968, pp. 887–8, 912–13.
5. **J. F. C. Harrison**, *Robert Owen and the Owenites in Britain and America*, Routledge and Kegan Paul 1969, pp. 7, 197–216.
6. **A. E. Musson**, *British Trade Unions 1800–1875*, Macmillan 1972, Ch. 5; **W. H. Fraser**, 'Trade unionism', in **J. T. Ward** (ed.), *Popular Movements c1830–1850*, MacMillan 1970, p. 108.
7. **J. Foster**, *Class Struggle and the Industrial Revolution*, Weidenfeld and Nicolson 1974.
8. **W. H. Oliver**, 'The Consolidated Trades' Union of 1834', *Econ. Hist. Rev.*, 2nd ser., XVII, **1** (1964–65).
9. **R. G. Kirby** and **A. E. Musson**, *The Voice of the People*, Manchester U. P. 1975; Musson, *British Trade Unions*, Chs. 4 and 5.
10. **Kirby** and **Musson**, *Voice of the People*, Chs. 6 and 7, provides a good, detailed account.
11. Ibid., pp. 153–4.
12. *Manchester Times*, 3 Oct. 1829.
13. **W. Longson**, *An Appeal to Masters, Workmen and the Public Showing the Cause of the Distress of the Labouring Classes*, Manchester 1827, p. 16.
14. For a discussion of the economic problems facing the main trades in the cotton district, see **R. A. Sykes**, 'Popular Politics and Trade Unionism in South-East Lancashire, 1829–1842' (Ph. D. thesis, Manchester, 1982), part 1.
15. **Kirby** and **Musson**, *Voice of the People*, pp. 153, 240, 320–33. My own reading of the evidence supports these conclusions.
16. See ibid. pp. 262–3, for the tables of total subscriptions, to which all

amounts (rounded to the nearest £1) refer, and especially pp. 196, 220–1, 259–61, for discussion of membership patterns.

17. **A. E. Musson**, *The Typographical Association*, Oxford U.P. 1954, p. 76.
18. Other metal-working trades, such as iron moulders and smiths are subsumed in the 'miscellaneous skilled trades' category used by Kirby and Musson, *Voice of the People*, p. 263.
19. See the table in ibid. p. 263; and Sykes, 'Popular Politics and Trade Unionism', pp. 308–15.
20. See **R. A. Sykes**, 'Early Chartism and trade unionism in South-east Lancashire', in **J. Epstein** and **D. Thompson**, (eds), *The Chartist Experience*, Macmillan 1982.
21. See **Kirby** and **Musson**, *Voice of the People*, pp. 181, 196, 231–2, 259.
22. *Voice of the People*, 30 Apr. 1831.
23. **Sykes**, 'Popular Politics and Trade Unionism', pp. 340–2.
24. See e.g. *Union Pilot and Co-operative Intelligencer*, **24**, 31 Mar., 7 Apr., 5 May 1832; and *Poor Man's Advocate*, 2 and 16 (June 1832).
25. **Oliver**, 'Consolidated Trades' Union', pp. 85–6.
26. **Kirby** and **Musson**, *Voice of the People*, pp. 172–5, 261, and for a re-assessment of the Yorkshire situation, see **J. R. Sanders**, 'Working Class Movements in the West Riding Textile District, 1829 to 1839, with emphasis on local leadership and organisation' (Ph.D. thesis, Manchester, 1984), pp. 109–14.
27. *Herald to the Trades Advocate*, 13 Nov. 1830.
28. E.g. see the general comment in *United Trades Co-operative Jn.*, 3 July 1830.
29. See especially ibid., 24 and 31 July 1830; and the 'Operative Voice' leaders in *Voice of the People*, July–Sept. 1831.
30. **Kirby** and **Musson**, *Voice of the People*, pp. 183–7.
31. *Manchester Times*, 3 Oct. 1829; *United Trades Co-operative Jn.*, 1 May 1830; *Voice of the People*, 10 Sept. 1831; *Proc. Second Co-operative Congress*, Birmingham 1831, p. 15.
32. For a full discussion, see Sykes, 'Popular Politics and Trade Unionism', Ch. 8.
33. *Voice of the People*, 5 Mar., 23 Apr. 1831.
34. **Harrison**, *Owen and the Owenites*, p. 7; **Barbara Taylor**, *Eve and the New Jerusalem*, Virago 1983; N. W. Thompson, *The People's Science*, C. U. P. 1984.
35. For the dyers, see especially *United Trades Co-operative Jn.*, 27 Mar. 1830; *Manchester Times*, 3 Mar. 1832; and for the calico printers, *Voice of the People*, 16 July 1831; Holyoake House, Manchester, Owen Papers, Carson to Owen, 1 March 1832.
36. **Sykes**, 'Popular Politics and Trade Unionism', pp. 300–1, 305, 312–13 and 332.
37. See especially *Brief History of the Proceedings of the Operative Builders' Trades Unions*, Manchester 1833; and *An Impartial Statement of the Proceedings of the Trade Union Societies and of the Steps Taken in Consequence by the Master Tradesmen of Liverpool*, Liverpool 1833.
38. *Crisis*, 7 and 21 September 1833. See also Owen Papers, Hansom to Owen, 25 August 1833, and the reports of delegate meetings in Manchester in September 1833, items no. 652 and 660.

39. *Crisis*, 19 Oct.; *Manchester Guardian* and *Manchester Courier*, 5 Oct. 1833. The strike was certainly not 're-kindled' by Owen as has been claimed, see **R. Postgate**, *The Builders History*, National Federation of Building Trades Operatives 1923, p. 97 and Ch. 4 and 5 *passim*. **R. Price**, *Masters, Unions and Men: work control in building and the rise of labour 1830–1914*, Cambridge U.P. 1980, p. 35, has rather uncritically followed Postgate in exaggerating the impact of Owenism.

40. *Pioneer*, 16 Nov., 7 Dec. 1833.

41. **Oliver**, 'Consolidated Trades' Union'; id., 'Organisations and Ideas behind the Efforts to Achieve a General Union of the Working Classes in the Early 1830s' Ph.D. thesis, Oxford 1954.

42. *Crisis*, 5 and 12 July 1834; *Poor Man's Guardian*, 12 July 1834.

43. For a detailed account, see Kirby and Musson, *Voice of the People*, pp. 273–301. For continued use of the Owenite label, see e.g. **R. K. Webb**, *Modern England*, Allen and Unwin, 2nd edn 1980, p. 241.

44. *Cobbett's Weekly Political Register*, 14 Dec. 1833.

45. *Manchester and Salford Advertiser*, 10 May 1834; PRO, HO 40/32/1, Bouverie to Phillipps, 19 March 1834.

46. **Harrison**, *Owen and the Owenites*, pp. 225–6.

47. **I. J. Prothero**, *Artisans and Politics in Early Nineteenth-Century London*, Dawson and Sons 1979, Chs. 13 and 15; Sanders, 'Working Class Movements in the West Riding', Ch. 4.

48. The attendance was variously estimated between 2000 and 6000, see *Manchester and Salford Advertiser, Manchester Guardian* and *Manchester Courier*, 10 May 1834; HO 40/32/3, Foster to Melbourne, 5 May; and Kennedy to Phillipps, 5 May 1834.

49. **Sykes**, 'Popular Politics and Trade Unionism', pp. 304–7; **T. M. Parssinen** and **I. J. Prothero**, 'The London tailors' strike of 1834 and the collapse of the Grand National Consolidated Trades' Union: a police spy's report', *International Review of Social History*, **22** (1977).

50. *Herald of the Rights of Industry*, 17 May 1834.

51. **Foster**, *Class Struggle*, pp. 73–4, 107–14, 125.

52. **A. E. Musson**, 'Class struggle and the labour aristocracy, 1830–60', *Social History*, **3** (1976), esp. pp. 338–40 and **J. Foster**, 'Some comments on Class struggle and the labour aristocracy, 1830–60', *Social History*, **3** (1976), esp. pp. 357–8.

53. Oldham Public Library, Butterworth diary, 14, 15, 16, 17 and 19 April 1834; *Manchester and Salford Advertiser*, 19 Apr. 1834; HO 52/24, Mills to Melbourne, 17 April 1834. For a more detailed account, see Sykes 'Popular Politics and Trade Unionism', pp. 509–13.

54. Butterworth diary, 18, 19 and 21 April 1834; HO 40/32/3, Doran to Kennedy, 17 April 1834.

55. **Foster**, *Class Struggle*, pp. 107, 109; and id., 'Some comments', p. 358, where Foster re-emphasises this point that '1834 was seen to mark a vital advance in the *ideological* quality of the leadership'. For further discussion of the issues raised by Foster's account of Oldham, see **R. A. Sykes**, 'Some aspects of working-class consciousness in Oldham, 1830–1842', *Historical Jn.*, Vol. 23, No. 1 (1980).

56. **Musson**, 'Class struggle', p. 339.

57. Butterworth diary, 16 April 1834; HO 52/24, Holme to Melbourne,

20 April 1834; Mills to Melbourne, 17 April 1834.

58. *Herald of the Rights of Industry*, 3, 10 and 17 May 1834.
59. HO 52/25, abstract of intercepted letter from Patterson of Oldham, 7 July 1834; *Weekly True Sun*, 24 Aug. 1834.
60. See e.g. HO 40/32/3, Foster to Phillips, 12 January 1834; Bouverie to Phillipps, 2 March 1834.
61. For further details about all these disputes, see Sykes, 'Popular Politics and Trade Unionism', part 1.
62. **Prothero**, *Artisans and Politics*, Ch. 15; Sanders, 'Working Class Movements in the West Riding', pp. 101–17.
63. **G. Rudé**, 'English rural and urban disturbances on the eve of the First Reform Bill, 1830–1831', *Past and Present*, **37** (1967), p. 83; Ch. 7, below.
64. **C. Beehag**, 'Custom, class and change: the trade societies of Birmingham', *Social History*, **4** (1979), p. 473; **M. Haynes**, 'Class and class conflict in the early Nineteenth Century: Northampton shoemakers and the G.N.C.T.U.', *Literature and History*, **5** (1977).
65. 'The Reminiscences of Thomas Dunning (1813–1894) and the Nantwich shoemakers' case of 1834', ed. W. H. Chaloner, *Transactions of the Lancashire and Cheshire Antiquarian Society*, (1947); HO 52/24, Exeter Mayor to Home Office, 18 January 1834; *True Sun*, 12 Apr. 1834.
66. **R. K. Webb**, *The British Working Class Reader, 1790–1850*, Allen and Unwin 1955, Ch. 7.
67. **G. Stedman Jones**, Rethinking Chartism', in *Languages of Class*, Cambridge U.P. 1983, Ch. 3 (*passim*), but esp. pp. 111, 113 and, for trade unionism generally, pp. 112–17.
68. This has been convincingly argued by Stedman Jones, see ibid. Ch. 1, esp. pp. 45–56.
69. **Thompson**, *Making of the English Working Class*, p. 912 (my emphasis).
70. **Stedman Jones**, *Languages of Class*, pp. 102, 117.
71. **R. A. Sykes**, 'Physical-Force Chartism: the cotton district and the Chartist crisis of 1839', *Inter. Rev. of Soc. Hist.*, **xxx**, **2** (1985), pp. 219–24.

CHAPTER NINE

Unionism, Class and Community in the 1830s: Aspects of the National Union of Operative Potters

Robert Fyson

The importance of the potters' union (NUOP) in the 1830s has long been recognised by historians. The Webbs described it as 'one of the five great unions' outside the ranks of the GNCTU (Grand National Consolidated Trades' Union); Tawney emphasised that it succeeded in recruiting a larger percentage of pottery workers than any other union before 1914; and Cole paid the union considerable attention in his study of early general unionism.[1] Three histories of trade unionism in the pottery industry provide useful narrative accounts of the development of the NUOP: each of these works focusses largely on the potters' major industrial grievances concerning wages and conditions and the strikes which resulted.[2]

The historiography of early trade unionism has, however, during the last twenty years, begun to encompass wider questions than those addressed by the traditional institutional kind of trade union history. E. P. Thompson's influential work first situated the unionism of the early 1830s in the context of the formation of working-class consciousness in these years; J. F. C. Harrison described working-class movements in the 1830s as 'not so much a collection of separate movements . . . as one massive, complex response to problems facing the working classes'. More recently, John Foster has discerned 'the development and decline of a revolutionary class consciousness in the second quarter of the century'. Foster's analysis, centred on Oldham, describes the town as 'more or less permanently under the control of the organized working-class: much of its local government was subordinated to the trade unions . . .' and he identifies the year 1834 as the high point, in Oldham, of revolutionary class struggle led by the trade unions. Foster's interpretation has provoked vigorous criticism and debate and has not found general acceptance, but has certainly stimulated fresh lines of historical inquiry. Towards the end of his book, he mentions North Staffordshire as one of the areas in which class consciousness was strongest in this period and on which further research needs to be done.[3]

This chapter re-examines aspects of the potters' unionism of the 1830s in the light of this recent historiography.

ORIGINS: THE NATIONAL ASSOCIATION FOR THE PROTECTION OF LABOUR 1830–31

The initial impetus for the foundation of the NUOP (National Union of Operative Potters) came from the extension of missionary activity to the Potteries in 1830 by the Manchester-based National Association for the Protection of Labour (NAPL) a movement which, E. P. Thompson points out, at last seemed to give body to the long-held aspiration of skilled workers for general national unionism and to provide 'a means of bringing the organized workers of the country into a common movement', at a time of widespread popular political excitement, in the Potteries as elsewhere.[4]

A large anti-truck demonstration in Hanley on 18 October, organised by a committee including both working-class spokesmen and leading manufacturers, was surprised by a dramatic and unscheduled intervention by 'a stranger' from the NAPL who appeared on the platform and claimed that not truck but low wages lay at the root of the potters' problems. A month later, on 15 November, John Doherty, leader of the NAPL, and two other union spokesmen, held their own open-air meeting at Wolstanton Marsh, just outside the Potteries, and a local NAPL committee was set up. In the meantime a leaflet had been circulated which promised that 'the great day of justice and retribution is at hand, when the workman will emerge from his present prostrate condition to the possession of that higher rank and enjoyment which are justly due to his merits' and the local paper, alarmed by such language, denounced 'the distribution of inflammatory tracts by strangers . . . from a dangerous society'.[5]

As previous historians have noted, a China and Earthenware Turners' Society had formally affiliated to the NAPL by March 1831. The major NAPL activity in the Potteries at this time, however, was not to do with the potters' own grievances, but with support for the Ashton-under-Lyne spinners' strike. John Joseph Betts, the strikers' leader, speaking in Hanley, declared that 'The Ashton spinners are fighting the battle of the working classes', a view supported by John Richards, Hanley shoemaker and future Chartist leader, who urged his audience to 'assist the spinners to fight your own battles'. Meetings were held and money collected, both at work and in pubs, from the potters and colliers of Hanley and Burslem and the hatters of Newcastle-under-Lyme. Thus the claims of a broad working-class solidarity took priority over local concerns.[6]

After the defeat of the spinners' strike, attention focussed on the North Staffordshire miners' strike in May and June. 'A numerous Meeting of Delegates from the different branches of the Potting Business' met in Hanley on 30 May and agreed to raise funds 'to aid and assist the miners in their present struggle in defence of their just rights'. On 6 June, shortly before the strike collapsed, the fund-raising committee, now describing itself as a committee of the Potters' Union, issued a placard denying reports that the potters were only supporting the miners because they intended to strike for an advance of wages themselves as soon as the miners' dispute was over. The perspective of class solidarity and general unionism was again pre-eminent.[7]

It was not until September that the NAPL embarked on a public campaign, with open-air meetings in Hanley and Longton, calling on the potters to join their own union, as part of the NAPL, in order to resist low wages, and affirming 'Labour is the Source of Wealth'. A local union, said John Richards, was not enough, as the collapse of the earlier potters' union of 1825–26 had shown. The speeches of Richards, the potter Jesse Buxton and other speakers demonstrate clearly the appeal of the idea of Union as something transcending trade unionism in its narrower sense. Speakers at NAPL meetings during the twelve months of its influence in the Potteries referred to a wide range of subjects of concern to working-class radicals: 'corruption in Church and State', the national debt, placemen, landed proprietors and the Corn Laws were all objects of attack; the repeal of the Test Acts, Catholic emancipation and the revolutions in France, Belgium and Poland were cited as examples of the power of the people. In the view of Richards, speaking at an NAPL meeting in Hanley in September 1831, 'The Union of the people has brought about the Reform measure; by being united and true to themselves, they will secure every measure for the extension of their liberties;

and the time is come when every government must attend to the voice of the people'.[8]

The NAPL collapsed shortly afterwards. In the view of Doherty's biographers, it should be seen as 'the product of a temporary coincidence of interest among the declining handicraft trades and the new factory workers during the 1829–31 trade depression, in fighting against wage reductions'. Yet the perspective of general unionism as a political and industrial force making for social change, which it embodied, was to continue to be an important influence on the development of potters' unionism.[9]

OWENISM: CO-OPERATION *C* 1833–35

Information on the potters' union from the autumn of 1831 to the summer of 1833 is very sparse, probably for three reasons: the concentration of public attention on the agitation for-parliamentary reform, the union's deliberate secrecy, and equally deliberate neglect by the local press. A large demonstration and procession held in April 1832 to welcome eleven potters, released on appeal from gaol sentences for neglect of work, was briefly reported; letters to the press in July give further evidence of union activity.[10] One correspondent emphasised that the Reform Act had done nothing to improve the lot of the pottery workers; and it may be surmised that after the Reform agitation, which had been dominated by middle-class leadership, had subsided, the union was able to become the unchallenged focus of working-class aspirations. It was during this period, invisibly to the historian, that the important groundwork of establishing the NUOP as an effective and powerful union, locally and on a national scale throughout the industry, was done. The union's four-day annual meeting in August 1833 at the Sea Lion Inn, Hanley, was attended by delegates from Bristol, Swansea, Newcastle-on-Tyne, Worcestershire, Derbyshire and Yorkshire. Thomas Simpson, potter turned publican, and union delegate to the Co-operative Congress in London in October, reported on the union's structure and organisation in lodges and claimed 8000 members: 6000 in the Potteries and 2000 in the 'out-potteries' outside North Staffordshire.[11]

According to J. F. C. Harrison, the Potteries was in 1833–34 one of the four main areas of Owenite strength in Britain and 'Owen's visits to the Potteries in the fall of 1833 swept them into the socialist maelstrom'.[12] The NUOP provides an interesting case history of the extent to which Owenite doctrines were able to make headway within a union which was already firmly established and organised on a national basis, before Owen began to devote his attention to it.

Working-class interest in co-operation already existed before Owen's visits: the potters' union of 1825 is said to have shown an interest in co-operative manufacturing; in 1830 the 'Pottery Co-operators' claimed over 200 members; and in May 1832 a visiting co-operative lecturer attracted a crowd of over 2000 in Longton, where the co-operative society intended to open a shop and begin to manufacture crockery. As Simpson told the Co-operative Congress of 1833, 'we have been studying the subject of labour exchange and co-operation'. Apparently as the result of an initial letter from a unionist, Owen visited the Potteries and spoke to union meetings at least three times in the autumn of 1833; he was impressed by 'the spirit and intelligence manifested by the pottery men, who seem to be far in advance of the rest of the trades in useful knowledge, and a right understanding of the proper means to be adopting for effecting their own deliverance'.[13]

Nevertheless Owen's correspondents in the Potteries, Simpson and Henry Pratt, reported substantial opposition to Owenism: 'There is a great hue and cry against you, all the religious world, so called, are opposed to you', wrote Simpson on 20 October; Pratt on 12 November, identified the opposition as emanating from Methodists, 'with all their sectarian bigotry', and also from the over-lookers or foremen, who in his view were opposed to the introduction of Owen's ideas into the union, because they had been put up to it by the masters. Many warehousemen, in particular, said Pratt, had withheld their union subscriptions in protest at the Owenite connection.[14]

The strategy adopted by Owen's supporters, who held the leading positions in the union, was to propagate his ideas vigorously while keeping his name in the background and making some concessions to conciliate his opponents. The Co-operative Society, started in November 1833, was organised by leading unionists, but kept nominally separate from the union. A network of stores throughout the Potteries was planned; subscribers would pay 6d. per week and become fully paid up shareholders after payment of £1 that is, in 40 weeks. Associated with the society was a plan for a Potters' Labour

Bank which would produce its own 'labour notes', like the Equitable Labour Exchanges in London and Birmingham. The society's constitution included clauses committing it to combat intemperance, avoid disputes over politics or religion, eschew Sunday trading, and not to organise lectures except 'by consent of the society'. It was intended in the future to open schools for the education of members' children, and 'that education shall be in accordance with the Christian faith'. A series of meetings was organised throughout the Potteries towns to promote the scheme; by the end of November, when Owen addressed an enthusiastic meeting at Burslem, there were said to be about 500 subscribers and Pratt was sure that 'the rapidity with which they are flocking to our standard warrants me in saying in a very little time we shall number one thousand'.[15]

The next stage in the development of the Owenite plan was co-operative production. Owen's correspondents discussed this in October and November: in Simpson's view the main problem was the large outlay of initial capital needed; Pratt hoped that it might be possible to find a capitalist who would put up £1000 or £2000, for which he would receive a 'remunerating price', so that the factory could be opened in the name of individual unionists. Several dealers from Liverpool, said Pratt, had approached William Stacey, union leader, 'in case the Union would Manufacture they would give ready money for all goods' but the time would not be ripe for the union to discuss this until February. A co-operative factory would employ surplus labour and sell its wares through the co-operative stores. Pratt and his colleagues would not support either a manufacturer's offer to open a factory to employ surplus hands with union backing, or a scheme by a small group of moneyed unionists to open a factory for their own benefit: nothing would do but a genuinely co-operative venture, establishing a principle of action which would lead to 'The Complete Emancipation of the Productive Classes from the Bodily and Mental Slavery they have been so long labouring under'.[16]

The letters preserved by Owen provide a fascinating inside view of Owenite unionist enthusiasm in the autumn of 1833, but later developments are obscure. In June 1834 Owen's emissary N. R. Wood, visiting Hanley, wrote that 'the popular feeling now arising is employing themselves and it appears they are just now about commencing to work at a very large establishment of their own'. Little is known of this venture. According to John Boyle, a factory at Burslem was taken on a lease by seven workmen with property, managed by two leading unionists, and supported by an advance of £800 from the union. By December 1834 the scheme had proved abortive, it was claimed, though Boyle says it lasted for a further twelve months. Certainly the union was involved throughout, since its accounts for the year 1834–35 show a loss of £183 on manufacturing. It is probable that the 'quantity of Earthenware . . . sent up from Staffordshire' to the Owenite Institution in London on sale in June 1835, for the benefit of the wives of the transported Tolpuddle labourers, was produced in this factory.[17]

The Co-operative Society was still in existence in November 1835 when it celebrated its anniversary with a tea-party; and the society's educational aims may have briefly found expression when the union ran schools for unemployed factory children at Burslem and Tunstall during the 1836 strike. The evidence is fragmentary, but sufficient to suggest that the Owenite ideal of co-operation made a considerable impact. Contrary to the view of A. E. Musson that the union can be characterised as 'pursuing bread and butter objectives', it was directly concerned, for perhaps two years, with co- operative enterprises linked to aspirations for the transformation of the social order.[18]

OWENISM: THE GRAND NATIONAL CONSOLIDATED TRADES' UNION OF 1834

The GNCTU, the short-lived and ambitious attempt at general union which lasted from February to August 1834, is generally agreed to be the project which most closely identified Robert Owen with the working-class movement of his day, and, indeed, put him briefly at its head. It is also well-known that the potters' union never formally affiliated to the GNCTU, which might appear to cast doubt on the general line of argument thus far. The circumstances require closer examination.

Because of the success achieved by their own union by 1833, the potters were wary of losing their independence through merging with any larger nation-wide body. They may also have been influenced by memories of the collapse of the NAPL. Thomas Simpson made it plain at the Co-operative Congress in October 1833 when Owen was concerned with his earlier plan for a 'National Moral Union of the Productive Classes', that he and his fellow delegate 'have no power from our constituents to form any alliance, or enter into arrangements with you', but they had no doubt that 'a solid union will shortly be effected between you and us'. He opposed any plan which would tend to destroy existing unions, but thought his union could not object to membership of a federation.[19]

The failure of the potters' union to join the GNCTU was at least partly due to a successful employers' counter-offensive. Henry Davenport, son of the Stoke-on-Trent MP and manufacturer, John Davenport, reported to his father in March 1834 that delegates from Birmingham, Worcester and elsewhere had arrived in the Potteries, where

they found the Hanley radicals of course ready to join them . . . I determined on trying to offer some resistance. Having caused all our own men from the different works to meet, without being seen in it myself, a set of resolutions determining to resist foreigners and keep by their own Union, was agreed to, which being sent thro' all the lodges, stayed the proceedings.

The outcome was a seven-hour meeting of the union's central committee, at which the radicals wishing to join the GNCTU had a narrow majority of eight votes. The minority then threatened to secede, and as a result, in order to avoid an irremediable split, the proposal to join the GNCTU was apparently dropped. Subsequently, there were difficulties in obtaining information from the London Headquarters of the GNCTU, whose organisation appears to have been inadequate: Simpson wrote complaining of this in April, and again in June, saying that due to a lack of 'true information relative to the principles of consolidation', there was now 'a Mountain of difficulties to fight through to get at the position we once were in possession of'.[20]

Failure by the potters' union to affiliate formally should not, however, obscure the importance of evidence which suggests considerable enthusiasm for the GNCTU, within the potters' union, as well as other trades in North Staffordshire. In April 1834 a meeting of delegates from lodges supporting it in Macclesfield, Newcastle (Staffs), Hanley, Stoke, Leek and Stone was held at the Sea Lion Inn, Hanley; they resolved to send delegates to London in order to formalise their membership. Contributors to the Derby silk-weavers' strike fund, listed in *The Pioneer*, the organ of the GNCTU in the first six months of 1834, include not only the potters of Hanley, Stoke and Burslem, but also the Newcastle clockmakers, tailors, hatters and sawyers, the Hanford and Stoke brick and tile-makers, the Burslem bricklayers, joiners and even shopkeepers, and the Hanley cratemakers. Inter-trade links must have existed. Thomas Simpson mentioned to Owen in June that 'The Grand Lodge of Operative Taylors is held at Our House'. In May the potters' union organised a demonstration to protest against the transportation of the Tolpuddle labourers, with a platform of speakers which included people from other trades; William Stacey, the chairman, was described in the press report as the 'Grand Master of the Pottery Branch of the Trade Union'. The Potteries sent a petition with 4000 signatures and between £40 and £50, and organised a similar meeting and petition a year later in April 1835.[21]

The surge of unionist activity, centred in the Potteries, penetrated deep into the rural hinterland. In July the agent of Ralph Sneyd, squire of Keele Hall, reported that 150 stone-masons working there, and at four other places, were on strike for higher wages; he complained indignantly that 'we must never submit to be dictated to by a committee held at Hanley in the Staffordshire Potteries what shall be done at Keel'. In the same month five men – one of them William Ball, a Leek delegate to the GNCTU meeting held in Hanley in April – were brought to trial at Stafford Assizes on a charge of administering illegal oaths to buttonmakers, in the remote moorland village of Alstonfield in February. Although they appeared before the same circuit judge, Williams, who had sentenced the Tolpuddle men, they escaped the same fate, and were bound over after showing contrition, because an example had already been made of the Dorset labourers, which had aroused widespread protest, and because by this time the GNCTU was on the verge of collapse, the wave of unionism was receding, and no longer seemed to threaten the social order.[22]

It is surely not fanciful to suggest that the natural focus for this activity in North Staffordshire was the potters' union, as by far the strongest trade union in the district. The union may indeed have avoided sharing in the collapse of the GNCTU by remaining a technically separate organisation, but the evidence suggests that nevertheless a large number of its leaders and members actively supported, in the hope of imminent social change, what they felt to be the general working-class cause, which heightened feelings of class consciousness and solidarity. The belief in co-operation, general unionism, and Owenite socialism was slow to fade: in March 1836 Richard Hall, Assistant Poor Law Commissioner, reported that 'The political, if not the religious, opinions of Mr. Owen have been disseminated by himself and his emissaries throughout the Potteries, and form the Creed of the Trades Union'.[23]

UNIONISM AND LOCAL POLITICS, 1834–37

The unionist enthusiasm of 1834 was accompanied by an upsurge of working-class interest and involvement in local politics, through active participation in parish vestry meetings. Opposition to the laying of church rates led in January to hotly contested polls in the parishes of Burslem and Stoke; in Burslem the rate was carried by only nine votes, but in Stoke, after a huge vestry meeting at which the floor of the Town Hall had to be propped from below, the poll resulted in the substitution of a 5d. rate for the original proposal of 13d. On this issue, working-class radicals were able to join forces with dissenting manufacturers like John Ridgway, whom even John Richards praised as 'a man whom to be able to call a friend should be esteemed one of the highest honours in social life'.[24]

At about the same time, another issue aroused even greater controversy. During the autumn of 1833, a series of meetings throughout the Potteries organised by leading manufacturers and gentry, had promoted the case for applying for incorporation of the Potteries towns as a united municipal borough with its own mayor, council, magistrates and police force. By January details of the proposed local electoral divisions were being discussed with visiting members of the Royal Commission on Municipal Reform, and incorporation seemed the likely outcome, until a number of town meetings held in Hanley, Burslem, Stoke and Tunstall from January to March demonstrated widespread popular opposition to the proposal, which was dropped as a result. As William White reported in his county directory, published in May, 'the workmen now raise their voices loudly against any incorporation whatever'. Local parochialism in each town was one element in this feeling, but working-class spokesmen at the public meetings, especially in Hanley and Stoke, including several leading unionists, opposed incorporation for other reasons: unnecessary expense to ratepayers, an unrepresentative local franchise, and suspicion of the magistracy and policing implications. There was no confidence in the ability of the local manufacturing elite to provide an impartial magistracy, and a fear of the introduction of 'armed police officers . . . looked upon an infringement on the liberties of the people, and as the emissaries of military rather than of civil law'. After the proposal had been withdrawn, working-class spokesmen continued to be suspicious of an alternative proposal for a full-time Potteries stipendiary magistrate (a measure ultimately to be implemented in 1839): Mark Lancaster, President of the Union, strongly opposed this at meetings in August

1836; he preferred the county magistracy of rural gentry and clergy, and argued that a stipendiary, 'residing in the midst of manufacturers, was likely to form connections with them, and have his judgement biassed by their influence on his friendship'.[25]

1834 also witnessed working-class intervention on a third issue, of enduring interest to working people, the administration of poor relief. William Stacey, President of the Union at that time, speaking at Burslem annual vestry meeting, objected unsuccessfully to the reappointment of the overseer, because of his harsh treatment of applicants for relief, but succeeded in forcing a poll to elect two new parish surgeons: it was alleged that their election was enforced by 'an order from the Union Lodge' to unionist rate-payers. In Stoke parish, where two thousand people attended the annual meeting, there was also controversy, and elections ensued for the posts of workhouse governor, and two of the poor-rate collectors: John Richards, a candidate for one of the latter posts, was recommended, to the parish meeting as 'a real reformer and unionist', won the show of hands but was not elected in the subsequent poll; the other working-class candidate for collector, a pawnbroker, was elected to serve as collector for Longton.[26]

The relief of poverty, especially in Stoke parish, which included four of the six Potteries towns (Hanley, Stoke, Fenton and Longton), was an issue with which the potters' union became increasingly concerned. Controversy flared up again in November 1835 when G. T. Taylor, overseer, was dismissed for alleged neglect of duty and acting in defiance of the select vestry. At a stormy general vestry meeting a few weeks later, it emerged that Taylor's chief offence had been to offer parish relief to the families of men imprisoned for striking at a factory owned by one of the select vestry's members. The meeting agreed that he should be reinstated temporarily until the arrival of a commissioner from London to supervise the implementation of the 1834 Poor Law Amendment Act in the parish. Tangled parochial finances, allegations of corruption and inefficiency, and the levying of four rates within a year to clear a backlog of debt, meant that working-class ratepayers, as well as middle-class manufacturers, wanted to see a fresh start.[27]

When Assistant Commissioner Richard Hall arrived in Stoke in March 1836, he was alarmed to find the Potteries suffering from 'the encroachments of a body of daily increasing influence . . . the confederated workmen'. The final decisive trial of strength between union and manufacturers was to take place in the winter of 1836–37, and Hall's assessment was a shrewd one: 'the two parties, masters and servants, might be said to be measuring their strength against each other, and it was become a question of vital importance which of them was to have the command of the parochial resources'. The key issue at stake was whether or not strikers could be relieved by the parish. Hall met a delegation from the potters' union, who pressed the case for a low qualification – occupation of property worth £6 a year – for membership of the Board of Guardians, which would make it possible for working-class guardians to be elected. With skilful duplicity, he gave the impression he would recommend their views to the Poor Law Commission, but in fact recommended a £20 qualification.[28]

The NUOP had been decisively out-manoeuvred. At the first elections for the new Board of Guardians, held in May on a £20 qualification, the union circulated a list of recommended candidates, mainly publicans and shopkeepers, but only one of those elected, Thomas Simpson, was a reliable supporter of the union. When the great strike and lock-out began in the autumn, Edwin Chadwick instructed the Board that relief must not be paid to those in receipt of strike pay; the Board concurred, and when union funds were ultimately exhausted, the strike was defeated and the union collapsed. It was, therefore, the union's failure to achieve political control of the local institution most crucially relevant to working-class life, which ensured the defeat of its industrial objectives.[29]

Working-class attendance at vestry meetings was a familiar phenomenon well before 1834, but prior to that date the workers' participation was largely confined to support for middle-class spokesmen, usually the liberal reforming employers, John and William Ridgway, or, more rarely, their Tory opponents. From 1834 on, parish politics became an arena in which working-class spokesmen expressed their own views on local issues. Although Robert Owen showed no interest in such matters, for many of his followers such activity on issues affecting their daily lives, in their own communities, was an appropriate way to work for social change and to contest the middle-class monopoly of local power; it expressed, and helped to develop further, the increasingly confident working-class consciousness, which the general unionism and reform agitation of the early 1830s had engendered.[30]

However, this did not rule out continued co-operation with middle-class spokesmen where there was ground for agreement, for example, in opposition to Church rates. As the union grew more powerful, and the employers more hostile, industrial and class conflict sharpened; but even on the crucial issue of poor relief, there was general acceptance of John Ridgway's proposal to introduce the provisions of the 1834 Act in Stoke, no campaign against the principles of the Act, but only an attempt to gain control of the Board of Guardians, which was a failure. Mark Lancaster, the most prominent union spokesman, usually claimed to be expressing only his individual views on local politics but his opponents believed he had in fact made it plain that the Union wished to control parish affairs. If so, his aim was not realised.[31]

The 1830s saw the beginnings of active working-class participation in the local politics of the Potteries, which was to be conspicuous for the next twenty years. But it was certainly an exaggeration to allege, as a London paper did of the NUOP in 1834, that 'All local and parish business is now wholly conducted under their influence and dictation, where they choose to interfere'. Whether or not John Foster's view of Oldham at this time as being 'under the control of the organized working-class' is correct, the same cannot be said of the Potteries towns.[32]

THE CHALLENGE OF UNIONISM

The NUOP's commitments to general unionism and Owenite co-operation and involvement in local politics, at various stages in its history, are important aspects of its activity which have often been ignored or underestimated. These aspects alone, however, are insufficient to explain why the union appeared to its opponents to pose a real threat to the existing social order.

Initially, the union's emergence as a powerful force in the Potteries was welcomed by some manufacturers. Charles James Mason of Fenton wrote an open letter to the union, published in the *Staffordshire Mercury* in July 1833, in which he recommended its activities as a means of maintaining and standardising both the prices of ware and the wages of workers, and preventing competitive price-cutting, and consequent cuts in wages, by some manufacturers. Mason asked his own workers to join the union, and nearly four hundred new members were enrolled. The Union responded enthusiastically, and in the autumn entered into negotiations with a committee of manufacturers, which resulted in the establishment of a new list of prices and wages, and the setting up of a joint committee of manufacturers and unionists to meet regularly and discuss their differences. But, inevitably, the attempt to regulate the trade foundered when some manufacturers refused to adhere to the agreement, and in April 1834 the joint committee collapsed. Even at this time, however, Henry Davenport could still write to his father about the union, 'I think more good than evil has resulted at present.'[33]

Others were less sympathetic: in November 1833 the semi-retired manufacturer and county magistrate, Ralph Bourne, wrote to the Home Secretary to complain about the 'system of combination and intimidation among the operatives' who broke their annual contracts by selective strikes against manufacturers who refused to accept their demands. These from 1833 onwards, concerned more than wages alone: the union's demands in the autumn of 1833 included not only 'No one to receive less than five shillings a day for his labour', but also the limitation of working hours to between 6 a.m. and 6 p.m., in order to provide more jobs by, in effect, banning overtime, and an end to the practice of sending consignments of pottery abroad without a definite order, to avoid a glut on the market and consequent slump. Later union practices, of which employers at individual factories complained, included a sympathetic strike to force the re-employment of sacked unionists, and a strike against the employment of non-unionists, that is, for a closed shop. In one case, it was alleged that union officials put pressure on a manufacturer to compel his men to pay their union subscription arrears.[34]

The employers' opposition to unionism was muffled until the late summer of 1834 when the GNCTU collapsed, but the potters' union obstinately continued to thrive. In the autumn, at the time of annual hiring, ten large manufacturers in Burslem and Tunstall refused to continue paying the union rates agreed in 1833, and attempted to enforce reductions said to be from 30 to 35 per cent. As a result, at least 3300 potters struck for fifteen weeks, from November 1834 to March 1835, when the employers capitulated. The strikers won largely due to financial support from the union subscriptions of those at work in the other Potteries towns: it was the most notable victory for the tactic of selective strikes. During the spring and summer of 1835 several manufacturers attempted to stop this by prosecuting strikers for neglect of work and breach of contract. Eighteen men received sentences of three months in April, and thirty in August, when four leading unionists, including Mark Lancaster, were also convicted of intimidation, but appealed successfully on technicalities. The use of the courts in this way merely hardened the unionists' resolve.[35]

The annual hiring in November passed off peacefully, with a

general advance in wages which reflected both the industry's prosperity and the unbroken strength of the union. The early months of 1836, it was alleged, were marked by intensified efforts to enforce a closed shop, recruit more members and build up the union's funds for future strike action. In March the employers formed a Chamber of Commerce and began to plan a counter-offensive. The stage was set for the final confrontation, in which the central issue was not pay but terms of employment. The union put forward a new form of agreement incorporating the end of annual hiring, the substitution of one month's notice on either side, and an obligation upon the employer to find work for his employees; they also demanded an end to payment 'good from oven', rather than 'good from hand', which the masters saw as an attempt to overturn a time-honoured usage of the trade. The masters' alternative new form of agreement included a 'suspension clause', whereby a strike at one factory would justify them in ordering a general lock-out. They now used this tactic successfully. In September the union called fourteen factories out on strike against the employers' refusal to accept the union's terms; in November the Chamber responded by calling a general lock-out by its 64 members who between them employed about 80 per cent of the labour force or 15,660 men, women and children. By the end of January the potters were forced back to work, substantially on the employers' terms. The union lingered on for two or three months, as a powerless shadow of its former self, before disappearing completely, at a time of severe depression of trade.[36]

Although the union throughout its life, even at times of severe crisis, maintained a disciplined, peaceful and non-violent strategy, the alarm of the authorities was such that for long periods troops were stationed in the vicinity of the Potteries: possibly in May 1834 at the height of GNCTU activity; briefly in November 1834 when the strike at Burslem and Tunstall began; continuously from April 1835 to January 1836, occasioned by the mood of tension arising from the prosecutions and sentences for neglect of work; and finally from October 1836 to February 1837 during the great strike and lock-out. Such evident fear of the threat to social order which the union seemed to represent should be seen not only in the context of particular moments of crisis, but also as a result of certain consistent features of union activity, which alarmed the union's opponents.[37]

First, the NUOP cloaked its proceedings in secrecy. Even in the 'honeymoon period' with the employers, in response to Mason's overtures in the summer of 1833, the unionists were adamant that they must keep their plans secret from gentlemen. An informer alleged that 'they are all sworn on the Gospels, and that a person with a drawn sword is the Door Keeper and they have a regular pass word'. Fines might be levied on members for communicating with the masters. Secrecy had obvious advantages in concealing union strategy, and hindering the persecution of activists, and was an increasing source of anxiety and irritation to the employers.[38]

Second, the union's strength was made openly apparent in large public demonstrations and processions. The demonstration held to welcome unionists released from prison in July 1835 involved several thousand unionists in five separate contingents with banners, and three bands; it was organised with military precision, with the demonstrators forming up in file and marching off in response to the sound of trumpets, and falling silent after three beats on the long drum. The union placard of instructions ended by stressing 'it is hoped that no Potter will be seen intoxicated on that memorable day. All Unionists are requested to keep the greatest order, and report to the proper authorities any person attempting any breach of the peace, or injuring either persons or property.' Throughout the union's history, violence was notable by its virtual absence. Even during the winter of 1836–37, as John Boyle conceded, 'no outrage was committed during the strike, either on the person or property of any manufacturer'. Such collective self-discipline was alarming, because it showed the authorities that they had to deal, not with the relatively familiar phenomenon of a riotous crowd, but with a highly organised movement enjoying mass support.[39]

Available fragments of information on membership, organisation and finances confirm this impression. The union may have included at its height three-quarters of the adult pottery workers of North Staffordshire, close to Richard Hall's estimate of 8000 members in the spring of 1836. This membership was organized in 54 lodges, 9 in each of the six Potteries towns, covering the main branches of the trade; the Grand Lodge, or Board of Management, included the President, Secretary, Treasurer, perhaps a District President for each town, and the Presidents of each of the separate lodges. There was also, at least during 1834–35, a separate women's union with its own finances. In 1834 the weekly subscription was sixpence for men, threepence for women; the union's accounts for 1834–35 showed an annual turnover of £3000.[40]

Finally, the union was not merely a local, but a national body. Its activities are known to have extended to Bristol, Swansea, Worcester. Coalport (Shropshire), Liverpool, Whitehaven, Newcastle-on-Tyne, Sunderland, Stockton-on-Tees, Swinton (Yorkshire), Ashby Wolds (near Horncastle, Lincolnshire) and Derby. It also had links with other unions, and the extent to which these unions rallied to the potters' support in 1836–37 provides important evidence of the continuation of such links after the failure of the GNCTU, and support for R. A. Leeson's view that in the history of craft unionism 'the post-1834 period is not a hiatus, but a richly active one'. The outstanding efforts of the Sheffield trades, headed by the saw and file makers and grinders, in raising over £2000 to support the potters, are well-known; there is also evidence of fund-raising efforts and meetings to support the strike in London, Birmingham, Lichfield, Wolverhampton, Kidderminster, Macclesfield, Liverpool and even, it was said, 'Edinburgh, Aberdeen and other principal towns in Scotland'. At the end of December 1836 about forty trades delegates from other towns came to the Potteries to give their support, and attempt to mediate with the employers: they included men from Bristol, Worcester, Wolverhampton, Birmingham, Congleton, Manchester, Ashton-under-Lyne, St Helen's, Derby, Sheffield, Huddersfield and Glasgow. These lists are doubtless incomplete, but they indicate the national importance attached by unionists generally to the potters' union, and the way in which the strike and lock-out of 1836–37 acted as a focus for the struggle between labour and capital.[41]

Both parties to the conflict saw the outcome as crucial and expressed their views in terms of an essentially defensive class-consciousness, wishing to secure what they felt to be their just rights. For the Chamber of Commerce, 'The plain question at issue is, whether the masters shall be the managers of their own business, or whether the Union shall usurp their places, and thus destroy the trade.' The NUOP claimed that 'We are the producers of all wealth – the capital of our employers is a dead weight without our labour', but also that 'We only want our place.' The high tide of Owenite enthusiasm for social reconstruction had ebbed by 1836, even if a powerful undercurrent was still evident. The confrontation of 1836–37 was a moment of intense class conflict and resulted in one of the 'glorious defeats' with which the history of the labour movement is so well-endowed, and which was to leave its mark on subsequent developments, especially Potteries Chartism. But the class-consciousness of 1836 was scarcely revolutionary; in Foster's terminology, it may be better described as 'labour consciousness'. Even this, however, was a threat to middle-class hegemony, as Richard Hall implicitly recognised when he described the Potteries as suffused by 'peculiar habits and modes of thinking and feeling. To investigate the structure of this singular community would, I think, be the death of a regular Conservative. He never could support the contemplation of such entire emancipation from all the prejudices of antiquity, as is enjoyed there.'[42]

NOTES AND REFERENCES

1. **S.** and **B. Webb**, *The History of Trade Unionism*, Longmans, Green and Co. 1920 edn, p. 147; **R. H. Tawney**, introduction to **W. H. Warburton**, *The History of Trade Union Organisation in the North Staffordshire Potteries*, Allen and Unwin 1931, p. 13; **G. D. H. Cole**, *Attempts at General Union*, Macmillan 1953, *passim*.
2. **H. Owen**, *The Staffordshire Potter*, repr. Kingsmead Reprints 1970, pp. 19–46; Warburton, op. cit., pp. 34–101; **F. Burchill** and **R. Ross**, *A History of the Potters' Union*, Ceramic and Allied Trades Union 1977, pp. 58–76.
3. **E. P. Thompson**, *The Making of the English Working Class*, Gollancz 1963; **J. F. C. Harrison**, *Robert Owen and the Owenites in Britain and America*, Routledge and Kegan Paul 1969, p. 200; **John Foster**, *Class Struggle and the Industrial Revolution*, Weidenfeld and Nicholson 1974, pp. 1–2, 252. For discussion of Foster, see: **G. Stedman-Jones**, *Languages of Class*, Cambridge U.P. 1983, Ch. 1; **A. E. Musson**, 'Class struggle and the labour aristocracy, 1830–60' and rejoinder by **Foster**, *Social History*, **3** (Oct. 1976), pp. 335–66; **R. J. Morris**, *Class and Class Consciousness in the Industrial Revolution 1780–1850*, Macmillan 1979, *passim*, esp. pp. 39–44; **D. S. Gadian**, 'Class consciousness in Oldham and other North-West industrial towns 1830–1850', *Historical Jn.*, Vol. 21, No. 1 (March 1978), pp. 161–72; **R. A. Sykes**, 'Some aspects of working-class consciousness in Oldham, 1830–1842', *Historical Jn.*, Vol. 23, No. 1 (March 1980), pp. 167–79. Further work on 'Foster's Oldham' by Michael Winstanley of Lancaster University is in progress.
4. Thompson, op. cit, Penguin 1968 edn, pp. 875–6.
5. *Staffordshire Mercury*, Oct. 23, Nov. 20 1830; *Staffordshire Advertiser*, 16 and 23 Oct., 20 Nov. 1830.
6. *Staffs Mercury*, 5 Feb. 1831; *Voice of the People*, 29 Jan., 5 and 12 Feb., 5 and 26 Mar., 9 and 16 Apr. 1831 lists donations to the spinners' strike fund from the Potteries and Newcastle totalling £26 19s. 0d.
7. *Staffs. Mercury, Staffs. Advertiser*, 4 June 1831; PRO, HO 52/15, f. 184; Stoke-on-Trent Museum, Enoch Wood Scrapbook, f. 204[A].
8. *Voice of the People*, 10 Sept. 1831; *Staffs. Mercury*, 17 Sept., 8 Oct. 1831; Enoch Wood Scrapbook, op. cit., f. 242[A].
9. **R. G. Kirby** and **A. E. Musson**, *The Voice of the People: John Doherty 1798–1854*, Manchester U.P. 1975, pp. 260–261.
10. *Staffs. Mercury*, 28 Apr., 14, 21 and 28 July 1832.
11. *Staffs. Mercury*, 17 Aug. 1833; *Crisis*, 19 Oct. 1833.

12. Harrison, op. cit., p. 210.
13. *Pottery Mercury*, 18 May 1825; **John Boyle**, 'An Account of Strikes in the Potteries, in the years 1834 and 1836', *Jn. Statistical Soc. of London*, Vol. I (1839), p. 38; *British Co-operator*, 12 May 1830; *Crisis*, 23 June 1832, 5 and 19 Oct. 1833.
14. Robert Owen documents, Co-operative Union, Manchester, 622, 618. These and some other letters from the same source are printed in abridged versions with some errors of transcription, in Warburton, op. cit., pp. 256–60.
15. *Crisis*, Dec. 14 1833; Robert Owen documents, op. cit., 613.
16. Robert Owen documents, op. cit., 622, 618, 613.
17. Robert Owen documents, op. cit., 703; John Boyle, op. cit. p. 38; *North Staffs Mercury*, 6 Dec. 1834, 11 June 1836; *New Moral World*, 27 June 1835, p. 280.
18. *N. Staffs. Mercury*, 14 Nov. 1835; *Staffs Examiner*, 26 Nov. 1836; **A. E. Musson**, *British Trade Unions 1800–1875*, Macmillan 1972, p. 30.
19. *Crisis*, 19 Oct 1833.
20. HO 52/25, ff. 149–50; HO 52/24, ff. 148–52; Robert Owen documents, op. cit., 702; **W. H. Oliver**, 'The Consolidated Trades' Union of 1834', *Econ. Hist. Rev.*, Vol. 17 (1964), pp. 87–8.
21. HO 52/24, op. cit.; Oliver, op. cit.; *Pioneer*, 25 Jan. 8, 15 and 22 Feb., 15 and 22 March, 28 June 1834; Robert Owen documents, op. cit., 702; *N. Staffs. Mercury*, 24 May 1834, 25 Apr. 1835.
22. **C. Harrison** (ed.), *Essays on The History of Keele*, University of Keele 1986, p. 83; *Staffs. Advertiser*, 2 Aug. 1834; *Poor Man's Guardian*, 2 Aug. 1834, for a radical comment on this case.
23. Public Record Office (PRO), M. H. 32/34, R. Hall to E. Chadwick, 26 Mar. 1836.
24. *Staffs. Mercury*, 26 Oct. 1833, 11, 18 and 25 Jan., 1, 8 and 22 Feb. 1834.
25. *Staffs. Mercury*, 9 Nov. 1833–8 Mar. 1834 *passim*; HO 44/27; **W. White**, *History, Gazetteer and Directory of Staffordshire*, 1834, pp. 533–4; *N. Staffs. Mercury*, 6 and 13 Aug. 1836.
26. *N. Staffs. Mercury*, 22 and 29, Mar., 5, 12 and 19 Apr. 1834.
27. *N. Staffs Mercury*, 7, Nov. 5 Dec. 1835; *Staffs. Advertiser*, 5 Dec. 1835.
28. PRO., M. H. 12/11458, Hall to George Nicholls, March 21 1836; M. H. 32/34, Hall to Chadwick, March 26 1836; *Second Annual Report of the Poor Law Commissioners*, 1836, pp. 438–41.
29. *N. Staffs. Mercury, Staffs. Advertiser*, 7 and 14 May 1836; M.H. 12/11458 for Stoke Board of Guardians' correspondence with the Poor Law Commission 1836–37.
30. See *Pottery Mercury*, 31 Mar. 1824, 11 Apr. 1827; *Staffs Mercury* 26 Mar. 1831, 23 Mar. 1833 for reports of vestry meetings.
31. *N. Staffs. Mercury*, 31 Dec. 1836.
32. *Albion*, n.d. cit. *N. Staffs. Mercury*, 12 Apr. 1834, also in HO 52/25, f. 152; Foster, op. cit, p. 2.
33. *Staffs. Mercury*, 15 June, 13 July, 3 Aug., 21 and 28 Sept., 12 and 19 Oct. Nov. 11 1833; for C. J. Mason, see **R. G. Haggar**, *The Masons of Lane Delph*, Lund Humphries and Co. 1952, Ch. 6, and **R. G. Haggar** and **E. Adams**, *Mason Porcelain and Ironstone, 1796–1853*, Faber 1977; *N. Staffs. Mercury*, 12 Apr. 1834; HO 52/25, f. 149.

34. HO. 52/23, Bourne to Melbourne, 4 Nov. 1833; *Crisis*, 5 Oct 1833; *Staffs. Advertiser*, 16 May, 27 June 1835.

35. *N. Staffs Mercury*, 23 Aug. 1834; Warburton, op. cit, pp. 80–6; Boyle, op. cit., p. 40; *N. Staffs. Mercury*, 25 Apr, 15 Aug., 24 Oct. 1835.

36. *N. Staffs. Mercury*, 14 Nov. 1835, 6, 13 and 27 Feb., 19 Mar. 1836; Boyle, op. cit. pp. 42–3; Warburton, op. cit., pp. 88–101; *Staffs. Examiner*, 1 Apr. 1837 for last newspaper report of NUOP activity.

37. *N. Staffs. Mercury*, 31 May 1834, letter from 'An Inhabitant'; HO 41/12 *passim*, 1834–7.

38. *Staffs. Mercury*, 3 Aug. 1833; HO 52/23, Bourne to Melbourne, 7 Nov 1833; *N. Staffs. Mercury*, 31 Dec. 1836.

39. HO 52/27, f. 64; Boyle, op. cit, p. 44.

40. *Second Annual Report of the Poor Law Commissioners*, p. 439; *N. Staffs. Mercury*, 11 June, 31 Dec. 1836; HO 52/25, ff. 149–50; HO 52/27, f. 95.

41. *N. Staffs. Mercury*, 17 Aug. 1833, 11 June, 13 Aug. 1836; **R. A. Leeson**, 'Business as usual – craft union developments 1834–1851', *Bull. of Soc. for Study of Lab. Hist.*, **49** (Autumn 1984), pp. 15–17; *Important Meeting of Delegates in the Potteries*, 1837, repr. in Warburton, op. cit., pp. 264–82.

42. *N. Staffs. Mercury*, 15 Oct. 1836; R. J. Morris, op. cit. pp. 37, 40 and J. Foster, op. cit., *passim*; M.H. 32/34, Hall to G. Nicholls, 26 Mar. 1836.

CHAPTER TEN
Bristol Trade Unions in the Chartist Years

David McNulty

INTRODUCTION

In the summer of 1848 a Bristol trade unionist calling himself 'Vent-wire', characterised the organised trades of the city in a series of newspaper articles:

At one period of trading prosperity – exacting, and exclusive; in adversity – complying and solicitous seeking by every method to augment their strength. Now on the brink of dissolution from the want of funds; anon in the height of vigour with funds large and increasing . . . The *ostensible* objects of trade unions are generally – support to sick members unable to follow their ordinary employment; an allowance to the relatives of deceased members; to the maimed by accident and to the unemployed. The *real* inducement is – resistance to what may be thought oppression on the part of employers; advancement of, or prevention of a reduction of wages; limiting the number of hands as much as possible so as to create a demand for labour; and the employment of unionist workmen . . . With a singleness of mind and independence of character highly creditable to him he prefers to depend for his subsistence in stagnation of trade like the present on the funds of his union society wrung as these have been from the wages of his toil in prosperity to incurring the tender mercies or submitting to the degra-dation of the union house.[1]

Their influence, he argued, should have been 'gigantic', for they were the 'advance guard of labour': 'It is generally admitted that trade unionists are the most expert workmen in their respective trades. The rules of most of their unions forbid the admission to membership of any but proved, competent workmen.'[2] Their labour, moreover, was an inexhaustible resource and through their loan and building societies they had shown that they had the intel-ligence to create and run the necessary institutions. These capabilities gave them the potential to become the 'moral Hengists and Horsas' of the nineteenth century. This had not yet happened because leadership had not been confined to 'intellectual and experienced' members whose counsels had been neglected for 'the frothy language and violent determination of the illiterate and prejudiced'. Like the fanatical followers of the Juggernaut, the unionist had clung to the 'old, worn out, demoralising health destroying and politically disfranchising tendencies' which had led him at last to 'a slough of moral filth and social wretchedness'.[3]

Ventwire was particularly opposed to strikes and to tramping. He recognised that there might be times at which resistance to 'aggression and thoughtless dictation' was a duty, but defensive strikes occurred at times when employers did not find a withdrawing of labour very painful while offensive ones were wrong because when there was a sufficient demand for labour, wages should be regulated by individual merit and exertion. Exclusiveness he recognised as a defensive reaction to the new ability of the employer class to create an excess supply of labour, but argued that if unions were too successful they would simply drive from their district the employers they sought to control. Tramping not only destroyed health, morals and domestic happiness, but was ineffective in the face of the increasing surplus of labour.[4]

He identified a 'capitalist juggle' in which the labouring classes were robbed of nine-tenths of the value of their labour: a process of degeneration which was creating a race of slaves. Parliament underpinned this system and further robbed the working people through unequal taxation. Ventwire feared that immediate franchise extension would lead to class war when working men tried to achieve equality with a ruling class unwilling to relinquish its position. He urged unionists to reject political demagogues, patronising aristocrats and state interference, and suggested five simple steps to redemption: establish fixed residence by a weekly allowance for the unemployed; use funds to provide productive employment for them; start a fund for registration and obtaining the franchise; start weekly discussions in the branch and stop meeting in public houses. Learning from the mistakes of Fourier and Owen, unions should move towards the 'mightiest engine of progress' – co-operative production. From this political power would gradually follow.[5]

These articles provide a useful starting point for a discussion of the organised trades in the 1830s and 1840s. In typifying the self-image of respectable working men, Ventwire points to their analysis of the situation which they faced. He indicates their sense of threat to status; experience of deterioration and their historical understanding of their decline. He lists the range of remedies which they considered and demonstrates the eclectic nature of an analysis which was additive rather than substitutive. Ambiguities are revealed, not least the problem – also at the heart of Chartism – of the tension between an elitist sensibility and a mass movement. Ventwire reflects the values which both led artisans to act and which weakened their response towards the challenge of structural change.

Most workers in the organised trades believed that their position had markedly deteriorated by the 1840s. They usually dated the start of this decline to twenty or thirty years before, and identified two major related causes: the intrusion of large-scale capital into marketing arrangements and the growth of surplus labour. The first increased the opportunities for 'dishonourable' or 'unfair' masters to set up and intensified the competition between them and the 'honourable' or 'fair' masters. Middlemen supplying cheap ready-made goods for shops employed 'sweaters' to work below the standard prices of the trade. Artisans forced to become outworkers could not get work without providing security and had to accept the intervention of the middlemen. These set to work more people than they needed both to make profits from meals, lodgings and other charges and to sustain competition among the workers. Competition within the 'dishonourable' branch of a trade and between it and the 'honourable' branch led to a downward spiral of undercutting through wage and price reductions. The 'honourable' branch became an ever smaller section of the trade, reflecting a switch from day to piece work and from work on an employer's premises to outwork. 'Slop' which had once meant shoddy work came to mean good work done for bad wages.

Surplus labour was increased by these practices and further by de-skilling through an increased division of labour, a limited mechanisation and the employment of women and other 'unskilled' workers. This intensified competition for work and produced undercutting between workers. Again there was a vicious spiral. Men forced to work for lower piece rates were accordingly driven to produce more, while wives and other family members had to assist to maintain the family income. Inevitably this led to even more overstocked markets and increased surplus labour.

This system affected most severely those trades which catered for the basic consumer needs of the growing population. During the 1840s members of these trades sought answers in the reinforcement of elements of common interest linking 'fair' masters to 'respectable' workmen, and in the creation or strengthening of links binding the latter within and between trades. It was hoped such improved organisation could tackle the fundamental problem of surplus labour by institutionalising the 'customs of the trade'. Land schemes were also advocated as a means of reducing the surplus.[6]

There was a pattern to their efforts at preventing further deterioration. An incident such as a court case, a newspaper letter from a shocked observer, or the breaking out of a dispute with a particular employer would provoke an interest in the 'state of the trade'. A meeting would be called to try to unite the men in the trade, from which a deputation would confer with 'honourable' masters to seek their support. Sympathy might be sought through a public meeting and the presentation of a petition of grievances. The artisans might then form a new society linked to a national body or to other local trades. This improved organisation could then be the basis for action in defence of their status and interests.

Links between trades were based on the values of 'respectability'. Obviously such words, like artisan itself, can become elastic holdalls for the assimilation of the experiences of a 'dozen diverse groups' that in fact require separate analysis.[7] Nevertheless there was a common and consistent set of concerns which led groups faced by similar problems to develop a common defence. These values, stemming from the 'custom of the trade', craft skill and status and the attendant virtues of 'improvement' could establish working men as fully respectable and respected members of society. This artisan consciousness as an ideal drew in diverse groups. The division between respectable and non-respectable in itself depended upon whether trades could give organised expression to it. Values subsumed under 'respectability' whether as affirmation, aspiration, defence or recall of status, underpinned working-class organisation in the first half of the nineteenth century. Originally 'respectability' derived from the traditional property right of a trade skill which enabled a worker to maintain himself by his own labour.[8] It also meant being treated with dignity and respect, some control over hours of work, self-respect, pride and a general 'independence'. The relationship between being respectable and being respected could suggest links to puritan values of hard work, thrift and sobriety, and to emerging ideas of cleanliness, decent appearance and education but: 'Its chief elements lay not in behaviour but in a position of independence and in a status derived from possession of a skill and membership of a respectable occupation such as an honourable trade of value to the community.'[9] The emphasis upon personal moral qualities and behaviour was increased as the status of skill was eroded. By the Chartist period behaviour was of at least equal importance in defining 'respectability'.

Habits of frugality, industry, temperance, knowledge, pride in appearance and that of one's family, prudence, discretion, decency of conduct and language all became crucial aspects of a sense of moral and mental worth which defined a man as respectable. Working men shared this language of 'improvement' with the middle class, but it really described two distinct sets of values, the conflict between which came to a head in the Chartist years to be resolved by the movement's defeat. Subsequently working men accepted those parts of the dominant middle-class version which reflected long-standing artisan aims and adopted calculatively other aspects for specific purposes without losing their independent stance.[10]

To an extent these values echoed the ideal of the sober, industrious workman of good character being able to save money and set up as a master.[11] This had long been an unlikely prospect. By the 1840s to some extent the aspiration which underlay it had been replaced with a bitter contempt for the 'aristocracy of labour' who sought to join the middle class. With the intensification of competition the sense of a shared trade interest between masters and men was increasingly undermined and as the idea of harmony disintegrated, the defence of 'respectability' assumed more class-conscious tones. The vital elements of respectability, independence and mutual improvement were expressed and consolidated by association: 'the honest, sober, and reflecting portion of every town and village in the kingdom linked together as a band of brothers'.[12] Mental and moral improvement put stress on personal responsibility and individual achievement. The distinction between the informed and the uninformed was tagged onto others such as that between honourable and dishonourable and idle and industrious. It was even argued that the spread of knowledge itself produced the difference between the skilled and the unskilled.[13]

The sense of superiority central to 'improvement' developed naturally from occupations with a history of apprenticeship and of initiation into the 'mysteries' of the trade. Now it imposed itself as a missionary duty to elevate the rest of one's fellows. Personal example was of paramount importance. While respectability established a distance from the 'unimproved' it was intended to provoke emulation.[14] The 'improved' saw themselves as a vanguard whose example if followed would lead to the raising up of the whole class. They accepted the burdens of leadership and they expected others to listen, mark and inwardly digest. Above all the virtuous must not be swamped:

[the] zeal for numerical strength produced a real weakness; it gave power of demolishing the reputation of the worthy into the hands of the unworthy – it gave the frugal and the faithful the bitter reward of being supplanted by the idle and profligate . . . the most prudent measures were shouted down by the ignorant and the idle. Previous to witnessing these scenes I was, sir, an enthusiast for democracy; but my experience has convinced me that the only sure government for a union of the working class will be a mixed one, consisting of different grades. There will have to be a senate of intelligence possessing of course no privileges save those which their mental superiority obtains for them; but it must be placed in a position where it can be effective and not buried in the hubbub of riot and drunkenness.[15]

Sentiments such as these had their roots in the hierarchical organisation of artisan trades with wage differentials or other customary distinctions such as different books for different grades of worker at the House of Call, and they were reinforced by the sacrifices increasingly needed to acquire and sustain respectability. But if hierarchy there was to be, then it would be among working men. Criticisms made of their fellows by the 'improved' would be vehemently rejected if made by the middle class. Any notion of middle-class leadership was fiercely resisted and independent working-class organisation insisted upon. Problems could arise if one element of respectability was over-emphasised and thereby came into conflict with others. This was the cause of some bitter disputes within Chartism.[16]

Respectability could, then, encompass values which seemed ambivalent and paradoxical. However it remained in important respects a positive amalgam of trade and social requirements designed to protect the status of working men. It included a customary rate agreed between masters and men; similarly fixed conditions of employment; the ability to ensure that one's security was not threatened by events outside one's control such as illness; adequate diet, clothing and housing; access to education, especially for children, free from religious and social hypocrisy and the self-respect and accorded dignity which followed from all these. As behavioural aspects of respectability assumed greater significance in the 1840s groups of workers regardless of skill level or strength or status of their trade could be included in the idea of a general union provided they were ready to act honourably and that the scale of levies and payments could be adjusted suitably. Without breaking down notions of hierarchy within and between trades, respectability was thus a crucial linking element in the development of trade unionism.

FIRST PHASE: 1840–45

Chartists drew many lessons from the Reform agitation, among which was the significance of unions in mobilising popular support. They tried continually to bring the trades into the movement. In Bristol their success was limited by the influence exerted over the trades by Liberals, a vital element of their interest during the Reform years. In the 1837 election 23 trades organised support for the Liberal candidate whom they later helped to defend against Tory efforts to unseat him. Trades' support was indispensable in a constituency where the Liberals, who had lost any prospect of controlling the council, were clinging to the second of the two parliamentary seats by only fifty votes. The trades were also prominent in an Anti-Corn Law campaign at the beginning of the 1840s and in free–port agitation during 1846–48. Although between these episodes Chartists developed close links with the trades and Bristol was one of the initiators of the National Association of United Trades, they were destroyed by the systematic reassertion of Liberal influence.[17]

During the first phase of the movement Bristol Chartists had little organised trade support. They were unable to capitalise on local strikes or on national issues. There is hardly any recorded activity in support of the Glasgow cotton spinners, although Chartists did convene a special meeting for members of trade societies and factory workers. Enthusiastic reports were sent to the *Operative* about a trades committee, but the only reported delegates were from the engineers and combmakers.[18] Chartists wooed the trades with standard arguments. They began with the widespread distress and explained it by bad laws and by the failure to regulate the 'reckless spirit of competition' among businessmen which reduced labour to a 'marketable thing to be sold at the lowest price', destroying the harmony which should exist between masters and men:

It is one of the most gross and damnable falsehoods ever invented to assert that labour and capital, as at present situated, have a mutual interest in each other's prosperity; it is the interest of the capitalist to grind as much as he can out of the produce of the workman's toil, and the workman vice versa;

and never can the interests of the two become amalgamated until labour and capital be wielded by one and the same class of individuals.[19]

On top of this, taxation and high rents threatened ruin to the whole community:

If, for instance, a master shoemaker pays the greater portion of his profits away in taxes, or exorbitant rents, his income is thereby diminished; and in proportion to that diminution will his capabilities in the way of trade be lessened. He will not be able to furnish his men with so much work; and consequently neither he nor they will give so much encouragement to the baker, the grocer or other tradesman.[20]

The present corrupt political system was based on a monopoly of land and capital which had been achieved by usurpation and was now sustained by class legislation secured by a monopoly of representation. It was reinforced by taxation and the national debt. Universal suffrage would eradicate distress and unemployment by eliminating class legislation and restoring to property its proper uses and duties: 'the advancement of our race in all that tends to dignify and ennoble it; the affording to all food, clothing and shelter; the preservation of life; the felicity of home; the improvement of society; the bringing up and education of youth'. People would regain their natural property rights: 'the land and all that it contains of use to mankind; the sea and all that it contains necessary to their comfort and sustenance of animal life'.[21]

It is a commonplace that from 1840 there was renewed stress upon the need for Chartist links with the unions. In particular McDouall's plans have been noted. Organisationally his idea of trade-based National Charter Association (NCA) localities was significant for large cities, but otherwise his proposals were not much of an advance.[22] Bristol Liberals kept their grip on the trades until the winter of 1841. They relied upon them in the election of that year and in developing anti-corn law agitation. The turning point was the London masons' strike. Chartists were active in support group meetings for the masons and links developed rapidly between them and the trades. The fast-growing Bedminster locality had three masons on its twelve-man committee. A separate Bristol Trades NCA was started. These links improved steadily over the next two years and culminated in the National Association of the United Trades, of which shoemakers, tailors and cabinet-makers formed the core.[23]

In mid 1843 shoemakers struck against wage cuts. Their complaint was that rates were not fixed but subject to the whims of employers who reduced them without lowering prices and that they were kept waiting for work. They appealed to members of other trades who were similarly suffering 'the pressure of monopoly and competition' to protect their order in all disputes in resistance to wage cuts. A 'bond of union and fellowship' with other trades should be formed before all were degraded: 'Though the use of machinery did not immediately affect the cordwainers, yet when other persons in their old age were driven into destitution by its widely devastating influence, the injury in some measure extended to them also'. At the same time they declared their willingness to co-operate fully with any master paying a fair wage and to display their loyalty when Prince Albert visited the city in the hope of gaining his patronage.[24]

Early in 1843 a tailor was summoned for pawning his employer's materials to buy food. Herapath, a radical magistrate, used the occasion to denounce unions, which by keeping wages artificially high encouraged people to use cheap slop shops. He wanted tailors to price themselves into work by allowing wages to fall to their 'proper' level and urged them not to spend the first three days of the week in the pub and then expect to work for exorbitant wages during the rest of the week. In reply the tailors stressed the harmony between 'respectable' masters and their men, and pointed out that wages were in such cases at a 'customary' level which long experience had proven to be necessary to keep workers in 'tolerable respectability'.[25]

Seven years later George Jenkins who had worked in the trade for 25 years following his father, described its deterioration:

In the time of his father every man had full compensation for their labour and were enabled to bring up their families as parents would wish to do and give their children a tolerably good education . . . The wages paid them by the honest portion of the trade they had no wish to alter . . . This was no movement against the masters for when they first commenced it they laid their intentions open to the honest portion of the employers, asking them for their support . . . The slop system . . . destructive of health and in many cases of the lives of those who are engaged in it; it had been destructive of every possible means of a man doing any good for himself or for his family, to cultivate his mind, or of rendering any service to the community. The middleman system . . . they take work from the shops at a low price and then employ others at a still lower rate to do the work for them; working men, women and children were huddled together in rooms which served for workshops, kitchens, sleeping rooms, and hospitals, thus destroying their health, happiness and morals, and spreading contagion around them.[26]

Now only 10 per cent of the men received a fair wage and this would persist until there was a return to the custom of master tailors employing their men on their own premises: 'the system of outdoor labour having called into existence a class of persons called sweaters who take out large quantities of work and who in order to have a large percentage employ persons in the last stage of destitution, at the lowest possible wages, in the lowest and most miserable neighbourhoods'. These traders without capital employed broken-down men, boys and girls and by providing board and lodging kept them permanently in debt. Similarly, the foremen at slop warehouses ran tommy shops and beer houses.[27]

At the end of 1842 the operative cabinetmakers met in the Chartist rooms to consider the state of their trade and measures to prevent further reductions. Sam Jacobs, secretary both of the cabinetmakers and of the Bristol Chartists, tried to persuade them to accept his plan for a National Trade Benefit Society.[28] A year later the cabinetmakers affiliated to the Manchester Union because, 'one great society' of the whole trade was needed to prevent the continual reductions in order to: 'preserve to ourselves a sufficiency of food, clothing and shelter, to maintain our wonted respectability and save our trade from that wretched fate that hath befallen too many of the hitherto flourishing and respectable occupations'.[29]

Within four months they had persuaded members of the old society to join and had agreed to Jacob's suggestion:

That for the further benefit of the trade, it is advisable that a union of all trade bodies in this city, and ultimately throughout the Empire, should be effected upon the principle of mutual protection, having for its first object the furnishing of employ to those members that may be thrown out of work by strikes, or any other causes over which they have no control; secondly the increase of the trade's funds with the profits; and lastly the relief of the sick.[30]

The United Trades Association of Bristol had begun in February 1844. Jacobs, Hyde the shoemakers' secretary and Rooke, a Chartist shoemaker, were delegated to visit lodges to recruit support. The cabinetmakers, shoemakers, tailors, masons, saddlers, corkcutters and tinplate workers joined immediately.[31] A little later the carpenters sent two delegates, both Chartists. This association was intended to give mutual protection without interfering with the 'established usage of any trade or body of operatives' thereby combining 'great utility with little expense – giving no cause for distrust nor offering any chance for peculation'.[32] They prepared proposals for a union of all trades in Bristol and the nation with the immediate objective of mutual assistance to resist cuts and relieve distress. They suggested a strikers' employment fund and their ultimate aim was the 'elevating (of) our order to their former respectability and comfort':

In pursuance of the above objects we have from time to time investigated our present position compared with that of former years – have sought out the causes of the strange anomalies that present themselves to our senses in abundance and poverty; but so conflicting was the mass of evidence with which we had to deal that it was found to be no ordinary labour to trace out the chief cause of the innumerable ills that afflict us, as the primary cause of our degraded position. After much mature deliberation, we came to the conclusion that over production was an evil with which we should immediately grapple – over production itself being but an effect of a negative cause, the want of regulation in supply to meet the demand. The business of regulation belongs of necessity to the operatives and should be the primary object of all trade societies. This regulation cannot be effected by single trade exertions but only by the conjoint labours of every trade society in a general union.

Regulation would be achieved by four means: stopping wage cuts and long hours as both were linked to over production in a continuous downward spiral; organising a boycott of 'trashy goods'; raising wages and shortening hours to produce an upward spiral that would expand home demand and, fourthly, if machinery or other factors made it necessary, guiding surplus labour into other channels.[33] Further local support was sought and, although only the wood sawyers were persuaded to join, they decided to circulate widely their plan of organisation for all the trades of the Empire and to link with the London United Trades.

The United Trades Association organised the campaign of 1844 in Bristol against the Master and Servant Bill.[34] When, however, they tried to arrange a testimonial for Duncombe, the Bill's main opponent in Parliament, they were superseded by a General Trades committee under Liberal influence. An arrangement was agreed by which the Liberals were to provide room, money and some 'respectable' speakers for a public meeting at which, in return, their MP, Berkeley, was to be praised. Some Chartists had agreed to this, but others disrupted the meeting by attacking Berkeley. The United Trades delegates supported the Liberals.[34]

SECOND PHASE: 1845–48

In January 1845 Jacobs sent his plan to the *Northern Star* which refused to insert it. He had wanted to avoid the expense of a

conference by getting each locality to put forward a plan for circulation, the best being then adopted.[35] Bristol United Trades, who
now included the brass founderers, sent a delegate to the founding
conference of the National Association of United Trades (NAUT).
Their plan was after discussion rejected as impracticable because it
combined the two principles of organisation of trades and of land
allocation: Jacobs having the idea of buying land for industrial buildings.[36] He was a leading figure at the 1846 NAUT conference where
he chaired the committee that drew up a scale of levies and payments
which divided the trades into five sections with respective ranges of
dues and payments. He suggested that a fund of £50,000 would be
sufficient to dissuade employers from provoking strikes and wanted
it to be an employment fund, opposing arguments that the NAUT
should only support defensive strikes. This, he thought, would allow
another organisation to emerge as a rival. He argued that strikes
could often not be avoided and could be successful, as in Bristol
where the cabinetmakers had gained 50 per cent on their wages after
a two-week strike that had cost £100.[37]

Jacobs in fact exaggerated the success of the Bristol strike. In
August 1846, after nine months' effort, the cabinetmakers still felt
dissatisfied with their prices. The strike had been well organised:

you all know something of our labours: we waited on most of you: you
joined – with your help we made the list. By November all was ready –
we all struck at once – the blow was decisive, the rise was quickly gained,
we began with the lowest and upward went. Since then some small fry have
been dealt with and higher shops have risen to more reasonable prices; there
have been here and there a little wriggling to break from the list but by
prompt action all has been righted and now the committee know of no journeymen that are working otherwise than at fixed prices.[38]

The strike had reclaimed 15 per cent towards book prices, but the
union was still not properly established and had not fully restored
previous losses. It found problems keeping new members. The strike
had depended upon recruiting members in shops throughout the
city. There were 33 members at the start and 181 by 1846, but Jacobs
was appealing to many of these to pay their subs.[39] He hoped that
the NAUT would help them to open a factory for strikers. Experience with the cabinetmakers confirmed his belief in inter-union
activity as the only security for working men, but not in the
exclusive sense of a labour 'aristocratic association' embracing the
'select of diverse crafts':

that portion of the working class who seek the offices of foremen in the
workshop, and when obtained are ten times more tyrannical than the middle

class themselves, serving the employers at the expense of the trade they rose in. They will have the aristocracy of labour who ape the gentlemen and despise the plain, sensible, honest operative; a class of selfish beings who have not the moral feeling and courage to make the least sacrifice to serve the cause of their suffering order.[40]

Trades must recognise that they were 'children of one common parent against their one common enemy' and destroy: 'the barriers of prejudice, party spirit, petty selfish feeling and aristocratic pride that had for years divided the different classes of workers'.[41] Jacobs was ready to join with anyone, even handloom weavers. The benefits of the NAUT were: a huge strike fund; an end to tramping; and an extensive home market, while the profits of self employment would guarantee comfort, independence and indissoluble ties of brotherhood.[42]

History offered lessons:

The trades have long tried local societies and found them powerless for good. They next tried general unions of particular trades and found that these could not successfully resist the encroachments of the task masters . . . They then attempted to form a National Trades Union; but it was broken to pieces through mismanagement before it had grown into a 'monster combination'. I thank God that the NAUT has arrived at that state.[43]

His view of strikes was simple:

all strikes had arisen from one cause – in encroachments effected or attempted on the wages, rights or privileges of labour – there have therefore occurred but two classes of strike, defensive or offensive or rather protective and reclaiming, the first to resist encroachments, the second to regain what had at some previous time of weakness been taken.[44]

At present strikes were unavoidable and all the NAUT could do was to provide employment during them. But soon arbitration would replace strikes. Eventually a 'new age of philosophy, truth and general happiness' would end the need for strikes.[45]

Jacobs worked successfully as a NAUT missionary in Scotland during 1846 and 1847. He was dismissed acrimoniously in May 1847 because he had not managed to persuade his own trade to affiliate. Bristol trades seem to have been slow to join the NAUT, but eventually the tailors, plasterers, painters, brushmakers, nailors, sailcloth weavers, curriers, masons, carpenters and joiners were involved.[46]

The city's trades had faced problems during these years. Hyde, leader of the shoemakers and first secretary of the United Trades, chaired the 1845 conference of the boot and shoemakers and called upon all trades to rid themselves of their 'aristocratic pretensions'.

A year later the shoemakers were not able even to send a delegate, though they hoped soon to regain their lost position. During 1846 the carpenters were in dispute over the method of recording their work.[47] Early in 1847 they circularised employers appealing for an advance because of the high price of provisions. By 1848 unemployment was severe. The union was paying 10s. a week to unemployed men. The masons had begun a bitter dispute in 1847 when they had sent an open letter stating their need for a rise, proper regulation of hours and the exclusion of unskilled men. The employers defeated them by using scabs and offering overtime and pay increases to some workers.[48]

Some trades responded to problems by looking to the NAUT for help, but for most trades the dominant concern became the agitation for a free port. This led to the reassertion of political influence over the trades by the Liberals. The port had been an issue for many years, but was revitalised in 1846 with the formation of a Free Port Association (FPA). Liberals organised an operatives' offshoot. Straightaway more than twenty trades affiliated and campaigned vigorously for a municipalised port accepting the argument that their situation depended on it. Their aim was achieved in 1848 and they were then left to pay off the debts of the parent Free Port Association.[49] The campaign had absorbed the energies of most of the trades, including all those who had been in the United Trades, as well as those of the individuals who had led Chartist and trades' activity over the previous five years. A renewal of Liberal control is obvious from a glance at the leading figures in the operatives' Free Port Association. The chairman, Davis, had helped the Liberals in the 1837 and 1841 elections and had organised support for the Anti-Corn Law campaign. The secretary, Johnson, had organised the Irish vote for Berkeley in 1841 and had been secretary of the city's Complete Suffrage Union. The treasurer, Matthias, had supported the Liberals since 1837. Most committee members had had similar careers.[50]

Chartists had recognised from the outset the importance of securing effective links with the organised trades. They had wanted the practical advantages of financial and organisational capacity, and they had had to combat the Liberals for whom the support of the trades had become a major part of their own political influence. The Chartists did not develop a specific analysis to appeal to the trades: rather they interpreted the problems facing them in terms of a more general radical critique of the political system. Although this perhaps seemed relevant in the first phase of Chartism, when events such as the persecution of the Glasgow cotton spinners seemed to confirm fears of a systematic onslaught against the labouring community, only preventable by ending the upper and middle class's monopoly of legislation, the Chartists still gained relatively little support.

After 1840 involving the trades became more central to Chartist thinking, but there was no significant extension by them of their analysis of the difficulties faced by working men. Although there was an increase in the formal support offered by the trades, the Chartists were still in competition for it with the Liberals. This support came mainly from the trades under pressure. From 1842 onwards the Chartist movement declined in a changing political context which made its strategy untenable while its critique lost its relevance and certainty. At this point trades which had developed specific analyses of their own decline began again to seek solutions in inter-trade co-operation. This was facilitated by a growing sense of class and, as important, a shared ideal of 'respectability'. Individual Chartists had a leading role in these efforts, but the Movement did not. When the Liberals introduced in the Free Port agitation a convincing local explanation for the decline of the trades, Chartist influence evaporated.

NOTES AND REFERENCES

1. *Bristol Mercury*, 17 June 1848. The articles appeared between 10 June and 29 July 1848.
2. Ibid. 10 and 17 June and 15 July 1848.
3. Ibid. 24 June and 1, 8 and 15 July 1848.
4. Ibid. 24 June 1848.
5. Ibid. 1, 8 and 15 July 1848.
6. See **E. P. Thompson** and **E. Yeo** (eds), *The Unknown Mayhew: selections from the Morning Chronicle 1849–1850*, Penguin 1971; **C. Behagg**, 'Custom, class and change: the trade societies of Birmingham', *Social History*, **4**, No 3, (1979), pp. 455–80.
7. **E. P. Thompson**, 'The very type of the "respectable artisan"', *New Society*, 3 May 1979.
8. See **J. G. Rule**, 'The property of skill in the period of manufacture', in **P. Joyce** (ed.), *Historical Meanings of Work*, C.U.P. 1986, pp. 99–118.
9. **I. J. Prothero**, *Artisans and Politics in early Nineteenth-Century London: John Gast and his times*, Dawson, Folkstone 1979, p. 27.
10. **P. Bailey**, 'Will the real Bill Banks please stand up? Towards a role analysis of mid-Victorian working-class respectability', *Jn. Soc. Hist.*, XII, 1979, pp. 336–53.

11. *Bath Guardian*, 19 July 1834.
12. *Wiltshire Independent*, 20 Dec. 1838, Prospectus of the East London Mental Improvement Association.
13. *Bath Guardian*, 19 July 1834, Francis Place; *Guantlet*, 15 Sept. 1833.
14. *National Vindicator*, 13 and 27 Nov. 1841, 'Pause'.
15. *Crisis*, 28 June, 5 July 1834; see also *Guantlet*, 15 Sept. 1833; *National Vindicator*, 27 Nov. 1841.
16. Ibid. 18 Sept. 1841, 'Pause'.
17. **R. G. A. Mackenzie**, 'The Parliamentary Representation of Bristol 1837–1859 and the Political Career of Henry Berkeley', M. Litt. thesis, Univ. of Bristol 1976; *Bristol Mercury*, 15 July 1837.
18. *Operative*, 25 Nov. 1838. Samuel Jacobs was a member of this committee.
19. *Bath Guardian*, 2 June, 24 Nov. 1838; *Western Vindicator*, 13 July, 24 Dec. 1839, Moses Clements.
20. *Western Vindicator*, 31 Aug. 1839, "Publicola".
21. *National Vindicator*, 11 and 18 Dec. 1841.
22. *McDouall's Chartist and Republican Journal*, 17 Apr., 21 and 28 Aug. 1841.
23. *Northern Star* (hereafter *NS*) 27 Nov., 4 Dec. 1841, 29 Jan., 5 Feb., 5 and 26 Mar., 30 Apr. 1842.
24. *Bristol Mercury*, 24 June 1843; *Bristol Times*, 24 June 1843. The 'pressure of monopoly and competition' refers to the slop system with a small number of slop warehouses at the top of the trade giving out all the work to a host of middlemen desperately undercutting each other.
25. *Bristol Mercury*, 1 Apr. 1843.
26. *Report of a Public Meeting of the Tailors of Bristol*, Bristol 1850.
27. Ibid. See also *Bristol Mercury*, 9 March 1844.
28. *NS*, 24 Sept. 1842.
29. *NS*, 28 Oct. 1843.
30. *NS*, 2 Mar. 1844.
31. *NS*, 24 Feb. 1844. The Webbs suggest that the NAUT began in 1845 following a letter to Duncombe after the defeat of the Master and Servant Bill, S. and B. Webb, *History of Trade Unionism*, rep. Clifton, 1973, pp. 186–95.
32. *NS*, 30 Mar. 1844. The tailors' delegate was George Jenkins.
33. *NS*, 29 June 1844.
34. *NS*, 13 Apr., 4 May 1844; *Bristol Mercury, Bristol Journal* and *Bristol Mirror*, 13 Apr. 1844; *Bristol Gazette*, 11 Apr. 1844. *NS*, 14 and 21 Sept. 1844; *Bristol Gazette*, 12 and 19 Sept. 1844; *Bristol Times, Bristol Mercury, Bristol Journal*, 14 Sept. 1844. There had been previous disputes between different Chartist associations in the city.
35. *NS*, 1 and 15 Feb. 1845.
36. *NS*, 2 Aug. 1845; *Bristol Mercury*, 2 Aug. 1845.
37. *NS*, 6 June 1846. See **M. A. Shepherd**, 'The origins and incidence of the term "Labour Aristocracy"', *Bull. of Soc. for Study of Lab. Hist.*, **37** (1978), pp. 51–67, and **D. McNulty**, 'Working Class Movements in Somerset and Wiltshire 1837–1848', Ph.D. University of Manchester 1981, appendix 2.

38. *NS*, 15 Aug. 1846.
39. Modern Records Centre, Univ. of Warwick, MSS 78/CU/4/1/1; 78/CU/4/1/2.
40. *NS*, 18 June 1842.
41. *NS*, 6 Feb. 1847.
42. *NS*, 30 Jan. 1847, 26 Sept. 1846, 27 Feb. 1847.
43. *NS*, 5 Dec. 1846.
44. *NS*, 17 Oct. 1846.
45 *NS*, 5 Dec. 1846.
46. *NS*, 12 June, 3 July, 25 Sept., 16 Oct., 13 Nov. 1847 and 4 Sept. 1847 to 19 Feb. 1848.
47. *NS*, 2 and 12 Apr. 1845, 16 May 1846. The establishment of 'mutual employment shops' was recommended. *Bristol Gazette*, 9 April 1846.
48. Ibid. 18 Feb. 1847; *Bristol Mercury*, 5 Feb. 1848, 27 Feb., 10 Apr. 1847; *Bristol Journal*, 17 Apr. 1847; *Bristol Gazette*, 15 and 22 Apr. 1847; *Bristol Times*, 24 Apr. 1847.
49. The campaign of the free port is reported in the Bristol press through October and November 1846. For the debt see: *Bristol Mirror*, 20 Oct. 1848.
50. See McNulty, 'Working Class Movements'.

CHAPTER ELEVEN
Employers and Trade Unions, 1824–1850

Michael Haynes

INTRODUCTION

Employers have been the missing item on the agenda of labour history.[1] Although there has been an attempt to remedy this for the later nineteenth century, with a few notable exceptions, the reactions of employers to unions before 1850 have been little explored.[2] Searching for employers in a trade union history is as frustrating as searching for trade unions in a business history. The two fields seem separate worlds, even when an historian is an acknowledged authority in both.[3] It is difficult to see who gains from this, when any understanding of the totality of class must deal with employers as well as with workers and when even the narrower debates over the nature of early trade unionism have to be related to employer strategies. Musson's insistence, for example, on the dominance of 'limited trade union interests' implicitly assumes that some employers were prepared to recognise at least tacitly that questions of wages, hours, apprenticeship and technical change were matters around which workers could legitimately organise. The opposite view, that trade unionism spilled over into politics, implies that employers could not accept the legitimacy of organisation, even in pursuit of narrow objectives.[4]

Given the neglect, there is a danger that a general survey of employers' attitudes might come out resembling one of those wonderful early maps of Africa; a geography of the imagination, where the coastline is reasonably firm but the interior a no-man's land. The odd landmark appears distorted by a lack of perspective while the vast spaces in between are populated either by mythical beasts who consume the living flesh of slave workers or are magical

Edens where men work in real and lasting contentment. Nevertheless the attempt must be made and not only to provoke others to
do better. Justification lies in the fact that thus far employer attitudes
and their rationale have been dealt with by assumption. To uncover
and if necessary challenge these assumptions is important.

THE 'TYRANNY OF THE MARKET'?

No assumption has been more pernicious than that which asserts that
employers' reactions were simply a product of their market situation.
Clearly accounts of employer strategies must start from the situation
of the firm, but they cannot be directly read off from its balance
sheet. Market situations are complex with employers able to look
at a number of different indicators of their position. Historians have
too often identified general pressures without specifying precisely
how they operated on employers. A clear example is the emphasis
on competition as the determining force in industrial relations,
according to which, employer or managerial discretion increases as
competition decreases. Monopoly gains can be shared between
employers and workers allowing the development of strategies in
which unions can be recognised and integrated. It is then suggested
that because of the level of competition before 1850, employers were
more hostile to unions except in those cases where their market was
protected, either in previously competitive industries beginning to be
monopolised, or where small master and artisan relationships had
yet to be subjected to the solvent of competition.

This seductive schema can be dismissed. In the first place it is not
clear that businessmen were in such a hostile competitive environment before 1850. Fierce competition has often been invoked by
historians without an empirical basis. Payne has questioned the
traditional picture of the 'embattled entrepreneur' and expressed
'doubts concerning the relative magnitude of the difficulties
confronting the entrepreneurs of the industrial revolution'.[5] Despite
a sharp response from Church, who thinks the judgment itself to
have a weak empirical basis, recent macro-economic stress on the
slowness of change seems to support Payne.[6]

Secondly it must be recognised that competitive structures are
relatively slow in changing. It is difficult to see them as a cause of
a change in an employers' level of hostility to unions except in the
very long term or in the special case of previously uncompetitive

markets suddenly made competitive. There were undoubtedly such cases, but Clapham's view that in general competition was sharper *after* 1850 better accords with what we know of the integration of the national and international economies. Competition was uneven both between regions and industries in the earlier period. Moreover internationally too, broadly similar competitive and industrial structures have given rise to a wide variety of employer strategies.[7]

These problems are no less evident if employer strategies are analysed over time in a single industry. In the pottery industry, for example, although by the 1830s an industrial structure had emerged that was to remain largely unchanged until the twentieth century, between 1825 and 1850 the employers moved from a degree of co-operation with their workers through to open confrontation and then to laying the basis for an arbitration system in the years immediately after 1850.[8]

Thirdly competition was never so intense as to prevent some employers maintaining an impressive degree of unity against unions reinforcing voluntary organisation with systems of bonds and fines. Although many contemporaries denied that employers' combinations existed or were even possible, a growing literature has revealed the tenacity with which they developed in some industries. They were often strengthened and consolidated by the threat of unions, but it is time to question the view that they were simply a response to combinations of workers.[9]

Another approach seeks explanation in terms of a surplus labour market. Surplus labour certainly reduced the costs of employer opposition and in some trades undercut the possibility of building unions altogether, but it is too broad an explanation. The costs of employer opposition were never zero, and further it cannot serve in industries where there was a minimum skill barrier. It is by no means clear that employers were more compromising in cases of this kind, or where they faced labour shortages.[10] In fact there was not a single but a multiplicity of labour markets in nineteenth-century Britain so arguments of this kind would require close specification. Even then an emphasis on labour surplus is not a dynamic explanation unless related to the trade cycle. We know too little about unemployment, and it has been argued that too much emphasis has been placed on misleading partial figures and that it is unlikely to have been worse before 1850 than after.[11] The preference of employers in some industries for short-time working also suggests that the costs of dispensing with labour were higher than the surplus labour argument allows.[12]

It is more sensible to regard both competition and surplus labour as helpful general explanations in the analysis of the pattern by which employer strategies change. Other things being equal a less competitive market structure where there is no labour surplus will make it easier to co-opt and incorporate unions, but other factors are also necessary to explain developments and changes in employer strategies. It is more appropriate to look at a relatively dynamic economic force such as variations in the rate of profit. Unfortunately evidence is difficult to trace here too. Foster has argued that the cotton industry developed an 'almost suicidal economics' and Church more generally that 'profit rates were relatively modest and came under constant pressure'.[13] But while certain industries did have problems, the evidence of a general profits crisis, even when dressed up as a Kondratiev downswing, remains tenuous. Even in an industry like cotton the majority of firms managed to survive the major crises.[14] Nor were general pressures ever so intense as to preclude different responses within the same industry. Henry Ashworth noted that Preston cottonmasters attempted to maintain wage rates through fluctuations while in Bolton they followed them.[15]

What lies behind these empirical difficulties is important and interesting. That similar economic backgrounds can give rise to dissimilar employer strategies towards labour reflects the fact that the economic situation of the firm does not precisely determine how labour is used. The problem is the assumption that the external market creates a despotic regime within the firm. In a simple economic model productivity and wages may be determinate, but labour is a process and productivity is variable even with a given technique – as more modern theory admits and as writings on the 'labour process' insist. Employers have a choice in how they seek to maximise profits in any given situation. If they respond to external factors through labour policies, then we have to explain why it is *labour* costs that they seek to cut as well as why any particular strategy is deployed to that end. At a crude level the second choice may be viewed as involving either a strategy of direct control in which worker responsibility is minimised by close supervision and coercion or of 'responsible autonomy' in which worker responsibility and co-operation is encouraged to the benefit of the firm. Less crudely there are a number of possible variations which makes it better to think of a repertoire of available labour strategies even when competition is sharp.[16] Indeed the competitive argument can be stood on its head. A competitive environment with rapid technological change can be seen as conducive to union recognition if employers see co-operation as a means of minimising disruption. Indeed this is one of the reasons advanced for the rise of conciliation and arbitration after 1850.[17] Thus even if we demonstrate that external economic pressures lay at the root of employer strategies, we still must show why those strategies developed in one direction rather than another.

But another dimension of employer reaction should also lead us away from reading strategy too directly from economics. Leaving aside both industrial and local differences, the responses of employers to unions were more generally structured and not least by the state. Employers are, in Marx's phrase, 'hostile brothers' – both united and divided by their role in production. The divisions are rooted in the economic, but overlaid and often consolidated by social and cultural divisions. This makes it difficult for all employers to act with one voice. To order their disparate interests and to try and define a collective interest is the task of the capitalist state. One does not need recourse to modern Marxist theories of the state to accept this. It was commonly enough accepted when presented to contemporaries, for example, throughout the debate on the repeal of the Combination Laws. *The Times* insisted that Parliament could not simply be guided by the views of the masters: 'there are so many cases in which the master has no objection to a combination, which he may allege as a pretext for raising the price of his article'. Others went further, believing that while employers would oppose unions in their own firms, they would support them in their competitors. Nassau Senior was so concerned about this that in 1831 he proposed to Melbourne that the law be changed to introduce severe penalties for any employer doing this.[18]

One of the clearest examples of the belief that employers were not the best judges of their collective interests is provided by Sir Archibald Alison. As Sheriff of Lanarkshire from 1834 and a leading Tory publicist, he was one of the more formidable foes of early trade unionism. Constantly he despaired of the spinelessness of local employers:

they invariably looked upon the Sheriff as a sort of machine which, without being supplied with men or money, or costing them one shilling of expense, was to conduct the whole detection and prosecution of crimes within his jurisdiction; and on the least appearance of the public tranquillity being threatened, was to rear up as if by magic a vast civil force capable of effecting anything, and possessing the admirable quality of costing nothing.

When he had succeeded in organising the routs of the Glasgow cotton spinners and the Lanarkshire iron workers and colliers in

1837–38, at the Glasgow Exchange, 'the whole persons in the room with one accord took off their hats' when he went in, but the local employers were still unwilling to pay for a proper county police force. After the terrors of the Spinners' strike a committee of cotton masters and associated country gentlemen joined with him to try to set up such a force but were soon trying to get him to pay for the cost of publicising their cause. An historian of the French Revolution, Alison soon found it increasingly hard to separate his views of his own local ruling class from his views of the French in 1789: 'in the terrors of moneyed men, of which on the occurrence of every crisis I received the most convincing proof, I perceived the truth of Mirabeau's observation that a "capitalist is the most timid animal in existence"'.[19]

His view of the local employers was overdrawn. But it is a necessary correction to the folk vision of entrepreneurs of this era. Few businessmen had the self-confidence of the leading cotton masters like Henry Ashworth and few industries had employers who shared the 'messianic sense of the cotton manufacturers' destiny as the nation's spirit of enterprise and social conscience'. Indeed we may question how accurate this view is even of the cotton masters.[20] The average employer, then as now, was more likely a 'plodding man of business', operating within a given environment rather than consciously trying to transform it.

Thus we have to see employer attitudes as being formed by the interaction of their own circumstances with the wider social, political and ideological structures of the day. To single out some of the latter, though it may do violence to the interaction, is a necessary task. In attempting it we can look two ways: towards those elements which encouraged and supported a hostile view of unions and towards those chinks and fissures which allowed a degree of freedom and were later widened to accommodate them within capitalist society without fundamentally challenging it.

THE STATE AND EMPLOYERS

Then as now the framework for union activity and employer response was set by the state. To understand how its role changed between 1825 and 1850 it is helpful to review the rationale for the repeal of the Combination Acts. Moves for repeal came to a head in 1823 when Peter Moore presented a bill that had been drawn up by Gravenor Henson and George White. Place dismissed it as 'a beautiful scheme of legislation, as complicated and absurd as two such ill-instructed men could well contrive'. Moore agreed under pressure to postpone its introduction until the following session when it was by-passed by the manoeuvrings of Place and Joseph Hume for the select committee which eventually paved the way for the 1824 Repeal Act. This was significantly narrowed in 1825 after a wave of strikes. However, for a full appreciation of events we must rescue the Henson–White Bill from the dustbin of history.[21]

It was 'absurd' only from the perspective of the emerging political economy at which well Place and Hume had drunk deeply. In fact it was the last and most comprehensive attempt to legislate in defence of a traditional artisan way of life and its interest went beyond simply freeing trade unions. A summary of more than 70 clauses repealing 44 statutes is impossible, but its main thrust was to attempt to put into law what artisans had traditionally thought of as good industrial relations. The artisan was to be protected from the unscrupulous master and the generous master to be protected from 'unprincipled servants'. At its root was a comprehensive reform of the master and servant legislation to include provision for written contracts; written recording of tools and materials lent out; of rates of pay and so on. Henson and White saw this aspect as more significant than removing combination legislation which they thought little used, 'it is the law against the finishing of work, which masters employ to harass and keep down wages'. If such laws were changed, then even if the Combination Acts remained, the workmen would think of them 'in great measure as waste paper'. The bill hit sharply at the use of the law as a disciplinary weapon by employers and would have given 'servants' considerable rights against their masters. It stood little chance of success, but it is not surprising that it drew petitions of protest from employers in Dudley, Halifax, Bradford, Nottingham and Coventry.[22]

What happened to these broader aims? Part of the answer is that they were lost by Place's wire-pulling which led to a much more restricted bill confined to repeal of the Acts and which drew protests only from Preston and Bolton. More crucially, prior to this, the thrust of the Henson–White Bill had been undercut by a hurriedly passed Act which consolidated much of the existing master and servant laws and made prosecutions by employers more straightforward.[23] The precise relation between this act and the Henson–White Bill is difficult to trace, but its effect was to strengthen the laws as a weapon of discipline. Its passing and the continued centrality of the master and servant legislation in the legal framework affecting workers became a key unspoken assumption in the debates of 1824 and 1825, appreciation of which narrows considerably the apparent radicalism of the repeal itself.

Three further aspects of the repeal also call for clarification. The Henson–White Bill deliberately sought to prevent conspiracy charges being brought against workers who combined. This was achieved by the 1824 Act, but was it intended? Probably so by Place, but most participants in the debates seem confused as to the distinction between prosecutions under the Combination Acts and those under the common law of conspiracy.[24] Hume had actually assured the House that his Act would not affect the common law and had apparently taken advice on the matter.[25] The Act however took a different course and when this was belatedly realised, it was one of the main reasons for *The Times* undertaking a last-minute campaign against it.[26] It is easy to see why, once the consequences were fully apparent, Huskisson, Peel and others quickly restored the common law in 1825.

The apparent radicalism of the repeal is also qualified by the clauses in both the 1824 and 1825 Acts creating various summary offences of violence, threat and intimidation. These were not after-thoughts, but considered weapons placed in the hands of magistrates to force unions to operate within narrow limits.[27] These repressive aspects have been little commented on, yet the provisions of the 1824 Act were widely used in its short life to imprison more than 250 workmen.[28] The wave of strikes which crested in late 1824 and 1825, stimulated both by the repeal and the trade cycle, led to the strengthening of the clauses in 1825. Finally the 1825 Act significantly narrowed the 1824 one by allowing union action only to change hours and wages, explicitly excluding action over working conditions. Controlling conditions had been central to the Henson–White Bill.[29]

Thus the net result of the Acts was to leave the master and servant legislation untouched, allow trade unions to organise over wages and hours, but to have in reserve both statutory powers to deal with any attempt at enforcement by picketing etc. and common law powers to bring more serious charges. *Provided employers were prepared to take the initiative*, the law provided a relatively cheap, short-cut method of harassing unions which consequently reduced the costs of employer opposition. Because both master and servant laws and the provisions of 1825 offered summary justice it is difficult to trace their use by employers before 1850.[30] It is clear that the former was more widely used. It was both simpler and had more value as a preventative weapon against strikes. Conviction was usual, partly because employers in the same trade could sit as magistrates and partly because the offence of breach of contract was relatively clear-cut. Simon's pioneering study of the 1850s and 60s suggested that it was mainly the weapon of the small employer, but this needs qualification for the years after 1850, and even more so for 1825–50. Probably there was a regional context. In areas where the dominant industry used long contracts and bonds a more general employer–magistrate culture could develop, encouraging use of the legislation at all levels. This seems to have been so in the Black Country. In other areas where the leading industry dispensed with long contracts, it may have been used more by smaller masters.[31]

Employer use was often quite cynical to control their workforces. The anticipation of pressure to increase wages and of possible disputes could lead to workers being required to sign long contracts. In the glass industry, for example, seven-year contracts for skilled workers were common. In 1845 when the excise duty on glass was removed, employers deliberately bound their workers anew, anticipating an increase in demand and consequent wage pressure. Pilkington's were then thrown into a 'labour crisis' when W. P. Roberts temporarily got their contracts discredited on a technicality. In justification for the long contract, Pilkington's insisted:

the trade could not go on without it . . . we are firmly resolved to maintain not only those rights, but also that proper discipline, obedience and order in our Works which are one great object of the contracts, and without which not only the master but every good and steady Workman might suffer from the misconduct and irregularity of others.[32]

The great value of the contract, especially the annual one, was that it enabled unions to be cut out except briefly at the point of renewal. This is one reason why employers in a number of industries strove to maintain them for so long.[33]

We lack detailed knowledge of the use made of the 1825 Act, but it appears to have been more widespread than has been allowed. The key part was Section Three with its penalties for 'violence, threats, intimidation, molestation and obstruction'. What these terms meant was a matter of debate and at the end of our period the higher courts gave them a wider definition in the cases of *R. v. Rowlands* and *R. v. Duffield* in 1851.[34] However the vaguer nature of the 1825 Act and the fact that under it magistrates had to come from outside the trade made it a less reliable method of using the law.

One of the more important of the other factors affecting the inclination of employers to use the law was working-class pressure. Because the onus to act was put on the employers, much depended upon their nerve, which, to judge from their pleas for help to the Home Office, was very often lacking. Foster has shown how in Oldham in the 1830s and early 1840s a combination of working-class control of local government and a general militancy acted to reduce employer control. Few workers were in quite this situation. Sometimes pressure took more basic forms. A leading South Shields magistrate was reputedly killed because of his support of employers in the courts.[35] In the Potteries in 1842 the house of a magistrate notorious for his support of the use of master and servant legislation was burned down.[36] Pressure was also possible within the system given the dubious legality of many magistrates' decisions. The activities of W. P. Roberts in the courts were sometimes successful and on two notable occasions in 1847 mass petitions were brought to Parliament against particular magistrates in Sheffield and Warrington, both to the embarrassment of government and the consternation of local society.[37] To the extent that trade unions began to win arguments within the system, they could both increase their respectability and change the climate in which the laws were enforced, but it would be difficult to argue that a major breakthrough occurred before 1850, especially in the light of *R. v. Duffield*. But what can be concluded is that although the legal framework provided a relatively simple route for legal harassment, its use reflected a complex interaction in which working-class pressure had a role to play.

A similar point needs to be made about the wider role of the state in relation to employers. It is clear from appeals to the Home Office that many employers expected the state to get them out of their labour difficulties, particularly by repressing strikes. From the point of view of the Home Office, even under the Combination Acts, the legal complications were a considerable constraint.[38] The problem tended to be pushed back to local magistrates and employers and this continued under the 1824–25 legislation. However when strikes became a matter of public order, employers could find a more sympathetic ear. As Home Secretaries both Peel and Melbourne were worried by union activity and until the mid-1830s it was by no means certain that the laws against it would not be strengthened.[39] Moreover, in matters of public order there was considerable scope for the Home Office to act in the general interest of local employers, even if it had no wish to appear their direct agent. When Melbourne left the Home Office, a marked change of attitude and tone became visible.

Russell was far less sympathetic than Peel or Melbourne had been with employers and magistrates who appealed to the Home Office. He thought it better to have working-class organisation of all sorts out in the open: 'there was fear when men were driven by force to secret combinations. There was the fear – there was the danger, and not in free discussion'.[40] This important new attitude was indicated when he was petitioned by pottery workers in the run up to their great strike of 1836. The Lord Lieutenant of Staffordshire had been used to sympathetic support, but Russell, instead of rejecting the petition, wrote to him: 'that the military have been frequently called into our county, talked of the petition and of establishing a stipendiary magistracy'. His shock was considerable: 'supported as I have been, and by no one more effectually and generously than by Melbourne I dare put myself in the breach, but if I am to be left in the lurch by those whose duty it is to stand by the Civil Power, I confess I tremble for the result'.[41]

Russell's attitude reflected not the abandonment of industrial relations matters by the state, but its relative retreat to the background except at times of crisis like the Plug Plot strikes in 1842. Apart from personality, what lay beneath this was the beginning of a policy directed more to containing labour troubles and political protest through controlled education and the lessening of press restrictions rather than through repression. As Russell's successor, Graham wrote, 'government will do what they can, but they cannot be everywhere and do everything . . . It is impossible even if you had a standing army ten times greater than the British, to provide troops for every town and village throughout the manufacturing districts'.[42]

But here too we should not neglect the impact of working-class pressure. Ironically the Tolpuddle incident made the position of unions more secure. The fact that in this fiasco the sentences were withdrawn within two years won the government little support, even from its own side.[43] This was followed by successful negotiation by the trade unions of both the Glasgow Spinners case and of the Select Committee on Combinations of 1838. Although opponents made much of its evidence which did have a major impact on public opinion, the fact that no legislation came out of it partly reflected the unions' effective defence of their position.[44] For these reasons unions could by the 1840s feel more secure and their employers correspondingly less hopeful of securing further legislation against them. The Plug Plots then served to confirm need for a different approach rather than to encourage a return to more repressive measures.[45]

The situation with respect to master and servant legislation was much less favourable. It had been strengthened against certain domestic workers without serious debate in 1843.[46] Then in 1844 came a major crisis in the shape of the Master and Servant Bill which appeared to have the support of the Home Secretary and would in its amended form have given employers draconian rights in enforcing labour discipline.[47] The vehemence of working-class reaction, organised through the unions and at mass meetings, deserves wider note. Parliament was flooded with 213 petitions claimed by T. S. Duncombe to represent 'nearly two millions of the working classes'. The weight of protest and his manoeuvrings were successful in thwarting the bill. But the wider necessity for a work contract enforceable by law continued to be taken for granted by employers, legislators, commentators and even some workers during this period.[48]

A further aspect of the relation between the state and employers is not only important in itself, but also serves as an example of the significance of the wider changes that were occurring in the local structure of the state. This is the development of the new police forces. Although there were still by 1850 a considerable minority of industrial boroughs and counties in which there were either no new police or in which they were of very recent origin, their overall development had begun to have a contradictory impact on industrial relations. On the one hand they made both the master and servant legislation and the Act of 1825 more effective by facilitating the apprehension of offenders and were a more effective form of control over strikes. Employers thus benefited and their role in industrial relations was without doubt part of what Storch has called the police's 'omnibus mandate'.[49] Although there was a conflict between employers' desire to have the police and their willingness to pay for them, the inadequate 'state of protection of manufacturing industry' was an argument much deployed by supporters of the new police.[50] On the other hand the development of the police as a bureaucratic professional organisation meant that they functioned less directly, though far from independently, of the local employer–magistrate nexus that had previously been responsible for law and order. To this extent more onus was placed on employers to sort out their own difficulties. Equally, by providing the Home Office with more objective information about the seriousness of disturbances, they enabled it to act with more discrimination.[51]

In summary, after 1825 the state provided a framework which allowed a small legal space for unions, but allowed employers ample reserves to harass union activity. To the extent that there was a widening of the space before 1850, and the evidence is contradictory, it reflected the interaction of a number of elements including a change in government policy and pressure from below.

IDEOLOGY AND THE PERCEPTION OF TRADE UNIONS

Within this framework employers' attitudes tended to be guided by the ideological prism through which they viewed union activity. If a few of the better-known employers had coherent and sophisticated world-views, the majority operated amid a mish-mash of ideas in which there was a 'complete absence of any science or teaching on the subject of labour management, apart from some *a priori* reasoning of the philosophers and political economists'. Pollard thinks this the 'greatest failure of all', but we cannot neglect the ideas that filled the gap left by 'the strange absence of management theory'.[52] It is not, however, easy to delineate the different elements in employer perceptions of unions for only exceptionally did they leave any account.[53] For the majority we have the evidence of some of the inputs into their thinking, for example the press they read, and of some of the outputs, for example anti-union propaganda. Clearly such evidence may not be representative. The diversity of employers' interests which we have noted found a reflection in ideological terms as well. The problem is somewhat mitigated by the relative uniformity of the condemnation of unions in the available evidence. This is not to say that employers did not come to terms with unions, but that when they did so it was on a grudging and pragmatic basis with the belief that unions could be dispensed with should opportunity arise.

Typically 'negotiation' involved an elected deputation of workmen 'waiting on the master', who might refuse to see them, or insist that it was his foreman's job to deal with labour. If the master was willing and the issue settled amicably, the meeting and delegation dissolved until the next issue arose. It is worth noting that years could elapse between such meetings, even decades in trades subject to little change where formal price lists lasted over very long periods. If conflict broke out then 'negotiations' tended to take place at arm's length through public claim and counterclaim. Direct negotiations tended to come at the end of disputes, and the majority of masters were reluctant to admit the legitimacy of an outside union representative being involved at any stage. Indirect contact was more common with each side meeting separately with a third party. If the initiative lay with the master, changes might simply be announced, but the better employers might explain them to representatives of the workmen. Whatever the precise form, it was the failure of employers and unions to give their relations a more permanent form that was the chief characteristic before 1850.

The size of the problem faced by unions seeking legitimacy can be illustrated by the failure of three different groups of employers to develop any kind of ideological rapprochement with unions before 1850, even in circumstances which hindsight might view as propitious. The first group is the urban craft employers. Traditional views that they were more tolerant now appear to be an oversimplification for the 1825–50 period. What might earlier have appeared as the 'slowly differentiating ambience of custom' accelerated from the 1820s as the crafts were pulled in different directions by their ties to industrial capitalism. The rapid growth of large dishonourable sections in trades like shoemaking and tailoring eliminated organisation in many towns for all but a minority 'honourable section'.[54] Attempts to maintain these created problems for employers in that workers were seeking to formalise craft practices at the time when employers were also being squeezed from other directions.[55] Traditional forms did not immediately disappear, but the struggle to maintain them became much more serious. These trades therefore continued to create complex political crosscurrents, but what they did not do was create a basis for a significant defence of the right to organise, and a challenge to anti-union ideologies did not emerge from outside the craft unions themselves, even in towns where the crafts predominated.

The experience of printing suggests that the need to qualify this general judgment in the case of particular trades is less than some historians have suggested. Musson has argued that 'good relations existed on the whole between employers and employed' but these were most evident when union action was directed against what the masters also saw as low-waged unfair competition.[56] Where unions tried to impose control over apprenticeship and hours or to raise wages, revealingly called by Musson 'arbitrary regulation', employer attitudes quickly hardened and there was a mass of small strikes and some more notable clashes. So far as contemporaries were concerned, it was these rather than good relations which character-ised the industry. Far from being a positive model, printing was viewed as presenting an example to be avoided. This then fed back into the attitudes of many of the employers. In spite of the fact that 'typographical societies almost invariably adopted a moderate and conciliatory attitude towards employers in disputes', the latter were quick to resort to traditional anti-union categories. The resulting uneven situation in the industry can be seen in the way in 1847 the Edinburgh employers defeated and destroyed the National Typo-graphical Association which with 4000 members had briefly emerged as a major craft union.[57] At the same time in London the Society of Compositors was able to reach a degree of accommodation with employers and formalise its collective bargaining procedures.[58]

If failure to build on other than a local basis in the relatively favourable conditions of printing shows the problems that unions had in gaining acceptance before 1850, the third example illustrates the difficulties in using the wider political system to gain a legitimacy which might influence employers. Attempts to build a Tory base among workers, especially in the North, are well known, but they fell short of supporting trade unions, the one factor that might have assisted consolidation.[59] Turning anti-manufacturer rhetoric into a *positive* defence of the right of workers to organise was impeded not only by the need for the support of Tory manufacturers, but also by the paternalism of popular Toryism in the face of 'self-governing' combinations of workers. It was convenient for most Tories to forget that supporters of campaigns like that for factory reform were often 'trade unionists in Sunday clothes' and both Ashley and Sadler were sensitive to the accusation that they were 'effecting what the Trades' Unions seek to obtain by other means' and formally disas-sociated themselves from them.[60] Only a few, of whom Richard Oastler is the best known, went further. They are sometimes used as examples of class collaboration, but the central point is the nature of their 'collaboration'. When Oastler, for example, was pulled round to support trade unionists and strikes he became cut off from most of his fellow Tories as well as from his employer enemies. However much he might squirm around the need for a real union of employers and employed, his actions were seen to be taking him in a different direction.[61]

The general condemnation of unions before 1850 assists us in solving a related problem: why the more conservative and narrow aspects of unions which later had a positive appeal for some employers were not sooner recognised. Although a number of commentators appreciated that unions were initially rooted in sectional interests, it was a view which co-existed with a more widespread exaggeration of the extent and power of trade unionism. Similarly union protestations of their concern to maintain the role of the employer, commonplace in their rulebooks, were either not believed or ignored. Nor was an emphasis on respectability enough. Under questioning in 1838, Alison admitted the respectability of trade unionists appearing in his courts, but concluded that as this was itself part of a union plot, they should not be allowed trial by jury.[62]

This suggests an ability to close the mind to aspects of early unionism that have impressed later historians. There is a danger that if we ignore the disparity between the ostensibly narrow aims of many unions and the employers' reactions, we will offer a misleading picture of the thrust of union development. The widespread failure of employers to reciprocate union overtures before 1850 must seriously qualify any assessment of the role and wider significance of unions in the working-class movement. However much they sought to distinguish between 'honourable' and 'dishonourable' masters, whether in workshop or factory, it always remained easier to unite employers to oppose unions than to reach accommodation, even in particular localities. Intransigent employers could always comfort themselves with the view that they were acting in the general interest and there was always strong outside support to bolster this view.

Before the late 1850s few outside the unions' own ranks were prepared to speak out in their defence. The limited nature of the breakthrough made by the unions can be seen in the response to the formation of the National Association of United Trades (NAUT) in 1845 with Thomas Duncumbe, the radical MP, as its president. One parliamentary critic suggested that Duncombe could 'hardly conceive the countenance which his name gave to such a society'. Duncombe felt obliged to stress the very limited aims of the NAUT: 'the object of which was to create a good understanding between workmen and their employers, and to obviate the necessity of strikes'. In these terms unions had to restrict themselves to 'legitimate objects' and 'legitimate means', which more often than not excluded effective trade unionism at all.[63]

One reason for the very slow acceptance of legitimacy, was the centrality of trade unionism to 'moral panics' over 'subversion'. Typical instances can be seen in the early 1830s, in 1837/8, stimulated by the Glasgow spinners' strike, the Select Committee of 1838 and in 1842.[64] Such panics flourished not only because unions were seen as class organisations, but also because their institutional forms themselves contained features which contemporaries found difficult to digest. At a time when so much of the working class was excluded from the political system, unions based on democratic self-organisation seemed, whatever their protestations to the contrary, to offer a fundamental challenge to the existing order.[65]

Such reactions did prompt some attempts to discuss unions more rationally, symptomatically in 1838 the London Statistical Society attempted a major survey of strikes, although the results were never published. The questions implied some awareness of the difficulties of calculating the cost of strikes, but the assumption that strikes were to be justified in narrow monetary cost-benefit terms remained the norm as did the consequent conclusion that they were therefore irrational.[66]

Classical economics provided the most rational attempt to deal with the unions ideologically. Few employers had the key works at their fingertips, but the laissez-faire argument, often shorn of all qualification, formed the backbone of the condemnation of trade unionism. Some historians have stressed the positive labour attitudes of the political economists. So far as trade unions are concerned much of their argument seems disingenuous and dependent upon an arbitrary distinction between 'scientific political economy' and 'unscientific laissez-faire', as well as on the marginalising of evident union opponents like Nassau Senior.[67] The best that can be said is that some economists like McCulloch held a qualified view recognising a limited role for unions in correcting the monopolistic power of employers. The assumption remained that most markets would clear normally.[68] It tended to be trade unionists themselves, armed with selective quotes from Smith and McCulloch, who argued to the contrary. McCulloch himself supported the extension of education to correct their misunderstandings of political economy.[69] In the dynamic economic context, unions were seen universally as barriers to technological change. Ironically this led to a further belief that attempts to defeat unions were a major cause of technical progress.[70]

None of these views served employers very well. They were led to underestimate consistently the strength of worker grievances, their determination and the competence and intelligence of their leaders. The treatment of John Doherty is illustrative. One does not have to accept fully a recent view of him as 'a staunch advocate of peaceful collective bargaining and co-operation with employers' to recognise the number of occasions when he and other spinners' leaders restrained their members and offered the olive branch to employers. Each time the result was rebuff by all but a handful, and Doherty was pilloried in the middle-class press for his pains.[71] Convinced of their own rationality and the irrationality of trade unions, employers were not forced to rethink fundamentally by the continued struggle to form unions. 'It is strange', wrote one observer, 'that though these unions have, in many trades, been successfully overthrown, still new ones arise . . . It bespokes deplorable ignorance of the mass of the operatives who have allowed themselves to be led on by a few designing and selfish men.'[72]

Some viewed this irrationality as inbred in the working class; others, a minority, as a consequence of circumstance and ignorance. When Henry Ashworth, for example, discovered that a riot leader had been educated in one of his schools, he concluded that still more education was needed. More agreed with Nassau Senior that workers worsened their own conditions by joining unions only because of union tyranny and they continued to argue for stronger restraint from the law, although not necessarily outright proscription.[73]

Whatever its form, the assuming of working–class irrationality neatly fitted in with 'paternalism'. In fact employers generally tend to see work relationships in a paternalistic light whatever their actual practice towards labour. Given the family base of many firms and the many reference points in the wider ideology of the time, it is not surprising that paternalist views were particularly intensely held before 1850. However it is necessary to distinguish between general feelings, expressed in the occasional tea party, and, much more rare, genuine paternalist strategies. Factory villages, often seen as outstanding paternalist examples, can be more usefully explained in terms of the provision of necessary amenities to retain labour, whatever their paternalist clothing. Genuine paternalist strategies for controlling labour were rare because the structural conditions for their success were more demanding than is often allowed.[74] In ideological terms they could develop only when a degree of recognition had been granted to the seriousness of the labour challenge. To the extent that unions were seen as illegitimate, impermanent and irrational there was no real need to go beyond the type of minimal gestures that most employers were capable of and which probably did more for their own self-esteem than anything else.

The intensity with which such views were held cannot, however, be explained solely in terms of the self-confirming nature of their underlying ideas. Breaks existed which were later prised open. This was difficult at the time because of the social value of the ideas to the employers. Most had been brought up with a degree of wealth and power, but the new responsibilities created by the emergence of industrial capitalism in a period of political turmoil presented challenges for which many were ill-prepared. The assumption that the employer was 'king of his domain' acted partly as self-reassurance, partly as a wider method of persuasion and partly as legitimation. Employers could be 'cruel to be kind' if they believed themselves the best guardians of their servants' interests. As Flanders has stressed, with such 'rich returns' it is not surprising that the paternalist ideas were long cherished, even after 1850.[75] Moreover they not only denied the legitimacy of union 'interference', but excluded outside arbitration as a possible route for union recognition. This is important because although arbitration legislation had existed from an early period, the routes were equally unappealing to workers and employers. Indeed, encouraged by their hostility to unions in principle, employers were often more reluctant than unions to accept offers of arbitration, like those frequently made by members of the local middle class such as shopkeepers suffering from disputes. Employers' opposition and fears cannot, however, be explained only in terms of a functional need. Their views also gained credibility in their own minds from apprehension of the probable impact of unions within their own firms, a matter we must now discuss.

THE IMPACT OF UNIONS ON THE FIRM

The essence of day-to-day union recognition, whether articulated or not, lies in a bargain by which employers expect to gain from the institutionalisation of conflict. For this to occur employers must first recognise that gains could be made and then have some confidence that they would be forthcoming. In fact there is considerable evidence that many found it difficult to identify costs at all. Pollard's pioneering study has shown the general difficulties they faced before 1830, many of which were not resolved until later in the century. With accounting practices so weakly developed, so much so that some firms did not even record data on the number of their employees or the hours they worked, it is not difficult to see the fog through which costs were often viewed. The problem of control was compounded by the frequency of partnerships with divided responsibilities and the lack of an overview. It was not unknown for an employer to deny knowledge of his workers' level of wages.[76] It has been argued that such problems allied with external financial constraints and the lack of technical economies led cotton employers to cautiously limit the size of their firms.[77] A French observer found that even the leading textile manufacturers emphasised caution and piecemeal change and came away with the impression that employers and managers needed an almost sensuous touch in the control of their businesses: 'take away the manager (the best of them are often the most hidebound) from his accustomed surroundings and he will not long accomplish anything'.[78]

In this situation the main focus of employers tended to be on the external problems of markets and prices and, among the better businessmen, product quality within the firm. A considered interest in other internal problems was more rare. When Brown visited the Leeds flax mills he found much to admire in Marshall's mill, but most of the rest were 'leading their life in the midst of dust, waste, confusion, dirt and discontentment'. This had the paradoxical consequence of throwing the burden of any adjustment onto wage rates because they were the most easily identifiable costs and accordingly the ones to which employers first turned, irrespective of their actual share in total costs or the real possibilities for saving which they offered. This view was further encouraged by the extensive use of payment by the piece, not piecework proper, both inside and outside the factory. From the late 1830s a number of management guides were published, but they were noticeably silent on labour matters.[79]

It is doubtful whether employers at this time felt that a worthwhile bargain could have been struck with labour. One of the assumptions they shared with other contemporaries was that labour productivity was constant or only variable downwards. When Owen attempted to show in 1816 that reduced hours meant increased labour productivity, he was greeted with bemused disbelief. Much more in line with employer thinking was Nassau Senior's argument of the 'last hour' against factory hour limitation nearly thirty years later. The failure to appreciate that much good could come of positive cooperation with labour accounts for the preponderance of the 'stick' in work discipline. Pollard's picture of a 'reign of terror' doing 'duty for factory discipline' perhaps exaggerates the situation, save for some well-known examples, but his related emphasis on the limited inventiveness of employers in using the 'carrot' seems well in accord with the evidence. The alternatives seem to have been polarised into discipline or slack. Although Pollard dates the beginnings of the shift away from 'labour administration in terms . . . [of] crude force, punishment or monetary reward' from 1830, there is only limited evidence of change before mid century.[80]

This in part reflected the transitional problems involved in recruiting a new factory labour force. The difficulty was that employers found it almost impossible to separate out elements of 'unorganised conflict' capable of being moderated by a more positive attitude to unionism, from those problems of labour turnover, absenteeism, the uneven pace of work and poor quality production which reflected the 'adjustment problems' of workers to changing contexts of work discipline. Nor were they advised that there was such a difference when Andrew Ure published his virulently anti-union *Philosophy of Manufactures* in 1835. He still held up Richard Arkwright as a model: 'a man of Napoleonic nerve and ambition', subduing 'the refractory tempers of work-people accustomed to irregular paroxysms of diligence' and who had had to face prejudice, passion and envy.[81]

It is misleading to generalise from the experiences of the better-known industrialists. The unevenness of the consolidation of explicit employer rule and work discipline is well known. Elements of traditional behaviour survived in many industries well into the second half of the century. The consequent slack was, according to Hobsbawm, in part mitigated from the employer point of view by the slowness with which skilled workers learned to push their advantages in the labour market rather than settle for customary expectations.[82] Danger would however threaten if unions intended action not only over hours and wages, but also to control working conditions and to formalise and extend customary practices. As has been noted, action over this area was deliberately not legalised in 1825 and we need to take the fear of the consequences of union action in it more seriously. Employers did not conceive that coming to terms with unions could lead to an 'effort bargain'. Instead they tended to see unions as being concerned to institutionalise indiscipline. Trade unionism according to a leading mid-century mine engineer tended: 'to the utter subversion of the necessary discipline in a pit'. Such an almost military articulation was less common among the 'Captains of Industry', but it is symptomatic to find such an anti-union attitude in coal-mining which was in most respects regarded as 'one of the most dynamic and fertile fields in the development of industrial management'.[83]

The outcome was that even though labour problems were not all of a piece, they appeared so to many employers, who were able to associate the development of union power with an intensification of their difficulties rather than with their reduction. John Boyle, a pottery manager, typically interpreted the consequences of a settlement with unions and subsequent wage rise:

the intemperate workmen had so much more time at their command to devote to dissipation. The indolent were better abled to indulge their habits without diminishing their earnings, and as it was one of the professed objects of the union to lessen the number of working hours, the best members were expected to show an example in this respect.[84]

The three components of this condemnation, drink, indolence and the loss of the leadership of the best workers, echo commonplaces in the accounts of employers of what would happen if unions were recognised.

It has often been suggested that employers were able to escape the most urgent and immediate problems of large-scale management by displacing them onto subordinate subcontractors. But in industries where this prevailed, the indirect control of the employers had produced a 'miasma of distrust'.[85] In organised craft industries this was to some extent mitigated by the possibility of upward advancement which meant a less firm line between master and workman and between master and union. An important side consequence was that few artisans seem to have had much respect for their masters. It is difficult to read the autobiographies of men like Francis Place, Charles Manby Smith or John Brown without realising that they saw themselves as responsible for the success of their employers' businesses.[86] But when 'honourable' trades came under pressure, and in the new factories, it often appeared to the employers that a necessary condition for success was the absence of unions. Union action, for example, over foremen, struck at the heart of indirect control: 'one of the crucial and most mischievous objects of the union has been to control the discretion of the masters in the selection of their foremen', complained the master builders, 'it is upon the vigilance and efficiency of the foremen that the honest execution of the works must in great measure depend'.[87]

Attempts to organise the sub-contractors themselves were even more threatening. Early industrial capitalism depended in a number of industries on 'autonomous workmen' who supplied skilled labour and some managerial services – typified in the factory by the cotton spinners. The strategic position of these groups placed them constantly at the forefront of attempts to build unions which were thus 'associations of internal contractors'.[88] For this reason, even if they cast their demands narrowly, it was difficult initially to win employer confidence that they would not 'abuse their power' over more than wages and hours. A Glasgow cottonmaster said in 1838: 'we have never had a single dispute with the workmen about wages till 1837; all our disputes, and all the operations of the unions, have been against our management of our works'.[89]

To this extent anti-union ideology did partly reflect genuine workplace problems for employers. The fact that workers were slow to learn 'the rules of the game' helped create a rigidity of output and employers reacted by trying to reduce costs, either by driving down wage or piece rates or through technological change. Both could be best done without the interference of unions. If short-term costs were incurred in defeating unions, they were justifiable in view of long-term gains. That labour might respond to defeat and to coercive discipline by what Veblen termed the 'withdrawal of efficiency' was not considered.

THE NATURE OF TRADE UNIONS

Finally we have to consider the extent to which employers' strategies responded to the nature of the unions themselves. Did they exist on a basis which might realistically have led employers to come to terms with them? The separation of cause and effect is difficult since many features of unions can be attributed to employer intransigence, but some aspects of union organisation and policy have been suggested as impediments to their legitimacy.

The first suggestion is that unions were prone to violence and employers understandably wanted nothing to do with them. More neutrally this can be reformulated as an argument about the 'immaturity' of much union activity. Historians have repeated contemporary claims of union violence and tried to suggest that they outweighed or balanced actions by the other side. Gash has written that whatever the sanctions of the employers and the state, 'the men had sanctions of their own – arson, vitriol throwing, gunpowder, and assassination – even more ferocious'. But much of this is the imagery of moral panic, as William Lovett protested, the unions' critics 'magnified isolated acts of violence into crimes of blackest atrocity; they have sought to prevent justice by slander; and what they failed to substantiate by facts, they have depicted in words of deadly meaning'[90] Frequent claims of arson in the cotton industry, for example, must be set in the context of the peculiar vulnerability of cotton mills to fire risk.[91] Claims of intimidation and especially of assassination of employers were much exaggerated. The evidence linking trade unionists to the most notorious example of the latter, Thomas Ashton of Hyde, is ambiguous and the union itself was almost certainly not involved.[92] Most violence was directed against fellow workers and took place in the context of community sanctions where the most extreme examples were related to the ends of bitterly fought disputes. Just how much actually took place is difficult to establish since the employers and the authorities had an interest in blaming every incident on trade unionists. Their success can be seen in the contemporary view that the 'crimes' of the Glasgow spinners were: 'without a parallel in the annals of criminal jurisprudence', which has been echoed by later historians. In fact the most detailed study of the dispute has concluded that it is surprising that historians rather than accept a verdict of not proven have accepted almost in its entirety the case for the prosecution.[93]

For their part (leaving aside the role of the state), employers and their agents were hardly less adverse to using violence. During an attack on a papermill in Buckinghamshire in 1830 four gallons of vitriol were reputedly thrown by a defender. Yet this remains an obscure incident whereas the Glasgow case became a national scandal. The thrower of the vitriol appears to have been punished only by a ducking. While unions scurried from any hint of violence to defend their respectability, when James Bently was shot by 'knobs' in Oldham in 1834, the anti-union *Wheelers Chronicle* could still contest the verdict of manslaughter claiming justifiable homicide.[94] The point of presenting these examples is not to redraw the balance sheet but to stress that both the terms and terrain of conflict are set by those who have power, not those who lack it.

'Immaturity' can be interpreted less pejoratively; it could be that unions were simply not strong enough to offer employers a worthwhile 'quid pro quo'. Any union weakness lowered the potential costs of employer opposition and there were many sections of the labour force that lacked basic sectional strength. Hunt has argued that in narrow labour market terms many early unions amounted to little more than 'strings of pretentious initials'. If organisations like the Grand National Consolidated Trades Union (GNCTU) are judged solely in terms of their power in the labour market, this judgment is difficult to contest, but it seems less valid for many individual unions.[95] Unions like those of the spinners could sustain long strikes and strike discipline as well as maintain a degree of control over the labour process. Rather than being unable to offer anything to employers, it seems in such cases more likely that the employers did not like what was on offer.

'Immaturity' might find expression in other ways. It has been suggested that union policy too often encouraged self-defeating actions in adverse economic circumstances. However, not only is the evidence on the general timing of strikes unclear (though recent work suggests that many unions were quite adept at trying to use the market), but the argument is also a mechanistic analysis of the determinants of strikes. This is not to minimise the organisational difficulties of the early unions. They could be quickly weakened by fluctuations in members' contributions and in this context the push to organisational maturity was itself difficult. Taylor has pointed to the significance of the Miners' Association of Great Britain's appointment of W. P. Roberts as their legal adviser, both for union development in the mines and for organisation more generally, but he has also shown the huge drain on finances that this type of activity entailed.[96] Faced with union difficulties, employers could easily come to believe that their own power and organisation made them a 'phalanx of strength' and, buoyed up by their own propaganda, look for quick and decisive victories.

It was a different facet of union organisation that was most problematical for employers. Many were fatally ambiguous about the nature and character of union leadership. On the one hand they tended to see union leaders as itinerant agitators with an interest to 'create and keep up ill-will between the masters as a class, and the men as their natural opponents'; as in fact, the 'astute opponents' of accommodation.[97] On the other hand they feared the leaders having insufficient control over their members and facing them with what the Webbs called 'primitive democracy', where 'each branch, in general meeting assembled, claimed the right to have any proposition whatsoever submitted to the vote of the society as a whole'. This can be seen in the difficulties of Doherty when he was pushed on a number of occasions to more militant postures by pressure from below. In the potteries in 1834 negotiations were broken off by the employers when a section of the potters 'refused to sanction the acts of their delegates'.[98] Specific examples like these apart, the appearance of primitive democracy was strengthened by the threat of victimisation which often led to unions deliberately hiding their leaderships. Behind this front there was often a reality of considerable stability of leaders in office. Nevertheless, although the Webbs probably exaggerate the degree of openness in early unions in order to show the 'rational' progress towards a centralised maturity by the turn of the century, the problems of union organisation cannot be ignored. Employers had yet to see the value of the influence of leaders of trade societies: 'known and responsible men; through them prejudices may be dispelled, and the laws of that political economy which, correctly understood, is the workman's best friend, gradually acquiesced in and obeyed'.[99]

CONCLUSIONS

Employers need to be brought more seriously into labour history. Caution is needed against simple economic explanations of their behaviour. Class formation is a two-sided process and employers' attitudes and strategies are important in the assessment of union development as well as important in their own right. Trade union organisation is an integral part of capitalism, continually oscillating between accommodation and resistance but unable to come down firmly on either side without losing its raison d'être. The variation between these two extremes is immense. Because both are always present it is possible to build up false continuities when it is the changing balance and context that is important.

It has been argued here that before 1850 the balance worked against accommodation and that this was not simply a product of workers and their unions failing to understand the 'rules of the game'. Employers too seemed uncertain about the game they were supposed to be playing. Seeing problems in their own workplaces and in society at large, they made connections which delegitimised most union activity and forced contact to take place on an ad hoc basis, if at all.

To insist on this is not to pose a sharp turning point in mid-nineteenth century. In a few instances changes had already begun, and more importantly many of the negative factors, such as the adverse legal situation, continued long after. Turning points however do exist in history. From the 1850s some unions began to find different routes which enabled them to negotiate a wider area of acceptance and the fact that this did not threaten the survival of British capitalism came to be more widely appreciated. To understand how this happened, it is as important to look at what employers were thinking and doing as at social changes within the working class or the character of working-class politics.

NOTES AND REFERENCES

1. **S.** and **B. Webb**, *History of Trade Unionism*, Longman 1920; **A. Flanders** (ed.), *Collective Bargaining*, Penguin 1969.
2. See **H. Gospel**, 'The development of management organisation in industrial relations: an historical perspective', in **K. Thurley** and **S. Wood** (eds), *Industrial Relations and Management Strategy*, Cambridge U.P. 1983; **H. Gospel** and **C. Littler** (eds), *Managerial Strategies and Industrial Relations: and historical and comparative perspective*, Heinemann 1983.
3. Despite their discussion of their role, **A. E. Musson** and **R. G. Kirby** do not index employers in their study of John Doherty, *The Voice of the People*, Manchester U.P. 1975.
4. **A. E. Musson**, *British Trade Unions, 1800–1875*, Macmillan 1975; **R. J. Morris**, *Class and Class Consciousness in the Industrial Revolution*, Macmillan 1979.
5. **P. Payne**, *British Entrepreneurship in the Nineteenth Century*, Macmillan 1974, pp. 30–45; id. 'Industrial Entrepreneurship and Management in Great Britain', in **P. Mathias** and **M. Postan** (eds), *Cambridge Economic History of Europe (CEHE)*, VII, Cambridge U.P. 1978, pp. 184–91.
6. **R. Church**, 'Problems and perspectives', in **R. Church** (ed.) *The Dynamics of Victorian Business: Problems and Perspectives*, Allen & Unwin 1980, pp. 19–44. See **N. F. R. Crafts**, *British Economic Growth during the Industrial Revolution*, Clarendon Press 1985.
7. See **R. Geary**, *European Labour Protest 1848–1939*, Croom Helm 1981.
8. **F. Burchill** and **R. Ross**, *History of the Potters' Union*, Ceramic and Allied Trades Union 1977, pp. 23–9, 57–140; **W. H. Warburton**, *History of Trade Union Organisation in the North Staffordshire Potteries*, Allen & Unwin 1939, *passim*; ch. 9; **R. Fyson** above, Ch. 9.
9. *The Times*, 5 June 1824; **J. Ridgeway**, *On Combinations of Trades*, 1831, pp. 20–5. Some of the pamphlets referred to below were reprinted in the series of volumes: H. E. Carpenter (ed.), *British Labour Struggles: Contemporary Pamphlets, 1727–1850* (32 bks), New York, Arno Press 1972. On employers' combinations see **S. J. Chapman**, 'An historical sketch of masters' associations in the cotton industry', *Manchester Stat. Soc. Trans.*, (1900–1), pp. 67–84; **D. C. Coleman**, 'Combinations of capital and labour in the English paper industry', *Economica*, NS, XXI, no. 2 (1954), pp. 103–34; **A. Fox**, 'The combinations of masters', *New Society*, IX, no. 230 23 Feb. 1967, pp. 268–70; **A. R.** and **C. P. Griffin**, 'The role of Coalowners Associations in the East Midlands in the Nineteenth Century', *Renaissance and Modern Studies*, XVII (1973), pp. 95–121; **A. H. Yarmie**, 'Employers' organisations in mid-Victorian England', *Inter. Rev. of Soc. Hist.*, XXV, no. 2 (1980).
10. **John Orth** relates the repeal of the Combination Acts to the growth of a labour surplus. See his 'The legal status of English trade unions, 1799–1871', in **A. Harding** (ed.), *Law-Making and Law Makers in British History*, R. Hist. Soc. (1978), pp. 195–207. See also Payne, 'Industrial entrepreneurship', p. 185. An important area where employer determination and control were sufficient to hinder unions taking advantage of a favourable labour market was coal mining.

11. See **S. Pollard**, 'Labour in Great Britain', in *CEHE*, VII, pp. 97–105; **E. H. Hunt**, *Regional Wage Variations in Britain, 1850–1914*, Weidenfeld & Nicolson 1981. **P. B. Lindert** and **J. G. Williamson**, 'English workers' living standards during the Industrial Revolution: a new look', *Econ. Hist. Rev.*, XXXVI no. 1 (1983), pp. 12–16. Pollard offers a more traditional view, pp. 125–8.

12. **B. M. Ratcliffe** and **W. H. Chaloner** (eds), *A French Sociologist looks at Britain: Gustave d'Eichthal and British Society*, Manchester U.P. 1977, p. 84.

13. **J. Foster**, *Class Struggle and the Industrial Revolution: early industrial capitalism in three English towns*, Methuen 1974, p. 82; Church, 'Problems and perspectives', pp. 20–34.

14. **R. Lloyd-Jones** and **A. Le Roux**, 'The size of firms in the cotton industry, Manchester, 1815–41', *Econ. Hist. Rev.*, XXXIII, no. 1 (1980), pp. 72–82 and 'Marshall and the birth and death of firms: the growth and size distribution of firms in the early nineteenth-century cotton industry', *Business History*, XXIV, no. 2 (1982), pp. 141–55.

15. **Henry Ashworth**, *An Inquiry into the Origin, Progress and Results of the Strike of the Operative Cotton Spinners of Preston . . .*, Manchester 1838, p. 2.

16. **A. Friedman**, 'Responsible autonomy versus direct control over the labour process', *Capital and Class*, no. 1; (1976), and Friedman, *Industry and Labour, Class Struggle and Monopoly Capitalism*, Macmillan 1977; **C. Littler**, *The Development of the Labour Process in Capitalist Societies*, Heinemann 1982.

17. **V. I. Allen**, 'The origins of industrial conciliation and arbitration', in his *The Sociology of Industrial Relations: Studies in Method*, Longman 1971, pp. 72–7

18. *The Times*, 5 June 1824; 4 May and 24 June 1825. Many contemporary accounts make this general claim. See for example: **E. C. Tufnell**, *Character, Object and Effects of Trade Unionism*, 1834. In 1838 the Glasgow spinners claimed to have been encouraged by the main body of masters to act against low-wage employers. The cynical view was that this was to waste their resources. *BPP*, 1838, VII, *S.C. on Combinations*, Qs. 683, 688–97, 813, 1073, 1085. See also the evidence of Alison, Qs. 1948, 2036. The masters denied the claim. **N. Senior**, 'Report on Combinations', repr. in **S. Levy**, *Nassau W. Senior 1790–1864*, David & Charles, Newton Abbot 1970.

19. **Sir Archibald Alison**, *Some Account of My Life and Writings*, I, pp. 340–402.

20. **S. Chapman**, *The Cotton Industry in the Industrial Revolution*, Macmillan 1973, p. 57; **R. Boyson**, *The Ashworth Cotton Enterprise*, Oxford U.P. 1970; **A. Howe**, *The Cotton Masters 1830–60*, Oxford U.P. 1984.

21. **G. Wallis**, *Life of Francis Place 1771–1854*, Allen & Unwin 1918, Ch. 8.

22. Their proposals were in the anonymously published pamphlet: *A Few Remarks on the State of the Laws at Present in Existence for Regulating Masters and Workpeople . . .*, 1823. The petition from Nottingham in support of the bill gives a good indication of its artisan basis, *Hansard*, 2nd Ser, VIII, 27 Mar. 1823, cl. 751–4. *Commons Journals*, LXXVIII (1823), pp. 345, 376, 391, 407, 439, 477. These in part reflect the areas where

the Henson–White campaign was well known and also where master and servant legislation was widely used.

23. Ibid. LXXIX, (1824), pp. 211, 297. Significantly these reflected the views of an important part of the cotton trade. *An Act to enlarge the powers of justices in determining complaints between masters and servants and between masters, apprentices, artificers and others*, 4 Geo. IV, c. 34. This became the main Act used in subsequent master and servant prosecutions. No discussion is noted in *Hansard* although *The Times* notes its introduction, 10 Apr. 1823, and a bare timetable can be gleaned from *Commons Journals*, LXXVIII (1823), pp. 187, 254, 285, 350, 358, 391, 399.

24. Some workmen were also confused especially in their evidence to the S.C. of 1824, but Henson and White were not, see *A Few Remarks . . .* and also the Nottingham petition.

25. *Hansard*, 2nd Ser. xx, 12 Feb. 1823 cl. 146. Resolution 8 of the S.C. of 1824 on Artisans and Machinery also suggests it had wanted to go less far: 'the Common Law under which peaceable meeting of masters or workmen might be prosecuted as a conspiracy should be altered'. The extent to which the 1824 Act actually repealed the common law was never tested, but the impression was that it did so on a blanket basis. This raises the general question of the link between Hume's Bill, the role of the Committee and that of Place. Hume's recent biography, apart from insisting on his independence from Place, adds little on this episode. **R. K. Hutch and P. R. Ziegler**, *Joseph Hume: the People's MP*, American Philosophical Society, Philadelphia 1985, pp. 33–45.

26. *The Times*, 4 and 5 June 1824.

27. Resolution 11 of the Committee said: 'it was absolutely necessary that any new law should efficiently and by summary process punish either workmen or masters who, by threats, intimidation, or acts or violence, should interfere with that perfect freedom which ought to be allowed to each party of employing his labour or capital in the manner he thought best'. Neither act imposed any limit on actions by masters.

28. *BPP*, XXIII (1825), *Return of the number of persons committed in the UK for offences under 5 Geo. IV c. 95*. The return is unclear in places, some of the sentences appear inconsistent with the Act, but these may reflect trials for conspiracy to violate the statute. 54 sentences were recorded for Scotland where the Combination Acts of 1799 and 1800 had not applied. See also: **J. L. Gray**, 'The Law of Combination in Scotland', Economica, VIII, no. 24 (1925), pp. 332–50.

29. Resolution 7 of the 1824 Committee said: 'masters and workmen should be freed from such restrictions, as regards the rates of wages and the hours of working'. Thus the 1825 Act restored the original intention.

30. The better known cases under the 1825 Act usually involve conspiracy to violate the Statute, a more serious offence tried by jury.

31. **D. Simon**, 'Master and servant', in J. Saville (ed.), *Democracy and the Labour Movement*, Lawrence & Wishart 1954; **G. Barnsby**, *Dictatorship of the Bourgeoisie: Social Control in the Nineteenth Century Black Country*, Communist Party, Our History pamphlet, no. 55 (1972); **D. C. Woods**, 'The operation of the Master and Servant Act in the Black Country, 1858–1875', *Midland History*, VII (1982), pp. 93–115; **H. I. Dutton** and **J. E. King**, 'The limits of paternalism: the Cotton Tyrants

of North Lancashire, 1836–54', *Social History*, VII, no. 1, (1982), pp. 66–7. Elimination of bonds and long contracts did not automatically mean free labour. In the coal industry in the 1840s some miners were tied by annual bonds, others by monthly contracts and still others informally by truck and debt. Each served to help keep the labour force intact and impede union development.

32. **T. C. Barker**, *The Glassmakers Pilkington: the rise of an international company 1826–1976*, Weidenfeld & Nicolson 1977, pp. 81–6, 437–9.

33. For its use in the Pottery industry see Burchill and Ross, *Potters' Union*, pp. 12–15.

34. These two related cases are discussed in **J. Orth**, 'English law and striking workmen: The Molestation of Workmen Act 1859', *Jn. of Legal Hist.*, II, no. 3 (1982), pp. 239–46.

35. Foster, *Class Struggle*, pp. 51–72; 105.

36. Rose, the magistrate, was admonished by the Home Office for his failure in the riots and after took at least as tough a line. **R. Fyson**, 'The crisis of 1842: Chartism, the colliers' strike and the outbreak in the Potteries', in **J. Epstein** and **D. Thompson** (eds), *The Chartist Experience*, Macmillan 1982, p. 214.

37. *Hansard*, 3rd Ser. XC, 2 Mar. 1847, cl. 679; XCII, 18 May 1847; 'James Gerrard and others: Copies of Information and Evidence' and 'Sheffield Petty Sessions William Overend Esq.,' *BPP*, XLVI, (1847).

38. See **A. Aspinall**, *The Early English Trade Unions*, Batchworth 1949. There is no reason to suppose that the situation changed much after 1825.

39. **N. Gash**, *Mr Secretary Peel*, Longman 1961, pp. 344–66, 618–22 and P. Ziegler, *Melbourne: A biography of William Lamb, 2nd Viscount Melbourne*, Collins 1976, pp. 156–61 offer what seems over-generous assessments of Home Office attitudes. Kirby and Musson, *Voice of the People*, offer a more complex view. **E. Rogers**, 'Labour struggles in Flintshire 1830–50', *Flintshire Hist. Soc. Pub.*, XIV, 1953, pp. 54–65 contains a valuable account of how the North Wales coalmasters used Melbourne's support against the miners in 1831. See also: **L. Sanders** (ed.), *Lord Melbourne's Papers*, 1889, pp. 120–65.

40. *The Times*, 9 Oct. 1838.

41. *Mr Gregory's Letterbox*, London 1898, pp. 343–4.

42. **C. S. Parker** (ed.), *Life and Letters of Sir James Graham*, I, 1907, pp. 323–4.

43. *Hansard*, 3rd Ser. XXII, 14 Apr. 1834, cl. 725–38; 16 Apr. cl. 860–3; 18 Apr. cl. 938–49.

44. **William Lovett**, *Life and Struggles*, rep. McGibbon & Key 1967, pp. 131–5. As well as the London Trades Committee with Lovett as secretary, there were mass meetings and petitions in support of the Glasgow spinners throughout the country. See, for example, *The Times*, 27 Jan. 1838.

45. **M. Jenkins**, *The General Strike of 1842*, Lawrence & Wishart 1980, pp. 219–38.

46. 6 & 7 Vict. c. 40. The act was directed against 'the frauds and abuses' of textile workers.

47. The ambiguous role of the government led to a sharp attack on Graham in *The Times*, 3 May 1844.

48. *Commons Journals*, IC, 1844, pp. 184, 212, 217, 224, 229, 232, 243, 252–3, 269, 282. *Hansard*, 3rd Ser. LXXIII, Feb–May. See *The Times*, 3 May 1844.

49. **R. D. Storch**, 'The plague of blue locusts: police reform and popular resistance in England, 1840–57', *Inter. Rev. of Soc. Hist.*, XX, no. 1 (1975), pp. 61–90. On the development of the police more generally see: **F. C. Mather**, *Public Order in the Age of the Chartists*, Manchester U.P. 1959, pp. 75–140.

50. The *Report of the Commission on the Constabulary Force in England and Wales* although concerned with rural areas devoted a very substantial section to the value of the police in industrial disturbances, *BPP*, XIX, 1839, pp. 68–88. See also Sir Archibald Alison, 'Practical working of trades' unions', *Blackwoods Magazine*, XLIII (1838), pp. 302–3.

51. The dangers of too close an identification of police and employers both in pointing to the class nature of the former and in affecting internal discipline were recognised by both police and government, Mather, *Public Order*, p. 105; Storch, 'Plague of Blue Locusts', p. 67.

52. **S. Pollard**, *The Genesis of Modern Management*, Arnold 1965, pp. 146–7.

53. See the outstanding diary of **William Brown**, a flax manufacturer, *Early Days in a Dundee Mill 1819–23*, ed. **J. Hume**, Dundee Abertay Historical Society Publication no. 20, 1980. See also the appeal from a Manchester builder, Samuel Holme, to his employees in: *Statement of Facts connected with the Turn-Out in the Lancashire Building Trades*, Manchester 1846, pp. 25–31. Henry Ashworth's attitudes are reconstructed in Boyson, *Cotton Enterprise*,

54. See **M. J. Haynes**, 'Class and class conflict in the early nineteenth century: Northampton shoemakers and the GNCTU', *Literature and History*, no. 5. (1977), pp. 77–94.

55. **C. Behagg**, 'Custom, class and change: the trade societies of Birmingham', *Social History*, IV, no. 3 (1979), pp. 455–80, **D. Goodway**, *London Chartism 1838–48* Cambridge U.P. 1982

56. **A. E. Musson**, *Trade Union and Social History*, Cass 1974, pp. 81–136.

57. Ibid. pp. 87, 89; **J. Child**, *Industrial Relations in the British Printing Industry*, Allen & Unwin, 1967, pp. 81–3.

58. **London Society of Compositors**, *Report of the Journeymen Members of the Arbitration Committee, or Conference of Employers and Employed*, London 1847. On the comparative position of the printers see **I. Prothero**, 'London Chartism', *Econ. Hist. Rev.*, XXXIV, no. 2 (1971).

59. **R. N. Soffer**, 'Attitudes and allegiances in the unskilled North, 1830–50', *Inter. Rev. of Soc. Hist*, X, no. 3 (1965), p. 446; **J. T. Ward**, 'Some aspects of working class conservatism in the nineteenth century', in **J. Butt** and **J. T. Ward** (eds), *Scottish Themes*, Scottish Academic Press, Edinburgh 1976, esp. pp. 141–56 Both evade serious discussion of the relationship of this type of Toryism to trade unions.

60. The best general study remains **R. L. Hill**, *Toryism and the People 1832–46*, Constable 1929, pp. 104–23.

61. In his reply to Musson's critique of his work on Oldham, Foster has observed that failure to note the terms on which 'collaboration' took place would mean that the 'Paris Commune could also be turned into an exercise in class collaboration'. ('Some comments on class struggle and the labour aristocracy', *Social History*, I, no. 3 (1976), p. 362.) For Oastler's movement for more open support for unions (despite his opposition in principle) see *BPP*, xx (1833), *Report of the S.C. on . . . Labour of Children . . . in Factories . . .*, Q. 9800, 9840; **R. Oastler**, *A Few words to the Friends and Enemies of Trades' Unions*, Huddersfield 1834 and *A Serious Address to the Millowners, Manufacturers and Cloth Dressers of Leeds*, Huddersfield 1834.

62. *BPP*, 1838, *S.C. on Combinations*, Q. 2013.

63. *Hansard*, 3rd Ser. xcii, 18 May 1847, cl. 1059. 'The moment this line is transgressed, that moment a complete change is effected in the character and operation of the body. From a positive good, it becomes a positive evil, and the results are dangerous in the extreme.' *Statement of Facts connected with the Turn-out in the Lancashire Building Trades . . .*, p. 6. On the NAUT see Prothero, 'London Chartism', pp. 213–19.

64. Like other moral panics there were elements of manipulation. Few historians seem to have appreciated that the major condemnations of the Glasgow spinners and of trade unions in general were written anonymously by **Alison**, 'Trades unions and strikes', *Edinburgh Review*, lxvii, (1838) and 'Practical working of trades' unions', *Blackwoods Magazine*, xliii (1838). The literary reflection of his success is discussed by **P. Brantlinger**, 'The case against trade unions in early Victorian fiction', *Victorian Studies*, xiii, no. 1 (1969).

65. The language of the attack on unions was the same as of that on Chartism and on democracy in general. It would be incorrect to think that it was only Tories like Alison who thought in this way.

66. *Jn. Statistical Soc. of London*, I, no. 1 (1838), pp. 11–13, 50–1. The first issue did publish an account of the strikes in the Potteries by a local manager, **J. Boyle** (pp. 37–45). Warburton has suggested that it was intended to influence the S.C. on Combinations. (*Trade Union Organisation*, p. 95).

67. **D. P. O'Brien**, *J. R. McCulloch: a study in classical economics*, Allen & Unwin 1970, pp. 366–70 and *The Classical Economists*, Clarendon Press, Oxford 1975, p. 274, 284, 292.

68. **J. R. McCulloch**, 'Combination laws, restraints on emigration', *Edinburgh Review*, xxxix (1824), pp. 330–3. **D. Read**, *Press and People, 1790–1850*, Arnold, 1961, suggests northern employers preferred the middle of the road provincial press where the laissez-faire position against trade unionism in principle was stated with less qualification than in some of the more doctrinaire papers.

69. See **J. R. McCulloch**, 'Causes and cure of disturbances and pauperism', *Edinburgh Review*, liii (1831), p. 63.

70. **Andrew Ure** advised employers 'when capital enlists science in its service, the refractory hand of labour will always be taught docility'. (*Philosophy of Manufactures*, 3rd ed. 1861, p. 368). **T. Bruland**, 'Industrial conflict as a cause of technical innovation: three cases', *Economy and*

Society, XI, no. 2 (1982), pp. 91–121 investigates the extent to which labour conflict encouraged innovation.

71. Brown, *Early Days*, pp. 60–2 for an example of employer miscalculation. Musson and Kirby, *Voice of the People*, for the treatment of Doherty.

72. **W. Cleland**, *Former and Present State of Glasgow*, Glasgow 1836, quoted in **J. T. Ward** and **W. H. Fraser** (eds), *Workers and Employers*, Macmillan 1980, p. 47. This should be compared with **J. M. Ludlow**, 'Trade societies and the Social Science Association', *Macmillans Magazine*, May 1860, pp. 313–15 where it is argued that the persistence of workers in forming unions shows that they must be rational.

73. Boyson, *Cotton Enterprise*, p. 132. **N. Senior**, 'Combinations and strikes', 1841, repr. in *Historical and Philosophical Essays*, II, 1865, pp. 116–72.

74. Dutton and King, 'Limits of Paternalism'; **G. M. Norris**, 'Industrial paternalist capitalism and local labour markets', *Sociology*, XXII, no. 3 (1978), pp. 469–89. By way of illustration of employers' paternalistic self-image, the London master builders presented their workers with the 'document' 'in a spirit of kindness and conciliation', *Statement of the Master Builders of the Metropolis*, 1834, pp. 11, 14–15.

75. This section draws much upon **A. Flanders**, 'Managerial Ideology and Labour Relations', *Brit. Jn. of Indust. Rel.*, IV, no. 3 (Nov. 1966).

76. Pollard, *Genesis*, pp. 245–90; *BPP*, VI (1833), *S.C. on Manufactures, Commerce, Shipping*, Evidence of Samuel Walker, Q. 9533.

77. **V. A. C. Gatrell**, 'Labour, power and the size of firms in Lancashire cotton in the second quarter of the nineteenth century', *Econ. Hist. Rev.*, XXX, no. 1 (1977), pp. 95–139; **S. Chapman**, 'Financial restraints on the growth of firms in the cotton industry, 1790–1850', *Econ. Hist. Rev.*, XXXII, no. 1 (1979), pp. 50–69.

78. d'Eichthal, *French sociologist*, pp. 98–9, 103. See Brown's maxims written for his own guidance, *Early Days* pp. 16–18, 34.

79. Ibid, pp. 92–106. For a list of management guides for textiles see E. J. Hobsbawm, 'Custom, wages and workload', in *Labouring Men*, Weidenfeld & Nicolson 1964, pp. 365–6.

80. Pollard, *Genesis*, pp. 221, 242.

81. Ure, *Philosophy of manufactures*, pp. 15–16, 277–83.

82. Hobsbawm, 'Custom, wages and workload', p. 348. Recent writing stresses the slowness of change. See, for example, **E. Hopkins**, 'Working hours and conditions during the Industrial Revolution: a reappraisal', *Econ. Hist. Rev.*, XXXV, no. 1 (1982), pp. 52–82. However caution is necessary. Even where traditional forms were maintained discipline could be tightened and pressure increased. This may partly explain the continuing volume of prosecutions under the master and servant laws. My research on provincial shoemaking suggests that from the 1830s employers gave out smaller quantities of material in order to increase their control and reduce costs.

83. **C. P. Giffen**, 'Colliery owners and trade unionism: the case of the South Derbyshire coalfield in the mid-nineteenth century', *Midland History*, VI, (1981), p. 110; Pollard, *Genesis*, p. 87.

84. Boyle, 'Strikes in the Potteries', p. 40.

85. Pollard, *Genesis*, pp. 51–63; Littler, *Development of Labour Process*, Ch. 6.
86. **F. Place**, *Autobiography*, ed. M. Thale, Cambridge U.P. 1977; **C. Manby Smith**, *The Working Man's Way in the World*, Printing Historical Society 1967; **J. Brown**, *Sixty Years Gleanings from Life's Harvest*, Cambridge 1858.
87. *Statement of the Master Builders*, p. 12.
88. Littler, *Development of the Labour Process*, p. 68. See also **B. Soffer**, 'A theory of trade union development: the role of the "autonomous workman"', *Labour History*, I, no. 1 (1961), pp. 141–63.
89. *S.C. on Combinations*, Q. 245. See also Henry Houldsworth's appeal to Peel fifteen years before in Aspinall, *Early Trade Unions*, pp. 363–7: 'I never yet knew a club satisfied . . . an *increase in wages has always been followed by a diminution of labour*', Holme, *Statement of Facts*, pp. 28–9 (original emphasis).
90. Gash, *Peel*, p. 345; Lovett, *An Address from the London Trades' Committee Appointed to Watch the Parliamentary Inquiry into Combinations of the Working Classes*, 1838, p. 2.
91. Chapman, *Cotton Industry*, p. 28; Brown, *Early Days*, pp. 51–2.
92. Musson and Kirby, *Voice of the People*, pp. 128–37.
93. *The Times*, 19 Jan. 1838; **W. H. Fraser**, 'The Glasgow cotton spinners, 1837', in Butt and Ward (eds), *Scottish Themes* pp. 96–7.
94. **P. Searby**, 'Paternalism, disturbance and parliamentary reform: society and politics in Coventry, 1819–32', *Inter. Rev. of Soc. Hist.*, XXII, no. 2 (1977), p. 222. On the killing of Bentley see: Kirby and Musson, *Voice of the People*, pp. 292–3; *Cobbett's Political Register*, LXXXIV, no. 3 (19 Apr. 1834), cl. 177–80; no. 4 (26 Apr.) cl. 197–9, 205–16, 247–8.
95. E. J. Hunt, *British Labour History 1815–1914*, Weidenfeld and Nicolson, 1981, pp. 203–4.
96. **A. J. Taylor**, 'The Miners' Association of Great Britain and Ireland 1842–8: a study in the problem of integration', *Economica*, NS, XXII, no. 85 (1955). Taylor suggests, 'Financial management is a touchstone by which the effectiveness of every union in the second quarter of the nineteenth century may well be judged' (pp. 48–9).
97. *The Times*, July 1850, quoted in **E. Perry**, *The Tinmen's Strike . . .*, Wolverhampton 1850, p. 6.
98. **S.** and **B. Webb**, *Industrial Democracy*, 1913, pp. 3–37; Boyle, 'Strikes in the Potteries', p. 39.
99. National Association for the Promotion of Social Science, *Trades' Societies and Strikes*, 1860, quoted in Ward and Fraser, *Workers and Employers*, p. 70.

Notes on Contributors

Clive Behagg: Senior Lecturer in History at the West Sussex Institute of Higher Education, Clive Behagg has published a number of articles on the social relations of production. This work is soon to be consolidated and extended in his book *Politics and Production* which deals particularly with the workshop trades of Birmingham. He is currently working on a book on the informal structure of control within the nineteenth-century workplace.

Maxine Berg: Senior Lecturer in Economic History at the Department of Economics, University of Warwick, and Wolfson Research Reader of the British Academy 1986–1988, Dr Berg is author of *The Machinery Question and the Making of Political Economy 1815–1848* (1980) and *The Age of Manufactures* (1985) and articles on the areas of proto-industrialisation, women's work, and political economy. She is also co-ordinator of the Seminar Group on Early Industrial Communities.

Alan Campbell: Lecturer in Sociology and Industrial Relations in the Department of Continuing Education, University of Liverpool, Alan Campbell's publications include *The Lanarkshire Miners: a social history of their trade unions, 1775–1874* (1979) and *Getting Organised* (1981). He has been an editor of the *Bulletin of the Society for the Study of Labour History* since 1982 and is currently researching a book on Communism and the Scottish miners.

Robert Fyson: Senior Lecturer in History at North Staffordshire Polytechnic, Robert Fyson's main research and publications have been concerned with popular movements in the Potteries *c.* 1790–1860. He was a contributor to *The Chartist Experience* (1982), and has recently completed his Lancaster University doctoral thesis on Chartism in North Staffordshire.

Michael Haynes: Lecturer in European Studies at Wolverhampton Polytechnic, Michael Haynes's published work in related areas of labour history includes articles on provincial shoemakers and strike dynamics in the nineteenth century. He has also written on Russian history and aspects of the development of capitalism.

David McNulty: Co-ordinator of Adult and Continuing Education at Weald Tertiary College, Dr McNulty has published work on politics in the 1830s and 1840s based on his Manchester doctoral thesis.

James Moher: National Legal Officer to the National Communications Union, Jim Moher is a graduate in law of the National University of Ireland. He is currently completing a postgraduate thesis on London millwrights and engineers 1775–1825, to be presented to the University of London, which will develop some of the themes outlined in his contribution.

Adrian Randall: Lecturer in Social History in the Department of Economic and Social History, University of Birmingham, Adrian Randall has published articles on early English trade unionism, industrial violence and popular protest. A study of the differing responses of industrial communities to mechanisation in the early Industrial Revolution, *Before the Luddites*, is forthcoming.

Robert Sykes: Head of the Sixth Form at Mellow Lane School, Hillingdon, Robert Sykes has published articles on Chartism and working-class consciousness. He is currently completing a book on work, popular politics and class conflict in early nineteenth – century Lancashire, which is largely based on his Manchester Ph.D.

Roger Wells: Senior Lecturer in Modern History at Brighton Polytechnic, Roger Wells' publications include *Insurrection: the British Experience 1795–1803* (1983) and *Wretched Faces: Famine in Wartime England 1793–1801* (1987). Forthcoming publications include *Poverty, Protest and Police in a Rural Society: South-Eastern England 1780–1880* and a micro-study of a nineteenth-century village, Burwash in the High Weald.

Index

Stevenson, John, 30
stonemasons, 18, 232
strike funds, 5, 6
Sussex, 99, 103, 105, 113, 117, 120–1
Swing riots, 113, 116, 118–22, 178
Sykes, Robert, 17, 19

tailors, 8, 11, 14, 15, 17, 78–80, 93,
106, 121, 189, 208, 227, 228, 232
Thompson, E. P., 7, 20, 29, 39, 40, 41,
48, 178, 200–1
Tolpuddle Martyrs, 15, 16, 17, 121,
187, 190, 208, 247, 190, 208, 247
tramping system, 8, 9
Tucker, Josiah, 56, 59
Tufnell, E. C., 172
Turner, H. A., 29, 149

United Brothers, 124–5

violence, 15, 43, 88, 125, 154, 171,
259–60
Von Tunzelman, G. K., 52, 58

weavers, 11
wool, 2, 8, 15, 33, 66, 69, 80, 106,
148, Ch. 2 29–51 *passim*
carpet, 58, 166, 169
sailcloth, 232
Webb, Sidney and Beatrice, 1, 3, 9, 17,
19, 29, 30, 87, 93, 178, 200, 261
Whitbread, Samuel, 104–5, 114
White, George, 11
Wilberforce, William, 12, 81
Wiltshire, 32, 33, 34, 42, 58, 125
Wolfe, James, 37
woolcombers, 2, 6, 15
woollen workers, 2, 5, 9, 47, 53, 55,
59, 60, 65, 77, Ch. 2 29–51 *passim*
see also shearmen, woolcombers,
weavers, woolsorters
woolsorters, 5

Yorkshire, 33, 53, 59, 67, 85, 86, 183,
184
Young, Arthur, 102, 103